ASPECTS OF ROTHERHAM

ASPECTS OF ROTHERHAM

Discovering Local History

Edited by
Melvyn Jones

Series Editor
Brian Elliott

Wharncliffe Publishing Limited

First published in 1995 by
Wharncliffe Publishing Limited

For up-to-date information on other titles produced under the Wharncliffe imprint, please telephone or write to:

Wharncliffe Publishing Limited
FREEPOST
47 Church Street
Barnsley
South Yorkshire S70 2BR
Telephone (24 hours): 01226-734555

ISBN: 1-871647-27-4

Cover illustration: *A View of Rotherham in 1828* Courtesy of Rotherham Metropolitan Borough Council,
Dept of Libraries Museum and Arts

A CIP catalogue record of this book is available from the British Library.

Printed in Great Britain by Redwood Books, Trowbridge, Wiltshire

CONTENTS

INTRODUCTION .... *Melvyn Jones* 7

1. SUMPTUOUSLY BUILDED OF BRICK: THOMAS ROTHERHAM'S COLLEGE, 1482-1550 .... *Stephen Cooper* 11

2. TRAVELLERS TO ROTHERHAM FROM THE SIXTEENTH TO THE EIGHTEENTH CENTURIES .... *Freda Casson* 30

3. EARLY WATERMILLS OF THE MALTBY AREA .... *Alice Rodgers* 47

4. THE DOMESTIC COMFORTS OF A SEVENTEENTH CENTURY KIMBERWORTH FARMING FAMILY .... *Melvyn & Joan Jones* 77

5. SANDBECK HALL AND PARK .... *Tom William Beastall* 89

6. THE THIRD EARL OF EFFINGHAM .... *John Goodchild* 99

7. RENTS, REMARKS AND OBSERVATIONS: THE FIRST MARQUIS OF ROCKINGHAM'S RENT ROLL BOOK .... *Melvyn Jones* 113

8. KIVETON: THE SEAT OF HIS GRACE THE DUKE OF LEEDS .... *Brian Elliott* 129

9. CHRISTMAS CAROLLING AT THORPE HESLEY .... *Ian Russell* 155

10. 'THE ODD CONFOUNDED SPEECH OF RAWMARSH LANE': ASPECTS OF THE GROWTH OF PARKGATE 1831-1891 .... *Tony Dodsworth* 175

11. A MAN AND HIS WORKS: THE LIFE OF GEORGE WILTON CHAMBERS OF ROTHERHAM .... *John Goodchild* 206

12. The Stirrings in Thorpe Hesley on Saturday Night .... *Stephen Cooper* **213**

13. Coal in the Valley: Coal Mining in the Dearne Valley at Wath .... *Alex Fleming* **220**

14. Rotherham's Railway Trades: an Early Chapter in Heavy Engineering .... *Trevor Lodge* **241**

15. From Slums to Council Houses: the Rotherham Experience .... *Tony Munford* **273**

16. Roger Dataller of Rawmarsh .... *Ray Hearne* **298**

CONTRIBUTORS *309*

INDEX *318*

INTRODUCTION

by Melvyn Jones

In recent years there has been an explosion of interest in the history of our local towns and rural communities. The enormous amount of research in family history and the steady flow of local history publications from individuals and groups have enhanced our appreciation of the life and work of our ancestors.

The *Aspects* series began in 1993 with the publication of *Aspects of Barnsley*. Its popularity and the subsequent publication of *Aspects of Barnsley 2* have confirmed that there is a place for quality publications containing essays on a variety of local subjects over a long time-scale. Although aimed at the general reader, each volume has included case studies of considerable regional importance. The series is virtually unique in the sense that it combines aspects of autobiography with family, community, social and economic history, in independent but linked volumes, and has encouraged original research from both new and experienced writers. The publication of *Aspects of Rotherham* marks the first stage in extending *Aspects* into other Yorkshire towns and districts.

The Rotherham area has a long and rich history and this is reflected in the contributions in this volume. There is something of interest to all readers wherever their principal interests lie: in the town itself, the surrounding communities, the development of industry, the domestic lives of ordinary citizens, civic dignitaries or local aristocratic families, or in local culture.

Stephen Cooper's meticulously researched study of the establishment and role of Thomas Rotherham's College in late fifteenth century Rotherham will surely become the definitive study of this aspect of the life of Rotherham's most famous son. Freda Casson's study draws on many years of collecting interesting items from the local collection in Rotherham Central Library and provides a fascinating insight into how travellers to the Rotherham area perceived the town and its people, and the surrounding district. It is all too easy to make facile generalisations about how the local landscape developed and how its natural resources were put to use by people in the past. Alice Rodgers's study of the harnessing of water power in Maltby parish illustrates what thorough research in original sources can achieve: a faultlessly compiled piece of historical detective work.

We are all fascinated by how our ancestors lived. Mel and Joan

Jones's close analysis of an inventory enables us to go on a guided tour of a seventeenth century Kimberworth farmhouse and to poke our noses into every nook and cranny. John Goodchild's study of the life of the Earl of Effingham, Brian Elliott's study of the building of Kiveton, Tom Beastall's account of the building of Sandbeck and the laying out of its park, and Mel Jones's analysis of the Marquis of Rockingham's 'remarks and observations' in his rent roll book allow us to revisit the eighteenth century and the lives and grandiose building schemes of the local aristocracy.

At the other end of the scale Tony Dodsworth's study of the growth of Parkgate, making full use of the Census enumerators' returns, reveals the way in which rapid industrial growth in the nineteenth century attracted migrants from far and wide into one of the fastest growing industrial communities in the area. In the town of Rotherham itself, the burgeoning population resulted in the development of very high population densities and slum conditions. Tony Munford's study graphically exposes these conditions and records the subsequent efforts to re-house the town centre's population in council estates.

Rotherham's period of most rapid expansion in the nineteenth century was the result of industrial development. This is the subject of Alex Fleming's wide-ranging economic and social study of coal mining in the Dearne Valley and Trevor Lodge's carefully researched and superbly illustrated study of Rotherham's railway engineering trades. Labour history in the area has had its ups and downs and Stephen Cooper's account of the bomb outrages in Thorpe Hesley, connected with a troubled period in the nailmaking trade, graphically illustrates the way that local newspapers and court proceedings can be used as the basis of historical research. Interestingly, the local magistrate who presided over the preliminary hearings of the Thorpe Hesley case was George Wilton Chambers, the subject of John Goodchild's study of one of Rotherham's Victorian civic patriarchs.

Local culture has not been ignored. Ian Russell's fascinating account of the local carol singing tradition of Thorpe Hesley is a model of how oral testimony can be used in writing about the local cultural heritage. Finally, Ray Hearne's celebration of the work of 'Roger Dataller' is a timely reminder of the stature of this fine writer whose work was nourished by the lives of the ordinary men and women among whom he grew up and worked.

The volume could not have been produced without the help and support of a number of key individuals. I would like to thank Timothy Hewitt, Managing Director of Wharncliffe Publishing, for his confidence in and support for the project, and Roni Wilkinson and

Caroline Cox for their sterling efforts at the production end. I also acknowledge the help of Hazel Undy in word processing and/or amending typescripts and Neil Donovan for technical help with disks. Brian Elliott, as Series Editor, also helped to keep me on track. Staff in Rotherham Central Library's Archives and Local Studies Section were, as usual, patient and helpful, and their assistance to a number of the contributors is gratefully acknowledged. Finally, I would like to thank the contributors themselves. They have met all my expectations and the result is a volume of studies of infinite variety and interest and, I hope, an encouragement to others with an interest in researching the history of the area and finding an outlet for that research.

Anyone interested in making a contribution to *Aspects of Rotherham 2* (subject to commercial viability) should, in the first instance, contact Melvyn Jones, c/o Wharncliffe Publishing Ltd., 47 Church Street, Barnsley, S70 2AS, enclosing a brief description of the proposed work. If suitable, guidelines will then be issued.

Figure 1. King Edward IV (left), Thomas Rotherham (centre), Queen Elizabeth Woodville (right) and members of the Luton Guild, kneeling before the Trinity. Frontispiece to Luton Guild Book, c.1475. *Luton Museum*

1. SUMPTUOUSLY BUILDED OF BRICK: THOMAS ROTHERHAM'S COLLEGE, 1482 — 1550

by Stephen Cooper

WHEN HE VISITED ROTHERHAM towards the end of Henry VIII's reign about 1539, John Leland noted its 'fair stone bridge of four arches' with its 'chapel of stone well wrought', its 'good smiths for all cutting tools' and the proximity of 'good pits of coal'; but above all he remarked on the town's 'large and fair collegiate church' and the college itself. As he explained, this was founded in 1482:

> *by one Scot, Archbishop of York, otherwise called Rotherham, even in the same place where now is a very fair college sumptuously builded of brick for a provost, five priests, a schoolmaster in song and six choristers, a schoolmaster in grammar and another in writing.*

Leland must have seen the College more or less as it was when the chantry commissioners visited it a few years later:

> *First, the mansion house... with a garden and an orchard within the clausture of the same of two acres and one house near unto the said college, wherein the three free schools be kept. Part of the said site or mansion house is covered with lead, viz., the gate house containing six yards in length and four yards in breadth with two little turrets thereunto annexed. The chapel on the east side the said gate house with a crested roof containing in length eighteen yards, and in width on either side the roof five yards. A chamber on the west side the said gate house with like roof containing in length twelve yards and in breadth on either side the said roof five yards.*

We know from another source that, in addition to gardens and orchards, the College had stables and dovecotes.[1]

This was a fine building and an impressive institution. The rest of South Yorkshire had nothing to compare with it and the town was 'worth a detour' on its account. How did this come about?

Foundation

Thomas Rotherham was born and educated here. He was of humble origins, but was talented. He went up to Cambridge, took a doctorate at Oxford and entered the Church. He gained the patronage of Elizabeth Woodville, a lady at the court of King Henry VI. When the saintly Henry was overthrown by Edward IV — a notorious womaniser —

Edward took a fancy to Elizabeth. She spurned him, 'thinking herself too base to be the king's wife but too good to be his harlot'. The consequence was that they were married; and Fabyan, a London draper, recorded what people said about their King:

> *After which spousals ended, he went to bed, and so tarried there upon three or four hours, and after departed and rode to Stony Stratford, and ... there went to bed again.*

With Elizabeth Woodville as Queen, Thomas Rotherham's career was assured (see Figure 1). He became Bishop of Rochester (1468-72), Bishop of Lincoln (1472-80) and Archbishop of York (1480-1500). In the 1470s and '80s, he was one of Edward IV's principal advisers, accompanying the King on his only expedition to France, and presiding over the peace made at Pécquigny, near Amiens in 1475. He held office as Lord Chancellor from 1474, earning a reputation as a good Parliamentary manager, and gaining popularity by a stringent Act, requiring all Irishmen in England to return home, or pay a tax. Thomas appears as counsellor and diplomat in Philippe de Commynes's memoirs and Dominic Mancini's history; but it is less well known that he was the first Lord Chancellor to give a judgment in Chancery on his own — rather than royal — authority. In the nineteenth century, Lord Chancellor Campbell wrote that Thomas was considered 'the greatest equity lawyer of his time'.[2]

Thomas Rotherham's career as Chancellor came to an end in 1483. Edward IV died and Richard of Gloucester seized the Crown. Queen Elizabeth Woodville was distraught, rightly afraid for her two young sons. As Shakespeare tells the story, it is Thomas who advises Elizabeth to take sanctuary to escape the attentions of the villainous Richard:

> *My gracious lady, go;*
> *And thither bear you treasure and your goods*
> *For my part, I'll resign unto your grace.*
> *The seal I keep................*[3]

The seal is the great seal of England; and Rotherham's idea is to support the Queen in her struggle with Gloucester; but the plan miscarries. In fact, Richard III dismissed Thomas and sent him to the Tower; but unlike Elizabeth Woodville's two young sons, Thomas emerged unscathed and remained Archbishop of York.

Thomas had a great interest in education, was Chancellor of Cambridge and drew up the statutes of Lincoln College, Oxford. The fifteenth century was the age of chantry chapels and collegiate churches and, in deciding to found a college in 1482, Thomas was only following the example of his contemporaries.[4] There was room for a religious foundation in Rotherham, for there was no friary in the town and no monastery closer than Roche Abbey. Thomas owned land near the parish church, and as Archbishop he could override any objections which might be raised to his scheme.

Thomas's own reasons for founding his college are not in doubt, for they are clearly stated in the college statutes and in his will. First, he was grateful for the education which he and his friends had received in Rotherham from an anonymous teacher of Latin grammar. The college was therefore to have a grammar school, providing free tuition for local boys. Second, he believed in the power of music to move men's hearts. He knew that most people found Latin difficult, but music could be enjoyed by all, even by the simple country people [*rudes et montani homines*] who flocked to Rotherham parish church. His college must therefore have a free song school with six choristers, chosen from the poor boys of Rotherham and Ecclesfield parishes.[5] Thirdly, Thomas wanted to assist boys who, though unsuitable for the priesthood, wanted to learn writing and arithmetic, so there was to be a third free school, to teach what would later become known as the 'three Rs'. It was this third school which was distinctive. Winchester and Eton were bigger, grander and richer, but even they had only two.

But the new college was to be more than just a collection of schools. In Thomas's view 'writing, music and grammar are subordinate to the divine law and to the Gospel' and he decreed that the college was to be governed by a provost, who must be a Cambridge theologian. This provost must preach 'the ladder of Jacob, the Word of Jesus [and] the shortest and most certain way to heaven', throughout the diocese of York, but particularly in Rotherham, Ecclesfield, Almondbury in West Yorkshire and Laxton in Nottinghamshire. The requirement to preach in these two far-flung places will shortly be explained.

There was another motive for the foundation. Throughout the later middle ages, there were recurrent worries about how chantry priests spent their time when they were not saying mass.[6] Rotherham's parish church had several chantries and Thomas had heard reports that some of the priests who served them had given themselves up to 'ease and idleness'. He blamed this on the fact that they lived in the town, 'eating and passing the night in different places'. It may be that some of them had been guilty of sins worse than sloth, for Thomas (who knew the ways of the world, from his time at the court of Edward IV) thought that '...in these days a scandal often arises from clerks and women dwelling together...' He considered it would be much easier to bring about a moral reformation if these men were separated from the laity. He therefore provided that all chantry or stipendiary priests ministering in Rotherham be given free lodging and meals at reasonable rates. Safe inside his college, they could occupy themselves with 'grammar, music, singing, the art of writing, hearing the Bible, studying in the library, or hearing some teaching from the provost'.

The college was itself a kind of enormous chantry for its founder. Thomas was an orthodox Catholic and he believed that when he died his soul would enter purgatory, to be suspended there and subjected to various torments before progressing to heaven or hell; but he also believed in the power of masses and prayers for the dead, to relieve this situation. In his last will, made in 1498, he directed that 1,000 masses be celebrated as quickly as possible after his death, so that his soul might be 'more mildly dealt with'. No less than three college statutes contain directions for masses and prayers. The cumulative effect was that not a day would go by without some intercession by the members of the College of Jesus for the soul of the founder.[7]

As Archbishop, Thomas Rotherham remained a powerful and wealthy man. He gave his College the churches of Laxton (1483) and Almondbury (1488). He confirmed this in his will and added various smaller properties in the Rotherham area. He also gave it numerous vessels and objects used in connection with the mass — chalices, cruets, pixes, basins, cups and spoons; and he also bequeathed vestments, including a mitre for the boy-bishop, and a total of 105 books, including a huge stock of sermons for use by the provost, but also works by Cicero, Lucan, Sallust, Terence, and even three copies of Ovid's *Art of Love*! Remarkably, he also gave his college a book by Nicholas of Lyra (c1270-1340), though some later quipped: 'If Lyra had not lyred, Luther would not have danced'. Thomas also left a fund of £200 so that 'my College of Jesus of Rotherham shall be defended...if it be wronged'.[8] Litigation was a constant menace, even in the fifteenth century.

Thomas was not the only benefactor of Rotherham College. When he died in 1495, John Bokyng the grammar master left land worth 8s a year to his wife for life and thereafter to the college. A month later, provost William Rawson left four books to the college library (including Lyra's commentary on the psalter). In 1501, provost Greybarn left the residue of his goods to fund scholarships for poor scholars at the grammar school and University. But the greatest benefactor, after the founder, was Henry Carnebull. Carnebull had been educated with Thomas Rotherham, and became Archdeacon of York and one of Thomas's executors. Thomas had also entrusted him and the treasurer at York with the college defence fund and had decreed that he was to be remembered in all prayers said in the college. Henry founded two chantries in Rotherham parish church and left the bulk of his estate to the college, when he fell ill and died there in 1512.[9]

The generosity of Thomas Rotherham, Henry Carnebull and others meant that the College of Jesus became relatively wealthy. The net income of the properties listed in the founder's will was £102-6s-2d. King Henry's *Valor* gives £74 (net) but the corresponding figure in the late 1540s was £122-16s-5d. The college goods were then worth £54-7s-8d and its plate a staggering £247-0s-4d. Its endowments included forty or fifty houses and some 400 acres of land.[10]

The Life of the College

The college was unfinished in 1498, when Thomas Rotherham's will tells us that he had 'begun to rear' it. He intended it to be 'perpetual', but it was dissolved soon after 1547. In the years in between, it was an independent corporation with its own statutes, livery, common chest and common seal. Its members went by the name of 'Provost and Fellows of the College of Jesus of Rotherham'. This lent distinction to the town, which otherwise had no charter. The college provided employment for a butler, cook, washerwomen, barber and other servants. It was an important consumer of salt, fish, flour, fuel and other goods. It was a source of alms for the poor: doles were paid on the anniversaries of the deaths of Thomas Rotherham and Henry Carnebull, the poor were sometimes given free food and drink and the college provided free board, clothing, lodging and education for the six choirboys from Rotherham and Ecclesfield parishes, and employed one pauper as janitor. It provided free lodging for the chantry priests, from whom the vicar was 'accustomed to have help' in his pastoral work. This was important, for Rotherham was a large parish and Tinsley Brinsworth, Orgeave and Catcliffe townships were difficult to get to, even on horseback, when the waters of the Rother and the Don were 'up'. The provost and fellows were learned men, bound by oath to reside in Rotherham and able to help their neighbours, for example by witnessing their wills and acting as their executors. They also had a library which other clergymen could use: an irate librarian noted that the Abbot of Kirkstead had borrowed a book of sermons but had failed to return it, and even denied that he had ever taken it![11]

The members of the college were required to attend the parish church (where they sat on the left-hand side of the choir) and added colour to town life, quite literally. Thomas Rotherham's statutes provided for gowns to be worn by his fellows and we know from the will of provost Rawson that these were colourful garments — red, blue, violet, green and russet. Some thirty years later Thomas Swift left provost Neville a crimson gown trimmed with marten fur, a surplice, a black velvet bag with a silver ring, and a belt decorated with silver, with a flower on the buckle. This provost must have cut a fine figure in church and around the town. The choir boys too made their contribution. They seem to have adopted the practice, prevalent in cathedral choirs, of electing one of their number as boy-bishop for part of the year; and this curious custom doubtless provided some amusement for the citizens of the town.

Some of the college fellows were generous to the town of Rotherham. John Bokyng's will of 1483 has become famous because he left 3s-4d for the fabric of the chapel to be built on Rotherham bridge, which enables this to be dated; but provost Greybarn left money for the repair of the bridge itself. The parish church was a favourite place for burial and received many bequests and legacies. Bokyng (true to form) left money for repairs. Provost Greybarn left 6s-8d for the church bells and provost Rawson (with his taste for fine cloth) left five yards of linen for an altar cloth. Henry Carnebull left money for the repair of a road in Rawmarsh ('Rawmarsh causey').

The funerals of provosts Greybarn and Rawson were great occasions. Greybarn left 10s for torches and candles to be burned around his body and a shilling to every priest who attended his funeral and mass, plus £5 for the poor. Rawson's instructions were more elaborate. At his funeral there were to be torches, candles and tapers, and money for twelve poor torch-bearers. Any priest in attendance was to receive fourpence. There was to be a requiem mass, with a further 6s-8d for the poor. Then there was to be a wake, with bread and beer. On the seventh day, the ceremonies were to be resumed: more torches, candles and tapers and a further two shillings for paupers to carry torches. The vicar was to get a further twelvepence, any other priest sixpence, any boy belonging to the College twopence, other boys a penny, the poor a further 6s-8d. Five shillings was set aside for a dinner at the college for 'strangers'. The beadle announcing the services was to get two shillings and other clerics twelvepence; and 6s-8d was provided to pay the bellringers. What days to remember, especially for the clergy and the poor!

In general, the college seems to have been well ordered. We know of no allegations of breaches of the statutes, nor of financial irregularity, such as were made about Warwick and Ripon colleges in the 1530s; and men continued to entrust the College of Jesus with the fate of their immortal souls. In 1525 Thomas Swift left seven marks a year to pay for a chantry for his soul to last for eight years: the money was to be kept by the provost and fellows, and the chantry priest was to be John Addy, master of the writing school.[12]

We have no materials with which to paint a picture of the education which boys received in the three schools. There are no registers and no account of the teaching methods employed, such as exists for the seventeenth century grammar school; but Michael Sherbrooke, who was an old boy and subsequently rector of Wickersley between 1567 and 1610 wrote that:

> *by the Foundation of Lincoln College, Oxford... the scholars that came from this College of Rotherham, were to be preferred to a fellowship of that college, before any other; which was performed very well so long as the house stood'.*

When the chantry commissioners surveyed the College, they reported that the purposes of the founder were being fulfilled.[13]

Generations of Rotherham boys must have benefitted from the tuition provided at Rotherham College. These boys sang in the parish church and in the chapel on the bridge, where the *mass of Jesus* and the *antiphone of the Blessed Mary* were regularly heard. The musical life of the town was greatly enriched.

Thomas Rotherham had hoped that, by appointing a Cambridge theologian as provost, he would promote religious knowledge, at a time when parish priests were not necessarily responsible for preaching. The provost was obliged to preach in Rotherham and this may have been even more appreciated after 1541 when Simon Clerkson, vicar of Rotherham, was given leave of absence for ten years so that he could preach more widely, though he remained under a duty to return to his parish at least four times a year.[14]

We know the names of most of the College provosts and in particular something of Robert Neville, who took office in 1518. In 1534, an unseemly quarrel broke out in Doncaster between John Bale, prior of the Carmelites (or Grey Friars), and the Warden of the Franciscans (or White Friars). These two held radically different ideas about theology, though they were both licensed preachers. Bale was to become famous as a Protestant reformer and propagandist; his opponent was a staunch conservative. They used 'opprobrious and undecent words' about each other, even going so far as to attack one another from the pulpit. The matter came to the notice of the authorities, who appointed a commission of enquiry, including Neville of Rotherham. Thomas Rotherham would have been pleased to see his provost investigating a cause of scandal in the Church in this way, having himself settled a long and bitter dispute between the abbots of Peterborough and Crowland.[15]

* * *

But the winds of change which blew through England in the 1530s affected Rotherham too. King Henry VIII broke with Rome and dissolved the monasteries, including Rufford Abbey — which had been sole lord of the manor of Rotherham since the thirteenth century.

Rufford was dissolved in 1536, following (highly dubious) allegations that six monks were sodomites and the abbot a multiple adulterer and fornicator. The manor of Rotherham was granted to the Earl of Shrewsbury, in compensation for the loss of certain estates in Ireland following the government's decision to impose direct rule there. Shrewsbury was glad to acquire the manor, for he already owned land in Rotherham and wished to consolidate his estates around Sheffield.

The King proved unable to halt the Reformation when he wanted to. New ideas flowed in from the Continent, mingling with the native Lollard heresy, which had never entirely died out. Men were able to obtain copies of the Bible in English, smuggling in Tyndale's translation or purchasing older Lollard versions and they obtained other illegal books, including 'A book made by John Frith'. Frith's works were regarded as highly subversive (not least by Sir Thomas More, who said that one of them 'teacheth in a few leaves shortly all the poison that Wycliffe, Oecolampadius, Huss, Tyndale and Zwingli have taught in all their books before'); and Frith himself was burned at the stake.[16]

When the new ideas reached Rotherham, they caused bitter disputes and provost Neville was unable to resolve the problem, despite his extensive powers. Because of the regular contact between college and town, the controversy spread, involving clergy and laity alike, and attracting the attention of the secular authorities. This was a situation which Thomas Rotherham would have deplored: his statutes for Lincoln College, Oxford had required every fellow to take an oath that he would not favour the Lollards — 'that pestilent sect which, reviving ancient heresies, attacks the sacraments, and the position, and the endowments of the Church', and Thomas's will closes with the affirmation: 'I hesitate in no article of the faith, nor have ever hesitated'.[17]

The master of Rotherham song school, William Senes, was arrested on 4 August 1537 and brought before the Earl of Shrewsbury. Shrewsbury was one of the King's most trusted lieutenants in the North, a faithful upholder of the Royal Supremacy, though Catholic in belief. He had helped to put down the Pilgrimage of Grace and was still on the lookout for troublemakers.[18] When Senes was brought before him, the Earl bawled: 'Come near, thou heretic and kneel near, ha, thou heretic, thou has books here!' Senes replied meekly: 'Yea my lord, the New Testament I have.' This was a banned book, so the Earl shouted more than once that it was 'nought' and added: 'Thou art an heretic and but for shame I should thrust my dagger into thee'. Senes was remanded in custody for a week.

In prison, Senes composed his defence. According to this, there had been two factions in Rotherham College in the late 1530s, one loyal to the King, the other treacherous, and Senes had belonged to the former.

The Lincolnshire rising in the autumn of 1536 had provoked a lively debate. Thomas Holden (priest in the chantry of Holy Cross) had spoken in support of the rebels saying: 'God was in Lincolnshire, for those was good lads, for they would put down those heretics Cromwell, Cranmer and Latimer...' Senes had protested that 'those who withstood the king were rebels'. William Drapper (master of the grammar school) had sided with Holden, saying that the Earl of Shrewsbury was a 'favourer of the common people'. Senes had challenged this, asserting that the Earl had 'always been true to the King'. Drapper had replied that if this was so, 'the Earl himself was nought'. 'Why' replied Senes, 'is all nought that doth hold with our King? Yonder is Mr Markham, he hath put out the Abbot of Rufford ...according to the King's commandment...' Drapper had said Sir John was a heretic too. Then, like many academic arguments before and since, the matter had become personal: Senes had called Drapper 'Sir John Lack-learning', and Drapper had called Senes 'Whoreson knave!' The argument had been reported to the provost; but he had merely told Senes to see the bailiff of Rotherham. The bailiff had washed his hands of the affair and rebuked the provost for failing to keep his house in order. Provost Neville had threatened to expel Senes if he brought the college into disrepute again.[19]

In spite of this defence, Senes was indicted for heresy. It was alleged that he had met Holden in church on 8 June 1537 and had shown him some printed ballads, attacking the prayers used for hallowing water and blessing bread and bells. Holden had commented that the ballads were not authorised by parliament, but Senes had replied 'that such books as were sent down to the curates was made by heretics and none of them true.' In Senes's view there was no such thing as purgatory! This was not only unorthodox, it was highly offensive to a chantry priest like Holden. It also attacked the *raison d'être* of Rotherham college.

There was another incident in the parish church on 4 May. William Ingram was there, as was Thomas Pilley, priest in one of the Carnebull chantries. Senes mocked Pilley for sprinkling water on Carnebull's tomb. Ingram came to Pilley's defence, saying that he 'believed as his father had done'. Senes said in that case 'Thy father was a liar and is in Hell', though conceding that his own father must also be in hell, since he 'never knew Scripture'. A few weeks later Senes asked Ingram: 'When didst thou see God?' Ingram said that he saw him every day at mass, in the priest's hands, but Senes ridiculed this, saying 'Thou sawest but bread'. This was to attack the central Catholic doctrine of transubstantiation — that the eucharist becomes the body of Christ.

Fresh charges were brought in June 1540. It was alleged that Senes had been writing, as well as reading, subversive material; and a witness claimed that he and two others had visited Senes in Rotherham, where the grammar master had used unusual language to explain his view of the eucharist: 'as the ale pole signifieth that there is ale to sell and yet no ale in the pole, so Frith said in his book, is the sacrament of the altar'. The use of this curious simile (which tells us something about Tudor alehouses as well as Protestant theology) suggests that Senes had read John Frith's book, Frith having adopted Zwingli's view that the sacrament was the body of Christ only in a figurative sense.

Eventually, Senes admitted his guilt and recanted. He did penance in York Minster and again in Rotherham. We can imagine the pleasure that the conservatives and Catholics must have taken in his public humiliation; but Senes was lucky, for an Act of 1539 prescribed death for anyone convicted of denying transubstantiation, even if the accused recanted. At least the Rotherham music master had escaped the stake.[20]

For his part, William Drapper did not stay long at Rotherham college, for he became rector of Thrybergh in 1542. But this appointment provoked another controversy, though the scandal was minor compared to the Senes affair. Objection was made to Drapper's appointment, on the grounds of pluralism. He had certainly applied for the rectory at Thrybergh before resigning his position at Rotherham — thereby infringing Thomas Rotherham's injunction that no-one should hold any living whilst he was a fellow of the college, unless it were a free chapel or prebend not requiring residence (which was not the case with Thrybergh). However, Drapper defended himself with some success, though he soon resigned his position at Rotherham. Not long afterwards, he sued one of his parishioners at Thrybergh for tithe of lamb.[21]

* * *

Thomas Rotherham would have been disappointed by the verdict passed by a nineteenth century vicar of Almondbury: 'It would appear that Almondbury church did not derive any benefit from Archbishop Rotherham's foundation except that a man of learning was appointed from the college on any vacancy as vicar...' This may be unfair: the college did pay for new building and the provost of Rotherham must have preached there. On the other hand, one of the college's last decisions was to appoint William Drapper of Thrybergh as vicar, in succession to Robert Neville, who had become vicar there after being provost at Rotherham. Thomas Rotherham had specified that the vicar should reside in Almondbury; but Drapper attempted to hold onto Thrybergh as well. The result was more litigation. It even appears that when Drapper arrived in Almondbury in 1550, local people initially prevented his induction, by holding a demonstration in the church and refusing to come out! But Drapper won the day by using his connections at court.[22]

Figure 2. Sculpture of Archbishop Rotherham, complete with cope, mitre and cross, on the roof of Laxton Parish Church, Nottinghamshire. *Joan Jones*

Despite this, those liable to pay tithes may have regretted the passing of Rotherham college. After its dissolution the tithes became the property of one Ramsden, who sued the men of Almondbury, including Edward Hirst and Edward Dyson. Numerous witnesses gave evidence, which suggests that the matter was keenly contested. Among them was William Nettleton, who had formerly collected tithes, using 'a rental delivered unto him by the provost and fellows'. Another was Peter Key, who testified for Dyson. It is surely no coincidence that Ramsden also brought an action against Key in the church courts, alleging that Key had called him 'a knave a harlot and a naughty fellow'.[23]

As for Laxton, we know that Thomas Rotherham was responsible for the construction of the rood screen, the clerestory with its figures of the apostles, and a series of remarkable gargoyles; and that he commissioned an effigy of himself complete with cope, mitre and cross, which stands on the roof of the church to this day (Figure 2). We also know that Laxton was one of the places where the provosts of Rotherham were supposed to preach; but, unlike its open-field agriculture, the history of the church of Laxton has been little studied and we do not know enough about the vicars appointed by the college to be able to say whether they were better than their predecessors. There was certainly scope for improvement, for in 1471 the vicar of Laxton had been accused of a 'jollity' with the wife of William Blyton, who lived in the adjoining parish of Wellow. Blyton had lured the offending priest to Lincoln, had him beaten up, put in the stocks at Wellow, and imprisoned at Nottingham, where he had remained for several months. The vicar of Laxton had contended that the accusations were nothing more than a plot to deprive him of his living. Whatever the truth of the matter, the affair must have brought the clergy into disrepute. Men would perhaps expect more of priests appointed by the provost and fellows of Thomas Rotherham's College.[24]

Dissolution

The Protestant Reformers regarded the belief in purgatory as the worst kind of superstition, an obstacle to a true understanding of salvation by Christ's sacrifice alone. They seized the levers of power when Edward VI succeeded Henry VIII, at a time when the monarchy needed money and the nobility's appetite for Church property had already been whetted. The Chantries Act of 1547 provided for the dissolution of all chantries and colleges which maintained and supported the 'vain opinion of purgatory'. Commissioners were appointed to survey the institutions condemned by the Act, though they were given power to continue grammar schools attached to those institutions, where appropriate.[25]

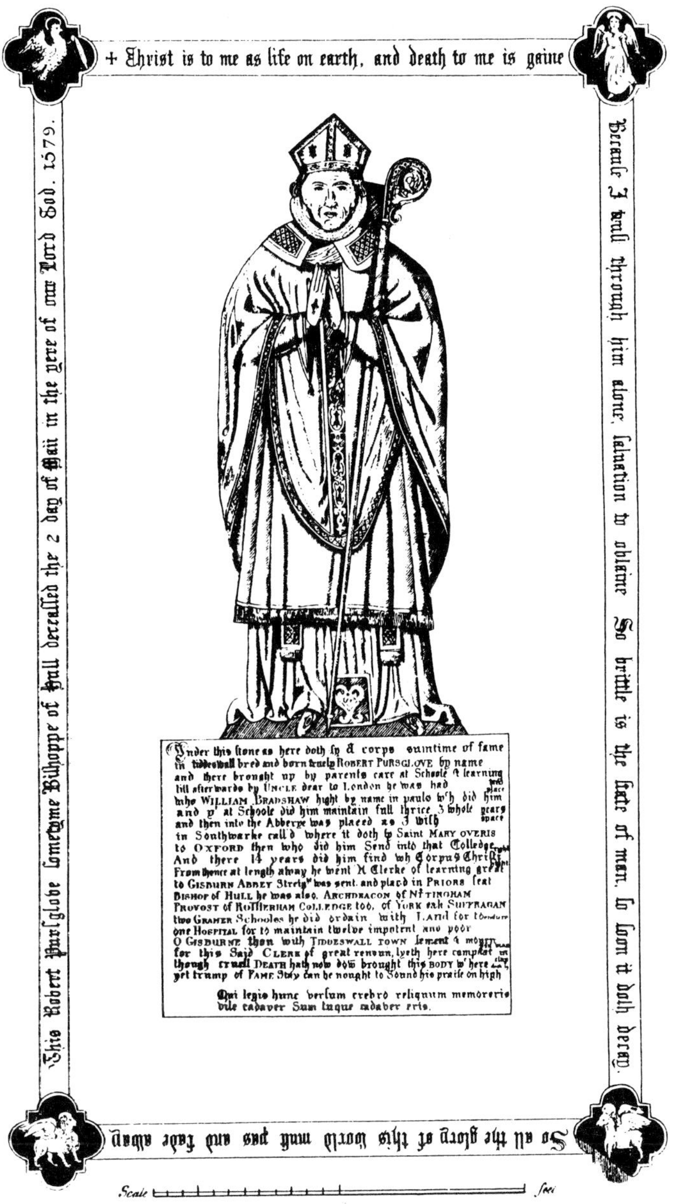

Figure 3. Brass of Robert Pursglove, the last provost of Rotherham College, in Tideswell parish church.

The chantry commissioners reported that there were six chantries in Rotherham, one at Tinsley and the other five in the parish church — Jesus and Our Lady, The Cross, Our Lady, St Katherine and Our Lady of the Carr. These chantries were not rich, though Henry Carnebull's had much valuable plate; but they were all swept away. The commissioners also surveyed Thomas Rotherham's college. They were not always complimentary about the schoolmasters they encountered, reporting for example that William Gegaltson of Acaster near York was 'indifferently learned in grammar'. But they thought that Thomas Snell of Rotherham was 'of honest conversation, qualities, and learning'; and they recommended that he continue as grammar master, at a stipend of £10-15s-4d, being the sum of his salary and 'fringe benefits' — clothing, fuel, barber and laundry. This sum was paid by the Court of Augmentations through its Receiver for Yorkshire, and the grammar school continued to exist, though there were problems in obtaining payment of the stipend during Queen Mary's short reign.[26]

But although the grammar school survived, the college itself was dissolved. The last provost was Robert Pursglove, whose brass is in Tideswell church in Derbyshire (Figure 3). Pursglove was pensioned off. The song and elementary schools were closed and the college servants dismissed. The college property was dispersed. The moveable property — plate, books and furniture — was probably the first to go.[27] As for the landed endowments, the Crown granted or sold these to various purchasers, the main one being Robert Swift, whose fine altar tomb and mural brass may ironically still be seen in Rotherham church (Figure 4). The Earl of Shrewsbury acquired the college itself, including the buildings and the lead on the roof, which the chantry commissioners had taken a careful note of. The grammar school may have continued to be housed in the College for a time, but it was soon moved. A document of 1583 refers to a 'house or building called the schoolhouse... in the street called Jesus Gate'; but Charles Hoole, who taught in Rotherham in the 1630s, thought that one of the Earls of Shrewsbury had ingratiated himself with the people of Rotherham by erecting a cockpit (perhaps in 1569) and had then taken the opportunity to move the school 'out of the College into a sorry house before the gate'. At the end of the sixteenth century the college was still, as Michael Sherbrooke noted, 'a fair House yet standing'. But he gave this warning: 'God knoweth how long it shall stand; for certain Brick Chimneys and other Brick Walls...is decayed and fallen down for lack of Use'.[28] The site was later occupied by the College Inn which incorporated considerable remains of the College (Figure 5).

After they had dealt with the chantries and colleges, the Protestants tackled the parish churches. The Rotherham churchwardens were

Figure 4. Brass of the Swift family in Rotherham parish church.

obliged to take down their rood loft, along with their high altar and 'tabernacles'; and they had to arrange for their service books to be taken first to Doncaster and then to York for destruction, while the parish clerk William Ingram was paid to write out a new version. All this must have been deeply upsetting for traditionalists, though committed Protestants may have welcomed it, and some men may have even have profited by the changes, like Thomas Bosvile of Tickhill, who got into the steeple at Laughton-en-le-Morthen and helped himself to a bell.[29]

But for Rotherham the crowning indignity must have been the loss of its college. William Camden (whose *Britannia* first appeared in 1586) informed his readers that this had been 'suppressed by the wicked avarice of the last age'. Charles Hoole (whose *Scholastic Discipline* was published in 1639) tells of 'the injury done to that school, which indeed... ought still to have been kept in the college'. Joseph Hunter (whose *South Yorkshire* was published between 1828-1831) wrote that: 'Few places have suffered more than Rotherham by the measures which accompanied the reformation of religion in England' and even thought that the morals of the town degenerated as a result. John Guest (whose *Historic Notices of Rotherham* appeared in 1879) idolised Thomas Rotherham and was astonished and ashamed by the 'relentless iconoclasm' which had destroyed his college. He thought that those responsible were quite simply 'beyond human forgiveness'.Arthur Leach (who edited *Early Yorkshire Schools* between 1899 and 1903) concluded that 'Rotherham suffered the most signally by the malversation of the Chantries Act'.

There is another view. Professor Dickens, whose magisterial *English Reformation* was published in 1964 pointed out that many Tudor Englishmen 'felt no more compunction in diverting chantry-funds to practical uses, both public and private than we should feel in demolishing the once-mighty Bethesda Chapel in some depopulated area of an industrial city'; and a Marxist or a materialist might say that the charity provided by the college benefited the souls of the dead rather more than the stomachs of the living. There are value judgements to be made here and much will depend on one's view of religion; but perhaps the last word should go to Michael Sherbrooke, who wrote his *Fall of Religious Houses* some forty years after the dissolution, in 1591. After describing Thomas Rotherham's purposes in founding his college, he protested: 'The Foundation whereof was not to make a Malt House, as it is now used'; and he issued this invitation:

> *Now let everyone consider what great loss this was to such a town, and the country round about it, not only for the cause of learning, but also for the help of the poor; that now in the town is not a few...*

Sherbrooke has been described as 'a stubborn believer in a mythical golden age before the Reformation', but for the present writer at least this lament from a local patriot still strikes the right chord.[30]

Figure 5. The former College Inn which stood on the site of Rotherham College and incorporated considerable remains of the medieval building.

Glossary

CHANTRY CHAPEL: It was common in the Middle Ages for a wealthy person to endow, on his death, a chapel, called a chantry, often attached to or inside a church. In such chapels chantry priests would celebrate masses for the soul of the founder. Chantry chapels were quite often built over the grave of the deceased.

COLLEGE: A community of clergy living together in a building or set of buildings for the purpose of religious service, study and instruction.

DOLE: The distribution of money or provisions to the poor.

EQUITY: A system of law existing beside common law and superseding it when it conflicts with it. In England equity was formerly administered by a special class of tribunals of which the Court of Chancery was chief.

HERETIC: A person holding (and often propagating) unorthodox religious beliefs.

LOLLARD: A term of contempt given to certain heretics.

PIX (PYX): The vessel in which the host or consecrated bread of the Sacrament is reserved.

PROVOST: The head of a community of religious persons.

TRANSUBSTANTIATION: According to the doctrine of the Roman Catholic Church, transubstantiation is the conversion in the Eucharist of the bread into the body of Christ and the wine into the blood of Christ.

VALOR: A valuation. On the Dissolution of the Monasteries by Henry VIII in the 1530s, a valuation of all religious property was made prior to its confiscation and acquisition by the Crown. Known as the *Valor Ecclesiasticus*, it was compiled by Royal Commissioners whose task was to value religious houses as real estate. The Commissioners were particularly interested in land holdings, rents and in the buildings themselves, particularly those with valuable lead roofs.

Notes and References

I have modernised spelling throughout.
Readers of a younger generation than mine will need to know that, before 1971, there were four farthings in a penny, twelve pennies in a shilling and twenty shillings in a pound; and the abbreviations for pounds, shillings and pence were £, s and d.

Abbreviations used in notes below:

Beckett: *A History of Laxton* by JV Beckett, Blackwell, 1989.
BIHR: Borthwick Institute of Historical Research, York.
Dickens, Lollards: *Lollards and Protestants in the Diocese of York 1509-1558* by AG Dickens, Oxford University Press, 1959.
Dickens, Reformation: *The English Reformation* by AG Dickens, Fontana, 1967.
DNB: *Dictionary of National Biography.*
EHD: *English Historical Documents*, ed DC Douglas et al (12 vols.; London, 1953-77.
Guest: *Historic Notices of Rotherham* by John Guest FSA, Robert White, Worksop, 1879.
HSY: *The History and Topography of the Deanery of Doncaster by Joseph Hunter, 1828-31*, re-published by EP Publishing in collaboration with Sheffield City Council, 1974.
Herbert: *Annals of the Church and Parish of Almondbury* by CA Herbert, London, Longmans, 1882.
Ivanhoe Review: Bulletin of the Archives and Local Studies Section, Central Library, Rotherham.
Keen, English Society: *English Society in the Later Middle Ages, 1348-1500*, MH Keen, Penguin, 1990.
LP: *Letters and Papers, Foreign and Domestic, of the Reign of King Henry VIII*, ed JS Brewer, J Gairdner, RH Brodie, et al (21 vols and Addenda; London, 1862-1932).
PRO: Public Record Office.
Rufford Charters: *Rufford Charters*, Thoroton Society Record Series, vols 29,30,32,34 ed CJ Holdsworth, Nottingham, 1972-80.
Surtees: Publications of the Surtees Society.
TRHS: Transactions of the Royal Historical Society.
Valor: *Valor Ecclesiasticus*, ed Joseph Hunter, 6 vols 1810-34.
VCH: Victoria County History, Yorkshire.
YAJ: Yorkshire Archaeological Journal.
YASRS: Yorkshire Archaeological Society Record Series.

1. *The Itinerary of John Leland the Antiquary* published by Thomas Hearne, Oxford, 1770, vol V, folios 91 & 92; Guest, p 105, p 149, p 160; Surtees vol 91(1892) *Yorkshire Chantry Surveys*, vol I, p 201.
2. DNB. For contemporary sources see J R Lander, *The Wars of the Roses*, Alan Sutton, 1990, p 158, p 169, p 171, p 176, p 177. Guest, p 164 cites the parliamentary material, including an amusing story about the sumptuary legislation of 1477. For Thomas's place in the development of equity, see EHD vol IV, 371-2 and docs 305 and 307, and Lord Campbell, *Lives of the Lord Chancellors*, London, 1868, vol I, pp 337- 343.
3. *Richard III*, Act II, Scene IV.
4. Guest, p 90, p 95; HSY vol II, 5; YASRS vol 33 *Early Yorkshire Schools*, vol II, pp 102-4; MH Keen, *England in the Later Middle Ages*, Methuen, 1973, p225; GM Trevelyan, *Illustrated English Social History*, Pelican 1964, vol 1, p 151; Dickens, Reformation, p 297; VCH vol I, pp 452-3.
5. Guest, p 106, p 136; see my article 'Music in Tudor Rotherham', *Ivanhoe Review*, No 7, Winter 1994. According to Michael Sherbrooke, boys stayed at the song-school until their voices broke and then transferred to the grammar school: Guest, p 96.
6. Keen, English Society, pp 259-60.
7. Guest, p107, pp 111-2, p 137, p 142, pp 113-4.
8. Herbert, pp441-445; BIHR, reg 23 ff 276-80v; Guest, pp 137-8; YASRS vol 33, xxxviii, p 164; Dickens, Reformation, p 99.
9. YASRS vol 33, pp 141-4, pp 169-71; YASRS vol 107 *Fasti Parochiales*, p133. One of Carnebull's first chantry priests was Thomas Gree, whose will is full of information about the College: BIHR, Abp Reg V 24, f 163v. Carnebull's monogram appears alongside Thomas Rotherham's on the roofbeams of Rotherham church: Guest, p 322.
10. Guest, p 144, p 149; YASRS vol 33, xxix; VCH vol III, p 374.
11. Valor, vol V, pp 44-5; Guest, p 75, p 79, p 107, p 112, p 115, p 116, p 137, pp 147-8; Surtees vol 91(1892), p380; YASRS vol 33, p 162(n), p 171, p 173. Thomas Reresby appointed provost Neville executor in 1522, and Thomas Swift's will of 1525 was witnessed by several members of the College.
12. YASRS vol 33, p 173, p 142, p 167, p 168, p 171. For Warwick and Ripon Colleges, see Alan Kreider, *English Chantries, The Road to Dissolution*, Harvard University Press, 1979, pp 35-7. For the boy-bishop see Guest pp 168-9, HSY vol II, p 8.

13. Guest, p 96; Surtees p 91, p 201. Teaching in Rotherham in the 1630s is described in Hoole's *A New Discovery of the Old Art of Teaching School*, written in 1637 though published later: Guest, p 340. Guest (1879) and Leach (1903) thought that the author of *The Fall of Religious Houses* was Cuthbert Sherbrooke, a relative of Michael Sherbrooke, the rector of Wickersley; but Dickens in YASRS vol 125 *Tudor Treatises*, establishes that Michael was the author.
14. Guest, pp 73-4; LP vol XIII part II, p 953; vol XVI (1540- 1) 1308(38). Clerkson took a wife in Edward VI's time, and was deprived of his post at Rotherham in 1554, when Queen Mary obliged married clergy to renounce their wives: Dickens, Lollards, pp 145-7 & p 200.
15. Guest, pp 120-3; HSY vol II, p 7 & p 9; Dickens, Lollards, pp 140-3; Dickens, Reformation, p 236; Guest, p 91(n), p 95(n).
16. LP vol X, p 138; Dom David Knowles, *The Religious Orders in England vol III The Tudor Age*, Cambridge University Press, 1961, pp 226-8 and Chapter XXIII; Rufford Charters vol 1, lvii and Charter 1004, pp 555-561; Guest, p 170; HSY vol II, p 10; L & P XII part 2, p 350, p 954; Roger Lockyer, *Tudor and Stuart Britain*, 1471-1714, Longman, 1985; Steven G Ellis, *Tudor Ireland*, Longman, 1985; Dickens, Reformation, p 107, p 109, p 116, p 188; Keen, English Society, p 294.
17. Joan Simon, *Education and Society in Tudor England*, p 43(n).
18. A G Dickens, *Sedition and Conspiracy in Yorkshire*, YAJ 34 (1939), pp 379-98.
19. YASRS, vol 107, p 133; HSY vol II, p 16, p 17; Guest, p 74, p 76, p 118. It has been suggested that Thomas Holden may have been the same man as the Robert Holdyne or Howden, arrested for involvement in the Yorkshire Plot of 1541: YAJ 34, pp 379-98.
20. LP XII part 2, p 175 etc; Dickens, Lollards, pp 37-44; Dickens, Reformation, p 96.
21. HSY vol II, p 42; Guest, p111; BIHR CP G 307 (Rotherham school), 790 (tithe of lamb). Hunter describes him as Richard Drapper, but I think it is the same man. In the case papers, he is referred to as rector of Thrybergh on 9 October 1542, having been grammar-master at Rotherham since at least 1539.
22. Herbert, p 94, p 130, pp 441-5, p 464, p 485; BIHR CP G 427, 435 (disputed presentation). Drapper died in 1552. His will suggests that he was not a poor man; but his nephews renounced probate, and the estate was insufficient to pay the debts and legacies: BIHR AB vol 29 f, 107.
23. BIHR, CP G 406,417,453,474,476. Litigation over words was becoming increasingly common: J A Sharpe, *Defamation and Sexual Slander in Early Modern England: The Church Courts at York*, BIHR, Borthwick Papers no 58, p 8.
24. Beckett; R L Storey, *A Fifteenth Century Vicar of Laxton*, Transactions of the Thoroton Society vol 88 (1984), pp 39-41.
25. EHD V, doc 107(iv).
26. Surtees vol 91, pp 205-9; Surtees vol 92, pp 378-80; Guest pp 74-9, p 147; HSY vol II, pp 16-17; YASRS vol 33, pp 184-5, p 187. Snell was refused payment after 1555. Professor Dickens thinks this was because the Marian government was Catholic and Snell was Protestant: *Reformation Studies*, The Hambledon Press, 1982, p 152, see also YASRS 33, p 189(n). The explanation may be more mundane: civil servants thought it would be more efficient if the Court of Augmentations were amalgamated with Exchequer. This produced chaos. Stipends paid under warrant of the chantry commissioners were stopped, and schoolmasters had to sue for them in Exchequer: VCH vol 1, p 453, p 456; G R Elton, *The Tudor Revolution in Government*, Cambridge University Press, 1960, pp 244-50.
27. We do not have figures for the college, but the West Riding as a whole produced 1611 ounces of plate and 29 fodders of lead, of which 8 were given to the Earl of Shrewsbury. The rest were sold off at 4 each: J J Scarisbrick, *The Reformation and the English People*, Blackwell, 1984, p 87.
28. Guest, p 144, pp 146-62, p 345, p 368, p 385; E W Bernard, *The Power of the Early Tudor Nobility, A Study of the 4th & 5th Earls of Shrewsbury*, The Harvester Press, 1985, pp 139-142; Sherbrooke added that the College 'is in the Earl of Shrewsbury his Hands; and as the Report is, it is concealed Land'. Under Elizabeth commissioners and informers extorted considerable sums from the holders of such land: C J Kitching, *The Quest for Concealed Lands in the Reign of Elizabeth I*, TRHS 1974, pp 63-78. In Rotherham, this quest was closely connected with the origins of the Feoffees of Common Lands.
29. The churchwardens' accounts were printed by Guest over 100 years ago, when they were already 'torn, tattered and not easily decipherable': Guest, pp 177-8. They have since disappeared. Robert Parkyn, conservative priest of Adwick le Street, left a critical account of the Reformation: English Historical Review 62 (1947). Michael Sherbrooke thought Bosvile 'a very shifter, I will not say a thief': Dickens, Lollards, p 208.
30. *Britannia, or a Chorographical Description of Great Britain and Ireland* revised by Edmund Gibson, 2nd edn., vol II, p 847; HSY vol II, pp 6-9; Guest, p 68, p 74, p 86, p 96, p 106, pp 143-6, p 362; YASRS vol 33, lxx,lxxi, p 125, pp 126- 7; Dickens, Reformation, p 147, pp298-9. Leach thought that the loss of the writing school left an educational gap which could be noticed 'in the vile writing and spelling of the Feoffees' minutes and accounts of the Elizabethan and Jacobean periods, forming as marked a contrast to the scholarly hand and accurate Latin of the few extant accounts of Henry VIII's time as can be well imagined'. There is a critical appreciation of Leach's work in W E Tate *AF Leach As A Historian of Yorkshire Education*, BIHR, St Anthony's Hall Publications no 23. In the nineteenth century the surviving bits of the College became the Old College Inn, pulled down in the twentieth century: Tony Munford, *Victorian Rotherham*, Quoin Publishing Ltd 1989, photos 29 & 30.

2. SOME TRAVELLERS TO ROTHERHAM FROM THE SIXTEENTH TO THE EIGHTEENTH CENTURIES

by Freda Casson

MOTIVES FOR TRAVEL ARE MANY and varied and have altered over the centuries. In the Middle Ages merchants, pilgrims and scholars travelled for material gain or spiritual wealth whilst in the eighteenth century many wealthy young men undertook the Grand Tour as an essential part of their education, preparing themselves for the role they would play in politics and diplomacy. The search for physical health made both men and women journey to spa towns in Great Britain and Europe to 'take the waters' and enjoy the social activities there.

Until comparatively recently travel for its own sake was largely undertaken by the wealthy, the poor travelling in search for work. The habit of touring their native land began in the sixteenth century when the road system began to develop and improve. Curiosity, love of the countryside and willingness to overcome discomfort would appear to have been the key criteria for these early travellers. With the development of the railway system in the nineteenth century travel became easier, with planned excursions and mass travel contrasting with the style of journey undertaken in previous centuries.

It seems natural for people to write about the things they saw and experienced. Whilst many such manuscripts remained unpublished and in private hands, others were published and became valuable commentaries on places, people, houses, countryside and industry.

John Leland appears to be the first writer to mention Rotherham in a published book. An orphan who became one of the most formidable scholars of his age, Leland was born in London about 1503. After attending St Paul's School he went on to become a student at Christ's College, Cambridge and after graduating became tutor to the Duke of Norfolk's son. He later went to study at Oxford, possibly taking Holy Orders, and from there he went to Paris, returning to England about 1529. Four years later he received a commission from the King which changed his life. He was 'to make a search after England's Antiquaries and peruse the Libraries of all Cathedrals, Abbies and Priories, Colleges, etc. as also all places wherein Records, Writings and secrets of Antiquities were reposed'. This started Leland on his travels and he was to write to the King to say that he was 'totally enflammed with a

Figure 1. The chapel on Rotherham bridge, erected in 1483, and one of only three such bridges in Britain.

love 'to see thoroughly all those partes of this your opulate and ample reaulme...'.

He visited Rotherham in 1539.

> *I entered Rotherham by a fine stone bridge of four arches which has a well made stone chapel on it. Rotherham is a reasonable large market town, with a large and fine collegiate church. The College was inaugurated by an Archbishop of York called Scot, and also known as Rotherham, on the same site as the present and lavishly built brick college; it has a provost, five priests, a schoolmaster who teaches singing, with six choristers, another who teaches grammar and a third who teaches writing. Although between Cawood and Rotherham there is a good supply of wood, yet the inhabitants burn predominantly coal, which is found in great abundance there, and is sold very cheaply. There are excellent coal pits a mile from Rotherham. The town has good smiths manufacturing all kinds of edged tools.*

William Camden next wrote about the town. An antiquary and historian, Camden was born in the Old Bailey, London in 1551. He started his education at Christ's Hospital, but at the age of twelve suffered an attack of the plague 'to the great loss of his learning'. After his recovery he then went to St Paul's School, where he stayed until going up to Oxford. He was at Magdalen College before going on to Broadgate's Hall (Pembroke College) under the patronage of Dr Thomas Thornton who supported him for the rest of his time at Oxford.

In 1571 Camden returned to London and, having no regular employment, was free to follow his antiquarian interests for the next few years. It was during that time that he travelled widely. After becoming a schoolmaster at Westminster School in 1575 he continued to travel during vacations.

In 1582 he came to Yorkshire after setting out on a journey from Suffolk. He published his book *Brittania* in 1586 to great acclaim as nothing similar had been attempted since Leland's work. By 1594 it had passed through four London editions. Written in Latin, it was first translated into English by Philomen Holland in 1610, and a further edition was published in 1637.

Camden approached Rotherham from Sheffield.

> *From thence Don clad with alders and other trees goeth to Rotheram, which glorieth in Thomas Rotherham, sometime Archbishop of York, a wise man bearing the name of the town, beeing borne therein, and a singular benefactor thereunto, who founded there a Colledge with three schooles in it to teach children writing, Grammar and musicke, which the greedy iniquity of these our times hath already swallowed.*

Joseph Hunter, in Volume 2 of his *South Yorkshire*, refers to a rhyme about Rotherham circulating at the end of the sixteenth century 'too gross to be more than alluded to'. The poem he refers to was by Dr Richard Edes (Eedes), 1555-1604, Dean of Worcester. It was part of an unpublished manuscript, being an account of a journey undertaken by Dr Toby Matthew[1] to take possession of the Church at Durham. The poem was in Latin, and John Guest in his work *Historic Notices of Rotherham* provides us with both the Latin and a translation:

Prima in Eboraci Comitatu nos Rotherama
Accipit; haec solis caruit lusoribus; illic
Quovis excellunt simul hospes et hospita lusu.

Quae Rotherama prius caruit lusoribus illis
Jam scatet; hospitio prohibans qui ludere nescit.
Nos licet indigne tulimus prohiberier, illinc
In melius tamen, et magis amplum forte venimus
Hospitium; quandoque juvat quod obesse videtur.

Rotherham, in the County of York, is the first to receive us; this town was free for gamesters only; both host and hostess are excellent gamesters. Rotherham, which before time was free from gamblers, now swarms with them; denying a sojourn to whosoever does not know how to gamble. Although we were indignant at being kept out (told to move on), yet we happened to find a better and more honourable place of sojourn. Now and then that which seems injurous to us is pleasant.

The town being known as a haunt for gamblers is corroborated in another poem *Barnabae Itinerarium*, or *Drunken Barnaby's Journal*. This was written by Richard Brathwaite, born in 1588. He went up to Oriel College, Oxford at the age of sixteen, becoming a Cavalier, a High Churchman and country gentleman. Fighting for the King during the Civil War, he dedicated some of his writings to the Earl of Strafford, and gave the name Strafford to one of his sons. Brathwaite suffered for his loyalty to the King, being heavily fined during the Commonwealth. He died at the age of eighty-five in 1673.

Brathwaite never admitted authorship of *Barnabae Itinerarium*. This was not established until the early nineteenth century when Joseph Haslewood identified its author by way of textual criticism. Of the fifty or so works by Brathwaite this was the only one to survive with any degree of popularity. Written in an Anglo-Latin text it records four journeys made in the North of England. On these trips Barnaby goes from one town to another, visiting the inns, sampling the ale, making advances to the hostesses and expressing his own prejudices. These are thought to be Brathwaite's own travels and opinions. He comes to Rotherham on his first journey, and it is one of the few places where he actually mentions the name of the inn where he stays.

Thence to the Bull, at Rothram came I,
Where my gold if I had any,
Left I: long I stoutly rored,
'Till o' the Bridge I broke my forehead,
Whence ashamed, while brows smarted,
I, by night-time thence departed.

From this verse we would think that Brathwaite lost money gambling at the Bull. According to John Guest, the Bull was situated in the Market Stede, and was kept by Thomas Oke, but we do know that the Angel Inn in Bridgegate was also known as the Bull before its change of name.

Someone who would be opposed to gambling visited the area in 1733. This was John Wesley (1703-1791), the founder of the Methodist Church. In 1733 he came with his father, who was engaged in some

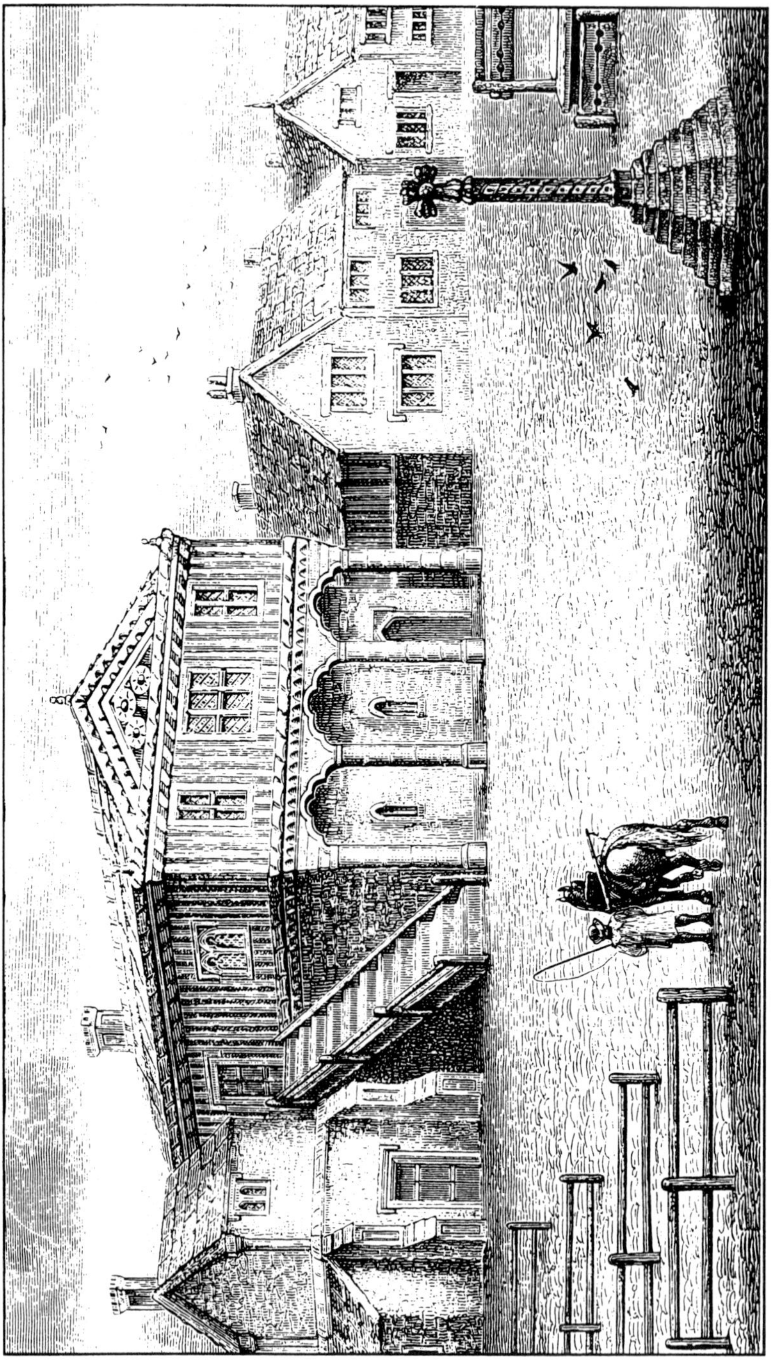

The old town of Rotherham with its market place, market cross, stocks and medieval town hall.

literary work, to stay at Wentworth Woodhouse where his father could use the library. During this stay John Wesley preached at Wentworth church. Some thirty years later he came to Rotherham and recorded the visit in his journal for 1764.

> *Saturday, March 31 (Rotherham). An odd circumstance occurred during the morning preaching. It was well only serious persons were present. An ass walked gravely in at the gate, came up to the door of the House, lifted up his head and stood stock-still, in a posture of deep attention: Might not the 'dumb beast reprove' many who have far less decency, and not much more understanding?...*

A notable woman traveller was Celia Fiennes, born in 1662 of Puritan stock. Her travels around Britain took place between 1682 and 1712. She died, unmarried, in 1741. Her first Northern Tour 'Begun to regain my health' was in 1697, when she visited Rotherham. Earlier journeys appear to have been rounds of visits combined with sightseeing, but from 1697 her travelling was more serious. She was an authority on prominent 'Spaws', where she drank the spa water and bathed. At Bath she wore a yellow canvas bathing dress 'stiff and made large... the water fills it up so that it is borne off that your shape is not seen'. In spite of taking the waters she must have had a robust constitution to undertake her arduous travelling, staying at inns as well as being entertained in private houses.

She came to Rotherham after receiving hospitality from the Rev Joshua Ferret, Vicar of All Saints, Pontefract.

> *Thence to Rotherham, its most deep clay ground, and now the ways are difficult and narrow. Rotherham is a good market town well built all of stone, the Church stands high in the middle of the town and looks finely, its all stone and carv'd very well all the outside.*

Another woman traveller was Johanna Schopenhauer. Born in Danzig (now Gdansk) in 1766, her father, Christian Heinrich Trosiener, was a man of progressive ideas who saw that his daughter received a liberal education, learning languages from an early age. When she was eighteen she married a man twenty years her senior, and together they undertook a series of long journeys in Europe. Following her husband's death she began to write novels and contributed articles to periodicals. As she had kept diaries of the travels she had undertaken with her husband, she also wrote books based on these. Johanna Schopenhauer died in Jena in 1806.

During her travels, many made on roads well away from the beaten track, she had also visited and made observations on the industry of

Figure 3. The Stable block, Wentworth Woodhouse.

the places she saw. She approached Rotherham from the 'large but not friendly manufacturing town of Sheffield, breathing fresh air again in nearby Wentworth House, the country residence of Lord Fitzwilliam.'

> *We were allowed to drive through the Park at Wentworth, but though it is large and pleasant we found it had nothing to distinguish it from any other... It is the splendid stables which are the remarkable thing here, more like a palace than a home for horses.*

She goes on to write about the stables, after which she toured the house, 'a little overloaded with ornamentation', before leaving to go to Rotherham and 'the abode of Vulcan'.

This was the Walker foundry where Mr Walker gave permission for the party to be shown round. She writes of vast quantities of sheet metal and says the raw material all came from Russia, partly in its crude state and part in bars. She comments that the Sunderland Bridge which she had seen had been made in the works, as had a bridge recently sent to Jamaica,[2] and that all kinds of work was carried out from flat irons to railing work. The visitors 'had the good fortune to see a twenty-four pound cannon being cast' and also to watch a cannon being bored, and she describes both processes.

Charles Hatchett, who made his journey through England and Scotland in 1796, also paid a visit to the Walker foundry. Born in

London in 1766, we do not know where Hatchett received his scientific training, but he is described as one of the first chemists in the organic field; he also carried on the family business of coach making. By 1821 it was said that 'Hatchett is taking care of his money... but is no longer doing anything in chemistry.' In the same year the mineral Hatchettite was named in his honour. He died in 1847, being buried at Upton-cum-Calvey in Buckinghamshire.

Hatchett saw and described collieries and a steel works in Sheffield before coming to Rotherham to meet Joseph Walker and to have breakfast with him in 'an elegant house about ½ mile from Rotherham on the Doncaster Road'[3]. After breakfast Mr Walker asked Mr Yates 'a superintendent' to show him the works in and near Rotherham. Hatchett describes the cannon making in a more scientific way than Johanna Schopenhauer. He visited the foundry, and then went to the forge. He remarks that 800 men were employed by the Walkers at their various sites in the area. He also visited the steel works of Mr Booth, a partner of the Walkers, where he again describes the processes he watches. After dining, Hatchett and his companions set out for Doncaster on a fine road through beautiful country after leaving Rotherham which was 'not a large town, neither does it appear to contain anything remarkable.'

The Rev William McRitchie, minister of the parish of Clunie, Perthshire, made his tour of Great Britain reaching Doncaster in August 1795, where he dined at the Reindeer Inn before getting the 4 pm coach to Sheffield. On his journey there he notes seeing Squire Finch's Castle,[4] a view of Wentworth, seat of Earl Fitzwilliam, Alric Hall,[5] and Joseph Walker's house, beautifully situated on a height on the south bank of the Don. He made a stop 'at Rotherham, to refresh', then after going about a mile on the journey 'look back at the town with its church and spire forming a fine object in the landscape. The rain falls heavily upon us. Go inside, and arrive at Sheffield, half past seven pm'.

The name Daniel Defoe (1660-1731) is nowadays largely associated with the book *Robinson Crusoe*, but in his time he was a prolific author and pamphleteer, being imprisoned and pilloried for writing *The shortest way with Dissenters* in 1703. He was also the writer of a three volume work, *A Tour through the whole island of Great Britain* published between 1724 and 1727. The work is primarily a guide to the social and economic conditions throughout the country. He prefers towns with clean, well built modern houses to the 'tumbledown picturesque', and the countryside full of corn and cattle rather than views and wilderness, and his interests were in the present not the past.

However, he did observe the past as he approached Rotherham from

Figure 4. Early eighteenth century Rotherham from the north. Sketch by Samuel Buck, 1723.

Sheffield. 'The remains of the Roman Fortification or encampment between Sheffield and Rotherham is there still and very plain to be seen and, I suppose, may remain to the end of time'. He also notes that 'Here also is the famous Bank or Trench which some call the Devil's Bank, or Dane's Bank, but 'tis frequent with us to give the Honour of such great Trenches, which they think was never worth the while for men to dig, to the Devil, as if he had more leisure...'.

In Rotherham he saw:

> *... nothing of note, except a fine stone bridge over the Don, which is here increased by the River Rother, from whence the Town, I suppose, took its name, as the famous Bishop Rotherham did his from the town: I will not say he is a foundling Child in the Streets, and was so sirnamed from the Place, as is often suggested in such Cases, though if he was so, it did not diminish his character, which was that of a great and good man. He was Archbishop of York, and was a Great Benefactor to this town, having founded a College here; but it seems it has been a long time ago.*

Arthur Young (1741-1820) was the son of a Suffolk clergyman and became well-known as an agricultural theorist although unsuccessful as a practical farmer. He wrote many works on agricultural subjects and became Secretary to the Board of Agriculture in 1793. He toured the North of England during 1769-70 and produced a three volume work on his findings. He tends to give accounts of good farming practices in order to encourage others to undertake improvements to their methods or equipment.

He entered Yorkshire by way of Bawtry, the road from Doncaster being 'Turnpike. Hilly but pretty good.' As well as noting road conditions Young also made brief notes on the inns where he stayed, commenting that he includes some prices 'as a matter of curiousity; to show that the North *yet continues*, beyond all comparison, cheaper than the South.' In Rotherham he stayed at the Crown, 'very disagreeable, and dirty, but very cheap. Hashed venison, potted mackerel, cold ham, tarts, cheese and a melon, at 1/- a head.'

Dedicated as he was to agriculture Young also observed the industrial side of Rotherham, and in doing so noted the rates of pay in the same way as he did for agriculture.

> *Rotherham is famous for its iron works of which it contains a large one belonging to Mr Walker and one or two smaller... The forgemen work by weight and earn from 8/- to 20/- a week but 12/- or 14/- the average; the foundry men are paid by the week from 7/- to 10/-. No*

> *boys are employed younger than 14. There are a few women employed, and only in piling old bits of scrap iron...*
>
> *Besides the iron manufactury they have a pottery... It employs about two or three and twenty men and forty boys, the men are paid 9/- a week for day work, but much is done by the piece, in which case they earn more... boys of nine or ten years old have 2/- or 2/- and 6d a week.*

Young soon turns to write about his prime interest. 'What gave me much greater satisfaction than the iron works of Rotherham was the cabbage culture of Samuel Tucker, Esq[6] who lives just out of the town... The excellent and accurate cultivator... was pleased to receive my inquiries with the utmost politeness...'. Young goes on to describe in great detail how three acres of cabbages were cultivated. Winter sown cabbage were the best, being 10lb in weight when Young saw them, and he estimated that they would weigh 30lb when 'in perfection'. The cabbages were used to feed milch cows, weaned calves and fattening beasts.

Apart from the cabbages Young also admired the view. 'Another circumstance, though not concerning agriculture I should not forget, which is the landscape from Mr Tucker's cabbage field, situated on top of a hill. I would, at any time, with the utmost pleasure, ride forty miles to view such another.' He went on to ride to Sheffield on a road 'excrably bad, very stony and excessively full of holes.'

He returned at a later date to visit Wentworth House. He begins by saying that 'the palace of the Marquis of Rockingham, is situated between Rotherham and Barnsley in the midst of a most beautiful country in a park which is one of the most exquisite spots in the world.' He goes on to describe the house, grounds and follies in great detail before writing that 'The husbandry of the Marquis of Rockingham is much more worthy of attention than any palace...', and then describes the crops and farming methods used on the estate in detail. On leaving Wentworth he rode to Kiveton Hall, the seat of the Duke of Leeds, by way of a good turnpike road, describing the soil, and rents of the land on his way. At Kiveton he visited and described the contents of the house.

Thomas Short (1690?-1772) was a Scot who settled in Sheffield after graduating in medicine. He undertook several journeys in order to visit mineral springs in Yorkshire and other parts of the country. In his book on the history of mineral waters, published in 1734, he describes a visit to Guilthwaite Spa (Spaw), near Whiston. Here, Mr George Westby had built 'a small house over the drinking well, and made below a large Receptacle or Bath for several people to go in it at once.' The spa had been abandoned by the time Dr Short paid his visit but he describes the chemical make-up of the water and the cures attributed to it. 'This water has done very great Cures in Vomitings, Belchings, Flatuencies, Hyppo's, Indegestion...' The clay around the spa was said to have been taken, dried and kept in a box, then moistened into a paste which was used to soften corns. The Duke of Leeds was said never to have been without this remedy.

Dr Richard Pococke was born at Southampton in 1704, and after attending school there went on to Corpus Christi College, Oxford, where he took the degree of Bachelor of Law in 1731, having the degree LL D conferred on him two years later when he was Precentor of Lismore in Ireland. His passion for travel is to be met when he starts to write a series of letters to his mother in the same year. The first letter is dated from Genoa in December 1733, and from then his letters tell of his travels away from his not too exacting duties in Ireland. He was Precentor of Waterford in 1744, then Archdeacon of Dublin, Bishop of Ossory, and finally Bishop of Meath six months before his death in 1765.

He made several prolonged visits to England in 1750 and 1751. In August 1750 he was writing a letter from Wentworth House, describing a visit to Hornby Castle, but it was not until a later letter that he described his visit to Wentworth itself. 'The Marquis of Rockingham invited me to dinner and my lady very politely engaged me to stay all night. I went with them to my Lady's wood where there is a little house in which a batchelor might live, offices underground.' The weather must have changed overnight as he spends most of the next day in the library as it was 'a terrible day'. The weather seems to have improved during the day as in the evening he went to see 'the poultry, the kine, the greenhouse, etc. and my lady engaged me to stay the next day and dine in the wood.' He ends this letter by saying that he would arrive in London in two days' time.

Another letter describes visiting Wentworth Castle before going on to Wentworth Woodhouse 'where the marquis invited me to dinner and I was engaged to stay there three days...' Pococke goes on to describe the house in great detail. In the library was:

> *a piece of antiquity I never saw before, called a Shepherd's Block; it is of yew, about two feet long and three inches square, it was a contrivance for an almanack before printing. At each corner the days of three months are marked by notches, the Sundays being marked by a larger notch, and the signs are cut out for each month.*

He writes of the gardens and the follies which were to be seen and

> *an invention for a gravel walk, where they have no gravel which is of sand, a red cinder of coals, and the spar of the lead mines, blue*

Figure 5. Rotherham parish church, which has dominated the town since the Middle Ages.

> *and white, broken into pieces laid on it, which does very well. A large walk behind the house is of gravel brought from Blackheath, near Greenwich.*

He adds a postscript that a Dr Wells, MD accompanied him to Rotherham, to a Roman Place, 'Temple-burgh', before going on to Worksop.

In another letter dated 18 August, 1750, he describes more fully what he did on his way to Worksop:

> *On the 10th I went four measured miles from Wentworth house to Rotherham, which has its name from the river Rother, on which it is situated, and by which there is navigation from the Don for large barges, by means of locks. This river is supposed to have its name from the red earth it runs through. There is a very handsome Gothick church in the town with a good spire. Thomas of Rotherham, Archbishop of York, and Bp Saunderson were born here. About a mile beyond the town is Temple brugh, which plainly appears to have been a Roman town; the circuit within the fossee is about 160 yards square, there being an entrance as in the middle, only on the east and west, and this is called Castle guard. A natural bank to the north is called Temple brugh, there seems on the south side to have been a double fossee. On the other side of the river, a little higher, is*

> *Kemberworth hill, from which I was informed a fossee and bank goes to Kemberworth, to Grape Brook...'*

From Rotherham he travelled to Conisbrough, and then by a circuitous route to Keighton (Kiveton), the seat of the Duke of Leeds 'which is a very grand house, with suitable offices, in the taste of the latter end of the last century', and from there continues to Worksop.

John Byng (1742-1813), later Viscount Torrington, was also an indefatigable traveller who came to these parts in 1789 and 1792. His diaries reveal that he was not in favour of industrialisation, believing that this was partly to blame for rural depopulation, the other cause being the 'Enclosing Acts'. He wrote 'I dread trade. I hate its Clamour' and that 'It is in trading towns where rioting and discord begin...'

Despite his dislike for industry he nevertheless visited the Walker ironworks in Rotherham. In 1789 he and his companions approached the town from Worksop, going through Carlton and 'Enter'd the wooded grounds of Mr Knight[7] and passed his ancient house, opposite which are new and spacious offices.' They then descended 'to the village of Stone' lost their way, and had to ask directions from some gentlemen 'of the Lumley family, I believe.' Finally they managed to approach 'the ruins of Roche Abbey:

> *and surely nothing was ever more happily placed for comfort and contemplation; on the one side the rocky cliffs where it derived its name, and on the other the most pastoral and translucent stream shaded by woods, for fishing there cannot be a better situation; or for love or contemplation. Our observation here was most hasty, for we sat down at several points. Tho' undemolished it is not properly guarded... and certainly there should not have been a modern lodge built close to this picturesque old gateway of entrance. A house and inhabitants are necessary but it should have been in concealment...'*

They then went on to Sandbeck Park Gate, which opened opposite the abbey garden, the 'chief beauty of this seat'. He went on, 'After having lately seen so many houses (and a modern house cannot be worth the trouble) and being drag'd about by a foolish housekeeper, I was not sorry at being refused admittance here.' The party then went to Tickhill, where they stayed at the Red Lion, and recommenced their journey the next day, going to Maltby 'in a pretty vale', and Bramley 'a neat well built village', where he stopped to drink a pint of milk and commented that 'Finer children than in this country I never saw.'

Finally he came to Rotherham.

> *We enter'd the town of Rotherham, and went to what is called the*

Figure 6. The ruins of Roche Abbey.

> *best inn, the Crown, but a more dreary, blacker, tumbledown, old casemented ruin co'ud not be. In a front room upstairs, uneven as a ploug'd field we drank tea, and then with melancholy faces survey'd our shatter'd beds, windows broken, paper hanging down, blankets and curtains torn, and everything numbered as if for sale, if purchasers can be found, for the master of the inn has got a patent*[8] *(a very odd one) for making marbles for children, which he can do of all descriptions as well, and expeditiously that he will soon supply all the school boys of the world. I proposed a walk when we pass'd thro' the churchyard by the church of great size, and with a very lofty steeple to the stone bridge over the River Don...'*

And as other travellers before him, he went to view Mr Walker's works, writing that Mr Walker 'not only maintains the neighbourhood, but has so honourably enrich'd himself, that he and his several sons live in magnificent villas, built on several eminences about the town... they ought to invent signals for invitations and announcements of all kinds.' In the iron works the party viewed an arch for an iron bridge, and then moved on to see the coal pits which were by the roadside, throwing stones into them and marvelling that children did not fall into them.

Returning to the Crown, Byng dined on thick chops and unscraped asparagus before spending an uncomfortable night in a bad bed. Next day, after rising early, he went and peeped through the windows of the church 'which contains nothing curious within, or without, but that all gravestones lie horizontally except one which was the old font.' He then went on his way to Sheffield. Although Byng made a second visit to the North in 1792 he did not return to Rotherham.

The books quoted here were written by some of the travellers before the nineteenth century, when travel began to be somewhat easier, and the advent of the railway made it a possibility for more and more people. The nineteenth century also saw more books written describing the Rotherham area, but they are beyond the scope of this article.

Notes and References

1. Tobias Matthew, Bishop of Durham, 1595-1606.
2. The Walker Bridge is at Spanish Town, Jamaica. It is now a National Monument.
3. Joseph Walker lived at Eastwood House, built in 1787, and now demolished.
4. Saville Finch, M P 1736-1788, of Thrybergh Hall.
5. Aldwark Hall, now demolished.
6. Samuel Tooker (or Tucker), 1736-1806. He lived at Moorgate Hall.
7. Henry Gally Knight, 1786-1846. He lived at Firbeck Hall.
8. J H Hohmann, Patent No 1635, granted in 1788.

Bibliography

Byng, John, *The Torrington Diaries*, Eyre and Spottiswoode, 1935.
Camden, William, *Britannia*, 1610.
Chandler, John, *John Leland's Itinerary: travels in Tudor England*, Sutton, 1993.
Defoe, Daniel, *A tour thro' the whole island of Great Britain*, Cass, 1968.
Everett, James, *Historial sketches of Wesleyan Methodism in Sheffield*, Sheffield, 1823.
Fiennes, Celia, *Illustrated journeys of Celia Fiennes*, edited by Christopher Morris, Webb and Bower, 1982.
Guest, John, *Historic Notices of Rotherham*, White, 1879.
Hatchett, Charles, *The Hatchett diary*, edited by Arthur Raistrick, Barton, Bradford, 1967.
Hunter, Joseph, *South Yorkshire*, London, 1828-1831.
Pococke, Richard, *Travels through England*, edited by J J Cartwright, Camden Society, 1888.
Schopenhauer, Johanna, *A lady travels*, Routledge, 1988.
Short, Thomas, *The natural, experimental and medicinal waters of Derbyshire, Lincolnshire and Yorkshire*, 1734.
Tate, W E, and Edmonds, E L, 'A commentary on Richard Brathwaite's "Barnabae Itinerarium" 1638', *Yorkshire Archaeological Journal*, Vol. 65, 1993.
Wesley, John, *Journal*, OUP, 1987.
Young, Arthur, *A six month's tour through the North of England*, Dublin, 1770.

3. EARLY WATERMILLS OF THE MALTBY AREA

by Alice Rodgers

LOCAL DOCUMENTARY SOURCES from the Domesday survey onwards contain abundant references to watermills in the Maltby area, but reconstruction of the history of single sites has, in the past, proved difficult because of their frequent identification only by tenant name or general location. In an attempt to overcome such problems this study sets out to put as many as possible of the references into their geographical context and to relate them to the landscape.

In an area dominated by large estates, title deeds and related documents are relatively abundant and wherever possible successive owners of individual sites have been traced. Although no cartulary of Roche Abbey survives, large numbers of deeds, some now lost, were transcribed or translated in the nineteenth century and these give an insight into the medieval picture.

This study also seeks to establish for how long individual mill sites remained in use and attempts to find the causes for their establishment or abandonment. Centred on Maltby Parish, the nature of local watercourses inevitably means that it extends into neighbouring areas from time to time. The Nottinghamshire mills of Goldthorpe and Oldcotes have, however, been regarded as beyond its scope.

The Medieval Settlement Pattern

In two separate entries, Domesday records, firstly, Maltby together with part of Hellaby (an association still visible in the nineteenth century in detached portions of the parish) and, secondly, Hooton (Levitt). There is no mention of Sandbeck, which is first recorded in 1148, but later medieval documents, including Roche Abbey charters, mention a number of outlying hamlets (see Figure 1).

What cannot be determined is if these hamlets were already in existence by the late eleventh century, or if they emerged later. All the settlements in the parish, apart from Hooton, are closely associated with watercourses which have at various times been dammed either to create fishponds or to power mills.

Drainage

Drainage in the western part of the parish is largely to the stream, which will, for convenience, throughout this article be termed Maltby Dike. This is fed by Hellaby Brook, Newhall Dike and Kingsforth

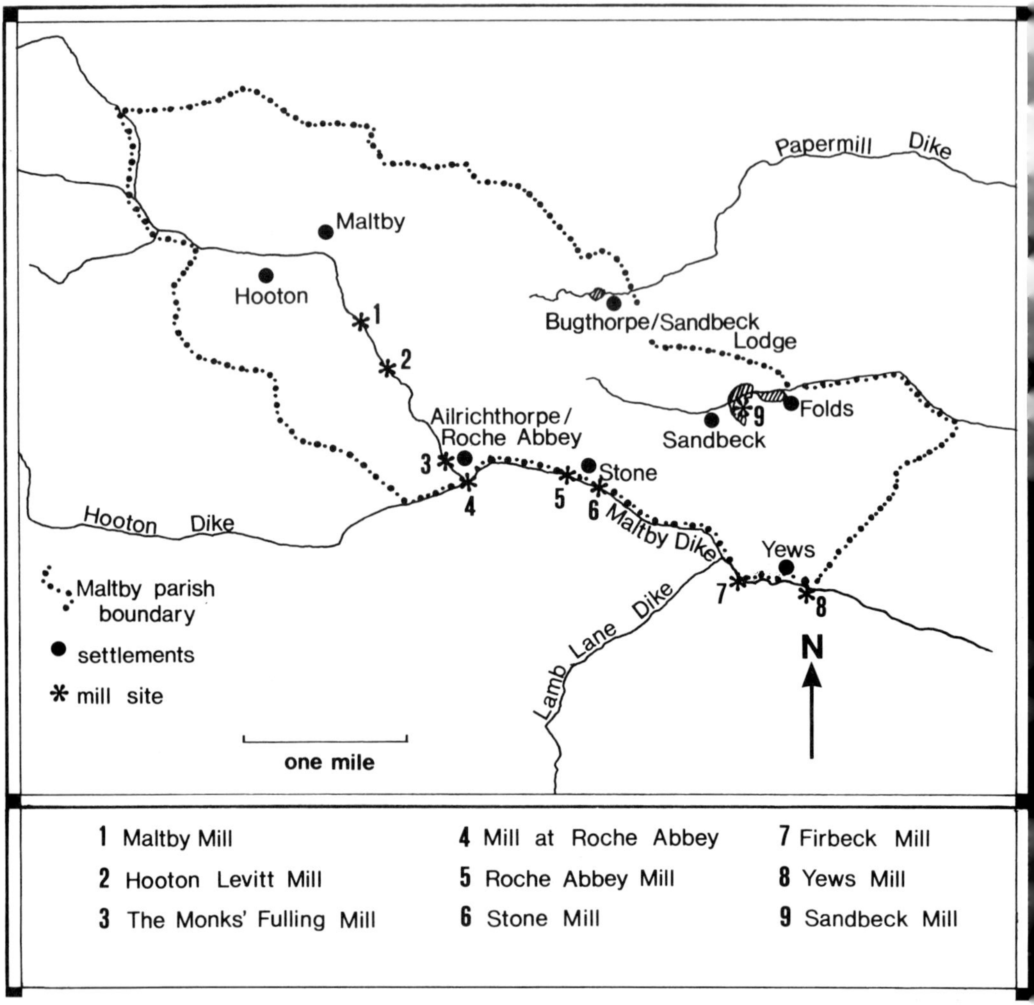

Figure 1. Maltby parish showing medieval settlements, water courses and mill sites.

Brook and gathers additional waters from Hooton Dike and Lamb Lane Dike. It flows via Roche Abbey and Oldcotes to the Ryton at Blyth and ultimately via the Idle to the Trent. The nameless watercourse which crosses Maltby Common and which is dammed to make fishponds at Sandbeck Lodge flows north-eastwards to Paper Mill Dike and so to the Torne at Tickhill. Another stream rises in Sandbeck Park and flows via Folds to the Torne south of Tickhill.

Domesday Mills

The two Domesday entries associated with Maltby Parish record a total of four mills. Hooton has one yielding 28d and Maltby/Hellaby has three paying 16 shillings. Although these mills are not particularly valuable, the number of sites seems totally disproportionate to the significance of the community, particularly when compared with other local vills. Rotherham is recorded as having only one mill worth 10 shillings, Conisbrough has two worth 32 shillings and the Dadsley (Tickhill), Stainton, Hellaby entry lists three mills paying 40 shillings. Laughton, a very significant place prior to the Conquest, has no mills recorded either for itself, or in its extensive, dependent territories.

The Mill Sites

It should be noted that of the mill sites identified or suggested in this article, only that of Maltby, and those within the part of Roche Abbey administered by English Heritage, are open to the public. The other sites may only be viewed by permission.

Maltby Mill (SK 532916)

The existence of a medieval mill in Maltby is indicated by Domesday and confirmed by a reference in a deed of 1336[1] in which Joan le Harpur grants to her son a toft and croft by the road leading from the vill to the mill of Maltby. A further reference is to be found in Richard Levet's undated grant to the monks of half the mill of Hooton Levet 'with free watercourse from Maltby Mill to the Monk's mill'.[2]

In spite of its proximity to Roche, there is no indication that Maltby Mill was ever held by the monks. What we have is a manorial mill associated with the de Busli family and their successors the Cliffords.

In 1585-6, George Clifford, third Earl of Cumberland, divided the manor and sold the half including the manorial mill to Sir Edward Stanhope. Sir Edward's son, Edward, sold it to Sir Nicholas Saunderson (of Sandbeck) in 1622.[3]

Shortly after this purchase, the mill became the subject of a dispute between Saunderson and Stanhope's former lessee George French.[4] French, in collusion with Stanhope's former steward Ralf Fretwell (who had retained the counterpart of the lease to the mill) had been underletting this and other property which was properly that of Saunderson and had 'been thereby a great gayner'. Further, French had failed 'sufficiently to repayre the said mill with millstones and other things needful and so to keep maintayne and leave in good and sufficient repayre as well the said mill and mill dam'. The dispute was apparently settled in Saunderson's favour because a 1633 Sandbeck Estate rental[5] reveals that William Elliot of Maltby was paying £15 per annum rent to Sir Nicholas for the mill.

Maltby Baptismal Registers[6] between 1620 and 1626 contain a number of references to the children of the Hibbes/Hibberd family 'de Milne', so it seems likely that their father was French's tenant. There are further parish register references to Maltby Mill when the children of William Elliot are baptised in 1632 and 1646. When in 1660 the mill is leased to John Daniell[7], William Elliot, deceased, is referred to as the previous tenant.

The 1660 lease reveals the property to consist of a 'dwelling house and water corne mill under one roof commonly called Maltby Mill ... with one croft or yard or garden ... and also all toll benefitte and custome for grindinge of corne and grain ... as well of the tenants of the said Manor of Maltby as others ...'.

Although no subsequent lease of the mill survives, Daniell apparently renewed because his name appears in the rentals of 1668 to 1677[8], and in the Manorial Court Rolls of the 1670s. In the 1674 Maltby Court Roll, John Daniell is fined 3s 4d 'for taking excessif tole and [illegible] Grest sent to the Lord's Mill'. The parish registers reveal that John Daniell died in 1680 but the mill appears to have remained in use because in the Maltby Court Roll of 1694, one Jervase Eyre Esq is fined 2s 6d for 'not grinding at The Lord's Mill'.[9]

The mill fell out of use shortly after this because its site is not recorded (as a mill) in the Dickinson Survey of the Sandbeck Estate of 1724.[10] Its general location is, however, easy to deduce as there is only one property indicated close to Maltby Dike and clearly linked by a wide track to Maltby Village. This track has beside it, near to Blyth Road, two small enclosures, also part of the Sandbeck Estate, either of which could match the description of Joan le Harpur's toft and croft.

The mill site below Maltby Crags is now marked only by an area of ill-drained land, full of bistort, which indicates the extent of its dam. Further confirmation of this site is found in the street name 'Millindale', which leads in the direction of the mill site, and in the Hooton Levitt fieldname 'Dam Close' recorded on the Maltby Tithe Award on the southern side of the dike opposite the ill-drained area.[11] The location of the mill is indicated on the extract from the 1854 Six-inch Ordnance Survey map (Figure 2).

Hooton Levitt Mill (SK 533912), alias Neithermiln, Upper Mill, Wood Lea Mill

Although long a part of Maltby Parish, Hooton is listed at Domesday as a distinct vill in a different lordship, both before and after the Conquest. At Domesday it had one mill worth 28d. The early medieval manor of Hooton apparently extended as far as Hooton Dike, which flows into Maltby Dike at Roche Abbey.

It was Richard Fitzturgis, Lord of Hooton, who joined with Richard de Busli, Lord of Maltby, to found Roche Abbey in about 1147. Fitzturgis granted extensive lands on the south side of Maltby Dike to enable the monks to build on whichever side of the water they pleased.[12]

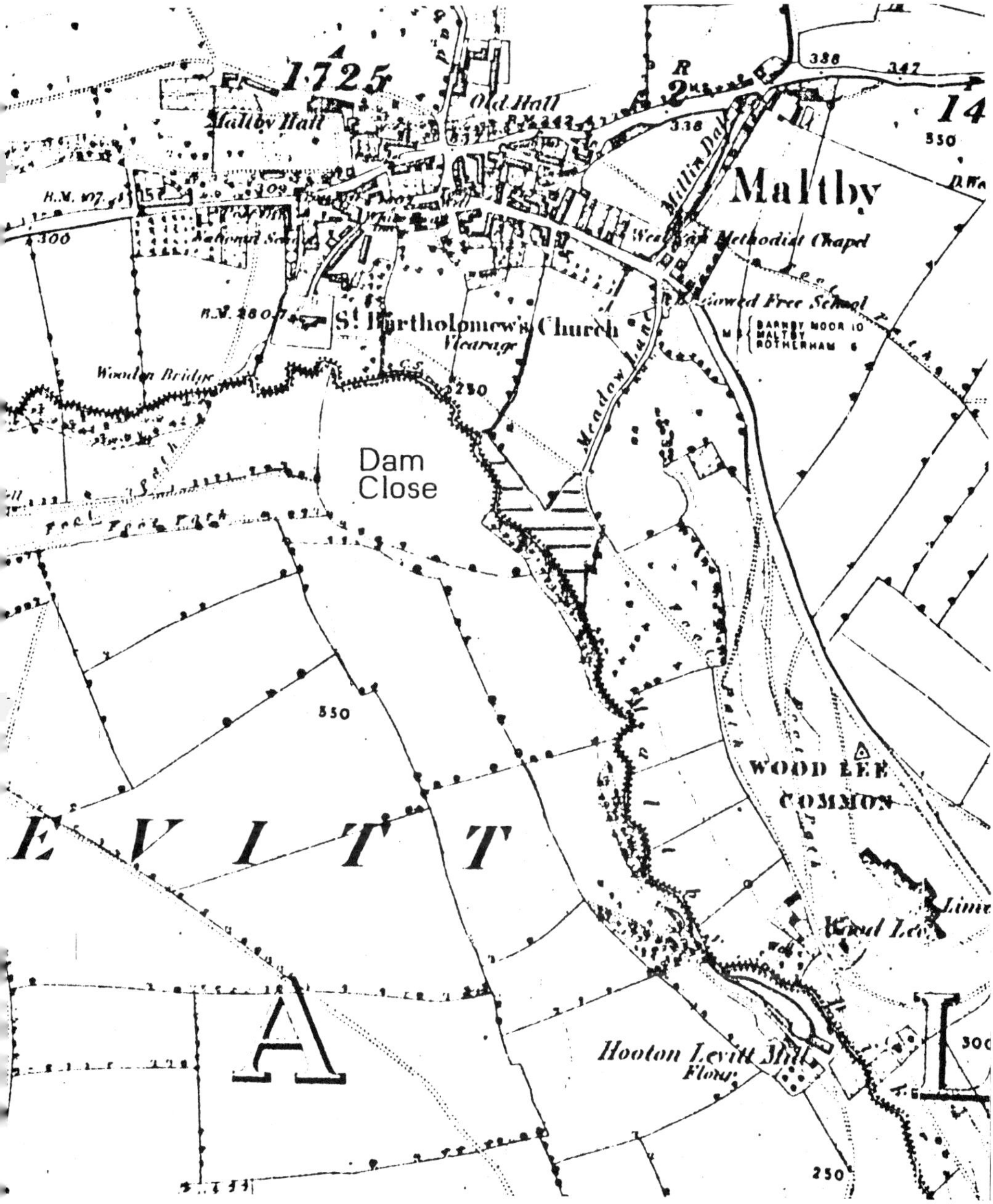

Figure 2. Extract from OS Six-inch Sheet 290, 1854 (enlarged), showing the street name Millindale. The field 'Dam Close' is indicated and the site of Maltby Mill is shown by diagonal shading.

The foundation deeds make no reference to mills which is consistent with the strictures of the Cistercian rule at this date.

Some time later, Richard Levet, possibly a great-grandson of Fitzturgis, granted the monks half a mill in Hooton 'with the pool and free water from Maltby Mill to the Monks Mill' reserving to himself the right to grind corn 'that shall grow on four oxgangs in Hooton at a multure of the sixteenth bowl'.[13] The implications of this grant are interesting. It places Hooton's watermill downstream of Maltby Mill and refers to the Monk's Mill, which is apparently upstream of the abbey (see below). As the mill's prime purpose had been to serve the needs of Hooton Levitt, there is a good case to be argued that the site mentioned in the grant is that still visible today opposite Wood Lea. This site was, until recently linked to Hooton by a somewhat circuitous track which rendered gradual the steep climb from Maltby Dike, making it suitable for beasts of burden. Could this, indeed, be the Domesday Hooton millsite? That notwithstanding, the connection between the site opposite Wood Lea and Roche is established by post-Dissolution documents.

In 1544 the Court of Augmentation (responsible for the sale of monastic land acquired by the Crown at the Dissolution) disposed of a number of Yorkshire manors, which had formerly belonged to Roche Abbey, to a syndicate of purchasers.[14] In 1549, amongst others, those of Sandbeck and Slade Hooton together with properties in Hooton Levitt were acquired by Robert Saunderson, as an initial step in the establishment of the Sandbeck Estate.[15] When, in 1620, various dues in connection with the Yorkshire manors were commuted, there is mention of property in Hooton Levitt including 'one water milne ... now in the hands of ... James Fretwell', which was valued at £3 6s 8d per annum.[16] This is probably the 'one corn mill' referred to in a Dissolution 'particular of grant' of the Manor of Hutton Slade with Carre, Hutton Leveyt and Hutton Robert quoted by Aveling.[17]

By the seventeenth century the site had acquired the name Neithermiln (that is the lower mill) which, in view of its relationship to Maltby Mill, is entirely logical. Maltby Parish Registers of the early seventeenth century associate the names of Fretwell, Elliot and Richardson with Neithermiln presumably, except in the case of Fretwell, names of mill tenants or servants. (The Fretwell family were substantial freeholders in Hooton, their holding, the Hooton Levitt Estate, descending by marriage to the Hoyle family).

The Ladyday 1672 Hearth Tax returns,[18] on which recent comparison with seventeenth century rentals has cast new light, reveals William Richinson to be the last person named in the Hooton entry, a place logically reserved for the tenant of the mill. He may be William

Figure 3. Hooton Mill, about 1910. *Rotherham Central Library, Archives and Local Studies Section*

Richardson, son of William Richardson listed in the 1643 baptismal register.

Following the demise of Maltby Mill, that of Hooton became known as the Upper Mill. The 1730 probate inventory of George Tyas of Woodley, Miller, refers to it as such.[19] The property consisted of a substantial house with buttery, parlour, house place, cellar, best chamber and chamber above the house together with a mill which appears to be detached from the dwelling (see Figure 3). In addition to the mill, Tyas had a small acreage of arable land and kept a variety of stock, including four horses.

The mill apparently continued in use throughout the eighteenth and nineteenth centuries meeting the needs of both Maltby and Hooton. It is marked on Jefferys' map (1767-71) and all subsequent surveys. It is found as part of the Hooton Levitt Hall Estate in 1919[20] and finally

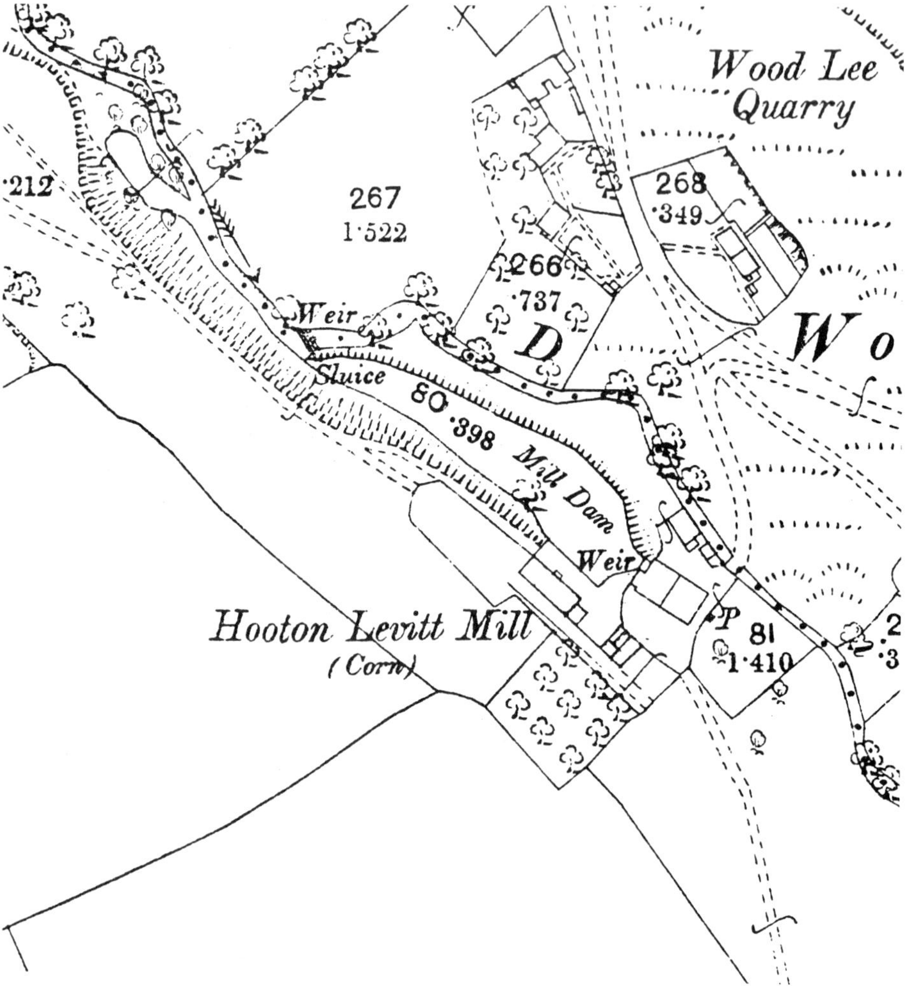

Figure 4. Part of OS Twenty-five Inch Sheet 290/15, 1892, showing Hooton Mill.

fell out of use within living memory. Figure 4 shows the mill and its dam as portrayed on the Twenty-five inch to one mile Ordnance Survey map of 1892.

The Monks' Fulling Mill

The mill mentioned in Richard Levet's grant (see above) lacks an obvious site although it is clearly downstream of Hooton Mill and upstream of the abbey. In a grant of 1377, John, son of William Levet, granted to Richard Barry founder's patronage of the abbey together with a half penny rent issuing out of the fulling mill 'situated in the aforesaid Abbey' and granted as parcel of the foundation of the said abbey.[21] Herein lies a confusion because the foundation grants make no mention of mills and the mechanisation of the fulling process (that of matting or felting loosely woven woollen cloth either by footwork or water-powered fulling stocks) did not occur until the thirteenth century.

The likely explanation appears to be that the monks chose to construct a mill upstream of the confluence of Maltby and Hooton Dikes and thus in the manor of Hooton and gave acknowledgement for the privilege to the manorial Lord. There has been much speculation by visiting archaeologists about a mill site next to the Abbey House where there are two sloping channels, apparently medieval, for the diversion of water. No documentary evidence has been found of the use of this site as a mill post-Dissolution, but it remains a possibility, although it seems uncomfortably close to the abbey church. Another suggestion is afforded by the name Walker Meadow on the Hooton side of Maltby Dike, which may recall the processing of textiles. The monks, whose main

Figure 5. Extract from Thomas Jefferys' map of the West Riding, 1767-71, showing the mill sites at Hooton, Brookhouse, Roche Abbey, Roche Abbey Mill, Stone, Firbeck and Yews, together with the windmill at Carr.

enterprise was the rearing of sheep and the export of wool, could clearly be at the leading edge of technological developments in the woollen industry. The 1379 Poll Tax returns for Maltby record three men whose trade is listed as 'Walker' and who pay the higher tax rate of 6d. This suggests a trade providing for more than local consumption.

Mills of Roche Abbey & Stone

Careful examination of Jefferys' map of 1767-71 (Figure 5) shows two mills marked near Roche Abbey, one close to the cross which marks the remains of the abbey church and the second beside the lane which leads to Kings Wood, this being the site now called Roche Abbey Mill. Downstream of that is marked the site of the modern Stone Mill. The close proximity of these mills and their use of the same name at different periods has led to considerable confusion in the past. The question of which of these is a medieval site, which was converted into a forge and which can be identified with Parish Register entries of mills bearing different names has proved an engaging puzzle.

The three mills will be distinguished for the purpose of this study as:

1. The Mill at Roche Abbey (Maltby Parish).
2. Roche Abbey Mill (Laughton Parish).
3. Stone Mill (Maltby Parish).

(1) The Mill at Roche Abbey (Maltby Parish, SK 545897)

The Dickinson map of the Sandbeck Estate of 1724[22] shows, as little pictures, two tall buildings associated with watercourses to the south-east of the abbey church. The survey reveals that this mill was tenanted together with 73½ acres of arable, pasture and meadow by one Thomas Taylor.

The will and probate inventory of Thomas Taylor's father, James, (also a miller of Roche Abbey) who died in 1721, survives.[23] The probate inventory shows James Taylor's house to consist of kitchen, brewhouse, cellar, coal house, parlour and three chambers. His bequest to his wife of 'the best bed in my chamber, the chest of drawers and one of the ovall tables... and alsoe one of the long settles and alsoe over and beside forty pounds of good and lawfull monye of England' casts light on the relative affluence of an early eighteenth century miller.

To his eldest son Thomas, James Taylor bequeathed his personal estate together with 'the propriety and tenant right of my house outhouseing ground and mill to enjoy the same dureing the term of my lease and afterwards during my Lds Castletons pleasure'. Lord Castleton (of Sandbeck), first and only Earl Castleton, was

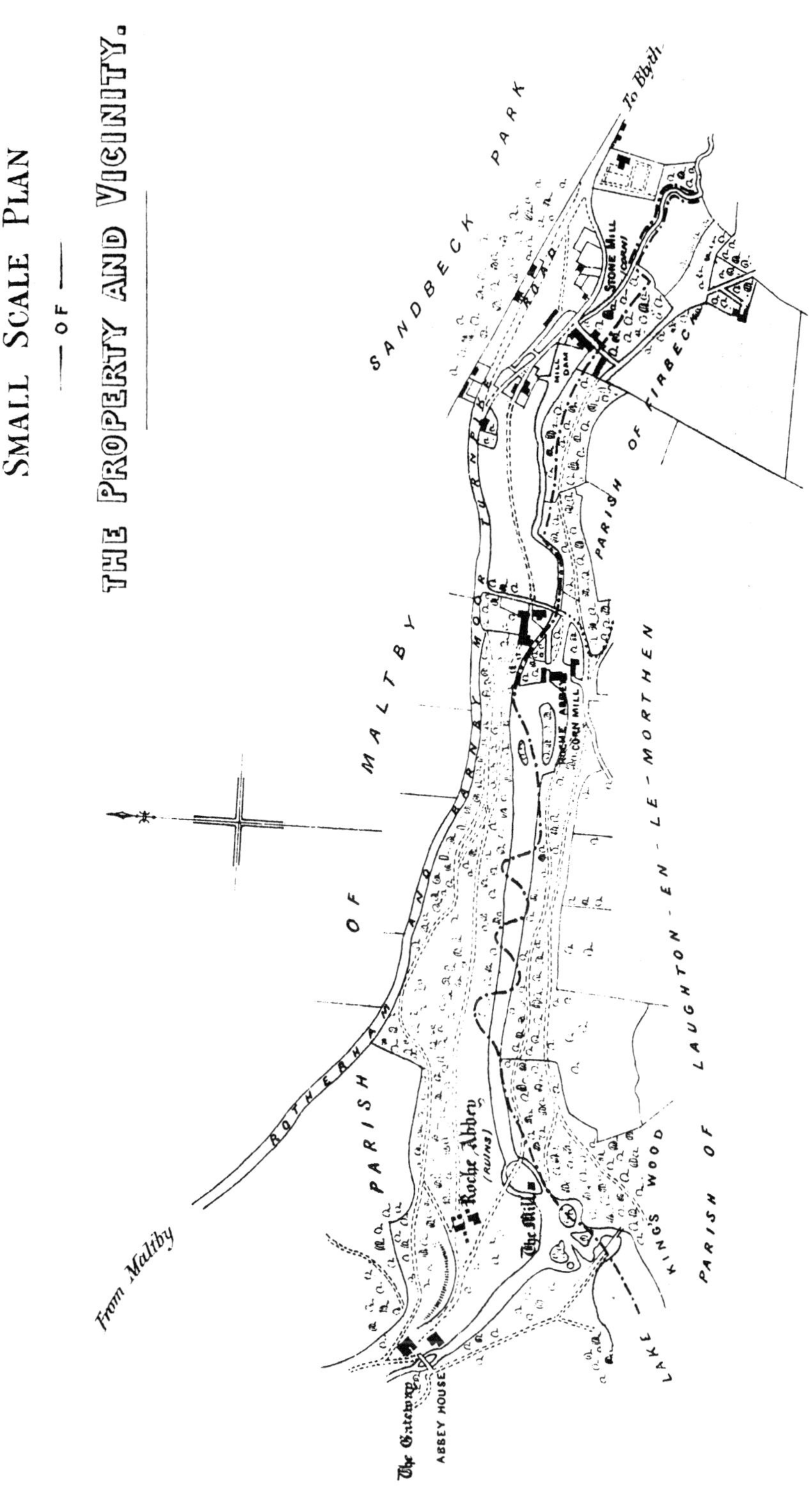

Figure 6. Plan from the 1867 sale particulars of Stone Mill showing the ruined mill at Roche Abbey, Roche Abbey Mill and Stone Mill.

great-grandson of Sir Nicholas Saunderson who had purchased the Roche estate in 1627.

A rental of Roche Abbey 'as it is now lett' of 1627[24] and a particular of Roche of 1628[25] both refer to a mill, but its context and tenure make clear that this is Roche Abbey Mill (see below) and not the Mill at Roche Abbey. It looks as if the latter was established in the later seventeenth century and reference to 'labour at Roche Abbey mill' in a 1695 account[26] supports this view. The location of the mill dam due south of the abbey (see Figure 6) meant that, in order to ensure a fall of water, it must have been built much higher than the medieval water level, presumably over the top of the abbey ruins. The additional mill was doubtless required because the conversion of Roche Abbey Mill into a forge meant that there was insufficient corn milling capacity in that part of the valley.

The mill at Roche Abbey continued in use until 1774 when a Sandbeck survey records its demolition.[27] This coincides with the landscaping of the Roche Valley by Capability Brown for the fourth Earl of Scarbrough (the Lumleys having inherited from the Saundersons in 1723).[28] Brown created a lake with an island which incorporated the mill and mill dam.

The mill, in ruins, remained on the island as a landscape feature and is recorded on Ordnance Survey maps in the nineteenth and early twentieth century. Excavations of the abbey site between the wars removed the island and revealed this ruinous mill as the upstanding portion of the infirmarers lodging.

(2)Roche Abbey Mill (Laughton Parish, SK 551897), alias: le Stonemiln, 1348; Molendinum de Petra; Backhouse/Barkhouse Miln; Stone Forge; Roche Abbey Forge.

Downstream of Roche Abbey, the converted buildings of Roche Abbey Mill and its former dam are visible today from the A634 (Figure 7). The buildings, apart from the late eighteenth century mill house, are south of Maltby Dike and thus in the ancient parish of Laughton en le Morthen and in that part of it which the 1672 Lady Day Hearth tax returns record as Stone.[29]

Laughton, it will be remembered, has no mills listed in the Domesday survey, but references in medieval and later deeds confirm that this site is of unquestionably medieval origin. A charter of Roche Abbey of 1319, transcribed by Addy,[30] reveals that Adelicia Countess of Eu, Lady Paramount of the Honour of Tickhill from about 1220, granted lands and properties in Hooton, Carr and Thurcroft (Laughton Parish) 'et molendinum de Petra' that is 'the mill of Stone' to the abbot and

Figure 7. Roche Abbey Mill now converted into a dwelling. Stone from its demolished dam is visible lower left.

convent of Foucarmont in Normandy. The charter reveals that this holding was later granted to the Cistercian house of Netley in Hampshire which in 1319 sold it for 380 marks sterling, to the abbey of Roche.

A Roche confirmation deed of 1342-3[31] records the mill as a landmark in the recital of the boundary of the wood of Lindric (part of Kings Wood) near to the abbey 'as it is enclosed by a ditch and from that ditch itself towards Bernehill and from Berneshill towards the mill of the same monks'.

A further reference to 'le Stonemilne' is to be found associated with a grant of 1348, of lands and tenements in Slade Hooton Manor (Laughton Parish)[32] and the mill's association with Slade Hooton Manor is confirmed by reference to a dispute of 1402 noted by Addy.[33] The cause of the dispute between the Abbot and Convent of Roche and one John Myrfin of Seton (Stone?) was a piece of land called 'le Milnecrofte' situated close to the wall of the abbey which had been considered the property of Seton (Stone?) Mill in which mill the inhabitants of Slade Hooton, Brookhouse, Thurcroft and Carrhouse were obliged to grind their corn. The proximity to the abbey wall can make this none other than the site of what is now called Roche Abbey Mill.

This mill appears to be subject to name changes. It is mentioned in a particular for grant supplied to William Ramsden and Henry Tyrrell in 1545-6[34], but this time it is referred to as Barkhouse (or Backhouse) Miln, its identification with the earlier Stone Mill being confirmed by the fieldname 'Barkhouse Green' adjacent to its dam recorded in the Dickinson survey of 1724.[35] This place name presents the alluring possibility that the mill was, at some stage, used to crush oak bark for tanning purposes. The relationship of the mill and its dam to Barkhouse Green is shown in Figure 8.

After the Dissolution, the Abbey Mill passed, with the site of the abbey, through a number of hands until it was purchased by Sir Nicholas Saunderson in 1627[36], thus becoming part of the Sandbeck Estate. The mill is recorded in a rental of Roche Abbey 'as it is now lett' of 1627[37], and in a particular of 1628[38], when it is in the tenure of Lawrence Yates, and in a high rent paid by Lawrence Yates in 1633.[39]

It must have been very shortly after this that the mill was converted into an iron forge because in 1640 George Sitwell and Henry Wigfall assigned to John Wright of Woodsetts the remaining term of the lease of the forge at Stone which they had originally had in association with Thomas Boseville of Warmsworth and Lionel Copley of Wadworth of Viscount Castleton as ground landlord.[40]

One continuity is clear, Nicholas Yates, recorded in Maltby Parish Register as son of Lawrence, is occupier of the only house recorded in Stone (Laughton Parish) in the Lady Day 1672 Hearth Tax return. This Nicholas Yates is referred to as previous tenant (presumably an undertenant of the syndicate of ironmasters who held the forge) in the 1681 lease of 'the forge at Roche Abbey' by George, Lord Viscount Castleton and his son to the Sheffield syndicate of William Simpson, Francis Barlow and Dionis Hayford.[41] When Simpson and Hayford renewed the lease in 1691 the property was referred to as 'the Stone Forge in Laughton'.[42]

The forge site is confirmed by the 1724 Dickinson survey and plan[43], it appears as a plume of smoke on Paul Sandby's mid-eighteenth century prospect of Roche, and is found in the tenancy of Richard Swallow (forgemaster) in 1774.[44]

The forge survived the comprehensive landscaping of its dam in the early 1770s and it appears in a lease of 1802 from George, Earl of Scarbrough to George Brookfield of Woodleigh Mill[45] when it is to be converted into a cornmill. The previous tenant is noted as Mr Richard

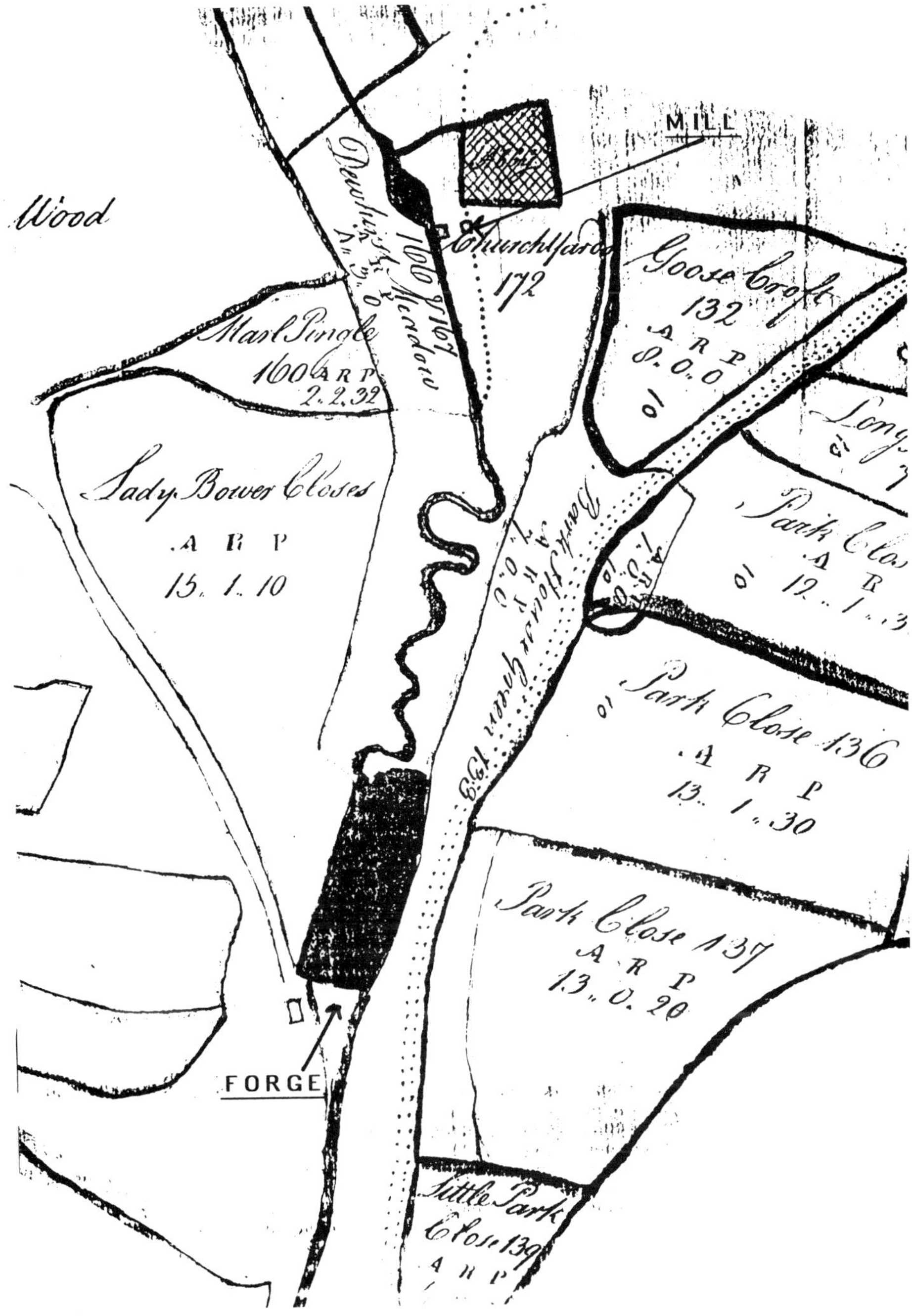

Figure 8. Copy of a section of a late eighteenth century estate plan showing Roche Abbey and the valley of Maltby Dike before it was landscaped. The course of Maltby Dike (dotted lines) and the site of the mill at Roche Abbey have been superimposed and are based on details from the Dickinson map of 1724. *Lumley Archive, reproduced with permission*

Swallow, the location is described as 'in the Dale in or near Stone in the Parish of Laughton en le Morthen' and its previous use is recorded as an iron forge.

Roche Abbey Mill, as has been demonstrated, was apparently the manorial mill associated with Slade Hooton in Laughton Parish and was somewhat inconveniently situated. The remainder of Laughton must have met its needs elsewhere.

The closest, modern, watermill site to Laughton is that of Brookhouse on Hooton Dike and this is indicated on Jefferys' map of 1767-71. This can probably be identified with the name Cawdwell Miln mentioned in a view of frankpledge of 1667.[46] This name is associated with the field name 'Scattercroft' which the Laughton Enclosure Award confirms is appropriately placed.[47] The Laughton Enclosure Award also refers to 'Windmill Field' situated on the east side of what is now School Road, but this mill had apparently gone by the late eighteenth century and no evidence of its earlier history has yet been traced. Also in need of investigation is the date of establishment of Carr Windmill whose ruins are still visible. This appears on Sandby's prospect of Roche of the mid-eighteenth century.

(3) Stone Mill (Maltby Parish), SK 554897, alias Newmiln.

Title deeds of the Firbeck Hall Estate reveal that the mill, known from the late eighteenth century as Stone Mill was in the late seventeenth century called Newmilne.[48] An earlier reference to this name is found in a 'Particular of Grant' supplied to William Ramsden and Henry Tyrrell in 1545-6 recorded by Aveling.[49] The latter lists land at Roche Abbey and contains sufficient field names which survived either to the Dickinson survey of 1724, or to the Maltby Tithe Award to enable the modern reader broadly to follow the surveyor's route. Thus, following a listing north-west to south-east of a number of fields on the Maltby side of Maltby Dike one called 'Milnefield abutting on the New milne Dam' is noted. Neither this dam nor its mill is listed as a property of Roche so they were, presumably, never acquired by the monks.

The Maltby Parish Registers of the first half of the seventeenth century record the name Newmilne in association with the personal names Edward Croft (1615), Thomas Wiggfall (1623, 1632, and 1633), John Dewhirst (1632) and Godfrey Dewhirst (1646). The baptism of Anne Dewhirst, daughter of John Dewhirst de Sido Milne' (1626) is also recorded, not it seems an additional mill name, but rather a delicious rendering of John Dewhirst's response 'side o' t'milne' when asked where he lived. In a prenuptual settlement of 27 October 1690[50], referring to property in Stone, in the ownership of John Dewhurst, his

Figure 9. Stone Mill watercourse showing re-use of Roche Abbey Stone. *Rotherham Central Library, Archives and Local Studies Section*

holding is described as 'all that messuage where Dewhurst dwells with buildings and gardens ... and all that Water Miln adjoining the messuage called the New Miln'.

As the place name element 'New' is quite often an indicator of antiquity, New Milne presents the problem of just how old it was in 1545. Examination of the site offers rather inconclusive suggestions. Like many buildings in the valley of Maltby Dike, the present structure includes much re-used Roche Abbey stone complete with masons' marks (Figure 9). This could have been gleaned in the orgy of destruction which followed the surrender of the abbey to the Crown. In an account written a generation after and quoted by Aveling[51], Cuthbert Shirebrook writes, 'for the church was the first thing put to spoil, then the abbot's lodging, dorter and frater and all the buildings thereabouts within the abbey walls'. It would have been easy enough, at the time, to cart stone to a new site only half a mile downstream of the abbey precinct. Equally likely is that the stone was acquired later to facilitate rebuilding. There is evidence to suggest that stone from the abbey ruins was being taken away as late as 1712.[52]

The mill remained with the Dewhurst family for the greater part of the eighteenth century being much mortgaged between 1758 and its conveyance by Robert Dewhurst to Joseph Bloom in trust to pay off debtors in 1784.[53] The extent of Robert Dewhurst's debts is recorded

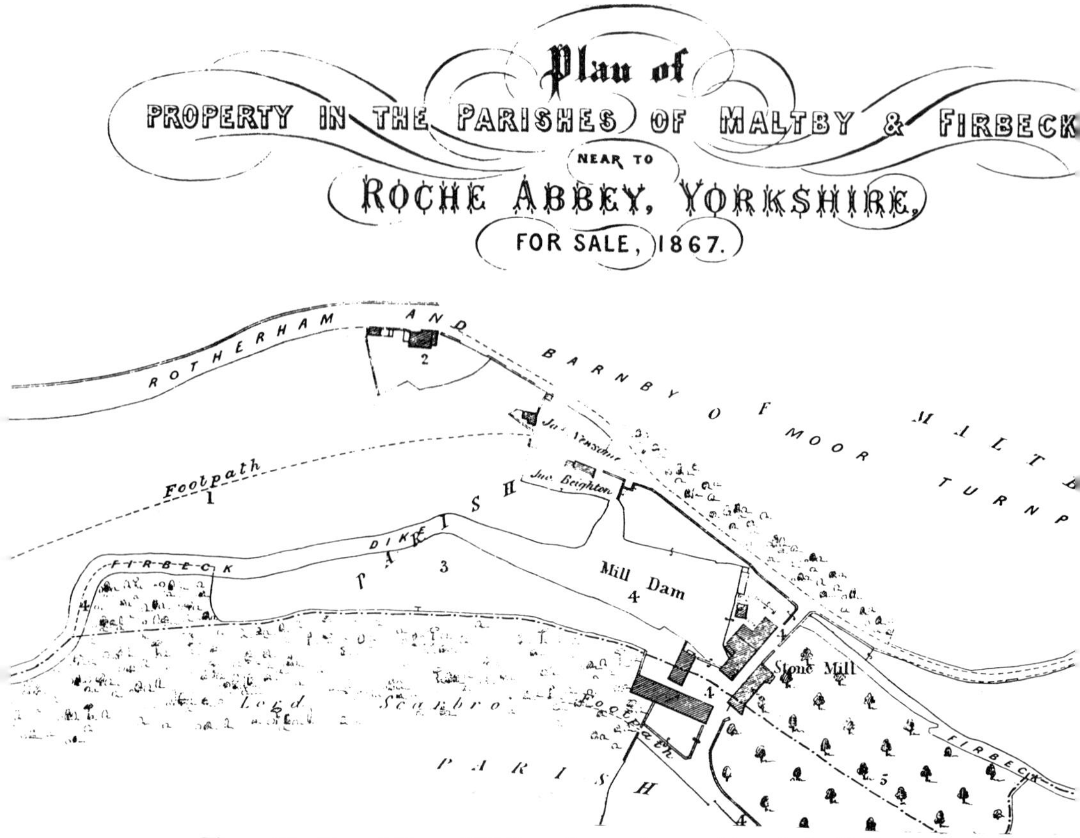

Figure 10. Plan of Stone Mill from the catalogue of its sale in 1867.

in an account of 1769-76[54] when he was found in 1776 to owe £334 11s 3d to Mr Banks (of Bawtry), £193 19s 9d to the Earl of Scarbrough (in arrears of rent) and £50 to the Curate of Scrooby. The Earl of Scarbrough had recovered interest on the debt in kind: 'Robert Dewhurst delivered to Sandbeck of the Roch Abbey (where he rented land) 18½ quarters of oats at 20 shillings the quarter'.

Following the conveyance of 1784, the mill was assigned to a succession of different parties being finally sold to Mrs Francis Harriett Miles of Firbeck Hall in 1867[55] and it remained with the Firbeck Estate until 1909[56]. Figures 10 and 11 are from the Sale Catalogue of 1867.

Firbeck Mill (SK 571888), originally Laughton Parish

Aveling notes that at the Dissolution the monks of Roche Abbey held property in Firbeck[57], but no reference has yet been traced linking the

Particulars and Plan

OF A

VALUABLE

FREEHOLD ESTATE,

COMPRISING

SMALL FARM, WATER CORN MILL,

DWELLING HOUSE,

COTTAGES AND BUILDINGS,

SITUATE AT

STONE, in the PARISHES of MALTBY and FIRBECK,

ADJOINING TO

ROCHE ABBEY, NEAR ROTHERHAM,

In the County of York,

CONTAINING IN THE WHOLE 19A. 2R. 31½P.

TO BE

SOLD BY AUCTION,

BY MR. JOSEPH NICHOLSON,

AT HIS AUCTION MART, HIGH STREET, SHEFFIELD,

On Tuesday, the 12th day of November, 1867,

AT FOUR O'CLOCK IN THE AFTERNOON,

IN ONE LOT, SUBJECT TO CONDITIONS.

The Premises may be viewed on application to Mr. GODFREY COWARD, one of the Tenants, and further Particulars may be obtained on application to the AUCTIONEER, in High Street, Sheffield; Messrs. WHATELEYS AND WHATELEY, Solicitors, BIRMINGHAM; or

BARNARD P. BROOMHEAD,

SOLICITOR, GEORGE STREET, SHEFFIELD.

Figure 11. Stone Mill, sale particulars, 1867.

abbey with Firbeck Mill. A settlement made in February 1663/4 prior to the marriage of Sir Francis Fane, the younger, refers to a water corn mill associated with the Firbeck Manor Estate[58] so it seems reasonable to assume that this mill was probably always manorial rather than monastic.

Firbeck Parish Registers[59] refer to millers in 1720 (Richard Hand) and 1759 (Samuel Foster) implying continuing use of this mill or its successor and both Jefferys' map of 1767-71 (see Figure 5) and Greenwood's map of 1817 indicate a similar, though not identical site, just downstream of the confluence of Maltby Dike and Lamb Lane Dike.

The Maltby Parish Register of 1799[60] records on 19 May, the baptism of Charles, son of John and Anne Cartlidge of Firbeck Mill, Miller, whilst the Firbeck Register of 1801 records that of Richard, son of the same John and Anne Cartlidge, Miller, on 9 November. The first entry seems something of a puzzle as Maltby Parish Church is some four miles distant from Firbeck Mill, whilst Firbeck Church is only half a mile away. The explanation lies in the fact that the mill house, as marked on the 1851 first edition Six-inch Ordnance Survey map (see Figure 12 below) lay north of Maltby Dike and, therefore, in Maltby

Figure 12. Part of OS Six-inch Sheet 297, 1854, showing the dam and former millhouse at Firbeck and the corn mill which replaced Yews papermill.

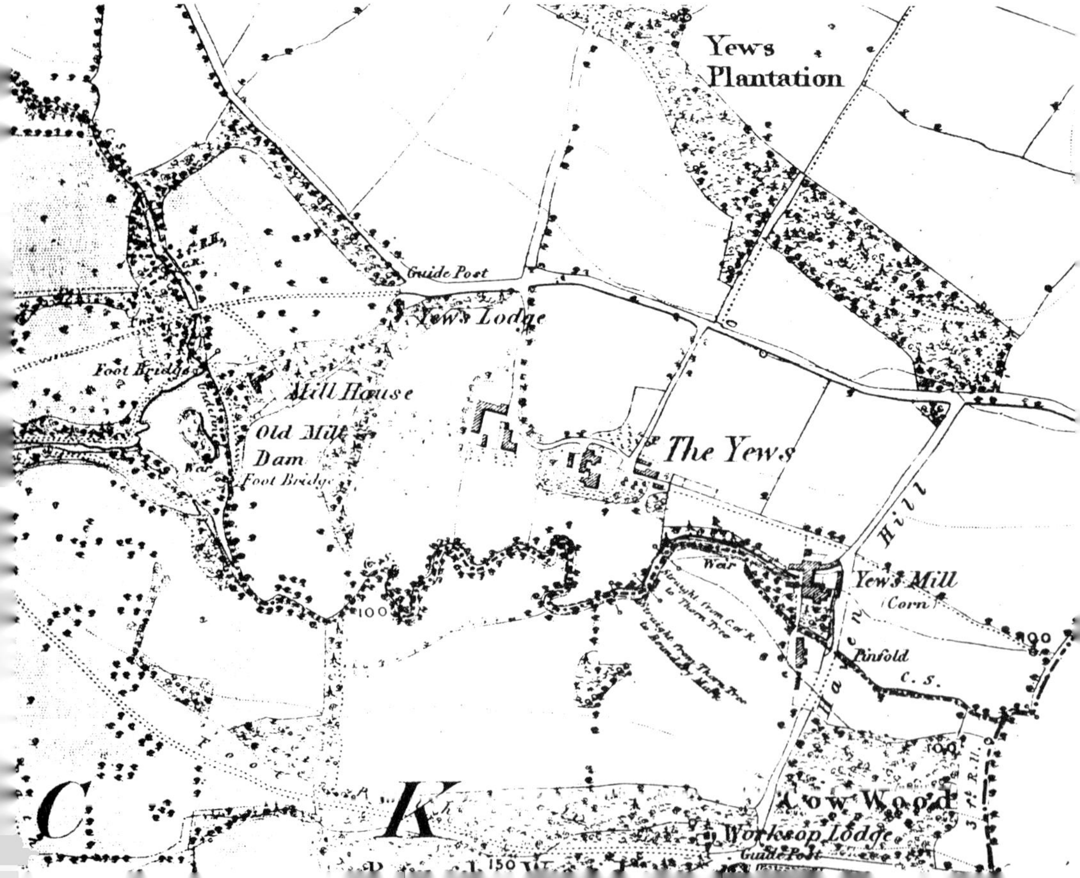

Parish. The younger Cartlidge, born in winter, seems to have had the rules relaxed for him. A Maltby Parish Church terrier of 1809 records a moduse (a money payment in lieu of tithe) of one shilling and sevenpence payable by John Knight of Langold out of Firbeck Mill.

It is not clear when this mill fell out of use, but the 1832 Maltby rating assessment shows that the area close to the mill was then part of the Firbeck Hall landscaping. Hunter, writing in the late 1820s, makes reference to the improvement of Firbeck undertaken by Henry Galley Knight, the younger, who held the property as he was writing.

> *'Henry Galley Knight esq., has much improved the ancient mansion without absolutely destroying its character and has surrounded it with beautiful gardens and pleasure grounds, to which, while in other hands it had been a stranger'.*[61]

Close to the Mill House, the first edition Six-inch Ordnance Survey map (surveyed in 1851) marks the Old Mill Dam (Figure 12). This area of water remains as an ornamental feature in the grounds of Lake House and is distinguished as the only former mill dam on Maltby Dike still to contain a substantial amount of water.

Yews Mill (SK 578887), Maltby Parish, alias Ewes Mill/Papermill

An inspeximus (an inspection and confirmation of an earlier charter) of Charles I of Letters Patent of Henry VIII (16 August, 1546) refers to a messuage, land and a mill in Ewes formerly belonging to the Abbey of Roche. This property was granted to Robert and John Thornhill[62]. Aveling records that land in Ewes was granted to the abbey by Walter, son of John of Wolverthwaite, but makes no mention of this including a mill. Ewes Mill may well have been established by the monks.

The 1379 Poll Tax Return for Maltby records Johannes del Ewes as a walker paying sixpence. This may suggest textile processing in the hamlet and the possible use of a mill for this purpose.

Maltby Parish Registers associate Ewes Mill with the surnames Nicholson (1619) and Haig (1644). By 1676 the mill had been converted to produce paper and had become part of the Firbeck Estate, then purchased by Jonathan Staniforth of Rotherham.[63] The Firbeck Registers record the burial of Anthony Walker, papermaker, in 1770 and James Spurr, papermarker, in 1771.

It is presumably this James Spurr, recorded as a papermarker, whom the Maltby Register reveals married Mary Stables in 1757. She was apparently not his first wife as he is recorded as father of a child born in 1753, as well as two others born in 1758 and 1760. As there was no other papermill in the parish, he must have practised his trade at Ewes. In 1788, this messuage, papermill and drying house was conveyed to his son, James Spurr, also a papermaker, together with William Nelson of Firbeck by Amelia Stanyforth of Firbeck Hall and others.[64]

This James Spurr's son, James Jeremiah, is shown in the Maltby rating assessment of 1832[65], as owner and occupier of the papermill and some twelve acres of land around it. The Maltby Tithe Award of 1844 shows him as landowner of the same estate, but this time a cottage and garden is let to William Bird and the mill and the greater part of the property is in the tenancy of William Jenkinson.[66] The holding is similarly described in both documents as consisting of a house, papermill with outbuildings and yard, front garden, orchard, garden and fishpond, shrubbery, a kitchen garden or cottage and garden, small plantation and four fields.

The 1841 Census lists four papermakers at the Yews, John Northage, John Sybery, and the aforementioned William Bird and William Jenkinson. The 1851 Census shows the site in the hands of William Winter, a miller and farmer of forty acres so it is clear that by this time it had ceased to work as a papermill. The first edition Six-inch Ordnance Survey Sheet, surveyed in 1851, marks it as a cornmill.

The mill continued in use throughout the nineteenth century being repurchased by the Firbeck Estate following the bankruptcy of James Jeremiah Spurr and it was sold as a parcel of that estate in 1909 (see Figure 13). By the time of the 1943 sale of the estate its status had been reduced to sawmill.[67]

Buildings on the site have now been converted into dwellings, but

Figure 13. Yews Mill, sales particulars, 1909.

Yews Farm and Yews Mill

EXTENDING TO ABOUT

284a. 0r. 39p.

And including a Stone-built FARMHOUSE, containing:—Attic, Four Bed Rooms, Two Sitting Rooms, Kitchen, Back Kitchen, Two Larders, Cellar, &c., and Pretty Garden adjoining.

The Buildings comprise:—Fold Yard, Granary, Cart Shed, Piggery, Barn with paved floor, Root House, Cart-horse Stable for six, Blacksmith's Shop, Cowhouse for four, Two Loose Boxes, Stack Yard, with Dutch Barn, Implement Shed, Two Loose Boxes, Cowhouse for six, &c.

On another part of the Farm, are Stone-built MILL, working two pairs of stones, with Granary over. FARMHOUSE, containing Four Bed Rooms, Two Sitting Rooms, Kitchen, Wash-house, Pantry, Cellar, &c., and adjoining is a FOUR-ROOMED COTTAGE.

Barn, Two Open Sheds, Fold Yard, Open Cart Shed, Yard, with Open Shed, Loose Box, with Loft over, Piggery, Two Calf Pens, Covered Fold Yard, Open Sheds, Root House, Stabling for six, Cowhouses for 12, Stack Yard, with Dutch Barn and Two Cattle Sheds.

Two Four-roomed Stone-built COTTAGES.

Figure 14. The head goit at Yews Mill.

still evident are mills of the early eighteenth century and the mid-nineteenth century. Figure 14 shows the head goit of the mill. Another particularly interesting survival is a small outbuilding to the south of the site, beside Maltby Dike, which shows evidence of a blocked-up water channel. This is built, in part, of what is apparently re-used Roche Abbey stone. It is similar in style to the late eighteenth century Gothick Roche Abbey House but crocketed pinnacles and ball finials make it even more fanciful (Figure 15). It is tempting to interpret this building as an eighteenth century adaptation into a summerhouse or fishing lodge of a seventeenth century or earlier mill.

Bugthorpe/Sandbeck Lodge, a possible millsite (SK 556915)

There is no documentary evidence of a mill at Bugthorpe, now Sandbeck Lodge, but a system of ponds is visible on the Dickinson Survey of 1724[68] and on subsequent maps. The site of the upper pond is indicated as disused on Maltby Tithe Map 1841[69] and can still be traced as

Figure 15. The eighteenth century Gothick building in the grounds of Yews Mill House which may be built on the foundations of a seventeenth century or earlier mill.

marshy ground. The lower ponds, somewhat altered, remain in use as fishponds (Figure 16).

Although it would have been a practical possibility to establish a mill here, this seems unlikely. The flow of water is very limited and such a small outlying settlement, bounded on the north by woodland and common, would hardly have produced sufficient corn to merit it.

Aveling erroneously identifies Bugthorpe in Maltby Parish with Bugthorpe in the East Riding.[70] He records that Idonea, wife of Nicholas de Bugthorpe granted two acres of land here to the monks of Roche, but he finds no mention of this at the Dissolution. The land

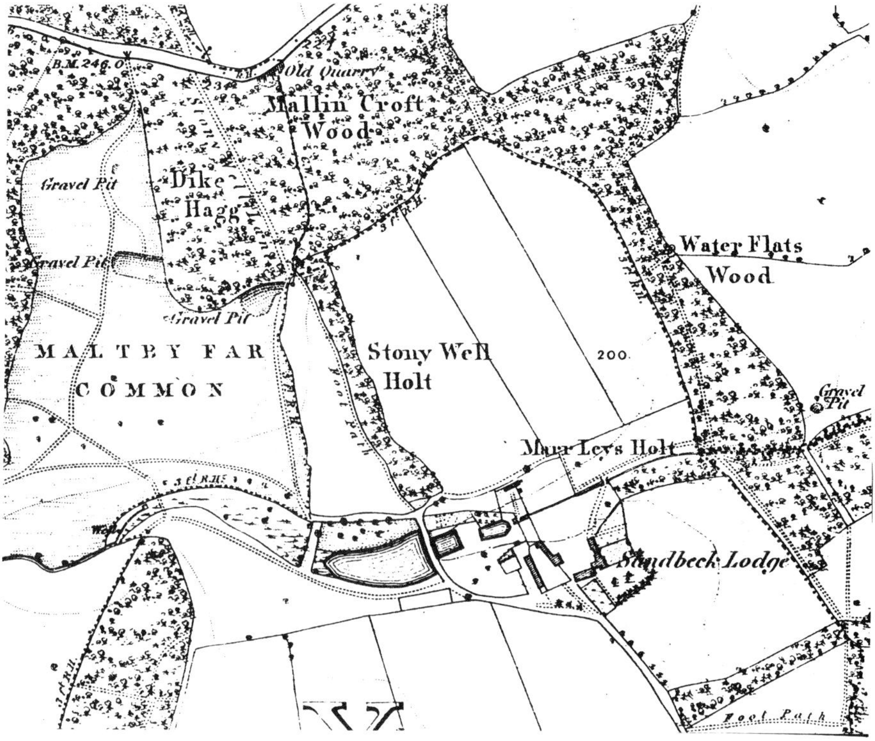

Figure 16. Part of OS Six-inch Sheet 290, 1854, showing the flight of fish ponds at Sandbeck Lodge.

in question may have become associated with the extensive monastic holding around Sandbeck.

Sandbeck Mill (SK 572905), not visible

Evidence of a medieval mill at Sandbeck is found in a single undated reference recorded by Aveling in his History of Roche Abbey.[71] This states that Hugh, Marshall of Sywardthorpe, gave his mill at Sandbeck with the pool and watercourse, to the monastery of Roche. The monks had a grange at Sandbeck thanks to the grant of the Manor to them by Idonea de Vipont in 1241.

After the Dissolution, Sandbeck passed in 1549 by purchase into the hands of Robert Saunderson.[72] Further evidence for a mill site is found in field names recorded in early seventeenth century written surveys of the estates. A particular of 1628[73] records 'Milside Close' and 'Upper Milside — a rough close' and an undated survey (of between 1627/1637) notes 'The Mylne Inge'.[74]

No mill names survive into the eighteenth century, but the Dickinson

Map and Survey of 1724 includes a field with a new name 'Pond Heads' which is almost identical in acreage to 'Upper Millside'.[75] A feature across the watercourse at the north end of this field, apparently a cascade, may well be a successor to the mill site.

Dickinson's map also demonstrates the extent to which the relatively small amount of water which rose on the estate was being impounded close to the house. To the north of the 'Lawn' are a flight of seven ponds fed by one spring and the field 'Pond Heads' includes three more ponds fed by a different spring. They may have been monastic or later fishponds or ponds provided for watering stock. All were removed in the extensive landscaping undertaken by Capability Brown in the 1770s (Figure 17). Pond Heads and the probable mill site were landscaped into the southern reach of the Upper Lake and the spring which fed the ponds and cascades is still visible at the lake's southern tip.

Summary and Conclusions

Of the nine certain mill sites described in this study, seven are of at least medieval origin, those at Maltby and Hooton perhaps finding themselves the best claimants to be two of the four Domesday mills in the Maltby valley. The five sites of Sandbeck, Hooton, The Monk's Fulling Mill, Roche Abbey Mill and Ewes were associated with Roche, but Hooton and Roche Abbey Mill apparently shared a manorial function with their monastic one. Maltby and Firbeck seem to have been exclusively manorial.

Following the Dissolution, the expanding estates of Sandbeck and Firbeck began a process of acquisition of land and property which included former manorial and monastic mills. The site of Sandbeck Mill together with Maltby Mill and Roche Abbey Mill became part of the Sandbeck estate which also had an interest in Hooton Mill and which held two mills in Tickhill. In the late seventeenth century the Firbeck estate added Ewes Papermill to its mill of manorial origin and these were subsequently joined by Goldthorpe Mill near Oldcotes and by Stone Mill. The latter mill was unusual in that it survived, independent of the great estates which surrounded it, until the latter part of the nineteenth century. Perhaps because of this it never seemed to make money.

Overall there was always greater capacity available from water powered sites than was necessary to meet purely local needs. The monks harnessed this for fulling and perhaps bark crushing for tanning. The estates, likewise, encouraged the application of non-local functions to old sites. The seventeenth century saw the development of an iron forge on land leased by the Sandbeck estate and Firbeck oversaw papermaking at Ewes.

Figure 17. The upper lake at Sandbeck Park, landscaped by Capability Brown. This work removed seventeenth century features which had in turn been built over the site of the medieval mill.

These applications seem largely opportunistic. The isolated forge at Roche required pig iron to be transported over long distances, but charcoal made from the abundant estate supplies of cordwood rendered this economic for a hundred and fifty years. Rags and old rope for papermaking doubtless reached Ewes via the port of Bawtry, but improved communications associated with the developing collieries in Barnsley and Sheffield encouraged papermaking to move westward as time went on. Local coal lay too deep to be exploited until the twentieth century so declining watermills were not superseded by steam.

The major estates not only contributed to the development of water powered sites, but also oversaw their destruction. Landscaping of Roche in the 1770s led to the demolition of the Mill at Roche Abbey whilst Firbeck Mill appears to have gone as the Hall grounds were extended.

From the eighteenth century the estates were concerned less with the productive capacity of mills than with amenity and they did much to preserve and enhance the natural beauty of the area. Thus sites, whose industrial function had ceased, reverted to the milling of corn and animal feed and to the crushing of bone for fertiliser, before gradually falling out of use. Figure 18 shows the known and conjectured periods of operation of the nine mills.

The valley of Maltby Dike now contains only four groups of mill buildings, all converted into dwellings. These are found at Hooton (Woodlea), Roche Abbey, Stone and Yews and are mainly of eighteenth and nineteenth century origin. Stone and Yews, however, show evidence of earlier work. Everything points to gradual development of individual sites over a long period rather than to more revolutionary change.

Today the sites lie silent, but one suspects that the still rapidly flowing Maltby Dike awaits only a catastrophic rise in the price of fossil fuels before its rediscovery as a renewable source of energy.

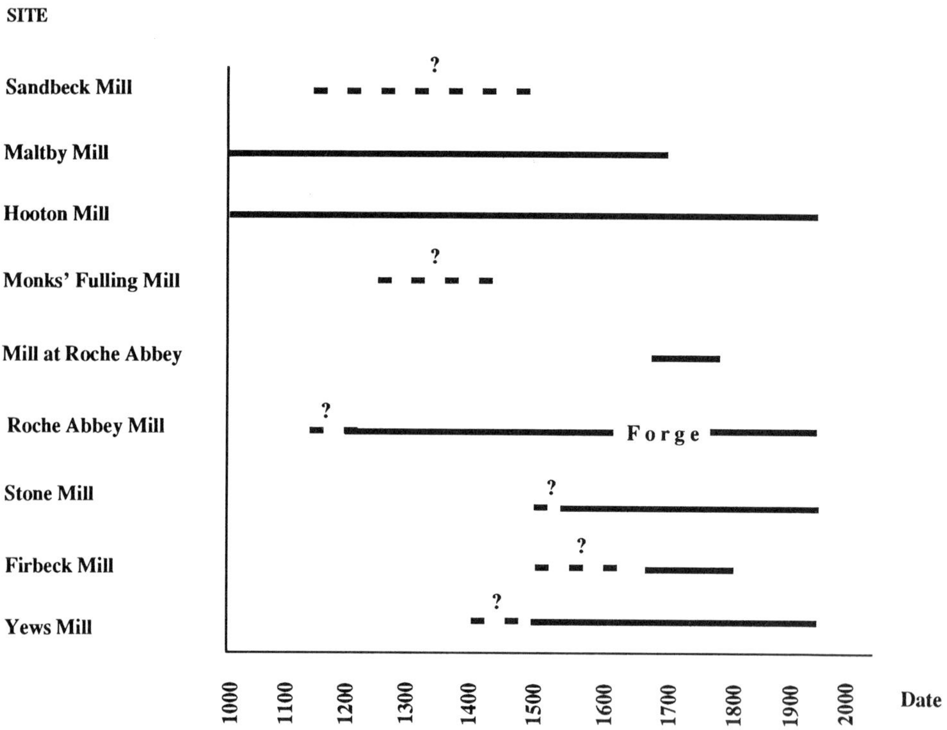

Figure 18. Diagram showing the known and conjectured periods of operation of the nine mills.

Notes and references

All references, unless otherwise stated, are to items in the Lumley Archive at Sandbeck Park.

1. MTD/B15/1.
2. J W Aveling, *Roche Abbey* — Worksop 1870, p 116.
3. MTD/B51/1b, MTD/B50/2, MTD/B50/4.
4. LPCP/9.
5. MTD/B30/40.
6. Yorkshire Parish Register Society, 1926.
7. MTD/B52/20.
8. EMA/4.
9. MAM/M/1-5, etc.
10. EMS/5.
11. ETI/12.
12. *Roche Abbey*, pp 3-5.
13. Ibid, p 116.
14. MTD/B37, etc.
15. MTD/B30/2.
16. MTD/B54/9.
17. *Roche Abbey*, p 144.
18. D Hey (Ed), *The Hearth Tax Returns for South Yorkshire: Ladyday 1672*, University of Sheffield 1991.
19. Borthwick Institute.
20. Sale Catalogue Hooton Levitt Estate, 8 September, 1919, 17/50c.
21. *Roche Abbey*, p 127.
22. EMS/5.
23. Borthwick Institute.
24. MTD/B30/33.
25. EMS/1/6.
26. EMA/139.
27. EMS/19.
28. Articles of Agreement (Lumley uncatalogued).
29. Hey, *Hearth Tax Returns.*
30. Transactions of the Hunter Archaeological Society, Vol 4 (1937), p 239.
31. Ibid, p 233 (translated C Castledine).
32. MTD/B59/2.
33. *Transactions of the Hunter Archaeological Society*, Vol 4 (1937), p 243 (translated C Castledine).
34. Roche Abbey, p 128.
35. EMS/5.
36. MTD/B30/34.
37. MTD/B30/33.
38. EMS/1/6.
39. MTD/B30/40.
40. Philip Riden (Ed), *George Sitwell's Letterbook 1662-1666*, Derbyshire Record Society, Vol X, 1985.
41. MTD/B8/4.
42. MTD/B85.
43. EMS/5.
44. EMS/19.
45. MTD/C20.
46. Sheffield (Mar. D60).
47. EEAW/2.
48. Sheffield (F H D 95-110 and 149-152).
49. *Roche Abbey*, p 129.
50. Sheffield (F H D 95).
51. *Roche Abbey*, p 90.
52. LPP/1/1.
53. Sheffield (F H D 95-103).
54. EMA/4.
55. Sheffield (F H D 152).
56. Firbeck Estate Sale Catalogues, 1909 & 1943 (Lumley 34/1a & 1b).
57. *Roche Abbey*, p 111.
58. Sheffield (F H D 7).

59. Transcribed by Gerald Stratford, 1985.
60. Maltby Parish Register, Yorkshire Parish Register Society, 1926.
61. Joseph Hunter, *South Yorkshire*, 1828-31, p 302.
62. Sheffield (F H D 1).
63. Sheffield (F H D 10).
64. Sheffield (F H D 51-53).
65. CPRB/3.
66. ETI/12.
67. 34/1a & 1b.
68. EMS/5.
69. ETI/12.
70. *Roche Abbey*, p 106.
71. Ibid, p 141.
72. MTD/B30/2.
73. EMS/1/6.
74. EMS/1/5.
75. EMS/5.

Acknowledgements

I am indebted to the Earl of Scarbrough for allowing access to papers in the Lumley Archive, to the staff of the Archives and Local Studies Section of Rotherham Central Library for prompt and good natured responses to unreasonable requests, and to the occupants of the former mills who kindly allowed access to their sites. Thanks are due to Tom Beastall who gave much guidance at the beginning of the project, to Peter Broadbent and the late John Howarth, in co-operation with whom much of the early research was undertaken, and to Kay Casey for help in the preparation of the manuscript for publication.

4. The Domestic Comforts of a Seventeenth Century Kimberworth Farming Family

by Melvyn and Joan Jones

THE THRILL OF BEING INVITED into someone's home and being offered a tour of the premises awaits the local historian opening and reading a probate inventory in a record office. A probate inventory is a list of the goods belonging to a recently deceased person, valued on oath by neighbours or executors as part of the process of obtaining administration of the movable estate, that is all possessions with the exception of any property. Such a record of belongings was required by the ecclesiastical courts from the early sixteenth to the mid-eighteenth century, especially where a person had died intestate.[1] Probate inventories for the South Yorkshire area are held in the Borthwick Institute in York.[2]

The layout of most inventories follows a standard pattern. First there is an introductory statement giving the name of the deceased, his or her former place of residence, and the date on which the inventory was taken. Next there is a valuation of the cash in the house and of the deceased's clothing and personal effects. This is then usually followed by a room by room survey with lists of furniture, eating and drinking vessels, cooking implements, beds and bedding, storage vessels, and if a farmer, agricultural equipment, animals, and, less commonly, crops stored in barns and growing in the fields. Even piles of manure in the farmyard are sometimes listed. Individual items and groups of items are all given a value. Debts, credits and leases, where appropriate, are also listed. Finally a total value is calculated and those taking the inventory (appraisers) append their names.

Obviously inventories are important to the historian from a number of different points of view. They give information about the size and layout of houses, food preparation and cooking arrangements, standards of domestic comfort, and working practices. Individual inventories are important in their own right but, of course, if a substantial number of inventories for a particular parish, area or region are analysed then broad social and economic characteristics and trends can be extrapolated. A well-known example of a district wide approach is S J Moore's study of five parishes in south Gloucestershire; nearer to home is an analysis of 160 inventories in Ecclesfield parish covering the period 1680-1790.[3]

All that is attempted here is a detailed analysis of one particular inventory to show the level of detail included in such documents and to reveal the domestic arrangements and level of comfort of one particular family who lived in the late seventeenth century in a house which still stands to this day.

The family and the house

The inventory in question is that of Thomas Yeardley (also spelled Yardley) of Kimberworth Park Gate who died at the early age of thirty-seven in the Spring of 1694.[4] Thomas Yeardley was the eldest son of Richard Yeardley who died about 1682. The earliest known record of Richard Yeardley was in 1672 when he was listed in the Hearth Tax returns for Kimberworth. He is named in a list of 115 taxpayers only four places away from Thomas Barnsley, the tenant of Park Gate Farm at that date, suggesting that they were close neighbours. Richard Yeardley's will is lodged in the Borthwick Institute and he is said to be of 'Kimberworth Parke'. This may have been the farm called Red House, the farmhouse of which was located where the Tarmac offices now stand near Keppel's Column, or Kimberworth Park Farm which lay at the junction of the modern Kimberworth Park Road and Wheatley Road on the Kimberworth Park estate.

Thomas Yeardley, Richard's son, was baptised in Rotherham Parish Church on 12 July 1656 and married Mary Barnsley sometime before 1683. The parish record of their marriage has not been located. They are known to have had four children: Mary baptised in 1683, Joseph baptised in 1685, Martha baptised in 1689 and Margaret baptised in 1691. Mary, Thomas' wife, was the daughter of Thomas Barnsley who was the tenant of the Duke of Norfolk at Park Gate Farm. The assumption is that on their marriage in or before 1683 Thomas and Mary took up residence at Park Gate Farm with Mary's parents. No records have been found of Thomas Barnsley after 1687 so that at the time of Thomas Yeardley's death in 1694 he (Thomas Yeardley) may have been running the farm in succession to his father-in-law. Thomas Barnsley had a son, another Thomas Barnsley (baptised 1646 in Sheffield) who, like his father, practised as a scrivener (ie, a professional penman, scribe, copyist, drafter of documents). No record of any association of Thomas Barnsley Junior with the tenancy and runnning of Park Gate Farm has been found. Thomas and Mary's son, Joseph, eventually came into the possession of the tenancy of the farm, and farmed there until his death in 1748.

The Park Gate Farm of 1694 is today the renovated group of buildings set around Kirkstead Abbey Mews off Upper Wortley Road at its junction with Scholes Lane. The farmhouse itself was the southern half of the long range of buildings that stands at right-angles to the main

Figure 1. Park Gate Farm, as it was before 1900, viewed from the east.

road. The northern half of the range was used as cowsheds and barns. The house and barns have long been believed to be of Norman construction, erected in the second half of the twelfth century by the Cistercian monks of Kirkstead Abbey in Lincolnshire. The range was renamed Kirkstead Abbey Grange by the Earl of Effingham in 1900. The history of the house, the farmland attached to the house and the families who have lived there during the last 350 years have been the subject of two recent articles in the *Ivanhoe Review* published by the Archives and Local Studies Section of Rotherham Central Library.[5]

Figure 1 shows an elevation of the house and barns viewed from the east as they would have looked shortly before the restoration in 1900.

Figure 2. Drawing of Park Gate Farm by Harold Armitage, published in the periodical *Young Sheffield* in 1898.

The building must have looked much the same when the late seventeenth century inventory was taken. It is made of local sandstone, mostly roughly shaped blocks, referred to as rubble. Occasionally, carefully shaped rectangular or square blocks (known as ashlar) have been used. The doorway surrounds, window sills, lintels and quoins (corner stones) are made of fine grained sandstone or gritstone, including the pink-stained Mexborough (or Rotherham Red) Rock. That part of the building that constituted the farmhouse was covered before 1900 by a thick layer of plaster to improve insulation. The roof is of sandstone slates. The dotted lines at the southern end of the building indicate the position of a wing that was built onto the main building but which was demolished during the 1900 restoration. Figure 2 is a drawing of the building published in 1898 when it had lain empty for more than forty years. The drawing shows clearly the wing at the southern end of the building, the unusual lateral chimney stack, and the flaking plaster on the farmhouse walls.

The land farmed by Thomas Yeardley in the late seventeenth century stretched away to the south-east of the house to the south of Upper

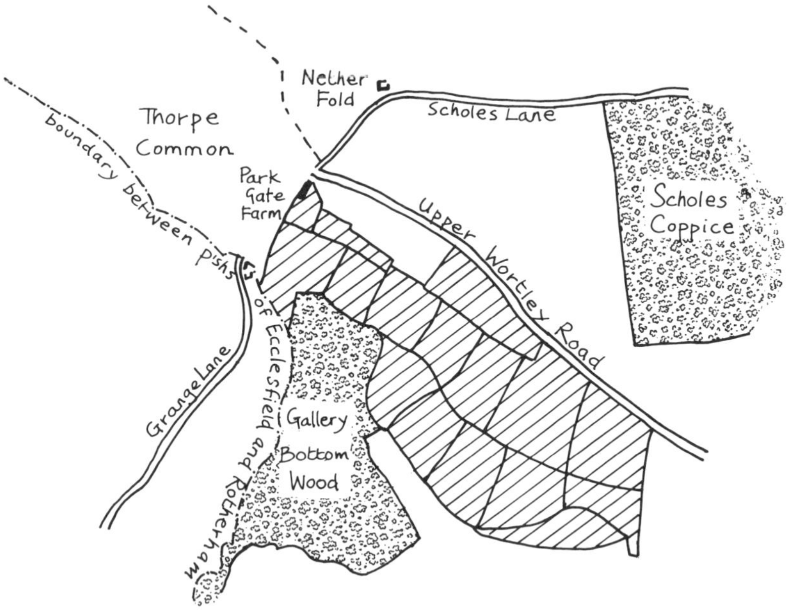

Figure 3. Map of Park Gate Farm in 1732. The fields attached to the farm are shown by diagonal shading. The farm tenant would also have had access to Thorpe Common for grazing. Source: Survey of the Manor of Kimberworth for the Earl of Effingham, 1732. The original survey book is lodged in Rotherham Central Library, Archives and Local Studies Section.

Wortley Road. According to a survey of the Manor of Kimberworth made in 1732 for the Earl of Effingham, who had succeeded the Dukes of Norfolk as Lord of the Manor of Kimberworth, Park Gate Farm covered sixty-seven acres. The farmer at that time was Joseph Yeardley, Thomas Yeardley's son. He would also have had access for grazing to Thorpe Common immediately to the northwest of the farmhouse (Figure 3).

The inventory

The inventory was made on 28 April 1694 by Francis Hellifield, Ezra Cawton, William Yardley and John Wainwright. William Yardley was the younger brother of the deceased and John Wainwright was a relative on his mother's side, probably his uncle, John Wainwright of Scholes. Nothing is known of Francis Hellifield or Ezra Cawton. The beginning of the inventory is shown in Figure 4.

They first valued his clothing and counted the money on his person and in the house: 'Inpris his purse & appel' [First his purse and apparel]. In total these came to £5.

They then proceeded on a room by room inspection of the house listing and valuing as they went. Before itemising and discussing what they found as they went on their tour it is worth pausing to consider the layout of the house. The first room they mention is ***the house***. This is the main room where the family cooked, ate and sat. It must be remembered that the Yeardley household consisted of at least Thomas and Mary, four children, and possibly Mary's mother. There may also have been indoor and farm servants living in the house. The appraisers next went to ***the buttery***, a cool storage place for food and drink. From there they climbed the stairs to ***the stair head chamber*** and after listing its contents they went on to inspect ***the great chamber*** and ***the little chamber***. They then came downstairs again to inspect ***the kitchen***. They completed their survey by inspecting the outbuildings and the farmyard. Figure 5 is a speculative drawing showing the possible arrangement of rooms in 1694.

The House

The appraisers began their list and valuation at the focus of family life: the fireplace. In the fireplace, which would have been of the inglenook type, there were froggs (horizontal bars on which the firewood was put), the rackings and pot hooks from which pots were suspended, a grid-iron which was a platform of iron bars for cooking meat over the fire, a spit on which cooking meat was turned supported on a pair of cobirons, together with two dripping pans to catch the juices.There was also an iron ladle, a beef fork and a container for salt (a 'salt pitch');

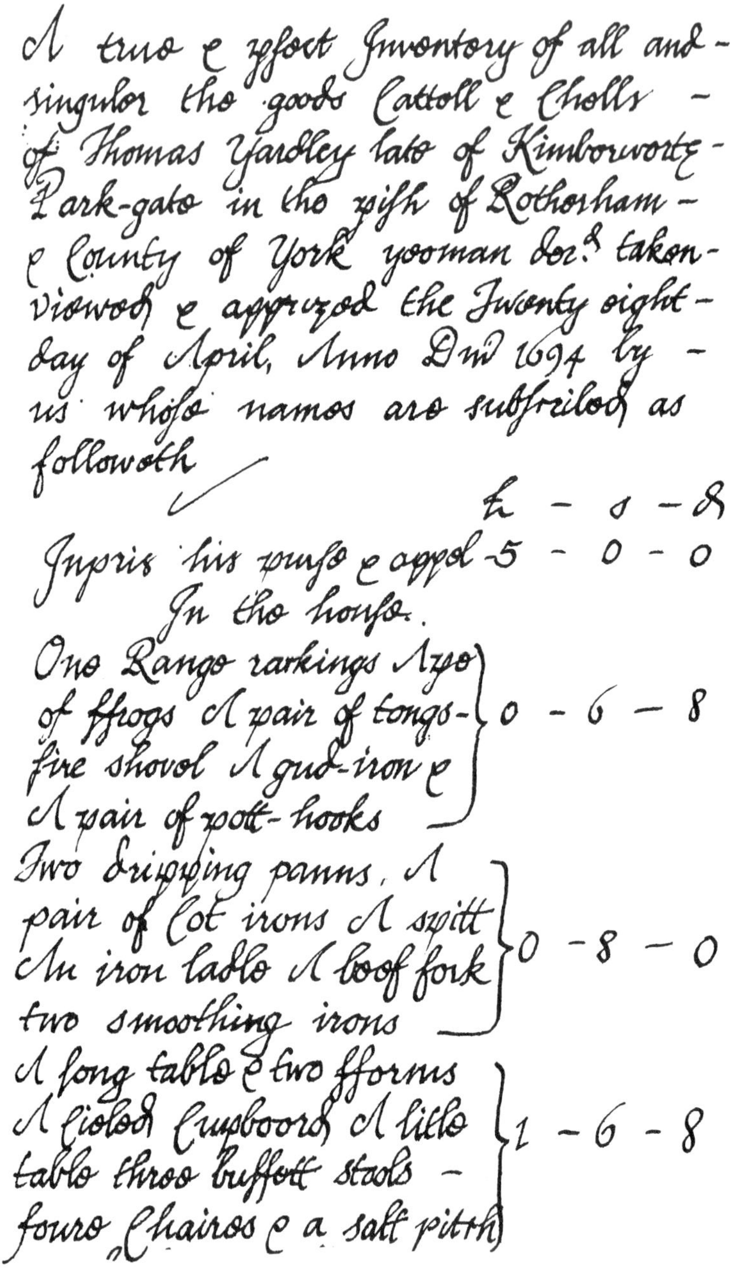
A true & perfect Inventory of all and singuler the goods Cattell & Chattells of Thomas Yeardley late of Kimberworth Park-gate in the parish of Rotherham & County of York yeoman decd taken viewed & apprized the Twenty eight day of April, Anno Dni 1694 by us whose names are subscribed as followeth

	£ - s - d
Imprimis his purse & apparel	5 - 0 - 0
In the house.	
One Range reckings A per of ffrogs A pair of tongs fire shovel A gud-iron & A pair of pott-hooks	0 - 6 - 8
Two dripping panns. A pair of Cot irons A spitt An iron ladle A beef fork two smoothing irons	0 - 8 - 0
A long table & two fformes A ceiled Cupboard A little table three buffett stools foure Chaires & a salt pitt	1 - 6 - 8

Figure 4. The beginning of Thomas Yeardley's inventory. See the Appendix for a full transcription.

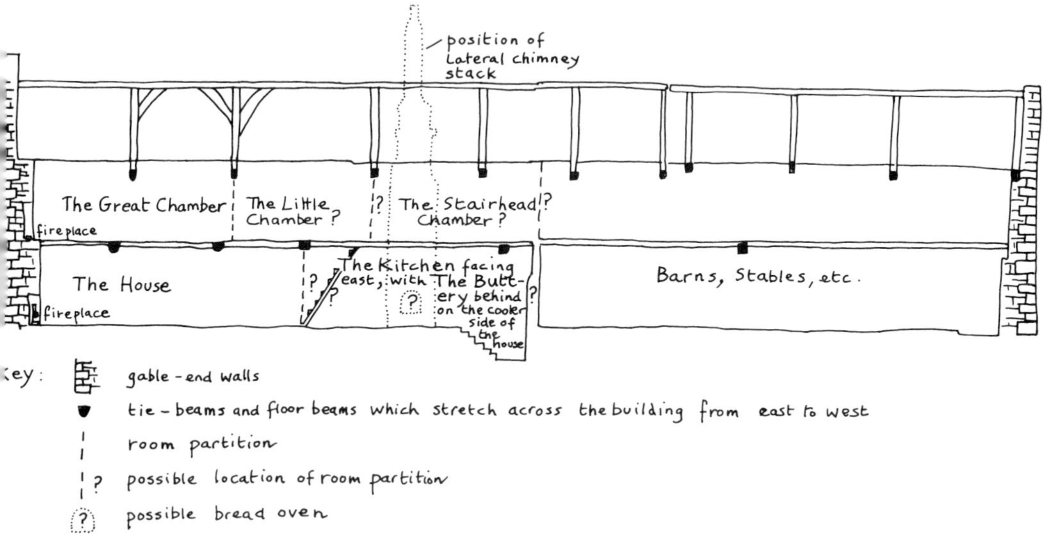

Figure 5. Speculative reconstruction of the arrangement of rooms at Park Gate Farm in 1694.

the latter would probably have been hung on the wall near the fire to keep it dry. Two smoothing irons were also on the hearth. For looking after the fire there were a pair of tongs and a fire shovel. There was also an assortment of pots and pans: two iron pans, one iron pot, a warming pan and two skelletts (a small cooking vessel with a long handle and three short feet allowing it to stand in a fire). Figure 6 illustrates some of the features described above.

Meals were taken at a long table with a form on either side. There was also a little table, three buffet stools and four chairs and four cushions ('quishions'). There was also a 'cieled cupboard'. In the seventeenth century a cupboard was literally a cup board, ie, a long table placed against a wall with one, two or three shelves, probably at this time without doors, used for displaying family silver, pewter and earthenware. 'Cieled' has two meanings; it sometimes means panelled, more often it means with a ceiling, presumably in this case possibly meaning a sideboard with a broad, flat top. It was probably on and in this cupboard that the nine pewter dishes, two tankards, four pottingers (silver, pewter or earthenware bowls with ear-shaped handles for porridge or soup), the salt pot, the mustard pot and an iron pestle and mortar were displayed. A candle stick is also mentioned but this must have been moved about the room as occasion demanded. The house also contained a wool wheel (presumably a spinning wheel) and an old chest. The total value of everything in the house was only £4-1s-4d.

Figure 6. A seventeenth century farmhouse fireplace. A pan and a cooking pot (cauldron) are suspended from a crane by pot hooks. In front of the fire, not in use, is a hand-operated spit supported on a pair of cob-irons. On the hearth is a grid-iron (left) and a skillet (centre), both with long handles and designed to stand in the fire. Standing beside the fire is a toasting fork and ladle. The iron pot or cauldron was the most versatile of the cooking containers. In it a whole meal could be boiled in one operation. Joints of meat could be placed directly in the boiling water or in an earthenware jar, accompanied by vegetables in net-bags and puddings tied up in cloths or floating in wooden bowls.

The Buttery

The buttery, which was usually small and in the coolest part of the building was, as has already been pointed out, used for storing liquids and food. The buttery at Park Gate Farm in 1694 contained only storage vessels, twelve in all. First, there was a kimnel, which was a wooden tub. Next is mentioned a flesh kitt. A kitt was a barrel, sometimes with a lid, for storing milk, butter and other foods. Flesh is derived from the Old English 'fleisch' meaning meat, and so it may have contained salted meat. The buttery also contained two wooden bottles, six milk pails, a tub and a barrel. The modern house contains a small room behind the kitchen which until 1984 had hooks in the ceiling, and leading off from it is a short flight of stone steps leading down to a cellar. Both of these areas may have been part of the seventeenth century buttery.

The Stairhead Chamber

There was probably an open stair leading to the upstairs rooms, the first of which, the stairhead chamber, may have been entered through a trap door. The stairhead chamber was used for storage. It contained wheel spokes, sections of the outer rim of wheels (the appraisers used the dialect word 'felks') and articles of farming equipment referred to as 'husbandry geare'.

The Great Chamber

This was the family bedroom. Figure 5 shows that we have assumed that this bedroom lay over the house. There are two reasons for this assumption. First, the room would have been warmed by the fact that there would have been a fire burning almost continuously in the room below and secondly, because the inventory refers to a 'range' or fireplace in the great chamber itself. There still exists in that room on the south wall a large inglenook fireplace with a stone surround.

The room contained three beds complete with bedding and linens. There were two cieled beds and one truckle bed. A cieled bed was a bed with a canopy (cieled = with a ceiling), a two poster as opposed to a four poster (Figure 7). The two cieled beds were said to be 'with the furniture' which means coverings, including the canopy and curtains of a two poster or four poster bed. The third bed was a truckle bed, which was a very low bed on wheels that could be stored under a bigger bed.

The room also contained two cupboards called presses, one large and one small, for storing linen and clothes; a chest; a table; two desks; four old chairs; and an old trunk. The furniture and other belongings in this room were valued at £14-10s-0d.

The Little Chamber

After inspecting and valuing the goods in the great chamber the appraisers retraced their steps to the little chamber. Here they found a halfheaded bed (ie, a bed with a wooden back but no canopy) with its 'furniture', together with a meal (meal = oatmeal) chest, a pair of weight scales and a pair of yarn windles. A yarn windle was used for winding wool.

The Kitchen

The appraisers must then have gone back to the stairhead chamber and descended the stairs to inspect the kitchen. The contents of the kitchen suggest that this was where baking was done, where butter was made and where clothes washing took place. It contained a water kitt, ie, a water tub, probably containing a supply of water brought from an outside well. Nineteenth century Ordnance Survey maps show a well in the orchard to the south of the farmhouse. There was also a flaskett in the kitchen which was an oblong or oval tub for washing clothes. The kitchen also contained a milking kitt and a churn for making butter. As far as baking is concerned, it must be remembered that on the outside of the kitchen was the large lateral chimney stack. This would almost certainly have been associated with a bread oven in the kitchen. The bread oven would have been of the beehive type, of domed construction and built into the thickness of the outside wall (the walls of the house are between thirty-two and thirty-six inches thick). Such ovens were heated by firing them with quickburning bundles of twigs, called faggots. When the oven was sufficiently heated the fire and ashes were swept out and the risen dough slipped inside with a long handled baking shovel or 'peel'. The oven door was then blocked with a stone and clay and the heat in the masonry in the oven baked the bread. After the bread had been baked, other items such as puddings, pasties and pies, requiring a lower temperature and a longer cooking time, could be sealed in place. Listed in the kitchen inventory and connected with baking was a 'leaven kitt', a container in which bread was kneaded and left to rise, like a pancheon. Also found in the kitchen was a 'great ark', a domed meal chest (Figure 8) in which oatmeal and flour were stored, and a hen 'call', ie a hen coop! Very handy when making Yorkshire puddings! Having hens in the kitchen is not as surprising as it sounds. E Estyn Evans in his book *Irish Folk Ways* describes how in Ireland hens used to spend the night in farm cottages on a rope or pole hung across the kitchen from eave to eave, and laid their eggs in 'handsome nesting baskets of woven straw'.[6] Also listed in the kitchen inventory was a dresser on the shelves of which some of the containers already mentioned may have stood.

The outbuildings, farmyard and fields

After valuing the possessions in the kitchen the appraisers moved outside and inspected the outbuildings, the farmyard or 'fold' and the farm beyond. They first listed a number of items of farming equipment: a farm wagon or 'wayn', two ploughs, a pair of horse harrows, a sledge - a wheel-less cart for use on steep and broken ground, a ladder and a stand-heck - a rack for fodder standing on four posts for use in the farmyard or pasture.

Finally they listed and valued the farmstock. This consisted of a pair of oxen, which would have been used for ploughing and for serving the cows. There were two cows (referred to as 'kine') and three calves.

There were also four horses, ten sheep and two pigs. The livestock were valued at £28 almost half the total valuation of Thomas Yeardley's belongings which came to £61.

Conclusion

Thomas Yeardley's inventory is full but there are some omissions which raise interesting questions. There is no mention of any floor coverings. Does this mean that all downstairs floors were made of beaten earth or flagstones without rugs, and the floors of the upstairs rooms just bare boards? No knives, forks or spoons are listed. Were they overlooked by the appraisers or did the Yeardleys eat all their food with their hands off their pewter plates? No books are mentioned, not even a bible. Were the Yeardleys illiterate?

Another set of questions relate to the Yeardley family in relation to other farming families in Kimberworth township and in surrounding townships and parishes. Were the Yeardleys' domestic comforts similar to, worse than or better than those of other late seventeenth century farming families in the locality? If other contemporary local farmers' inventories are examined, how likely are we to find a retiring room (a parlour) separate from the house where the cooking and eating took place? How widespread were luxuries such as pictures, mirrors, clocks and glassware? What evidence will be found of literacy?

All these questions and others are the subject of further research.

Figure 7. A 'cieled' bed.

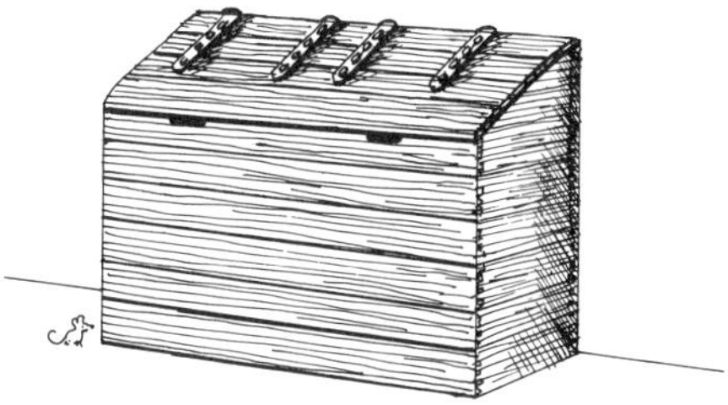

Figure 8. A great ark.

Notes and References

An invaluable guide to the archaic and technical terms encountered in probate inventories, and used by the present authors, is Rosemary Milward's, *A Glossary of Household, Farming and Trade Terms from Probate Inventories*, Derbyshire Record Society, Occasional Paper No 1, third edition, 1986.

1. In England and Wales the ecclesiastical authorities undertook the probate (ie, the official proving) of wills and related documents from the middle ages until 1858. In 1858 the power of ecclesiastical courts over probate was replaced by a principal probate registry at Somerset House, London, and district registries thoughout England and Wales.
2. Borthwick Institute of Historical Research, University of York, St Anthony's Hall, Peasholme Green, York YO1 2PW.
3. J S Moore (Ed), *The Goods and Chattels of Our Forefathers: Frampton Cotterell and District Probate inventories, 1539-1804*, Phillimore, London and Chichester, 1976; Mr and Mrs W Morton, 'Houses in Ecclesfield Parish, 1680-1790' in *The South Yorkshire Historian*, No 2, Spring 1973, pp 20-31.
4. The original inventory is in the Borthwick Institute: Thomas Yeardley, Kimberworth, Doncaster D. April 1694.
5. Melvyn Jones, 'Kirkstead Abbey Grange 1: Speculations on its Origins', *Ivanhoe Review*, No 4, Spring 1993, pp 3-12; Melvyn Jones, 'Kirkstead Abbey Grange 2: The House, its Land and its Inhabitants 1649-1993', *Ivanhoe Review*, No 5, Autumn 1993, pp 4-20.
6. E Estyn Evans, *Irish Folk Ways*, Routledge & Kegan Paul, London, 1957, p 60.

Appendix: Thomas Yeardley's Inventory in full.

A true and perfect Inventory of all and singular the goods Cattell & Ch[att]ells of Thomas Yardley late of Kimberworth Park-gate in the p[ar]ish of Rotherham & County of York yeoman deceased taken viewed and apprized the Twenty eight day of April Anno D[omi]ni 1694 by us whose names are subscribed below.

Inpris his purse and apparel £5-0-0
In the house
One Range, rackings A pair of ffroggs A pair of tongs fire shovel A gridiron & A pair of pott hooks £0-6-8
Two dripping panns A pair of Cob irons A spitt An iron ladle A beef fork two smoothing irons £0-8-0
A long table & two fforms A Cieled Cupboard A litle table three buffet stools four Chaires & a salt pitch £1-6-8
One brass pan A warming pan two skelletts One Iron pott two Iron panns nine pewter dishes two tankards A candle stick one salt A mustard pott & foure pottingers £1-15-0
ffive quishions An Iron Morter & A pestell £0-2-0
An old chest & a wool wheel £0-3-0
In the Buttery
One Kimnel A flesh kitt two woden botles & six milk pales A tubb and A barrell £0-13-4
In the Staire head Chamber
Certaine spolkes felks and husbandry Geare £2-0-0
In the great Chamber
One Cieled bed with the furniture, another Cield bed with the furniture one truckle bed, bedding and Linnens £10-10-0
A large Cieled press another less press one Cieled Chest A Table two Desks four old Chairs An old Trunk & A range £4-0-0
In the little Chamber
One half headed bed & furniture A meal-chest & a pair of weigh scales & A pair of Yarn windles £1-10-0
In the Kitchen
A great Ark A Dresser A tubb A churn A leaven kitt A flaskett A botle A hen Call A milking kitt & A water kitt £1-0-0
One iron pott £0-1-6

Item A cartwayn two ploughs A pair of horse harrowes & A sledge £4-0-0
A pair of Oxen two kine and three Calves £18-0-0
foure horses £7-0-0
Ten sheep & two piggs £3-0-0
A stand heck & a Ladder £0-2-0
huslam[en]t in & about the house £0-3-4
Summa totalis bonorum £61-6-6

Apprizers
ffrancis Hellifield
Ezra Cawton
William Yardley
John Wainwright

5. SANDBECK HALL AND PARK

by Tom William Beastall

THOUGH SITUATED IN A HIGHLY POPULATED PART of Yorkshire, Sandbeck Hall is one of England's more secluded houses. Built of magnesian limestone it retires within a spacious park laid out in the 1770s by Lancelot 'Capability' Brown (Figure 1).

James Paine rebuilt a house which dated from 1626-27 to create the present essay in Palladian architecture. He worked at Sandbeck from about 1762 to 1770 for the fourth Earl of Scarbrough though he was probably called there by the third Earl as early as 1750 when a 'new house' was built at the Folds to the east of the hall in a style which anticipated Paine's later work on many buildings on the estate including the Hall itself.

No very clear impression of the house Paine transformed exists. A map of 1724 by Joseph Dickinson drawn for Sir Thomas Lumley-Saunderson, later the third Earl, has a representation of the south gable of the 1620s house.[1] It gives the only indication we have of the structure James Paine started with. The drawings of the original house for which the building accounts record payment have been lost. Tall, narrow,

Figure 1. Sandbeck Hall and Park in 1779, engraved by W Watts from a painting by W Hodges. *Rotherham Central Library, Archives and Local Studies Section*

gabled with three prominent string courses and lofty chimney stacks it has a steeply hipped roof and a central doorway on the west side. A window-doorway opened up on the south side while the ground appears to slope fairly steeply from the west side down to the eastern side of the house.

Sir Nicholas Saunderson, later Viscount Castleton, a prominent landowner in Lincolnshire and southern Yorkshire had built it using a Robert Marshall of Ashby and Richard Barkworth of Nettleham both from Lincolnshire as his masons. Their contract mentions an obligation to keep eight men working there continuously, to build chimneys that would not smoke, to decorate the outside with 'handsome sculped stones' and to have a room in which their workmen could 'lay their bedds'. This provision suggests that the house was a rebuilding of an existing structure; perhaps the original manor house of Sandbeck. The contract is endorsed in a hand likely to be that of Sir Nicholas Saunderson, 'Arrant Knaves both for they performed nothing accordingly but got my money and would never measure their work.'[2]

The spirit of this and the original house is perhaps present in the Sandbeck Hall of today. Some masonry in the basement and the remains of a mullioned window formerly in the house and located now near the north-western side of the hall suggest it but, it has been argued, the most compelling evidence of a link is in the thick interior walls and in the saloon on the first floor which runs across the house from west to east. By the mid-eighteenth century this was an obsolete arrangement in house design. Isolated among bedrooms away from other reception rooms and thus inconvenient it lacks explanation except as the remains

Figure 2. The 'new house' at the Folds.

of the great chamber of a cross-hall house with a large hall below on the ground floor as in, for example, Manor Lodge at Worksop dating from about 1590.[3]

The new house at the Folds (Figure 2) was started in 1749 as part of the creation of a leisure area on the estate with a lake or pond, new walks, a menagerie and a bowling green. John Thompson received 16s for twenty-four days 'digging cellar and foundations at ye new House at ye Folds'. In June 1750 Francis Oxenforth received 18s for 24 days 'digging and levelling about the new house at ye Folds'. John Newland, John Rich, Francis Sydall and John England received similar payments for work at foundations level in 1749-50. In 1751 there is the first reference to Mr John Platt, the Rotherham mason, who was paid for work on the new house. He received £63 and a further payment of £93 11s 0d on account '...for building ye new House at the Folds as appears by his Acquittance'. Estate tenants provided transport for Roche Abbey stone from the quarry and payments were made for glazing and painting.[4]

Digging for the new pond, now known as the lower lake (Figure 3), was paid for in 1753 while tenants and estate workers were paid for leading earth, digging and ploughing. William and Simon Eastwood, local contractors, completed stone work around the lake; iron work was done by Robert Fowler and Westmorland slate for the house arrived via the inland ports of Airmyn and Bawtry.

Work at the Folds was accompanied by expenditure on houses at Braithwell and Roche Abbey in the 1750s. In the next decade work on

Figure 3. The lower lake near the Folds.

the Hall itself was preceded by rebuilding in other parts of the estate and the demolition of some of the offices of the old hall to make way for a new stable block with its clock tower, the steward's premises and the chapel in the south-eastern corner of the stable quadrangle. In 1764 there are references in the accounts to the building of Sandbeck Lodge farm house, to the removal of slates from the steward's old room and to the purchase of gunpowder to demolish an old 'waterhouse'.

James Paine received £10 10s for '...Making Plans of the old Offices etc. at Sandbeck and to sundry designs made for the Farm yard Stabling etc.' A further payment of £105 was made for plans of the old house and offices, for designing the alterations and additions with 'a set of Fair Drawings of the same. Comparing and examining them with the old Buildings etc., etc.' More drawings of alterations in the front of the house and instructions to workmen by Lord Scarbrough's orders followed. It is clear that the fourth Earl had a personal interest in both the designs and in their execution and that the whole scheme was an ambitious rebuilding of the old house. 'Directing the Building of the North and South Ends and the intermediate part of the East Front,' cost a further £52 10s.[5]

The mason was probably Edward Jackson of Doncaster. On 31

Figure 4. Sandbeck Hall from the south-cast showing the east front portico.

December 1762 the household accounts note a small payment, 'To John Morris Going to Doncaster for Mr Jackson to meet Mr Paine at Sandbeck.' As the architect's bills seem to have been submitted for work done over long periods of time and probably well after the developments were finished the building accounts are less helpful for dating the process and pace of building than the humble household accounts. These give some idea of when stages of rebuilding were reached if only because the necessary domestic clearing up activity was undertaken and paid for at particular times.[6]

20th May 1763, 'To Mary Robinson and Elizabeth Wright eleven days carrying out Rubbish and Clearing Staircase and Hall after the masons had gone at 6d a day'.

14th August 1766, 'To Ann Ainley for forty-seven days making fires in the new Rooms and cleaning them out and helping in the Kitchen when the Family was at Sandbeck at 6d per day to August 15th'.

1st September 1766, 'To the Chimney Sweep for cleaning down twenty-three chimneys of Mortar Rubbish'.

Estate correspondence from the steward John Hopkinson to Lord Scarbrough describes the setting up of the splendid east front portico without, sadly, giving this the most dramatic stage of rebuilding a precise date:-[7]

'May it please yr. Lordship. The Collum's Capitals Architraves and frise is all safe up, and Chain Barr'd quite round the Top of 'em, to the old partition walls, and God be praised, no person has received the least damage...'

Clearly a nerve-racking operation had been seen to a safe and happy conclusion but in his relief John Hopkinson ends his letter, 'Sandbeck, Satterday morning'! Other evidence, however, points to the late autumn of 1766 as its date. Figures 4, 5 and 6 show the house today, from the south-east, south and south-west respectively.

James Paine was engaged on many other projects for the fourth Earl.[8] He surveyed a house in Downing Street then in Lord Scarbrough's hands and he was paid £74 for the engagement and supervision of twelve tradesmen and workmen whose total cost exceeded £1000. In 1757 he was looking for a suitable London site on which to build a town house for the Earl. He submitted a detailed description of plots off Piccadilly, one with views of 'the Green Park, St. James's Park, Chelsea and all the Surrey Hills'. When on the death of his uncle the honourable James Lumley, the fourth Earl inherited Lumley Castle, the Durham estate and Lumley House in South Audley Street, James Paine was called in to make significant alterations and improvements to the Earl's London home. Plans for development and rebuilding at Glentworth in Lincolnshire had been prepared by Paine but there only

Figure 5. The Hall from the south showing the bow window of the dining room.

the stable block was completed.

Sandbeck then remains the most important memorial to Paine's long and apparently harmonious association with the fourth Earl. Yet, as with many buildings time soon revealed faults and weaknesses for by 1775 when James Paine was no longer active in the North, John Carr the Yorkshire architect was called to Sandbeck. He was well regarded by Paine who saw him as a colleague rather than a rival. He had worked on Raby Castle after Paine had moved away and so, perhaps, he was the obvious architect to turn to when Sandbeck needed attention. Slating on the main roof had to be replaced by 'a better workman' and well pointed on the inside. Better draining from the roof's new skylight was essential and the balustrade on the south side and bow window was to be raised to the height of the house balustrade.[9]

Paine had introduced to Sandbeck artists and craftsmen who made contributions to interior decoration under his supervision. Robert Ansell the carver and the plasterers Gervase and Thomas Ledger were among them. William Jelfe the mason worked on Lumley House, South Audley Street and William Collins the sculptor was responsible for the magnificent composition in the east front pediment at Sandbeck depicting Ceres in a scene of plenty. Joseph Rose the decorative plasterer supplied items under Paine's direction. He was paid in July 1768 for making forty roses for the ceiling and twenty-two half roses, for 102 feet of Vitruvian scroll for a cove for decoration between columns and for a large flower for the staircase.

Payment was made for '...an Ionick Jasper Collumn Chimney Piece with an Alto Relievo Tablet for the Bow Window Dining Room at Sandbeck'. This item included 'Cube Statutory Marble', 'Moulded Work' and 'Cube Sicilian Jasper Marble in Collumns'. 'Masoning 2 Ionick Antique Capitals and fitting in two brass pins to fasten the collumns', cost £2 15s. The tablet showing a shepherd, shepherdess and flock cost £21 0s 0d. Carving eight faces of Ionick Antique capitals with 'Cornucopia's and Flowers' cost £10 10s 0d. The whole chimney piece cost £143 9s 1d. Lord Scarbrough examined the piece in London before it was sent to Sandbeck. Ready for despatch to Yorkshire it was unpacked and laid out for his inspection at an extra cost of 5s on 26

Figure 6. The Hall from the south-west.

October 1765. By January 1766 it was at Sandbeck in its deal container. A workman was paid in April and May 1767 for ten days lodging and labour when installing the piece. Even so all was not complete for a further nine days work were paid for 'Taking down and resetting the Chimney Piece..'

Interior decoration was designed by Paine, drawn up and made into workmen's instructions at a cost of £52 10s 0d. Two marble tablets with 'Sienna Borders' were sent by him to Sandbeck in 1768.

Sandbeck park was already landscaped at the time of the 1724 survey by Joseph Dickinson. His map shows woodland, walks, plantations, orchards and formal gardens to the east and south of the old hall with

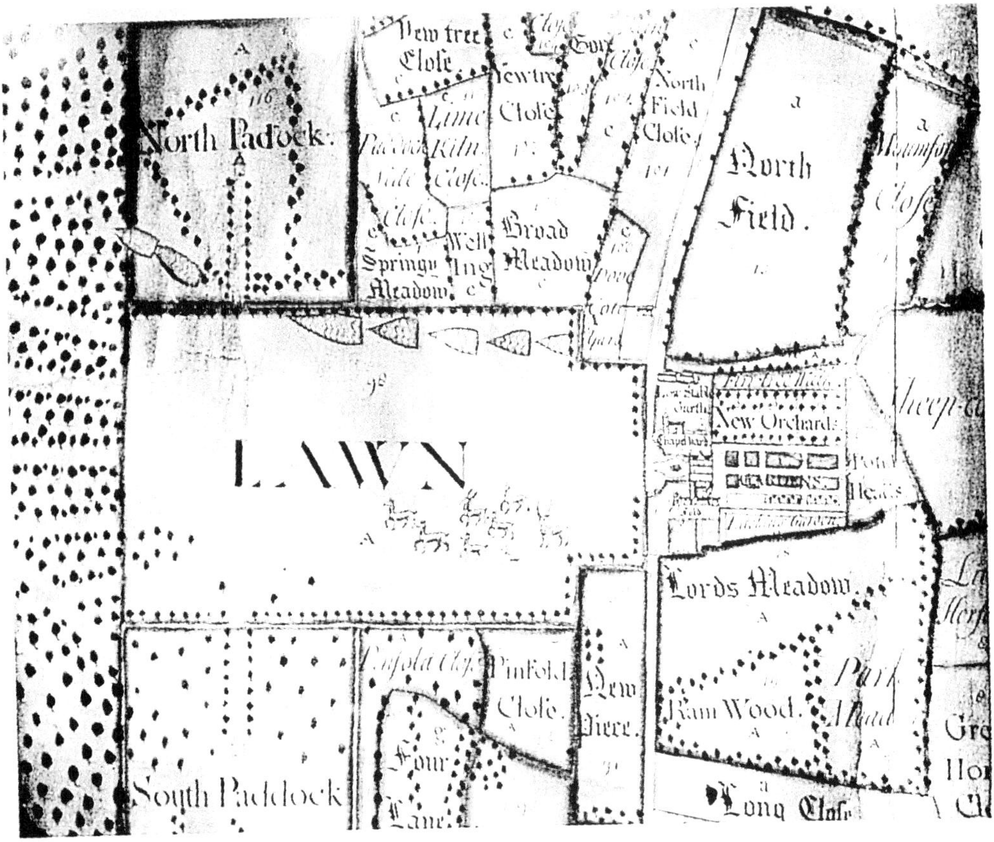

Figure 7. Details of Sandbeck Park from Joseph Dickinson's estate map of 1724 showing the house built for Sir Nicholas Saunderson about 100 years earlier and the gardens and park before their transformation by Lancelot Brown in the last quarter of the eighteenth century.
By kind permission of Rt Hon the Earl of Scarbrough

a 'lawn' containing deer lying to the west (Figure 7). In 1774 a transformation of this layout was undertaken and the Roche Abbey valley was included in the plan. The fourth Earl's Countess preferred Sandbeck to Glentworth their Lincolnshire home. As early as 1756 she wrote that it was '...inexpressibly charming, and which improves every year'. Sandbeck was to become the family's favourite home, the setting for an almost classical style of eighteenth century country living.

Lancelot Brown and the fourth Earl entered into a contract in September 1774.[10] A sunk fence was to be built (Figure 8), the old ponds in the lawn were to be drained and levelled. A pond for the stables was to be made and the Roche Abbey valley was to be 'dressed' or landscaped, the plans being executed with 'a poet's feeling and a painter's eye' from the Hammer pond near the forge up the valley towards Laughton. This involved covering some of the foundations of the Abbey. They were not to be seen again until the excavations begun by the tenth Earl soon after his succession in 1884. Completion was to be in December 1777 and the total cost was to be £3000. Sandbeck received the Capability Brown treatment. Lakes, woodland, walks and a carriage way were arranged to give the impression of Nature embracing the house itself in a man-made landscape whose mature beauty would not be fully appreciated until well into the next century. There were at times seventy workmen employed on the project.[11] By 1780 the house, grounds and park were complete. The Doncaster road entrance gates were in place on the Balby to Worksop turnpike road as were gates on the Rotherham to Barnby Moor turnpike near the junction with Firbeck Lane. Gates to the north were made on the lane to Sandbeck Lodge and Woolthwaite. The setting, little changed in its essentials to this day, was finished. It remained to mature gradually and to grow old gracefully. This it has done with the dignified results evident in the late twentieth century.

In 1782 the fourth Earl died. His son and heir spent much time away from Sandbeck but his successor, his brother Richard as the sixth Earl, spent time and effort in improving the estate and maintaining the Hall. All three estates in Yorkshire, Lincolnshire and Durham were run from Sandbeck which became the administrative centre for the three distinct properties with different economic concerns though the work of developing tenanted farms was basic to them all. County Durham with the family's ancestral home at Lumley Castle near Chester-le-Street had small farms and colliery workings which supplied the London coal market by way of the river Wear and the east coast shipping trade. In Lincolnshire large farms became places of interest to agricultural improvers in the nineteenth century as the rolling sheep walks and rabbit warrens of the Wolds and Lincoln Edge were converted

Figure 8. A section of Lancelot Brown's sunk fence.

into productive arable acreages. Farmland at Skegness was turned into a sea bathing resort for holidaymakers from Nottingham and Leicester. Sandbeck meanwhile was to be the least affected by urban or industrial development until the sinking of Maltby colliery early this century. It has seen, with many other settlements in Rotherham, heavy industry relaxing its hold on southern Yorkshire leaving behind an older, more rural landscape in which light industry has found a home in some of the abandoned farm complexes of a pre-industrial district.

Notes and References

1. Joseph Dickinson. Map of 1724. Earl of Scarbrough's collection.
2. Lumley Mss, MTD/B8/3.
3. *James Paine*, Peter Leach, Zwemmer, London, 1988, has many references to Sandbeck. pp79-80, 119-20, 207-8. Additional observations were made in correspondence.
4. Lumley Mss, EMA/10, EMR/32, EMR/3/1.
5. Lumley Mss, EMBA/9.
6. Lumley Mss, HMA, EMR/8.
7. Lumley Mss, EMC/39.
8. Lumley Mss, EMC/2/1-7.
9. Lumley Mss, MTD/C16/9.
10. The Earl of Scarbrough's collection.
11. Lumley Mss, EMA/25.

Acknowledgements

I thank the Rt Hon the Earl of Scarbrough for access to the Lumley archives at Sandbeck, for allowing me to quote from them and for giving permission for photographs to be taken of Sandbeck Hall and its surroundings.
I am grateful to Brenda Lowe for preparation of the typescript of this chapter.

6. MATTERS OF CONCERN: THE LIFE STORY OF THE THIRD EARL OF EFFINGHAM

by John Goodchild M Univ

THE ACTIVE PRESENCE IN THE ROTHERHAM area of Thomas Howard, third Earl of Effingham, is as well marked physically today as it was in the eighteenth century, for Thundercliffe Grange which he built and his Boston Castle are, curiously, perhaps more publicly observable now than then they were, the one standing in our day next to the M1 and the other in a public park. But Effingham was a man with far wider than a local landowner's interests: he took a leading part in local affairs and in national government, and even served as Governor of Jamaica, and it is the purpose here to study this range of his concerns — economic, political, social.

The third Earl of Effingham was baptised as Thomas Howard at St George's, Hanover Square, in London, early in 1747 at eight days of age: his father, a soldier, was already Earl of Effingham and the son carried the title of Lord Howard from birth. He was educated at Eton, but entered the army at fifteen and at sixteen succeeded on his father's death to the title as third Earl, in 1763. His personal interest in Yorkshire appears to have begun through the person of the under-aged Catherine Procter of Thorpe Hall, near Middleton on the southern outskirts of modern Leeds: the lady's home still stands, in great ruin. As runaways, the young couple married in Scotland in 1765 when he was only nineteen, and they married again, more formally, at Rotherham parish church, eleven months later, in August 1766. They seem to have been a happy couple, and they set up home not at Great Bookham in Surrey, whence the family came, but rather at the modest Holmes Hall in then rural Kimberworth, adjoining the market town of Rotherham: this property had come down in the Earl's branch of the Howard family. He seems to have had tastes which were as modest as his means: he had married socially beneath himself, and his wife brought a dowry of only £10,000, and he never held rank as a professional soldier beyond that of a lieutenant colonel. He may have come into modest funds upon his mother's remarriage, which coincided with his building of his own grand new mansion near Rotherham.

But the lack of a major fortune was no hindrance to the Effinghams' enjoyment of life in Yorkshire, so much cheaper then, as now, than in the south. For example, Lord and Lady Effingham were at the opening of the new Assembly Rooms in Leeds in 1777, when a celebratory ball attracted some 200 guests from the socially influential. In 1783 the Earl and Colonel Thornton of Allerton Park had a bet on the success of their respective packs of hounds when they were both at the Boroughbridge Races, and the Earl was Honorary Steward of the Sheffield Races in 1777. The Effinghams were obviously a young couuple who enjoyed the social life of the well-to-do in the West Riding, but the Earl was a man who also took his due part in the chore of county administration.

The Earl was a radical by political inclination, and one on friendly terms with the radical gentry of the West Riding. Effingham much disapproved of the War with the revolting North American colonists, and showed his disapproval by publicly renouncing his commission in the army, as the newspapers of the day reported at length. His resignation was much approved of in Yorkshire where there was much support for the American cause, and where of course the great Triumphal Arch at Parlington was built to celebrate the defeat of the British forces; we will come across Effingham's own celebration of these events later in this paper. Effingham was active in his attendance in the House of Lords, and he was obviously a near neighbour as well as being a friend of the great second Marquess of Rockingham, sometime Whig Premier of Great Britain, and they visited and corresponded frequently.

The Marquess was perhaps rather more of a sobersides than was Lord Effingham, and certainly he did not have Effingham's eccentricities: Effingham liked a joke, and wrote witty words for singing, commenting upon the politicians of his day, people of course like the politicians of our day. But it must be remembered that he was an eminent politician himself, becoming a member of Rockingham's Cabinet in 1782. A thin man in person, he caused comment by insisting upon carrying in Parliamentary processions both his baton as hereditary Deputy Earl Marshal of England, with that of his Cabinet rank of Treasurer of the Household: he was nicknamed the devil with two sticks (see Figure 1). Earlier, in 1780, he was said to have both sympathised with and joined in the anti-Roman Catholic Gordon Riots; he was said to have been killed in the streets; a wag said that as the body found and said to be Effingham's had ruffles at its wrists, it could be his. He was indeed notorious for his lack of interest in fashion, and indeed for his dirtiness. Another Tory wag suggested that the coat in which Effingham appeared at Court was that in which he had been killed in the Gordon Riots — it was so disreputable.

The Rev Joseph Hunter, the great historian of South Yorkshire, commented fifty years later, that by the 1770s the old Effingham mansion at the Holmes near Rotherham had 'become almost uninhabitable, by the extension in that direction of the manufacturers

Figure 1. Thomas Howard, third Earl of Effingham.

of Rotherham', and that in consequence Effingham had built for himself a new mansion, 'more befitting' the earldom. Holmes Hall (see Figure 2), the Earl's old home in the West Riding, was a modest mansion of stone which was to stand until the mid-nineteenth century, although by then long surrounded by industrial buildings and used for purposes other than the housing of a nobleman. In 1745, the partners in the Walker ironfounding business which was eventually to grow to proportions of worldwide significance had built two furnaces and a

Figure 2. Holmes Hall. *Ivanhoe Review, Vol 2, 1899*

casting house nearby, and in 1757 they took larger areas close by, while a lease of 1760 made provision for grinding and boring mills. As Hunter was to comment, by the 1760s and 1770s something rather grander in the way of accommodation might be expected from a nobleman. A new estate was purchased from one John Mellor, and had as its centrepiece a small, old house called The Grange or Thundercliffe Grange, and unlike so many places with the name Grange in the West Riding, this had been a medieval grange or administrative settlement, for Kirkstead Abbey in Lincolnshire. The old house stood on the opposite side of the Blackburn Brook from the site chosen by Lord Effingham for his new home: he chose a site within Rotherham parish, where he was Lord of the Manor and patron of the parish church.

John Platt of Rotherham, the Great South Yorkshire mason cum architect, records in his notebook that in December 1776 he was 'At Grange setting out ye House' and that the masons' work of the new

Figure 3. Thundercliffe Grange.

building was subsequently let to one H Ibbotson; Platt the architect-builder had already done work for Lord Effingham in Rotherham, and the new house at Thundercliffe Grange was apparently built during 1777 to the satisfaction of its owner, for Platt designed a new wing for the Grange in 1782, and the new house still stands, close to the M1 motorway just to the north of the Tinsley Viaduct (see Figure 3).

The Earl seems to have had no objection to the increased industrialisation of his ancestral estate at the Holmes on the edge of growing Rotherham, which of course brought him much-needed capital. In fact, he seems to have encouraged developments of an industrial kind and when his estate lawyer and agent, Thomas John Foljambe of Rotherham, became interested in glassmaking, Lord Effingham built a glassworks on his estate to let to him, and employed a technical expert to build it, while the industrial potential of the old estate, which offered coal, iron and good cheap transport to the investor, was developed yet further. It was doubtless to the Earl's chagrin that his tenants the great Walkers, ironmasters, had supplied cannon for the use of the British government during the American War, and as the War ended, in 1782, they purchased much of the Earl's estate at Kimberworth and took outlying parts on lease later. The Earl's estate included valuable coal and iron, one John Barber being paid £5 a year from 1772 'for Superintending the Management of his Lordships Collierys within the Manor of Rotherham'; in 1774 railings were put up 'at Owld Engen' probably a disused steam pumping engine house, and one B Downes was charged £10 in rent for a colliery road across the estate, perhaps an early railway.

The Earl owned the manorial mills, worked from the power of the River Don, a valuable source of power which was to be used for industrial purposes other than corn grinding, and in 1775 new stonebuilt salmon leaps and hecks were put down in the Don at his mills. The Earl was Lord of the Manors of Rotherham and Kimberworth and he kept up the manorial courts, which brought in a substantial £80 a year, less the costs: seventeen men had to be called for the manor court jury, and all dined, suppered, wined, aled and spirited on each occasion; knowing Lord Effingham's interest in local affairs, it is not at all impossible that he sat in on his own manorial courts. He was patron of the living of the great church and parish of Rotherham, and it fell to his lot to appoint one vicar of Rotherham, in 1782. He was also responsible for the repair of the great chancel of Rotherham Church as lay rector, and he had his own pews there in the chancel. He and his friend Lord Rockingham headed the subscription list when a new organ was built by the famous Snetzler in 1777 for Rotherham Church, and I have a bundle of papers relating to its supply, installation and financing, including letters from Snetzler.

It was in the mid-1770s that Lord Effingham became a very prominent freemason, at the same time becoming a prominent politician. After thirteen years in the army, in 1775, he resigned his commission in the army in protest against the Tory government's handling of the North American colonists' grievances: this he did with maximum publicity, and he made some most able speeches in the House of Lords as well as signing seventeen protests against the Government's actions which are recorded in the Journals of the House of Lords.

After the American War of Independence, Effingham resumed his commission as an officer in the army. Many people of his time thought him an interesting character; he was verbally painted as 'an able but eccentric and needy nobelman', while the great Horace Walpole called him 'a rough soldier with no sound sense' and 'a wild sort of head'. But in the West Riding Effingham was sufficiently well thought of to act as chairman of Quarter Sessions equivalent to the later office of chairman of the County Council, a position unsuited to a fool, and at home either in his old or new house, he was most unusual among the nobility in taking an active part in very local affairs: he served actively as a Rotherham Town Trustee, and sat on a working committee of that body, and he even sat on a committee appointed by the annual Rotherham ratepayers' meeting, to manage the affairs of their fellow inhabitants.

Although one of the scurrilous magazines of the period said in 1782 that Lord Effingham had a mistress, he and his wife seem to have got on quite well, appearing at balls and races together and ultimately going together to live in one of the colonies, despite again what the fashionable unkind in London said about his dirty clothes.

Lady Effingham kept a pet pony, and she was notorious as a horsewoman, afraid of no five-barred gate; she also kept a pet dog — in 1774 there is an account for 'curing my Lady's Pud'. New furniture was bought for Holmes Hall — three dining tables, twelve chairs at only four shillings and sixpence each, three window stools at five shillings, a large writing desk at fifteen shillings — surely secondhand — and there were shelves built to set 'the Globes on' and various pictures. The larder at Holmes Hall contained a canvas-fronted keeping safe and possessed a kitchen with its spit before the fire, a dresser and a plate cratch, and the servants' hall had a large table and forms for sitting on, and there were pantry, bakehouse and cellar. The family's rooms included a parlour which was fitted up with fireplace and a 'bright' or polished steel stove and a Blue Room and one which contained a bath bought in 1774-75. It seems likely that the family took their beds with them when they travelled, as references occur to the taking-down and setting-up of some beds; perhaps too they needed the boot jack which was at home, when travelling. A perhaps less pleasant sight at Holmes Hall was the 'Six Spiting Boxes' which were bought in 1773 at one shilling each.

The men servants were provided with breeches made of buck and ram-skin, and six male servants were provided in 1775 with velvet caps, while the servants were summoned by wire-operated bells. At Holmes Hall, Lady Effingham received five guineas a week for housekeeping, paid her by the estate lawyer cum steward fortnightly, but the servants' wages were not paid out of this: apparently the servants were nearly all males and in August 1774 Jones received ten shillings and sixpence a week, his wife nine shillings and their daughter Ruth six shillings, while four male servants were paid between six shillings and ten shillings and sixpence and two females sixpence; a total of nine living-in servants received £3 8s 0d in all. By January 1775 £4 10s 0d was being paid to thirteen servants, ten of whom were men, still at between six shillings and ten shillings and sixpence weekly, and in 1780, for which year the male servant tax returns survive, Effingham paid tax on fourteen males at his new Thundercliffe Grange, the same number as were employed at the nearby and considerably grander Nostell Priory. The working quarters at Holmes Hall included a laundry with clothes horses and mangle, a clothes drying ground with posts, and a linen press. Water for household purposes came from a well with pump and a new, fourteen yard deep well was proved by boring and then sunk in 1775, and there was a 'Whater cart' available in which to carry water about. The ordinary foodstuffs needed by the household cost in one half-year £59 and included candles. The chimneys at Holmes Hall required cleaning and on one occasion 'a Chimney Doctor' was brought in and eventually a 'snook Jack' put up. The matter of strong drink was important. The household had its own brewhouse and its own malt mill in preparation for brewing, there was a cellar and bottle racks, and cognac brandy, Jamaica rum, red and white port, sherry and Madeira were bought.

Owing to the great interest of the Earl and his lady in horses and riding and racing, the stable department was important. The farm horses had their separate accommodation in the carthorse stable; the riding horses were in part at least, shoed by the great local firm of Samuel Walker & Co, the ironmasters, and thirteen boards were fitted up with the horses' names on them, while above the stables were outdoor servants' bedroom or bedrooms. New horses were of course bought — for example, 'a Black Coach Gelding rising four Years Old' and costing fourteen guineas in 1775. What seems to have been a new coachhouse for Holmes Hall was built in 1766, and there was a harness room too. In 1774, Effingham paid £2 tax on 'one Chair with Two-wheel Carriage'. In 1771 the horse *Lesang* from Newmarket was dosed with physic at a cost of two guineas.

Both the Earl and Lady Effingham, as she was always known, rather than as Countess, were gregarious, and in the two months of December 1774 and January 1775 chaise fares were paid to Sheffield (twice), Barnsley, Bramley, Worksop, Banktop (near Barnsley), Doncaster and Crookhill, although in August 1774 the Earl paid £2 carriage tax on his own chaise. In May 1775 Lady Effingham and friends visited 'the Concert' and were regaled with negus and food, the Sheffield Theatre was visited, and Lord Effingham paid a five guinea subscription to the Doncaster Races and the Sheffield Races in 1775, although his name never appears among those of the winners of the St Leger or the Doncaster Cup. He was one of the two Stewards of the Sheffield Races in 1777.

The Earl had been a foundation member of the social Monthly Club in Sheffield, established in 1783 upon the occasion of the Cutler's Feast there; Lady Effingham played the guitar and an account of 1775 refers to her instrument being repaired and tuned, while perhaps the 'Quilting frame' bought in 1774 may have been for her use. The family had 'a Magick box', bought in 1774, and this may have been for the projection of pictures and silhouettes, while there was a set of skittles and ebony bowls and a large floor cloth painted in diamonds, all of which were presumably for entertainment. But sport engrossed much of their attention. As well as the 'Leaping Barr' for horse jumping, they hunted, fished and fowled. Dog kennels were built behind the stable block at Thundercliffe and hounds were kept — both hunting dogs and pointers, each dog being provided with a collar with an engraved plate presumably bearing its own name. The dogs were treated carefully and the huntsman Nathaniel Wilkinson was paid £9 17s 6d a quarter plus clothes and the keep of the dogs; occasionally payment had to be made for sheep killed by the Earl's hounds. A keeper preserved the pheasants on the Holmes estate, and there were turkeys there too. The Effinghams had a boat, the *Eagle*, and references occur to her repair, her rudder pulleys, her oars and her mast and a willow basket for keeping the victuals or perhaps the fish in; fishing rods, fish boxes, salmon in the Don, and payment was made for an otter cage, a box for partridges, a squirrel case, for the killing of crows and magpies at threepence a head, and hawks at one shilling. Rabbits abounded, especially on Rotherham Common, where a special gate was built 'to keep the Rabbits in', and rabbit nets were bought. The garrets of Holmes Hall included a room fitted out with pegs for guns, and powder and shot were bought, guns repaired, a brace of pistols cleaned, balls bought and a pair of shot moulds. Effingham also had lark nets, and in August 1775 he paid for 'Expenses on the Moors', including breakfasts, dinners and liquor.

More sedately, reference is made in the accounts to 'the Card Club', when five shillings was paid for twenty nights' absence. The Earl had even more sedentary pursuits, as he wrote letters extensively and even published a pamphlet or two of his own composing; he bought ink, quills, paper, a 'Spelling Book', and 'Shining Sand' in lieu of blotting paper. He had published a work with the title *A Collection of Letters* on Parliamentary Party Reform in 1783, 'a matter of which he approved and for which he had joined the Yorkshire Association for Parliamentary Reform, and he published on Pitt's scheme for a national sinking fund in 1787'.

Effingham was apparently short of money, regularly. His banking account was kept with James Meyrick of Parliament Street, London, and probably also with Hanbury & Co, also of London, but upon occasion he had to borrow considerable sums — £300 in July 1774, for example, from his then newly-appointed estate steward and lawyer, to be paid out of the next estate rents, and he owed £4,532 0s 1d to his previous steward for principal and interest, paid off in October 1775, while an eighty guinea a year annuity had been bought for ready money by Capt Thomas Buck, and other large sums were borrowed, the exact details of which cannot be gathered from the surviving papers; in January 1775 Effingham was wanting to raise a further £5,000 mortgage.

Taxes and rates were also substantial. Land Tax had to be paid on land and the tithes which he owned; rates included those for the expenses of poor, constable, church and highways and the annual Easter Dues for the vicar. There was also the Window Tax to meet. The estates were carefully surveyed in the years 1773-1775 by Bartholomew Rotherham, who produced detailed maps and written surveys of them at a cost of £32 16s 0d; Mr Rotherham's plan table was altered at the Earl's expense in May 1771, while in October 1768 a board had been bought for Mr Rotherham to draw a map upon, at eight shillings.

A little is recorded of how the family dressed. What were the 'White skins' bought in 1774 at one shilling each — were they for the Earl's Masonic costume? In 1773 his Lordship had five pairs of breeches and in 1774 he had three pairs washed and the buttons covered, while in 1773-74 he was supplied with a waistcoat, breeches, 'Drawers', a silk waistcoat, a shooting coat and waistcoat, a riding coat and a nightgown, while the Countess had a new riding coat, habits, ribbon of various types and colours, gauze, caps, lace, muslin, a cloak and various waistcoats. The indoor and outdoor servants were all provided with outer clothing, the indoor males having scarlet jackets and waistcoats and white breeches, the outdoor ones with frocks and waistoats, and the hunt staff with appropriate clothing.

The Effingham estates in and around Holmes Hall were in part parkland and in part used for heavy industry, while another part was worked as a farm. The farm was part in pasture — sheep and cows were kept, and pigs which were at least in part fed on purchased acorns — and part arable, hay, wheat and white clover seeds being bought and a barn rented at four guineas. There was a dairy, and a cowhouse. In July 1775 thirty acres were mowed; lime was bought for the land, manure led and spread, drains cut to improve the land, fences repaired with hedgewood and with rails and posts. Large quantities of oats were bought, coming in part at least by water on the Don Navigation, and malt, presumably for brewing, was also bought in. A waggon and a cart were used, a new stile erected, gates mended, and new wheels and spokes bought.

The Effinghams were certainly interested in their gardens on the Holmes estate; an ornamental fishpond, railed round, with trees and shrubs — gooseberry, green walnut, bay, many ashes — and Wm & John Perfect, the Pontefract seedsmen, provided seeds and broccoli,

Figure 4. Boston Castle. *J Guest,* Historic Notices of Rotherham

cauliflower, and Italian broccoli for the Thundercliffe Grange. There was also a garden house, papered and with blinds and shelving, at Holmes Hall, painted garden seats, garden frames, a roller for the lawn(s) and perhaps the 'trellise window' at the Holmes was in the gardens. The garden wall had had to be propped and wedged — industry was indeed creeping nearer! Despite the Earl's reputation for wearing dirty clothes, Holmes Hall was not without its bath, built in 1771. The eating vessels were quite sumptuous and some were engraved with his Lordship's arms; they included silver loops for wine bottles, gilt goblets, scalloped silver shells, Sheffield plate candlesticks, snuffers and snuffer stand, and a plate basket. A clock stood on the staircase at Holmes Hall, repaired and cleaned in 1771 and 1773, the house had blinds and the new Grange at least, was wallpapered, £4 5s 6d being paid in 1775 'for 19 Dozn of Paper'. In the middle of 1775, slightly less expensive wallpaper at three shillings and sixpence a dozen (as against four shillings and sixpence for the Grange) was bought, together with border strips; payment was made for hanging it and for the 'flower for Paist'.

His Lordship had his own lockable workshop, and in 1775 Henry Watson was paid a substantial £21 for 'A compleat Set of Specimens of Marbles, Crystals, figured fossils ores &c as described by a Catalogue with them' and they were housed in a wainscotted box with drawers. The Earl's watch was repaired upon occasion and in 1773 the Countess' watch required a new glass. The domestic arrangements are illustrated in some detail. Lady Effingham received her ten guineas a fortnight housekeeping money, but malt, beef, bacon and groceries were bought in bulk. There certainly were visitors: Lady Effingham wrote in mid-December 1775 to their Rotherham lawyer and agent that 'we expect you both to dinner & to stay all night according to promise'. When the family travelled, their trunks, hampers and boxes were carried to and from London by water; Lord Effingham also had a sea chest. Medical attention was of course sometimes required: Benjamin Wainwright charged thirty guineas 'for attendance upon the Family' in 1775 and in the January of that year two weeks' board and lodging were provided 'when Master Lindsey was innoculated'.

The mid-1770s was an important period in the Earl's life; he became well known as a politician, he became a freemason, and he began to build on a large scale. His advocacy of the American colonists' cause was in fact to be closely related to one of his major estate developments in a curious way. In the earlier 1770s Effingham owned some rough land on the southwestern outskirts of Rotherham which he had probably been awarded under the Rotherham Enclosure of 1761-64. The land was described as quarry hills; it was adjacent to these quarry hills that he began to build in 1773.

In commemoration of the so-called Boston Tea Party, the building was ultimately named Boston Castle, but was apparently begun with an intention of building nothing more ambitious than a gothic folly which would be used as a shooting box and rural retreat. During December 1773 the foundations for the intended new buildings were being dug and stone and lime led 'to Common'; possibly the commencement of the new buildings was the occasion for festivities marked by the purchase of the '17 Rockit sticks at 2d each', a 'standard for the soldiers' (two shillings and sixpence), 'a Board with Letters on for the fire Works' (four shillings) and 'a frame makeing to fix a Cannon upon' (one shilling and tenpence) which are all recorded in the accounts at the end of 1773. By March 1774 the new buildings were sufficiently advanced to require scaffolding being erected, in April 1774 work was proceeding on the guttering and in June 1774 the door snecks were put on. The joiner's bill for the work at 'House upon the common' includes references to architraves, a plinth, shelves and window seats, wainscot, sashes, 'Oval's', banister and hand rails and a fourteen-rise staircase; the glazing was done at the 'new Building on Rotherham Common' in April and June 1774 and the painting in oak and stone colours in the latter month.

In July 1774 accounts refer to the buildings as 'Boston Castle, although a fireplace provided in that month was 'for the great Room at Common'. The building was to be battlemented and to be surmounted initially with gothic pinnacles (see Figure 4). Four dowels were charged for, to hold these pinnacles in May 1774, but they had to be taken down a couple of months later. The builders' account, from John and James Bagshaw, refers to two foot walls, broached quoins, stone and brick work, and specifies a passage, two little chambers, the best chamber, a cellar with a stone keeping table and the Little House. The immense number of bricks which were being made for Effingham at the Holmes by Marmaduke Bailey may have been in part intended for the new Castle: how many were made is unknown, but in the period June and September 1774 Bailey charged for 75,800 bricks at seven shillings ninepence per 1,000, and between July 1774 and December 1775 he charged (apart from the bricks made specifically for the glassworks) the large sum of 142 guineas. Certainly a new farmhouse was also being built during this period and major developments were also beginning at Thundercliffe Grange; Bailey curiously charged for his brickmaking in multiples of half a guinea.

No tea was drunk at Boston Castle in its early days, that liquid being prohibited there on account of the building's 'dedication', although tea was purchased in large quantities for use at Holmes Hall: Hyson, single and greene tea at (in 1774) sixteen shillings, ten shillings and eight shillings per pound. Boston Castle stands today in a public park which was itself formally opened in 1876.

Effingham was much interested in Freemasonry, and held very high office: indeed, he was one of only two men to hold the office of Acting Grand Master. It was proposed at a Communication (ie, meeting) of the premier Grand Lodge in April 1782 that whenever a Royal prince should become Grand Master, he should be at liberty to nominate a peer to be Acting Grand Master: the Duke of Cumberland, a grandson of George the Second, had just been appointed to that office, at the age of 36, and he appointed Effingham, also in his late thirties, as the first to hold the new office. That office he held until 1789.

In what turned out to be his last years, Effingham accepted the office of Governor of Jamaica, a colony of which his own mother had been a native and where she had been brought up. The Effinghams went out to Jamaica in 1789, he resigning his offices as Master of the Mint and as Acting Grand Master of the Modern Freemasons. But Lady Effingham was to die of liver disease on board HMS *Diana* in October 1791, and he died only a month later at Government House, Jamaica, aged only forty-four. A monument to both of them was placed in the English Church at Spanish Town, where both were buried. That he was a man of parts is evident: capable of making major speeches in the House of Lords, of resigning his commission on a matter of principle, of holding a Government post of great responsibility and then that of Master of the Mint, of being Governor of Jamaica, and of being a Privy Councillor. At the same time he was a man of character, not altogether liked by the political establishment, respected in Masonic circles and highly regarded and usefully active here in the West Riding. Diary references show that others too thought well of him.

Sources

The John Goodchild Collection, Wakefield: Effingham Estate papers.
The Complete Peerage, Vol 5, St Catherine's Press, 1926, p 13.
Masonic Year Book, Historical Supplement.
John Guest, *Historic Notices of Rotherham*, 1877.
Frederic Reynold's *Life*, Vol 2, 1826, pp 98-101.
E Rhodes, *Yorkshire Scenery*, 1826, pp 60-64.
M H Habershon, 'The Old Holmes Hall', *The Ivanhoe Review*, Vol 2, No 1, Jan 1899, p 6.

7. RENTS, REMARKS AND OBSERVATIONS: THE FIRST MARQUIS OF ROCKINGHAM'S RENT ROLL BOOK

by Melvyn Jones

SOON AFTER COMING INTO HIS INHERITANCE, on his father's death in 1723, Thomas Watson-Wentworth, the future first Marquis of Rockingham, arranged for the details of his estate to be set out in a large volume of some 130 leaves of vellum, bound in the same material and secured by two metal clasps. The volume seems to have begun as a record of manorial courts in 1654. Records of the courts baron of Offham, Meopham and Bury occupy eleven pages at the back of the book. The book was then turned round and the rental details of the future Marquis' estate begun at the other end. It is now part of the Wentworth Woodhouse Muniments in Sheffield Archives, catalogued as WWM A1273. Interesting and important as the rental details are, giving a detailed summary of his landed inheritance, the volume's over-riding interest lies in the fact that the Marquis used the volume to record, in his own hand, what are called on the back cover, 'many remarks & observations...', from 1724 almost until the day he died in 1750. His jottings include details of his purchases and sales, the building of his great new mansion at Wentworth Woodhouse, the laying out and expansion of the park at Wentworth, the building of Hoober Stand, his son's birthday party, being the first person in Yorkshire to grow pineapples and breed goldfish, woodland management schemes, the death of two of his sons, an account of a fire at Wentworth Woodhouse, and his outlook on life.

The Man

Thomas Watson-Wentworth, the future first Marquis of Rockingham (Figure 1), was the son of the Honorable Thomas Watson and his wife Alice (daughter of Sir Thomas Proby of Elton Hall, Huntingdonshire). He was born in 1693 at Tidmington in Worcestershire. His father, the Honorable Thomas Watson was the third son of the Earl of Rockingham of Rockingham Castle in Northamptonshire and his wife Anne. Anne was the younger sister of the second Earl of Strafford, and on the latter's death, childless, in 1693, her third son Thomas inherited his uncle's vast estates in England and Ireland. A condition of the will was that he adopt the name 'Wentworth' and reside at Wentworth Woodhouse. The Hon Thomas Watson-Wentworth then set about

Figure 1. Thomas Watson-Wentworth, first Marquis of Rockingham, 1693-1750. *Rotherham Central Library, Archives and Local Studies Section*

improving and expanding the Strafford inheritance so that on his death in 1723 he was able to pass on to the future Marquis of Rockingham a substantially enlarged country estate.

In 1707 the future first Marquis of Rockingham entered St John's College, Cambridge and was awarded an MA in 1708. In 1716 he married Mary, daughter of Daniel Finch, second Earl of Nottingham and sixth Earl of Winchelsea and succeeded to the entire family estate seven years later. He was a strong supporter of the Hanoverian succession and was the organiser of Whig power in Yorkshire. He was MP for Malton from 1715 to 1727 and for the County of Yorkshire from 1727-28. His support for the Whig cause and later his role in the suppression of the 1745 Jacobite rebellion brought him a succession of honours. In 1728 he was created Baron Wentworth of Malton and in 1734 Baron of Harrowden and Viscount Higham of Higham Ferrers and Baron of Wath and Earl of Malton. In 1745, on the death of his cousin Thomas Watson, third Earl of Rockingham, he succeeded to the barony of Rockingam (the earldom ceasing to exist). Finally, in 1746 he was created Marquis of Rockingham. He was Lord Lieutenant of the West Riding of Yorkshire from 1733 till his death in 1750. He was buried in York Minster. His widow died in 1761.

His Children

The Marquis has much to say about his children in his Rent Roll book. For five of them: Anne (born 1722, and who married Earl Fitzwilliam in 1744), Mary (b 1727), William (b 1728), Charlotte (b 1732) and Henrietta Alicia (b 1737) he compiled a list not only giving their exact dates of birth but also their (mostly aristocratic) godparents. The other children to whom he refers were Thomas (b 1720) and Charles, the future second Marquis of Rockingham, (b 1730). On the 9 January 1733, which was Thomas' birthday, he gave a large party at Wentworth Woodhouse. The party had a double significance: it also marked the near completion of the new mansion that faced west (see below). The Marquis described the entertainment in some detail:

> *Upon the Hanselling [ie, inaugurating] the new offices Jany 9th 1732/33 my Son Thomas's Birthday I gave a large Entertainment to all my Tenants in the Neighbourhood & some Neighbouring Gentlemen also came... one Hogshead of Ale was given to the Poor the following day... The number of Guests was about one Thousand.*

He describes how the food was laid out in the dining room, prayer room, old laundry, old store room and old kitchen. All the guests had tickets telling them 'which room to repair to'. Men and women were separated and they were taken to 'the best Rooms & the Inferior according to their Rank'. He then goes on to list all the dishes that were served — 225 in all — comprising 'of beef 43, of Pork 30, Venison Pastys 24, Turkeys 15, Geese 21, Puddings 30, Apple or minced Pyes 16, Fowls 14, Boar's Heads 4, Mutton 28, one hundred sixpenny loaves of White Bread, about eight Hogsheads of Ale, and three of small Beer, twelve Dozen of Wine and Two Hogsheads of Punch.'

Unfortunately, one guest died: 'a too melancholy thing happened, a poor man dyed, as supposed by a Fall, in the Courtyard being in Liquor.' He also recorded the deaths of his sons Thomas and William. Thomas 'dyed of the Small Pox at Leyden' on 14 August 1734. The fourteenth day of August was a generally unlucky day for the Watson-Wentworths as the Marquis related:

> *...the same day was very remarkable to my present Eldest Son William. On 14th August he fell into the Bason in the Garden when no Body but a Boy was by, who providentially helped him out else he had probably been drowned being very young & on 14 August 1732 as he hastily shut a Door, a large Picture which hung over it fell down with that violence as to shatter the frame to pieces & by God's providence fell over the child so as he remained unhurt between the Door and the Picture.*

William only survived until 1739, the Marquis recording his early death, aged eleven, thus: '... after a Feaverish Illness of about a month's continuance dyed at Hampstead' William's death and the earlier death of Thomas, gave the Marquis pause for thought at the end of 1739:

> *... so that this Unfortunate Year when I lost my Dear Eldest Son William Lord Higham for whom I hoped to have prepared these Conveniencys [ie, his new mansion at Wentworth Woodhouse] I had laid out in the whole as near as I could compute fifty six thousand pound — God prevent our being attached to the Honours Grandeur or State of the World above what we ought, & Bless my now Dear & only son Charles to a long and Christian Life to the enjoyment of these so as to be fit at leaving them to enjoy Everlasting Glory.*

His House

Strictly speaking the title of this section should be 'Houses', because in 1724 the future Marquis started building a new mansion in the Baroque style facing west (Figure 2) but before he had finished building and furnishing it [1734], he had already commenced the erection of another, bigger house, in the Palladian style, facing east (Figure 3). It is this latter mansion, which was not completed until after his death, that we are familiar with today.

He meticulously recorded progress, setbacks and expenditure on his building projects, although, interestingly, he never mentions his

Figure 2. Wentworth Woodhouse: the Baroque mansion (west front).

builder/architects Tunnicliff (till 1736) and Flitcroft.

He noted that in 1724 he had 'articled for the Library Wing' and that these had been 'built in 1725 and furnished inside in 1726'. He went on to record that he had 'articled' for the 'rest of the Garden front in 1725 ' which had been built in 1726 and 1727 and the inside finished in 1728. The kitchen was articled for in 1730 and made use of in 1733. He computed that the outlay on building work between 1722 and 1733 was more than £27,000.

By the Spring of 1736 building expenditure had risen to more than £36,000 and included the building of part of the new front '7 windows in length'. In 1737 he noted that the new parlour and drawing room were finished, furnished and in use and the great hall and portico begun. By 1738 the great hall was built and covered and the 'supping room' finished. In 1739 the 'great porticoe' of the east front was complete. He said of this that 'considering the Size of the Stones & the Quantity of Carving, etc [it] was the greatest piece of Building I had ever done in one Year.' By the Spring of 1739 his building expenditure at Wentworth had risen to £56,800 and by 1744, by which time he was buying Cumberland slate for the main roof, it was £74,000.

By 1748 he was able to record that there was 'nothing but Furnishing, Finishing and Levelling' to be done. At the end of that year his total building expenses had reached an astonishing £86,000 including £3,500 for 'Statues bought ... by Ld Malton [the future second Marquis] at Rome and other places'. By the time the first Marquis died in 1850 the building expenses had reached £90,000.

Amongst the recitation of building achievements and monetary outlay he describes a fire that occurred during the morning of 18 September 1732. Having described how it was thought to have started by some burning coal having set light to floor joists which then spread and caused damage in some bedrooms, he goes on to say:

> ... *God's Providence be praised that it happened in the daytime & was immediately discovered & by his Goodness at a time when there were near 200 people at hand to assist in getting Water etc, which lay convenient, & we had two Engines. his name be praised, for had it lain undiscovered one Hour longer the danger had been exceeding great or if in the Night probably all our Lives had been lost & the whole Fabrick destroyed in a few Hours. Praise God for His deliverence from Fire Septr 18th 1732.*

His pleasure grounds and park

The expenses itemised above had been incurred not just on building one mansion and then another, but also in laying out and furnishing the pleasure grounds immediately around the house(s) and the park beyond. He recorded the completion of a ha-ha and the setting up of obelisks in the garden in 1729 (see figure 4), and in 1732 a keeper's lodge, park wall, a greenhouse and an obelisk in Lee Wood are mentioned. In 1735 and 1736 the 'Terrass' was made and an ice house and 'The Tempiatto' built. The terrace which stretched westwards for 500 yards from the southern end of the Palladian mansion was flanked by a bastion wall which collapsed and had to be rebuilt. Both the terrace and the bastion wall survive to the present day.

In 1739 he reported that 'a piece of water of three Acres was made to flow from the Terras between Shire Oaks & Old Hague and other lesser Waters for a Serpentine river'. He also records the building of a number of park monuments which still stand including a Doric temple and an Ionic temple. Outside the park on one of the highest points in the estate he built Hoober Stand. This 'Pyramidal Building', as he called it, was begun in 1747 in honour of King George II and the suppression of the 1745 Jacobite Rebellion. His son Charles, the future second Marquis, at the age of fifteen, had run away and joined the

Figure 3. Wentworth Woodhouse: the Palladian mansion (east front). The Palladian mansion has the distinction of having the largest front (just over 600 feet) of any English country house.

King's army under the Duke of Cumberland. The monument was probably also built in relief at the safe return of his only surviving son and heir!

At the same time that he was laying out the park and embellishing it with monuments, he was also extending it. In the early 1740s he wrote that:

> *The Totall Circumference of the whole Park at Wentworth House, following the Angles of the Wall & including Scholes Wood & the new Park viz Greasborough Common is six miles & seventeen Hundred & twenty two yards that is nearly seven Miles and now since the turning of the Road and enclosing the Bower's Pond &c it amounts to seven compleat miles & near a Quarter of a mile more which is added to the Garden... but in the year 1743 was encreased about a Mile by going down to the little Brook below the Old Hague Wood & taking in my wife's new Farm to the obelisk in Lee Wood & thence on the Brow of the Hill by Street Farm to Hoober Hill & so down by Flint Wood into the old Fall & thence quite round Skoles Wood as above the whole Circumference exceeds nine miles Anno 1744.*

The park as it is depicted on Peter Perez Burdett's map of Derbyshire, first published in 1767 and then reprinted with corrections and additions

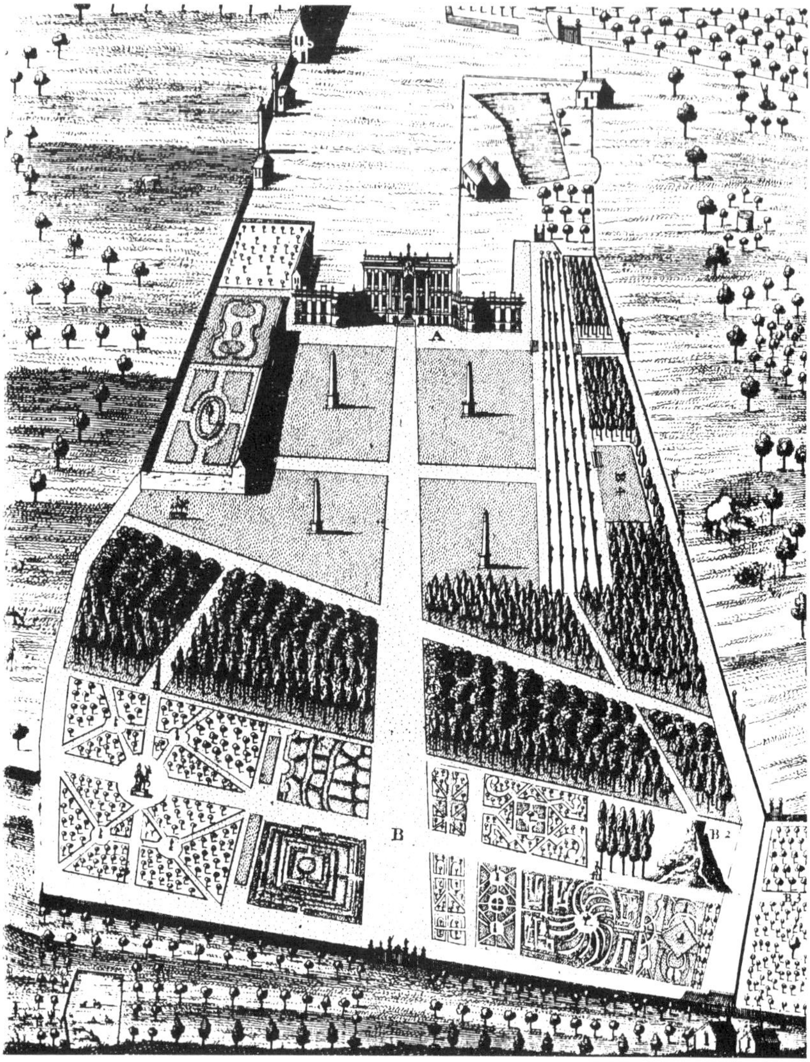

Figure 4. The pleasure grounds stretching westwards from the Baroque mansion c 1730. Immediately next to the house is a large lawn divided into four by wide paths and a central drive. In each quarter of the lawn stands a large obelisk which the first Marquis said were in place by 1729. On the south side of the lawn are five rows of pleached fruit trees and beyond these are areas of planted trees amongst which is a bowling green. To the north of the lawn are two small gardens with flower beds arranged in geometrical patterns (parterres). West of the lawn is another area of planted trees and beyond this and extending as far as the lane between Wentworth village and Thorpe Hesley is a large garden area laid out as a series of elaborate parterres.
Bodleian Library, Oxford, Gough Maps 35, folio 48

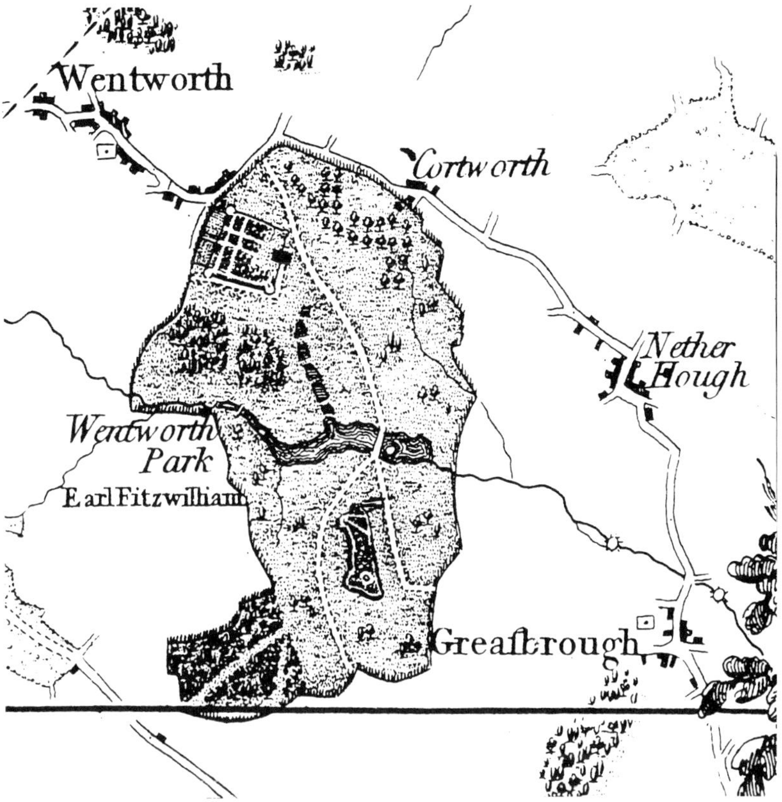

Figure 5. Wentworth Park as depicted on Peter Perez Burdett's map of Derbyshire, first published in 1767 and reprinted with additions and corrections in 1791. The map shows the 'serpentine river' referred to by the first Marquis in 1739 (the predecessor of Morley Pond and Dog Kennel Pond), Lady Rockingham's Wood (an ornamental plantation created on the former Greasbrough Common) and, in the south-west, Scholes Coppice which was purchased in 1714 and which according the first Marquis in 1726 was 'being cut into Walks for Beauty and intended to be thrown in the Park'.

in 1791, is shown in Figure 5. The map extended northwards into the West Riding as far as Worsbrough.

The Marquis also recorded some interesting details about his fruit growing and fish breeding. According to Prof Keith Thomas in his book *Man and the Natural World* (1983), at the beginning of the eighteenth century the most highly esteemed fruit was the pineapple, because it was so difficult and so expensive to grow. The Marquis seems to have started to cultivate pineapples in his heated greenhouses or 'stoves' at Wentworth in 1737, stating that they were then 'very scarce in England'. By 1740 he notes that he had got their cultivation 'to great perfection' and had produced one that weighed 3½lb which was '20 inches in girth the long way round and 16 inches the other'. In 1745 he says some were ripe as early as 24 March and he had them sent to London 'for an Entertainment I made' at which the Duke of Richmond, the Earl of Lincoln, Earl Fitzwilliam and Lord Harcourt were present. He noted that by the second week in June that year he had cut more than 200, sometimes as many as sixteen a day. He also noted that he cut several hundred in 1747.

He also cultivated grapes, 'Sweet water or Early Grapes' and also 'Hambergh and Frontiniak'. He noted that in April 1746:

> *I presented His Majesty with one Bunch of Frontiniak Grapes & one of Muscadine perfectly ripe, which He eat the Day after He Received the news of the Dukes Victory over The Rebells in Scotland.*

Surprisingly, he also bred goldfish! He notes that he brought down (presumably from London) a number in 1746 to 'try to propagate them in Yorkshire'. They bred successfully and by the following year he had several hundred, making presents of some to the Earl of Kingston, the Earl of Strafford (of Wentworth Castle) and Rowland Winn (of Nostell Priory).

His Estate

In 1723, when he became head of the family, he inherited a vast estate, part of which had already been passed to him on his marriage in 1716. This estate consisted of the estate inherited by his father from the second Earl of Strafford ('the Strafford estate') and land purchased by his father to which he continued to add throughout his lifetime ('the purchased estate').

The Strafford estate consisted of two separate sets of properties. The smaller of these two sets of properties was the 'home estate' in South Yorkshire which stretched away in all directions from Wentworth Woodhouse and included property in Wentworth, Hoyland Nether, Tankersley, Brampton, Wath, Hooton Roberts, Kimberworth, Greasbrough and Tinsley. The rents due from all these properties at the beginning of the future Marquis' stewardship in the early 1720s are listed in meticulous detail in the rent Roll book. Also valued, although the details of the properties and rents are not given, were the Irish properties which his father had inherited from the second Earl of Strafford. These properties, which covered an astonishing 90,000 acres, were in counties Kildare and Wicklow, in what is now the Irish Republic (Figure 6). The income from rents and from the sale of wood and timber on the Irish estates were crucial factors in enabling the building activity and estate expansion (see below) to take place on the

Figure 6. The Marquis of Rockingham's Irish properties.

scale that it did in South Yorkshire.

The Irish estates were not added to, but nearly 4,000 more acres were added to the South Yorkshire property by the first Marquis and his father. His father purchased about 1,650 acres surrounding the inherited South Yorkshire estate in forty-two different transactions costing £16,000 between 1695 and 1723, and the Marquis improved on this by adding a further 2,116 acres in 24 transactions costing nearly £37,000. Figure 7 shows the location of the South Yorkshire properties by township and parish in 1782 (ie, they also include the 726 acres purchased by the second Marquis between 1750-82 and the Bright estate that the second Marquis acquired through his marriage to Mary Bright in 1752), distinguishing between the amount inherited from the second Earl of Strafford in 1695, and the amount subsequently added by purchase.

The Marquis' father had also been active in the property market in another part of Yorkshire, and in Northamptonshire and parts of neighbouring counties, and the rents for these purchases are meticulously recorded in the rent roll. His father had acquired the majority property interest in the town of Malton in the East Riding and Higham Ferrers in Northamptonshire, so that they became the 'pocket boroughs' of his son and himself respectively (ie, they or their nominees represented the town in Parliament). In Northamptonshire the Marquis' father had also acquired a number of country properties (which were added to by the Marquis), including 'Great Harrowden House, Gardens and Park & Demesnes' which were 'in the Occupation of The Honble Mrs Wentworth [his mother]' in 1723. The Marquis also notes that he bought a house in Grosvenor Square, London in 1741.

After listing all his properties as they stood in 1723 and itemising all the rents, there is an overall valuation for the entire estate. The rents from South Yorkshire amounted to £4,448, for the Malton area in the East Riding it was £2,020, Northamptonshire, etc £3,050, and Ireland £6,446, making a grand total of nearly £16,000. In addition he reckoned he could expect an annual income of about £1,000 from his English and Irish coppice woods. He also put the value of his timber trees on his English and Irish properties at £25,000. In one of his last entries in 1748 he put his annual rental income at £19,000.

His Woods

The Marquis took a particular interest in the woods on his estate. With the exception of the 'demesne' woods (ie, those within his pleasure grounds and park) the woods on his South Yorkshire estate (nearly 900 acres) and on the Irish estate (more than 2,000 acres) were managed as coppices with standards (what the Marquis called 'spring woods').

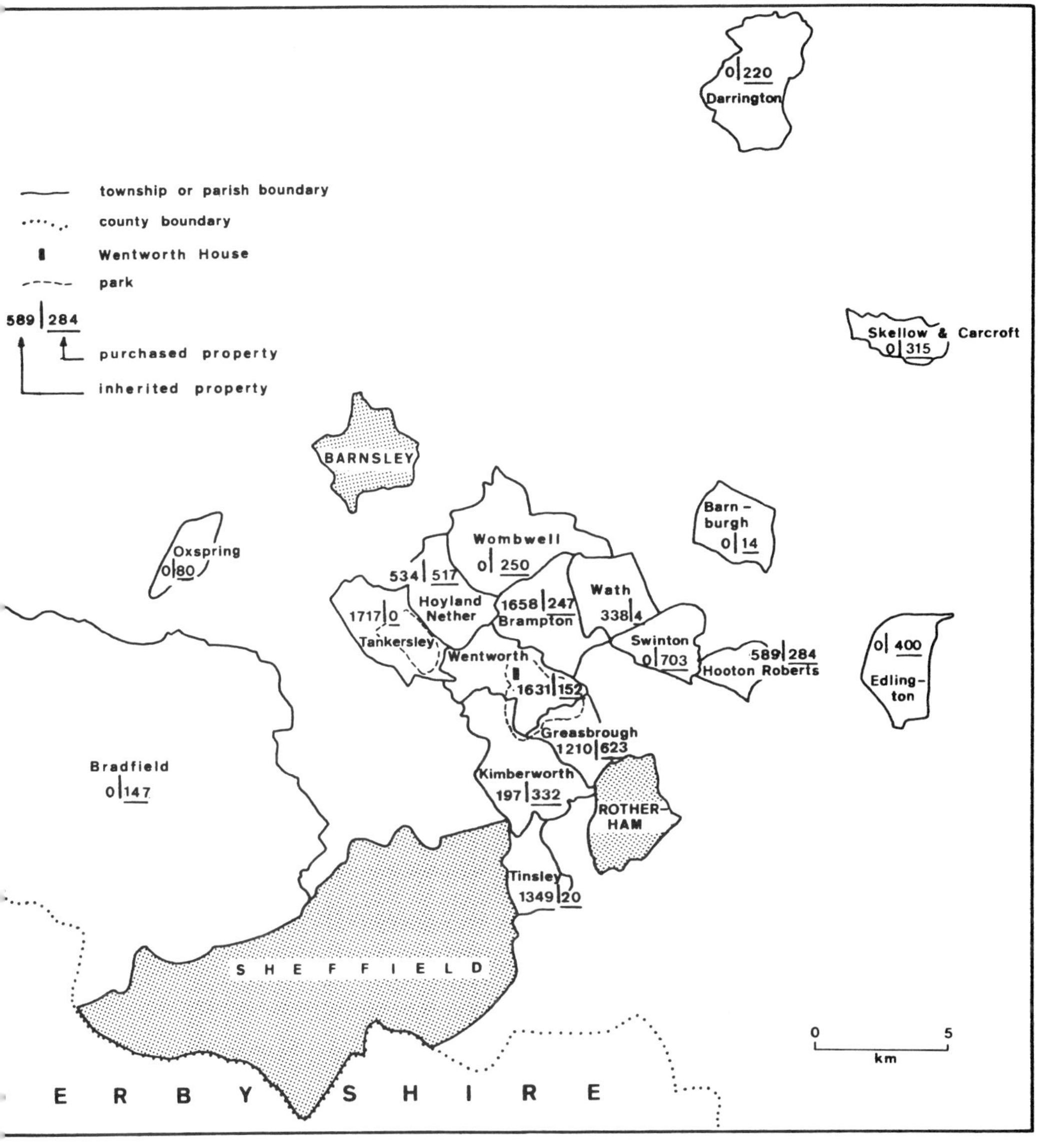

Figure 7. The Rockingham estate in 1782. The purchased properties include those bought by the first Marquis' father between 1695 and 1723 (1,643 acres), by the first Marquis himself between 1723 and 1750 (2,161 acres) and by his son the second Marquis between 1750 and 1782 (726 acres). In addition to the purchased properties a further 530 acres were added to the estate in the first half of the eighteenth century from the family's share of common land following the enclosure of commons.

A Scheme for a Regular Fall of Wood for 21 Years to come from the Year 1749 of about 42 Acres a Year the Coppice Woods in Yorkshire amounting to about nine Hundred Acres, in which Calculation Scholes Wood, all timber Trees & Woods in the Park at Wentworth are not included, nor the Woods in Northamptonshire, particularly Withmail Park of 100 Acres nor a Wood of about 30 Acres at Yesthrop Park which was felled Anno 1726 – Reserves to be at least 5 Black Barks & 70 Wavers – Philip Wood 2 Acres 2 Roods being Holted is not included nor the Wood by the Pyramide.

			Acres
Tinsley Park at Nine Falls for the Years 1749, 1750, 1751, 1752 1753, 1754, 1755, 1756 & 1757			350
Anno 1758	Bassingthorp Spring		37
Anno 1759	Great Thorncliffe		37
Anno 1760	Harley Spring 18^{A} Luke Spring 8 – 2 Goss Wood 8 Acres Bank Spring 4 Acres	totall	38 – 2
Anno 1761	Giles Wood 24 Acres King's Wood 11 Normandale Springs 5 Bolderfall 2A 2R	totall	42 – 2
Anno 1762	Tindle Brig Spring 4A 2R Wadsworth Spring 1 – 2R Westfield Ing Spring 3 Acres Simon Wood 25 – 2R Birkfield Spring 7^{A} – 2^{R} Coney Garth Spring 2^{A} – 2^{R}	totall	43 – 2
1763	Law Wood – 40 Acres		40 – 0
1764	Street Wood – 13 Rowing Spring 4^{A} – 2^{R} Littlewood Ing Spg 5 Acres 2 Roods Thorncliff Bottoms 5^{A} Blackmoor Bottoms 1^{A} Longland Spring & Longley Bottoms 5^{A} Little Thorncliffe 3	totall	37 – 0
1765, 1766, 1767 being three Years Fall	upper Linthwait 5^{A} – 2^{R} Golden Smithys 4 Rainbergh 115	totall	124 – 2
38 acres Per Annum			
Anno 1768, 1769 & 1770	Westwood exclusive of all Wasts being a Fall of 42 Acres Per Year. & so begin the Circle again excluding all wast to fall		126 – 0
			876

N.B. no Spinneys or Plantations in Wentworth Park & Demesnes are Included – There are also some little Reins & Spinneys up and down not taken notice of – also hedge Rows A Wood at Yesthorpe Park 30 Acres

1749

have now bought 400 Acres more called Edlington Wood 1750 bought Ld Gallway's Estate in Hoyland on which is 60 acres of wood so now the woodland is encreased near one half of that which may be brought into Regular Falls

Figure 8. The first Marquis of Rockingham's coppicing scheme for his South Yorkshire woods, 1749.

In this form of woodland management most of the trees in a wood are cut to ground level periodically, usually about every twenty years, and grow back as multiple stemmed trees. These provide the raw materials for a myriad of woodland crafts including chair and furniture making, wood turning for the manufacture of bowls, spoons and ladles, besom making, fence and gate-making and charcoal making. Among the coppice certain trees, principally oak, but also elm and alder, were allowed to grow — usually through a number of coppice cycles — to become large single stemmed timber trees for use in major building projects. Oak bark from the coppice poles and standard trees was also important in the leather tanning process. The rent roll book contains two major coppicing schemes (including preliminary versions which were abandoned) for his South Yorkshire woods. The first one, designed to run from 1727, was called 'A Scheme for making a yearly considerable Profit of Spring Woods in Yorkshire' and the second, designed to run from 1749, was entitled 'A Scheme for a Regular Fall of Wood for 21 years...'. In the 1749 scheme a 21 year coppice cycle was used so that the wooded area coppiced in 1749 (part of Tinsley Park which was then a wood of 350 acres) would be cut again in 1771. This meant that the Marquis' 876 acres of coppice woods in South Yorkshire would produce a regular crop of about 40 acres of coppice a year for 21 years at which point the crop in the wood cut in 1849 would be ready to be cut again. Two of the woods in the scheme were so big that they were divided into compartments and cut at different times. The Marquis was very specific about the timber trees in the coppice woods: there were to be five reserves (mature timber trees called black barks) and 70 wavers (young timber trees) per acre. The full 1749 scheme is shown in Figure 8. His notes show that large amounts of timber from his South Yorkshire woods were used in the building of his new mansion at Wentworth Woodhouse and that much of the coppice wood was sold to make charcoal for use at Tinsley Forge and Chapeltown Furnace.

Conclusion

It is unusual to be able to put together a coherent study of one estate at a particular period from just one source and this is what makes the first Marquis of Rockingham's rent roll book so interesting. The combined force of the formal rental entries, together with his own informal records, observations and marginal notes makes this a unique document and provides a real insight into his preoccupation with his estate and its enlargement and embellishment, his political leanings and his dynastic and personal preoccupations. But it is his estate that lies at the centre of his concerns. Let the Marquis have the last word. In 1750 the year of his death, in a letter to his son Charles, the future second

Marquis and prime minister (twice), he said 'If you lay out your money in improving your seat, land, gardens, etc, you beautifye the country and do the work ordered by God himself'.

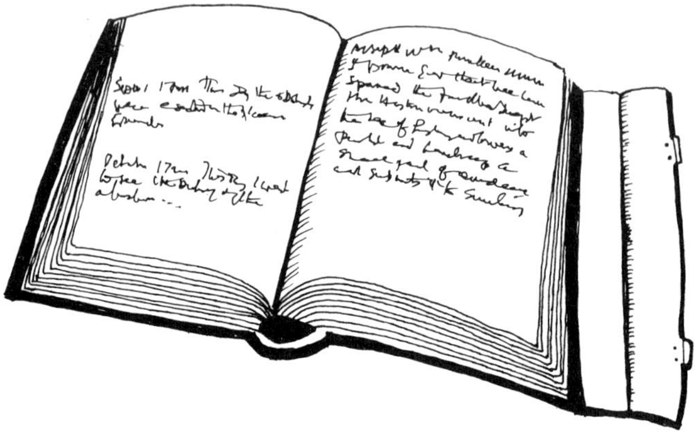

Acknowledgements

I am grateful to Olive, Countess Fitzwilliam's Wentworth Settlement Trustees and the Director of Sheffield City Libraries for permission to quote from the Wentworth Woodhouse Muniments in Sheffield Archives.

8. KIVETON : THE SEAT OF HIS GRACE THE DUKE OF LEEDS

by Brian Elliott

THE 'MANIA FOR ARCHITECTURE' of the first few decades of the eighteenth century caused Defoe in the preface of his *Tour Through England and Wales* to remark that:

> *Even while the sheets were in the press, new beauties appear in several places, and almost to every part we are oblig'd to add appendixes, and supplement accounts of fine houses, new undertakings, buildings etc.*[1]

The building boom had its roots 'in the displays of wealth and prestige constructed by the newly powerful and newly secure Whig ruling class in the wake of the Glorious Revolution'.[2] William III set about remodelling Hampton Court and his most loyal supporters, whose new wealth was based on the reward of high office and noble title, followed suit, rebuilding on their own estates from the late 1680s to the early 1700s: the Duke of Devonshire at Chatsworth, the Duke of Leeds at Kiveton, the Earl of Carlisle at Castle Howard, the Duke of Newcastle at Welbeck Abbey and Houghton (Notts), William Blathwayt, the King's Secretary of State for War, at Dyrham Park (Avon) and, further down the social scale, the royal gardener George London at Thames Ditton, Surrey. All the above had some association with William Talman who has been described as the architect *par excellence* of the Williamite Court.[3]

This article presents new findings on Kiveton Park, demolished as long ago as 1811, after little more than a century of occupation. When new, with splendid red brick contrasting with white decorative limestone (as at Hampton Court) Kiveton was, as we can visualise from Badeslade's later engraving (Figure 1), one of the most fashionable and therefore most envied houses for miles around. Writing from Berlin, in 1710, to his relative William Wentworth of Bretton, the Earl of Strafford appears to have considered using brick and stone for his new front at Stainborough, 'like that of the Duke of Leeds at Keton [Kiveton]'.[4] Kiveton's short life and ultimate demise has also made it one of the most enigmatic of our region's country houses. The Duke of Leeds' archives, held by the Yorkshire Archaeological Society, include detailed building accounts of the house but the identity of its designer is not, as we shall see, as certain as was once thought. Thankfully, however, we

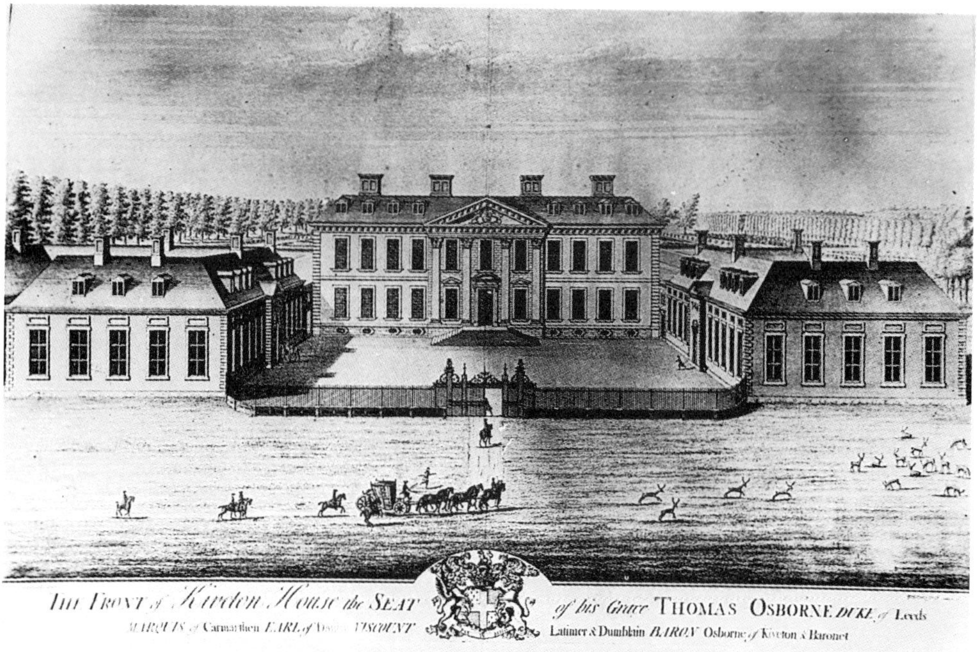

Figure 1. Badeslade's engraving of c 1730. Here we can see the showpiece front and its connecting wings forming a square courtyard separated from the park by means of an ornamental fence or screen, almost certainly the work of the foremost decorative metalworker of the age: Jean Tijou. Originally it was probably painted and partly enamelled as was the exceptional example at Hampton Court, currently under restoration. The impressive classical facade of two principal storeys and eleven bays has a central entrance framed by four giant pilasters crowned by a triangular pediment enclosing the Osborne arms. The noble owner is shown arriving by his carriage, the park deer scattering at his approach. The lodge keeper can be seen opening the courtyard gates whilst servants rush to greet their master. We also have a glimpse of what appears to be the formal avenue of trees and, in the distance, parkland plantings. *Rotherham Central Library, Archives and Local Studies*

are left with some valuable contemporary descriptions of the house and its contents. Of equal importance to the new country houses were the gardens and parks surrounding them. Although recognising the need for further research, new information will be presented about the garden and park, not least from an examination of the present local landscape that once formed 'His Grace's the Duke of Leeds' Seat' at Kiveton.

The Osbornes of Old Kiveton and Thorpe Salvin

Edward Osborne was a successful merchant who was knighted in 1585 when lord mayor of London. His grandson and namesake settled in the extreme southern part of Yorkshire in about 1618, purchasing a house and small estate at Kiveton in the ancient parish of Harthill. The second Sir Edward soon established friendly relations with neighbouring landed families, including Sir Thomas Wentworth (first Earl of Strafford) of Wentworth Woodhouse. The Kiveton estate was extended in 1636 through the acquisition of Thorpe Salvin, shown in Figures 2 and 3, the Elizabethan hall of the Sandfords which was used as an alternative residence.

Edward's heir, Thomas, born at Thorpe Salvin Hall in 1632, succeeded to the Osborne estate (and to a baronetcy) in his teens and before he reached thirty years was introduced at the Court of Charles I. Appointed Treasurer of the Navy in 1671, he had already come into contact with Pepys who found him a somewhat 'comely gentleman'. In practice he proved to be one of the most able and politically shrewd of the Restoration hierarchy, surviving impeachment and imprisonment in the Tower of London, to march from dignity to dignity. As Earl of Danby he joined William Cavendish, the Earl of Devonshire, his 'partner in the secret trust about the revolution', in supporting the future King William III who gratefully 'crowned' him Marquis of Carmarthen (1689) and later (1694) the first Duke of Leeds (after Leeds Castle in Kent). White's head and shoulders engraving of Osborne (Figure 4), probably dating from 1694, celebrates his new status, above a long list of titles, beginning with 'The most Noble and Mighty Prince ...', who was, after all, chief minister to the king; whilst a later full length canvas (Figure 5) shows him holding the white wand of the office of Secretary of State.

The principal outcome of such royal patronage was a huge increase in personal wealth which in turn provided the opportunity to found a noble dynasty. Both were impossible in the eyes of contemporaries without the trappings of a suitable residence, tastefully furnished and in a pleasant setting. The old house at Kiveton did not meet these needs — nor did Thorpe Salvin. Such properties were deemed old fashioned, too small and inappropriate for the new taste in decor and thirst for fine works of art. What was needed was a fine new house in keeping with the high status of its owner. It was modern buildings, enhanced by the latest craze for ornamental gardens, in a style influenced by French and Dutch examples, that attracted detailed comment and great praise. At Chatsworth, for example, Celia Fiennes, probably the most

Figure 2. Thorpe Salvin Hall. Today, only part of the south front and gatehouse survive of the fine Elizabethan house of the Sandfords and Osbornes; but the corner towers and massive chimney stacks make it an impressive ruin, now under the care of English Heritage. Although 'abandoned' in favour of Kiveton Park, and later Hornby Castle, it has outlived its fashionable successors. *The Author*

Figure 3. Thorpe Salvin Hall in c 1820. The engraving provides us with a useful impression of the house before the main body of the building was dismantled. Its romantic appearance and setting appealed to Sir Walter Scott, Thorpe Salvin reputedly being 'Torquilstone' in his famous novel *Ivanhoe*.

famous of the early tourists, was full of admiration of the Laguerre murals, the elaborate waterworks, and the 'curious carving'.[5] Not surprisingly, the most talented continental artists and craftsmen, including Louis Laguerre and the greatest wrought ironworker of the age, Jean Tijou, both with experience at Versailles and Hampton

Figure 4. Thomas Osborne, First Duke of Leeds, etc., from an engraving by Robert White, c 1694. *National Portrait Gallery*

Court, were to be employed at Kiveton, along with one of the best English royal country house painters, James Thornhill.

New Kiveton

Although the old house at Kiveton was in effect redundant, its site and setting had considerable promise as the seat of a noble lord. Here, on the fertile Magnesian Limestone, the estate and park was in an ideal position for managing adjoining interests, the manors of Todwick and Harthill having been added by the Duke during the 1670s (and North and South Anston manors in 1701). The ancient road running northwards from Harthill to Todwick ascends the escarpment and, almost at the crest, near to the Todwick boundary, was the principal park entrance. Fine panoramic views were (and are) to be had from here: especially westwards to Wales, south towards Harthill, and eastwards in the direction of South Anston, whilst the attractive spire of Laughton-en-le-Morthen's ancient church adds interest to the north-east. The park boundary and site of the new house are marked prominently on John Warburton's Yorkshire map of 1718-20 (Figure 6) and in more detail on Thomas Jefferys's map, surveyed 1767-72 (Figure 7).

William Talman: Architect of Kiveton ?

William Talman (1650-1719), appointed as Comptroller of the King's Works in 1689, virtually monopolised all major commissions in the field until ousted from Castle Howard in 1699. For someone who 'meddled in more country houses than all his chief contemporaries put together' it is a little surprising that, compared with Wren, Hawksmoor and Vanbrugh, his work has remained somewhat neglected.[6] Fragmentary and incomplete source material has resulted in very few detailed studies, Dr Margaret Whinney's lone paper of 1955 and John Harris's short but authoritative monograph, *William Talman: Maverick Architect*, published in 1982, being rare exceptions.[7] Given such a sparse bibliography it is understandable that general and regional books on architecture may refer to Talman as the architect of Kiveton.[8] However, in Dr Lynn Pearson's recent regional study, *Building the West Riding* (1994), where there is a brief reference to Kiveton, Talman is regarded as not completing the final commission, possibly due to his quarrelsome nature.[9] Information for the latter may have been based on Harris or, locally, from the Planning Department of Rotherham M.B.C.[10]

Talman's apparently quarrelsome disposition which resulted in sudden exits from projects and a collection of uncompleted designs for others does indeed make, as Harris suggests, attributions far from easy:

Figure 5. Thomas Osborne, First Duke of Leeds, canvas by Johann Kerseboom, 1704. *National Portrait Gallery*

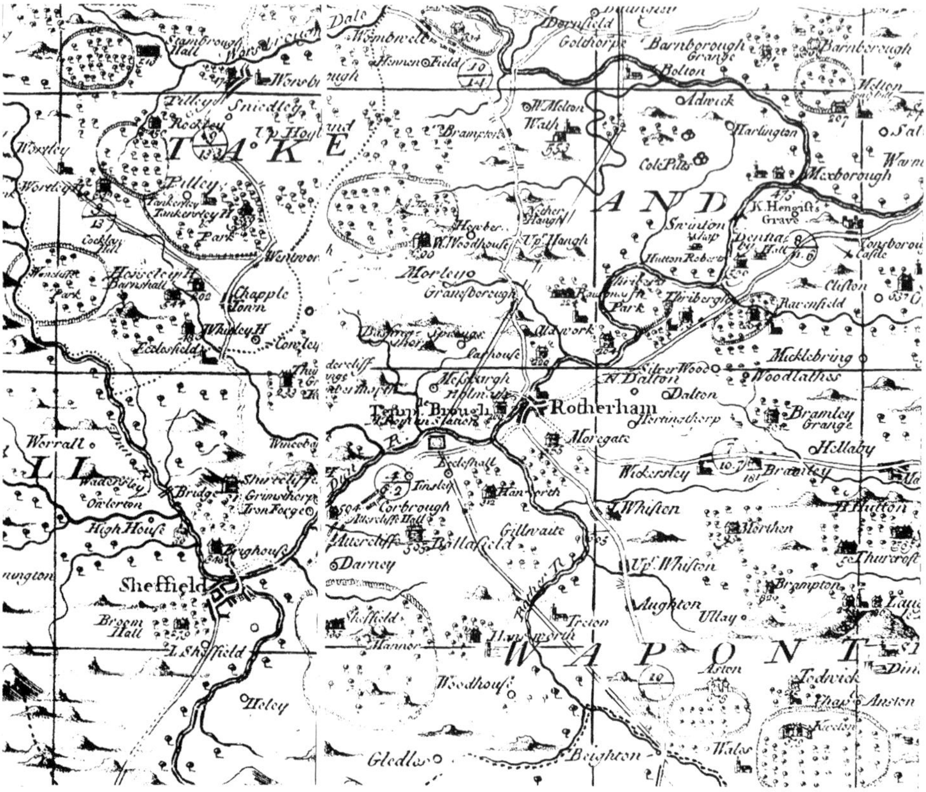

Figure 6. Thomas Warburton's map of Yorkshire, surveyed 1718-20 (detail).

> *Talman's professional behaviour as an officer was autocratic. He was by no means subservient, either with his official dealings or his personal relations with his clients. He never practised civility, and this frequently led to the termination of his appointment. He was simply a man of colic and irritability, of an affluent station in life which made him feel that there was no need to bow and scrape.*[11]

Talman's surviving portrait (Figure 8), shows him in a Wren-like pose, though he would have hated the comparison.

There is no doubt that Talman enhanced his architectural reputation when working at Chatsworth from about 1686 to 1696 when rebuilding, in a magnificent new style, the south and east fronts but fell out with William Cavendish, apparently after the Earl dismissed his favourite mason.[12] But despite this and other recorded instances of Talman 'standing-up' to noble patrons there must have also been many satisfied customers, despite the silence of the records.

Figure 7. Thomas Jefferys's map of Yorkshire, 1767-72 (detail).

Figure 8. William Talman, 1650-1719, architect *par excellence* of the Court of William II, 1650-1719.

Dr Margaret Whinney was probably the first to doubt Talman as the complete designer of Kiveton, suspecting that high fees were as much to blame as personality:

> *Talman possibly started the house, and when the foundations had been laid, fell out with his client. His ideas and still more his fees, which are likely to have been exorbitant, may well have been distasteful to the Duchess of Leeds, who was notoriously parsimonious. Alternatively....he may have been commissioned for a design only.*[13]

Talman did produce a design, inscribed *For the D. of Leeds at Keiton in Yorkshire* (Figure 9), housed in the Drawings Collection of the British Architectural (R.I.B.A.) Library.[14] It is for a very large house, 160 feet long with fifteen windows on the long fronts, though the exterior

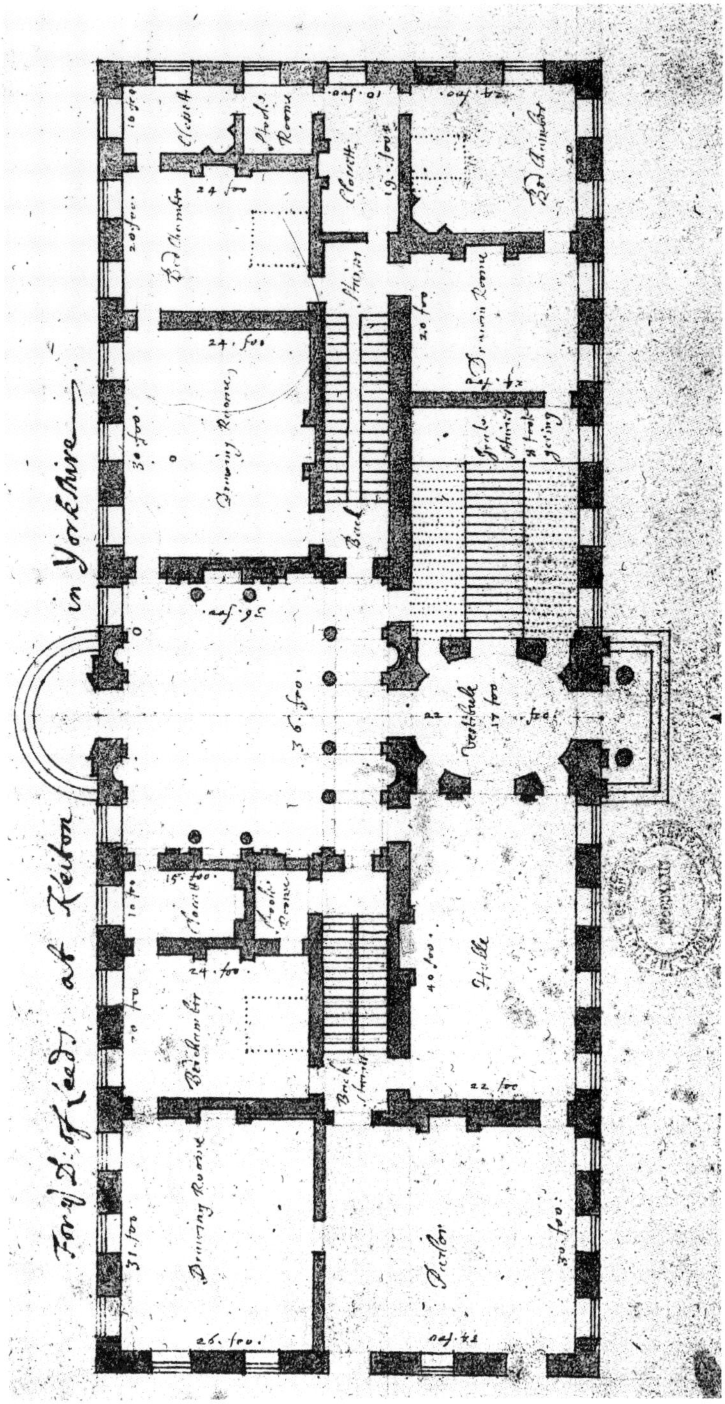

Figure 9. Talman's unexecuted plan of Kiveton. *Drawings Collection, British Architectural Library*

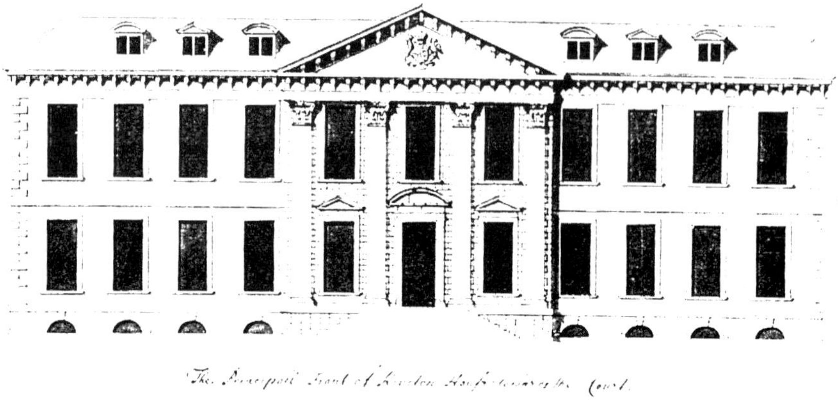

Figure 10. The architect James Gibbs, in many ways influenced by Talman, produced a series of measured drawings of the house, the manuscript title page reading *A Book of Drawings of Kiveton in Yorkshire/The Seat of His Grace the Duke of Leeds* and dated 1741. The above example shows the principal front which does not correspond with Talman's original design. *Ashmolean Museum, Oxford*

features appear to be plain, without pilasters, and with only a small porch. Whinney speculates that 'some kind of cupola' may have been planned for the roof.[15] The stairs are 'lavish', typically Talman and there are two main suites in which rooms are labelled *drawing room, bedchamber, closett and stoole-room*. However, it is an **unexecuted** design. The executed house is much smaller (eleven bays rather than fifteen) and the wording of the building contract suggests that the *vestibule* had been dropped. Harris tends to dismiss Talman as architect of Kiveton on stylistic grounds, its plain facade lacking any signs of the 'quirks' and 'idiosyncrasies' associated with other certain commissions, whilst the keyed *oeil de boeuf* motifs were 'quite foreign to Talman's vocabulary'.[16] The architect James Gibbs (1682-1754) produced a series of measured drawings of Kiveton in 1741 and, using the 'Principal Front' (Figure 10) as an example, Harris concluded that the 'elevation bears no resemblance to Talman's preliminary plan'. Talman certainly did produce 'fronts and elevations which charm by their difference to anything else' and we can see this at, for example, Chatsworth and Dyrham; and also on early projects such as the (now demolished) Blyth Hall but some of his later designs, as Harris also shows, were relatively austere.

Yet another puzzling feature of the finished design is the pitched roof and dormer windows, perhaps more traditional mid-seventeenth century than 'modern'. It is possible that Talman was only commissioned for the design and referred to on a consultancy basis since his services were in such great demand at this time.[17] Another possibility is that the house was completed by another (more amenable?) London architect or indeed under the influence of the Duke himself. One fact that previous publications appear to have ignored relates to the Duke's needs. Here was a noble lord certainly requiring a new and fashionable country residence but a good deal of his time would have been spent in London and in Wimbledon where he had a house; also most of his mature family appear to have taken up residence elsewhere. Even towards the end of his life, Kiveton was occupied by the Duke's bachelor brother. He may not, despite all the trappings of power, actually have needed such a large house as originally outlined. We may never know who actually completed the commission, but this situation was probably not entirely unusual given the relatively informal processes at work. Perhaps the most sensible approach would be to say that Talman was **associated** with Kiveton Park rather than regarding him as its indisputed architect.

Building the House

The contract for building Kiveton, dated 3 March 1698, was assigned to Daniel Brand who is described as 'of the Minores near Little Tower Hill, London, carpenter'.[18] Nothing is known of Brand but he must have been of some repute, perhaps with experience of royal work, to have been employed on such a prestigious project. The contractor was responsible for:

> *erecting building and finishing the main body of an intended mansion house....of such dimensions and with such materials and ornaments and in such form and manner as in designs for the same in draughts of the ground platt the first and ground storey and the uprights thereof hereunto affixed is delineated and sett forth...*[19]

The house had to be completed by 29 September 1699, a year and a half after the agreement. Since work was to be suspended during the winter when the structure was to be 'covered with straw and other materials', and the windows and doors boarded as protection 'from the injury of the frost', the actual construction time was probably little more than fourteen months which must have been a tight schedule for Brand, though the foundations had already been dug.

A small army of craftsmen and labourers would have been employed on the site, probably housed in temporary accommodation and there would have been a constant flow of materials carted to Kiveton from outlying areas. The contract document refers to the use of bricklayers, masons, plasterers, carpenters, sawyers, plumbers and glaziers and painters. An indication of the materials is shown in the building accounts:

New bricks at 9s per thousand
Old bricks at 7s per thousand
Tiles at 14s per thousand
Roche Abbey stone at 4s per ton
Other local stone at 2s per ton
Paving at 2d per foot
Lime at 4s per cauldron
Timber at 10d per foot girth measure

The reference to 'Roche Abbey stone' shows that the Duke wanted only the finest material for the decorative exterior features of the house. Sir Christopher Wren considered Roche Abbey the best building stone in England after Portland.[20] A likely source of supply was the quarry at Hell Green, near Roche, marked on Dickinson's 1724 survey of Sandbeck.[21] The quality and appearance of the exterior was to be ensured with the use of 'well-burnt brick, good mortar and stone well puttyed with hot lime, every three courses, to retain distance'.[22]

The Duke made an initial payment of £1 1s 0d when signing the contract and 'after Daniel Brand had set many hands at work', agreed to pay £40 'of good and lawful English money for every flat square of building work'.[23]

The Park and Gardens

While the house was being built 'plans and plantings' were taking place to create a suitable formal garden within the parkland setting. We do know that a great deal of planting took place in the early years after completion, with, for example, many varieties of tulips and other bulbs mentioned in the estate papers.[24] Given the rudimentary state of English nurseries at this time it is likely that bulbs were imported from Dutch nurseries.[25] Any new garden scheme would certainly have been influenced by French and Dutch schemes as at Hampton Court; and there were local examples to admire at Aston and Sprotbrough Hall.

Osborne may have turned to the royal gardeners, George London and Henry Wise, at the same time as consulting Talman. It was quite common for the chief country house architect of the Williamite Court to work alongside the king's gardeners, though confirmation of such collaboration at Kiveton has yet to be found. London may have been involved at Stainborough (Wentworth Castle) and Knyff's bird's-eye view (Figure 11) gives us an impression of the kind of grand design that might have been adopted at Kiveton.[26] The most prestigious nursery for correctly named plants was at Brompton Park in Kensington where London was a partner, though, as we shall see, local gardeners also serviced Kiveton.

It had become important to connect visually the house and garden

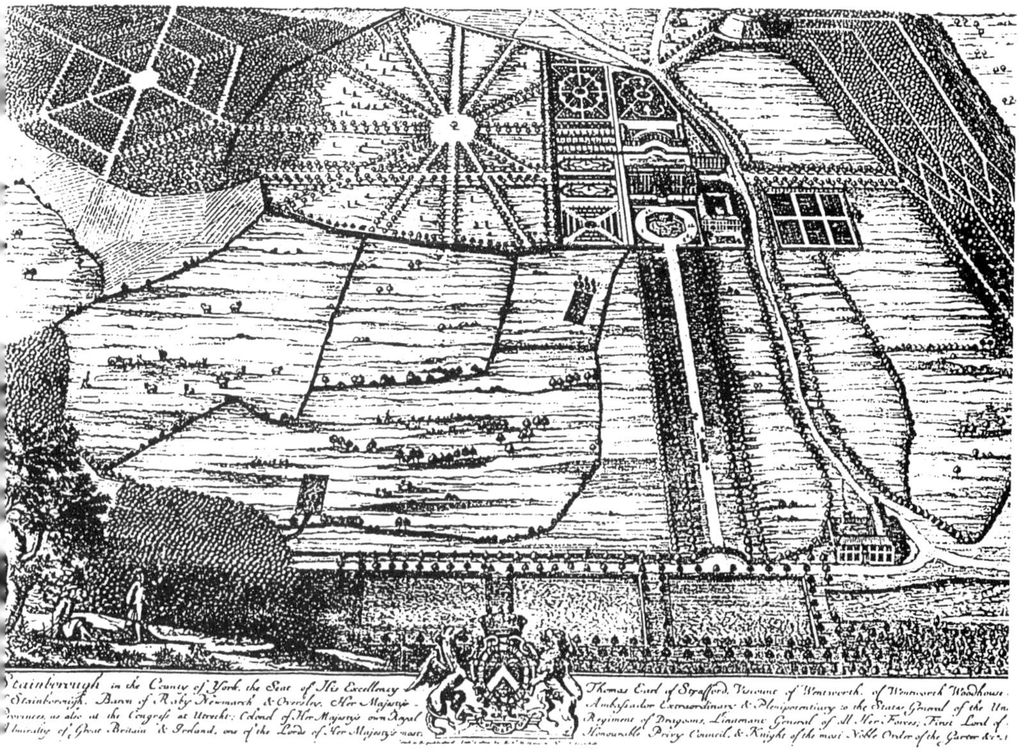

Figure 11. Stainborough Hall and its gardens as portrayed by Leendert Knyff and engraved by Jan Kip, c 1714.

with the park, often by means of 'avenues' of the kind that we can see on Warburton's map (Figure 6) which also shows a straight avenue or driveway extending from the house, directly eastwards through the park boundary to South Anston and what is now the A57 road. As one writer has remarked, 'The garden was an antechamber to the park, the whole landscape became a frame for the house and a status symbol'. The term 'landscape', adopted from the Dutch *landskip* paintings of the period, was introduced into our English vocabulary.[27] Tree planting took precedence over the chase; and a good design could make the park appear more extensive than reality, emphasising ownership and power.

Kiveton had its own nursery to service the great demands of the park and estate. A memorandum of 26 August 1708 itemised 'ye numbers of Forest Trees and Plants in ye nursery...:

Number of Limes fitt for removing next	Limes	
Under ye Cikamoores pretty large	13	
In ye Nursery of different sizes but all		
fitt to plant out next season	240	253
Limes in ye Nursery wch at this time		
twelve moneths season will bee fitt to		200
plant out Limes for two yeares season		250
Elmes fitt for planting out this season		260
Ditto for ye next season after this		050
Cikamores fitt to plant out this season		040
Chesnutts but not yett fitt to plant out		030
Ashes of about 2 yeares growth	120	
Oakes of ditto or more		350

There are no forest trees in ye Pond garden
quarters unless some few Cikamores
But there are severall young wallnutt trees
Some Mulberry trees young
Some Quince trees ditto there & in ye Nursery
Some Cherries trees & Cherry stocks
Some Pare trees and some Pare tree stocks
Ewes and Hollies in every quarter of ye Pond garden
& in many place besides as in ye old & new orchard’[28]

Aesthetic motives thus combined with demand at a time when there was a great shortage of timber.

In later years named varieties of apples were bought from John Perfect of Pontefract (1744), a well-known nurseryman who seems to have started business in the late seventeenth century Pontefract was well-sited alongside the Great North Road for distribution purposes. It must have been a lucrative enterprise, Perfect becoming Mayor of Pontefract in 1737 and 1754.[29] However, the main source of seeds, shrubs (eg, roses) and trees was Francis Noble (died 1756) of Newark-upon-Trent.[30] Other early Nottinghamshire nurseries that may have supplied the estate were at Blyth (before 1718); Mansfield (by 1717); and Worksop. William Aram (born 1689) ran the Mansfield nursery and may have had family connections with Nottinghamshire gardener Peter Aram who was assistant to George London at Bishop Compton’s gardens and later worked at Newby Hall.[31]

A large early nursery that almost certainly had links with Kiveton was based at Hodsack Woodhouse in Blyth parish, six miles eastwards, under the care of William Leeson who died in 1722 and whose substantial probate inventory survives.[32] His son, also William, inherited the garden and became head gardener at Kiveton, involved in large works and extensive plantings. Leeson is known to have subscribed, for at least twenty years, to Philip Miller's *Gardener's Dictionary*, first issued in c 1730. A son, a third William Leeson, appears to have assisted his father.

The post of Head Gardener at Kiveton had considerable merit in horticultural circles. In 1767 John Abercrombie, a gardener at Kew, produced *Every Man His Own Gardener* but, fearing that he was too little known for the book to do well, offered the Duke of Leeds's head gardener, Thomas Maw, £20 for the use of his name![33] The book proved to be a great success, the seventh edition being issued by Abercrombie and Maw in 1776.

Not surprisingly the increasing significance of the park was such that the word itself began to replace 'hall' as the suffix: Kiveton Park was 'born'.

In conclusion we can refer to an early description of the park by Edward Southwell, a traveller, whose manuscript diary of c 1727 can be found in the archives of the Yorkshire Archaeological Society:

> *The park is three miles around and full of ancient oaks. The parterre in the gardens is very large and adorned with many statues and large vases. On the right lies a wilderness and beyond it a bowling green. The situation commands a fine prospect and answers many avenues of great length in the park.*[34]

Thus, some of the main elements of a formal garden of the grand scale were present: parterre, statuary, wilderness, bowling green and avenues cutting through 'the prospect'; and the spectre of water features was highly likely, as suggested by the term 'Pond Garden' in the 1708 list quoted above. George London, working with Talman at Chatsworth, had created, as we can see from a detail of Kynff's view of c 1700 (Figure 12) showing impressive parterres and a bowling green with a temple. Kiveton had a similar arrangement.

Visitors and Guests

There were many visitors to Kiveton and where contemporary descriptions survive, in manuscript or printed form, they are an important source of information, as has been shown in Arthur Twibell's recent study.[35] An early example is that of Cassandra Willoughby of Wollaton Park, Nottingham, whose journal of her travels included a visit to Kiveton in c 1710. She refers to a garden room paved with marble, 'sometimes used for an eating room'. There is also mention of the use of two wings of the mansion:

Figure 12. Chatsworth and its garden (detail) by Knyff and Kip in c 1700.

one is divided into lodging rooms and closets which you go into from a passage, ye length of ye buildings, there is six of these rooms in a floor and in this building, ye Duke and all ye family lodge, ye other wing is stables and rooms for servants.[36]

Returning to Edward Southwell, we have a very useful visitor's account of the house:

After dinner we returned 4 miles and lay at Mr Wentworths [Thomas, of Wentworth Woodhouse]. *We came 9 miles to Kiveton, the fine modern brick house of the Marquis of Carmarthen. Thirteen windows in the main front two wings of offices each of eleven windows. The house has nine fine rooms on the floor. The hall painted by*

> *S.J.Thornhill, the staircase by Legare* [Laguerre]. *The rooms were richly furnished with damask velvet and rich tapestry, full of gold, with figures of horses and horsemen in perfection. Here were a great number of curious pictures. Part of one piece of the four quarters of the world, another of the Evangalists, an Italian concert of musick, God's appearance to Solomon, Rubens' Mistresses painted by himself. Harry and two sisters, St Peter, St Andrew and the Shepherds' Adoration. The maid and the candle, the musician and the base viol, King Charles I family. Two originals of King Charles II and Loyal Earl of Montrose, both on horseback, the Earl of Newport at full length, Lord Strafford and his Secretary, The Holy Family, two of St Sebastian. There were fourteen antique small statues in marble brought from Italy, very curious and on the staircase was painted 'The History of Phyphe'. There are two square courts one side and one on the other of the house.*[37]

The most detailed description of the house and its works of art was published in 1769 'By a Society of Gentlemen' and titled *England Displayed*.[38] The entry for Kiveton takes the reader on a tour of the principal rooms, drawing attention to paintings and statues. We start in the hall 'which is 50′ x 50′, painted by Sir James Thornhill' and five classical statues are listed and commented on, 'Lucretia', for example, having 'drapery admirably light and fine; and the hair of the head beautiful', whereas Diana had good drapery but 'the folds rather too small'. The adjoining 'anteroom' had a Holbein, and a Van Dyck of the 'Marquis of Montrose inimitably fine: the features and counternance noble and the attitude easy and elegant'. Moving through a 'Drawing Room, 24′ square, we enter the substantial dining room which has a Ruebens, 'The four parts of the world', its 'pure fleshy female' contrasting with the 'beast surprisingly fine' and panther 'equal to anything ever painted'; the crocodile 'admirably done' but 'The group vile'.

Paul Vernese's 'Marriage of Cana' and 'David and Nathan' received pleasing remarks, though the colours were said to be 'bad'; whilst Joshua Reynolds had created 'a most sweet attitude and exquisite eyes' in his portrait of the Duchess of Leeds. Another drawing room (25 feet square) contained a portrait of the Earl of Strafford, two more Reubens, a Schalken, Holbein (Erasmus and Thomas More), Carlo Marrat, Van Dyck and various landscapes. The staircase, painted by 'Le Guere' (Laguerre) was 32 feet square and 60 feet high. In the 'saloon' (54′ x 34′) could be found statues of Nero, Paris, Venus and Cupid; and Cleopatra ('nothing could be finer than this drapery'); also pictures by Guido and Titian. The 'vestible' (23 feet square) contained six views of Venice by Canaletto and yet another Reubens; next to it a dressing room which had an 'exceedingly fine' portrait by Titian of Philip II of Spain, 'the same as at Devonshire House [Chatsworth]'.

Rooms mentioned on the first floor consisted of the Red Chamber (23′ x 21′); Dressing Room (25′ x 24′); Closet; Bed Chamber (34′ x 24′) and Drawing Room, all with fine portraits, including another Van Dyck and Titian. Finally 'other pictures not hung in order' included a Holbein ('Alderman Hewet very fine'), a Van Dyck of the Earl of Strafford and his secretary, two Titians ('Lot and his daughters: very vile'; Portrait of the Duke of Newburgh, very fine') and a Bassan landscape.

The preponderance of continental paintings and sculptures on display were essential requirements for the new mansions of the nobility, reflecting also an interest in 'art objects' and not just portraits of the family. There was, as Adrian Tinniswood has shown, a great interest in the European art market.[39]

A group of tourists, led by Arthur Young, called at neighbouring south Yorkshire ducal estates in 1770. Young describes the journey in Letter VI of his *A Six Months Tour Through the North of England*:

> *From Wentworth Woodhouse we took the road to Kiveton, the seat of his Grace, the Duke of Leeds. From Rotherham to Kiveton the land is of various sorts, near that town, as I remarked in another place, the rents are exceedingly high... some farms of £200 a year and upwards, but in the general from £20 to £60 throughout this road'.*[40]

After Young had described the pictures of the house (as per *England Displayed*), the party proceeded to visit Worksop Manor and Welbeck. Kiveton had become an essential stopping place for the new tourists and travellers.

A final glimpse of the social life at Kiveton, under the sixth Duke, who was a keen race-goer, can be had by reference to the letters of Lady Stuart Wortley (Caroline Creighton) who appears to have been a frequent visitor, especially when races were held at Doncaster. On 18 September 1806 she writes:

> *We slept at Kiveton last night, & the Jerseys* [Earl of Jersey & Family] *arrived there in the middle of the night...*[41]

The Wortleys' remained at Kiveton for a further eight days, staying on in anticipation of a visit from the Prince of Wales who wanted to see the Duke's horses. The Prince's visit is described in a letter written from Wortley, on 29 September 1806:

> *After watching the road across the park till we were all fidgetty and nervous, the Duke came suddenly running round the house saying they*

were coming the other way & would be at the house before we could get into the hall! Imagine our fuss & hurry! Up the steps we flew & breathless & trembling got into the hall just in time. The Prince led the Duchess, and the Duke of Clarence offer'd an arm apiece to Lady Anne & me. The collation prepared for them in the eating room was really beautiful & in perfect taste.[42]

Country house life at Kiveton in the early nineteenth century seems to have been one of incessant entertaining. Lady Caroline was again at Kiveton in February 1807 when she met 'the Newarks and the Foljambes' and tells us that the Duke:

has discovered loads of music, some of his own, but mostly of his father's, and we are at it all day. There is food for many days yet to come. We found one opera by Paisello, which is beautiful.[43]

The health-conscious Duke 'wished someone would invent a machine to shake one up and down for a few seconds very fast as the apothecary does a draught before he pours it out of a phial'. 'Riding', he said, 'did it only partially'.[44] Within four years the house itself had succumbed to deliberate shaking and, to use Joseph Hunter's phrase, 'was levelled with the ground'.[45]

Figure 13. Hornby Castle in c 1720, from a sketch by Samuel Buck. *Wakefield Historical Publications*

The Dream of an Old English Gentleman

Writing in about 1828, Joseph Hunter, who is usually a reliable authority, states that the house was 'taken down by the order of the present duke [George William Frederick, sixth Duke, 1775-1838]' in 1811, describing it as 'a brick building of no great beauty'.[46] This comment certainly contrasts with Hunter's 'spacious and magnificent' description of the house when it was first erected.[47] Although only 112 years old, Kiveton seems to have been in a poor state of repair and had become something of a liability. The sixth Duke was in the process of converting the old park into a more viable farm holding and had taken to residing at his other principal residence, Hornby Castle, Bedale, which his father had acquired through marriage to Amelia Holderness.[48] Hornby, as can be seen in Buck's sketch (Figure13), was a large and impressive Gothic house in a parkland setting; and the Duke is believed to have commissioned considerable 'improvements'. What were considered to be the most important contents of Kiveton were probably transferred to Hornby. The expense of keeping two substantial properties, one of them needing a great deal of attention and somewhat out of fashion, may have been the main reason for demolition.

There is no sound historical evidence that the sixth Duke pulled down his ancestral home in consequence of a bet with the Prince of Wales, though this has been a popular explanation for the demolition of Kiveton.[49]

Figure 14. Gate piers at entrance to Kiveton Hall Farm, Kiveton Lane, probably re-used material. Notice the scrolled decoration on panels buttressing the piers. This was probably the original main entrance to the park. *The Author*

Figure 15. End section of a modern building using material from Kiveton Park: red brick and blind twin *oeil-de-boeufs* with keyed limestone ashlar. The oval *oeil-de-boeuf* features can be seen *in situ* by reference to the basement floor of the house as shown in the Badeslade print (Figure 1). *The Author*

Figure 16. Kiveton Hall Farm (left) and modern buildings at the crest of the escarpment with the site of part of the old park and garden in the foreground. *The Author*

The Kiveton estate was sold by the family in the early 1920s, following the considerable post-war demand for good quality farmland.[50] Remains and relics of the park and house are still visible, as can be seen by reference to Figures 14 and 15, and are indeed listed via the Planning Department of Rotherham MBC, based on advice from English Heritage. Walk along the public footpath from Kiveton Lane in the direction of South Anston, look back towards the present Kiveton Hall Farm (Figure 16) and, with a little imagination, some idea of the shape of the formal park may come to mind. An aerial view of 1967, shown as Figure 17, with the help of Jefferys's eighteenth century map, enables us to identify most of the park.

Although there is still much to discover, especially in relation to the gardens and park, and also on the events leading to the demolition of the house and break-up of the estate, this article may make a contribution to our understanding of one of the most important lost country 'seats' of our area.

Writing about Kiveton, John Thomas in his *Walks in the Neighbourhood of Sheffield*, published in 1844, provides us with a fitting final quote:

> *In this year* [1811] *the family roof was obedient to its doom — fashion frowned on its limited and rustic proportions — it fell — and the park, the gardens, and the fine harbours, vanished like the dream of an 'old English gentleman', and gave place to young enclosures, new surveys, and right tightly valued farms.*[51]

Notes and References

1. Defoe, Daniel, *A Tour Through England and Wales* (2 vols, J M Dent, nd {1928}), I, p 4.
2. Tinniswood, Adrian, *A History of Country House Visiting*, 1989, p 66.
3. Harris, John, 'The Hampton Court Trianon Designs of William and John Talman', *Journal of the Warburg and Courtauld Institutes*, XXIII, 1960, pp 139-149.
4. Wilkinson, Joseph, *Worthies, Families and Celebrities of Barnsley and the District*, nd [c 1880], p 353.
5. Morris, Christopher (Ed), *The Journeys of Celia Fiennes* (Macdonald, 1983), p 19.
6. Harris, John, *William Talman: Maverick Architect*, 1982, p 14.
7 .Whinney, Margaret, 'William Talman' *Journal of the Warburg and Courtauld Institutes*, XVIII, 1955, pp 123-129.
8. See, for example, Downes K, *English Baroque Architecture*, 1966; Colvin, H A, *Biographical Dictionary of British Architects, 1600-1840*, 1978; Hall, I (Ed), *Samuel Buck's Yorkshire Sketchbook* (Wakefield Historical Publications),1979; Hey D, *Buildings of Britain 1550-1750: Yorkshire*, 1981.
9. Pearson, Lynn, *Building the West Riding*, 1994, p 162.
10. Listed building information at Rotherham MBC Planning Department, based on advice from English Heritage.
11. Harris, *op cit*, p 20.
12. For confirmation of Talman's work at Chatsworth see Thompson, Francis, *History of Chatsworth*, 1950.
13. Whinney, *op cit*, pp 130-131.

Figure 17. Aerial view of Kiveton taken on 13 June 1967. The white line marks the approximate boundary (wall) of the park. *Rotherham Central Library, Local Studies and Archives*

14. British Architectural Library Drawings Collection, London: Kiveton Park (5), Yorkshire, under 'Talman'.
15. Whinney, *op cit*, p 130.
16. Harris, *op cit*, p 26.
17. Between 1680-1700, apart from official work as 'Comptroller', Talman was involved in at least 19 projects.
18. Twibell, Arthur, *Kiveton Hall, a Study in South Yorkshire History* (W.E.A. [S. Yorks], 1989, p 6.
19. Whinney, *op cit*, p 131.
20. Clifton-Taylor, Alec, *The Pattern of English Building*, 1972, p 94.
21. I am indebted to Mrs Alice Rodgers for this advice.
22. Twibell, *op cit*, p 7.
23. *Ibid.*
24. Information courtesy of Mrs Sylvia Thomas, Archivist-in-Charge, Yorkshire Archaelogical Society, Leeds.
25. Bisgrove, Richard, *The National Trust Book of the Garden*, 1990, p 62.
26. Hey, David, *Wentworth Castle: A Short History*, 1991, p 4.

27. Lasdun, Susan, *The English Park*, 1991, p 47.
28. Harvey, John, *Early Nurserymen*, 1974, pp 67-68.
29. Harvey, *op cit*, p 66.
30. Harvey, *op cit*, p 68.
31. *Ibid.*
32. Harvey, *op cit*, pp 160-166.
33. Bisgrove, *op cit*, p 145.
34. MS 328; Twibell, *op cit*, p 145.
35. *Kiveton Hall, A Study in South Yorkshire*, W.E.A., 1989.
36. Twibell, *op cit*, p 2.
37. *Ibid.*
38. Twibell, *op cit*, pp 10-11.
39. Tinniswood, *op cit*, p 70.
40. Twibell, *op cit*, p 11.
41. Grosvenor, Caroline & Beilby, Charles, *The First Lady Wharncliffe and her Family 1779-1856*, vol I, 1927, p 124; the Duke's horse *Octavion* won the St. Leger in 1810.
42. Grosvenor & Beilby, *op cit*, pp 126-127.
43. Grosvenor & Beilby, *op cit*, p 135.
44. *Ibid.*
45. Hunter, Joseph, *South Yorkshire* I, p 139.
46. Hunter, *op cit*, p 144.
47. *Ibid.*
48. Waterson, Edward & Meadows, Peter, *Lost Houses of York and the North Riding*, 1990, pp 48-49.
49. Twibell, *op cit*, p 13; Garbett, *History of Harthill-in-Woodall*, n.d. [1950], p 30.
50. Twibell, *op cit*, p 13.
51. p 59.

Acknowledgements

The writer takes full responsibility for any errors in the above article and would like to express appreciation to the following individuals and organisations for their help and kindness:

Archives and Local Studies staff at Rotherham Central Library; Colin Harrison, Supervisor of the Print Room, Ashmolean Museum, Oxford; Professor David Hey, University of Sheffield; Dr Neil Bingham and Andrew Norris, British Architectural Library (RIBA), Drawings Collection, London; Tracy Ingle, Conservation Officer, Planning Department, Rotherham MBC; James Kilvington, Picture Library, National Portrait Gallery, London; Sylvia Thomas and A J Jamieson, Yorkshire Archaeological Society Archives, Leeds; Mrs N Roome, Rother Valley College Librarian; Alice Rodgers; thanks are also due to Sally-Anne, Margaret and Ann, secretarial staff at Rother Valley College for WP assistance; and to Mel Jones for being so patient!

Picture Credits are shown at the end of each caption (where relevant).

9. CHRISTMAS CAROLLING AT THORPE HESLEY

by Ian Russell

IN MANY VILLAGES IN SOUTH YORKSHIRE and North Derbyshire there exists or has existed in the recent past distinctively local traditions of Christmas carol singing.[1] This is also the case to a lesser extent in other parts of England especially the West Country.[2] In this respect Thorpe Hesley provides a particularly notable example, combining a delightfully rich repertoire of carols with what was, until recently, a vigorous active tradition.

Thorpe Hesley lies about five miles north-west of the centre of Rotherham and six miles north-east of the centre of Sheffield, on the east side of the M1 at Junction 35. The motorway sliced across the top of the village above Hesley Bar in the 1960s, leaving the *Travellers Rest* and the cricket field isolated on the west side. In the early nineteenth century the small metal trades of nail, bolt and screw making were the main industry alongside ironstone and coal mining, and agriculture.[3] The 1841 Census records 86 employed in farming, 130 in nailmaking and 202 in mining, out of a total population of 1622 (including the outlying hamlets).[4] By the end of the century the metal trades had disappeared. After the First World War, the only local industries were the two coal mines, Thorpe and Barley Hall, and fourteen farms, plus the usual trades and crafts such as the blacksmiths. The main employer outside the village was Newton Chambers and Co Ltd of Chapeltown (founded 1793), who mined coal and ironstone and made iron products and disinfectants. Thorpe Pit ceased production in 1972 and Barley Hall was closed a year or two earlier. Since the Second World War a number of new housing developments have been built, greenfield sites have been infilled, and the village has become a suburb of Rotherham, housing mostly Sheffield commuters. According to the 1991 Census, Thorpe Hesley ward then had a population of 11,094.

In order to understand how the tradition at Thorpe Hesley came about, it is helpful to look briefly at the larger context of vernacular sacred music and its cultural setting during the seventeenth, eighteenth and nineteenth centuries.[5] During the seventeenth century, church music and especially the singing of Christmas carols had suffered greatly at the hands of the Puritans. What emerged from this period of suppression was a style of singing that was very slow and deliberate. For instance, each line of a hymn (a metrical psalm) would be 'lined out' in turn by a singer and the congregation would laboriously repeat it unaccompanied. The classic example of such a tune that is in the modern repertoire is 'Old Hundredth' (usually sung to 'All People that on Earth Do Dwell').[6] Harmony and part singing was unusual.

During the latter half of the eighteenth century, partly as a result of the inspiration of such composers as Bach and Handel, vernacular sacred music and singing enjoyed a great renaissance. It became much more exciting, more intricate and more elaborate. Singing in parts was introduced. At first this was normally treble (male and female voices) and bass; a third part, where it was introduced, took the form of a counter to the melody and was usually performed by female voices. The convention of modern four-part harmony singing only took hold in the latter part of the nineteenth century in villages in South Yorkshire and replaced a different four-part configuration in which male voices sang the melody, the tenor, and the bass, while female voices were restricted to the counter melody.[7] Evidence of these older forms of part singing are to be found in the local carol singing traditions.

Hand in hand with these developments in part singing came the introduction of accompaniment. The first to be used was provided by a bass instrument, usually a cello (often termed a bass viol) in South Yorkshire but sometimes a bass wind instrument such as a bassoon, serpent or ophicleide. For example, at Ecclesfield there are references to the purchase and repair of a cello known as the 'Ecclesfield Bass'.[8] By the end of the eighteenth century other instruments played with the bass to form an ensemble or church band. The violin was the preferred instrument in South Yorkshire, although wind instruments such as oboes, flutes, clarinets and keyed bugles were also used. In Thorpe Hesley before 1840 one such group of musicians, string players, were members of the Butcher family. They played for the Lord of the Manor, Earl Fitzwilliam of Wentworth Woodhouse, at Wentworth Church, which was about a mile and a half from Thorpe Hesley. In fact, the Fitzwilliams had a footpath made especially to help the group cross the fields without getting muddy for the Sunday service.[9]

The style of music performed by such groups had a character and form all of its own. It was not merely imitative of the classical or rather baroque repertoire — a top-down model of cultural diffusion — but rather was distinctive and innovative, a grass-roots cultural effusion fuelled by the creativity and religious fervour of local musical genius. Two such composers, whose music became part of the Thorpe Hesley carol repertoire, were John Hall of Sheffield Park (d 1794) and John Foster of High Green (1752-1822). Hall was an artisan, a blacksmith who ended his days in the workhouse penniless, unable to attract a suitably generous patron.[10] Foster was a professional man, a county coroner, who attracted the patronage of the Earl of Scarbrough.[11] The characteristics of their music included melismata (that is the singing of one syllable of a word to several notes), a fuguing or contrapuntal section (the different parts set off at different times perhaps imitating or reflecting each other), and symphonies (instrumental interludes between the verses that sometimes provide a new musical strain or more usually variation of the melody).

The cultural phenomenon that this music embodied ground to an acrimonious halt during the nineteenth century in the established church as a result of the systematic suppression by Oxbridge high churchmen who saw in its success a threat to the power and influence of the clergy.[12] It was a campaign which they conducted in the name of Reform. It had a broad target ranging from church music and bell ringing, to church interior design (for example, the removal of singing galleries from the west end of churches). Thus from about 1820 the parish churches in South Yorkshire became subject to this reform movement. Parts of Thorpe Hesley at that time fell within three parishes, Ecclesfield, Wath and Rotherham. At Ecclesfield, for example, the church band was dismissed in 1826, and an organ installed. The adult choir survived into the 1850s. A new surpliced choir of boys, in imitation of a cathedral choir, was trained on a seemly diet of *Hymns Ancient and Modern* (published 1861) without a fuguing tune in sight. They first performed in 1872 and were sponsored by Lord Wharncliffe. Meanwhile the ousted church band kept up their playing and annual perambulations at Christmas to sing their local carols.[13]

During subsequent years a similar reforming zeal ousted the local musicians, choirs and their music from most non-conformist places of worship in South Yorkshire. The Butcher family, father and son, mentioned above were, in 1840, playing for the Wesleyan Methodists for their Sunday School Anniversary at Thorpe Street Chapel and were described as the pride of the neighbourhood.[14] In 1849 Henry Butcher, believed to be the son, who was a grocer, joined the Reform Methodists and was one of the founders of Hope Chapel in 1856. The evidence of the manuscripts confirms that instrumental music accompanied the singing at Hope Chapel in its early years. A harmonium was bought in 1874. The reaction of the instrumentalists is not known, but the singers seem to have found the change hard to take and their attitude is reflected in the chapel records: 'The harmoniumist was thanked [by the trustees] for his first year of service [1875], but they would have preferred him to cooperate better with the choir'.[15]

The history of religion in the village has been well documented, especially the visits by John Wesley to Barley Hall to preach there on the 16 June 1742, and by his brother Charles on 27 May 1743 and his encounter with a local mob.[16] The first Wesleyan Methodist chapel was built in 1797 under the direction of Samuel Birks on Thorpe Street.

This was rebuilt in 1902 and recently closed in 1993, the Hope Chapel on Brook Hill having closed previously in June 1990. A third chapel, the Zion Chapel, was built in 1859 off Hesley Lane on Heslow Grove by the Primitive Methodists but this closed for worship just before the Second World War. All three buildings still remain. Thorpe Hesley gained its own parish church under the Million Act of 1818. This building, sponsored by Earl Fitzwilliam and the Earl of Effingham among others, was consecrated for worship in 1840 as the Church of the Holy Trinity.[17]

There is evidence that the members of Hope Chapel attached great importance to singing and music-making, and resisted the demands of reforming zeal, at least so far as their choice of music was concerned. The very fine set of manuscripts, 'Hope Chapel Musick', discovered when the Hope Chapel closed and rescued by Annie Chesman, are in four volumes, one for each singing part, and date from the opening of the Chapel. They include the music for over a hundred hymn tunes, among which are several examples of fuguing tunes. Moreover, pride of place is given over to local Christmas carols, such as 'John Foster's 47th Psalm', 'Liverpool', and 'Old Israel'. These occupy the first dozen or so pages (see the Appendix). The manuscripts also include the music for several symphonies confirming the existence of a tradition of instrumental accompaniment. It has been the members of the chapels rather the parish church who were largely responsible for the maintenance of a tradition of carol singing in the village right up to the 1970s. The manifestation of this tradition as an annual perambulation of the village will be discussed below.

By 1900 carol singing had become firmly established in other contexts in the village, especially in the public houses. Although there is no documentation to corroborate this fact, oral testimony is unequivocal.[18] It would seem that this happened when carol singing became unwelcome and was ousted from the repertoire of the established church (ie, at Ecclesfield, Wath and Rotherham), in the 1830s, 1840s and 1850s. It seems unlikely that the tradition was ever established in the newly created parish church of Thorpe Hesley, although during the 1930s, 1940s and 1950s the carols were sung by churchgoers, particularly when Arthur Walsh was organist. There were thus three constituencies in the village for whom singing carols in the pubs had an attraction. Firstly the Anglican male parishioners, secondly non-churchgoers, and thirdly the working men who did not support the nonconformists' call for abstinence from alcohol.

The three main pubs for carol singing after 1900 were the *Red Lion*, the *Mason's Arms*, and the *Sportsman Inn*, although other pubs, some of which have closed down, also featured. Don Batty (65 years) recalls his first encounter with carolling in the pubs before the Second World War:

> *When I was a little lad, I remember in the old days walking down past the Masons, there were a little pub there called the Victoria, on the corner. It's been shut down since about 1960 as a public house. I can remember hearing them singing Christmas carols as I was walking down. Taproom'd [had] bare windows. I can remember jumping up and looking inside and listening to them singing and going into corner of room where door is and listening. That sounds great, that! That does sound lovely, that! I got really into it.*[19]

Each of the main pubs produced its own carol sheet and often employed a pianist to provide the accompaniment. Arthur Walsh played at the *Sportsman*. The most popular occasion for carol singing in the pubs seems to have been the last Sunday lunchtime before Christmas, known locally as Holly Sunday, when a large number of singers would gather at the *Sportsman Inn*. There is some confusion as to the reason for the name Holly Sunday and also its date (a number of interviewees insisted that it was held on the first Sunday in December). Don Batty was given the following explanation. Six men had been out cutting holly on the morning of the Sunday before Christmas. They called at the *Sportsman* carrying their bunches of holly and the day was named, simply denoting the occasion on which holly is gathered for home decoration. Another less pragmatic explanation may result from the confusion of 'holly' with 'holy'.

In the other pubs the main occasions for singing carols were Friday, Saturday and Sunday evenings, when the local carol repertoire replaced the normal communal weekly singsong to the piano. The season would start seven weeks before Christmas, that is on the weekend after Bonfire Night (5 November). Don Batty quipped: 'They were humming them in October!' In the heyday of carol singing in the pubs, from 1920 to 1960, singers would go from one pub to the next to find 'the best' carol singing session. Nor was it simply a question of which pub was 'best' (more often than not the *Red Lion*), because within one pub there might be two or three sessions running simultaneously in different rooms. There is a general consensus among older members of the community, both drinkers and teetotallers, that the best carol singing was to be heard in the village pubs. It was the conversion of public house interiors (to make larger bars), the installation of juke boxes and the removal of pub pianos in the 1960s and 1970s that prompted the decline of carol singing in the local pubs. In the last few years, there has been a bold attempt at a revival of the local carols prompted by residents of Thundercliffe Grange supported by Derek and Janet Renshaw, but this has yet to take hold.

Two other contexts for carol singing deserve a mention, the home and the workplace. There is no doubt that several local families have cherished the local tradition over many years and that the singing of carols provided the focus for get-togethers over the Christmas season. This aspect of the tradition like the pub singing, would seem to go back to the reforms and probably predates them. One family who had such parties were the Goddards. In the years since the First World War, they would have as many as six different gatherings starting on Christmas Eve and finishing up late in January to coincide with the birthday celebration of one member of the family (John Goddard). Gertie Chesman (88 years, née Wood) remembers the Christmas Day parties of her childhood at her grandma's (Jane Law) house in the hamlet of Scholes, just half a mile from the *Sportsman Inn*:

> *We all used to go to my grandmas at Christmas. It was a big family. There used to be about 36 of us for dinner and tea. We had two turkeys. Then at night my uncle [Matthew Law] used to play the carols and everybody was singing . . . We used to be partying until three in the morning. I thought that was lovely, when I was young, to stop up like that.*[20]

The importance of this context for carol singing is supported by the number of local family manuscripts that have been encountered in the village. The family names associated with these include Almond, Burgin, Cooper, Law, Waller, and Willis. Understandably these family manuscripts were considered to be very precious to their owners and were (and are) carefully guarded, a fact that has often brought comment:

> *Now D– W– was very very shy about letting anybody have that book. He lent it to me. "Now think on, you don't lend it anyone. You can have it [borrow it] and you're only one can have it." Like some women are with their cookbooks.* (The non-attribution of this quote is deliberate.)

The writing out and/or copying of family manuscripts has continued almost up until the present day. Clifford Chesman (88 years) transposed and arranged his own collection in the late 1960s and 1970s, whereas Derek and Janet Renshaw produced their set by photocopying existing manuscripts, typing out the words, and by cutting and pasting. At the time of writing there is no published collection of the Thorpe carols.

The main source of local employment for most of this century has been the collieries. Walter Goddard (87 years) worked in Thorpe Pit until January 1947 when a roof collapse rendered him paralysed from below the waist. Previously he had worked at Barley Hall Colliery and he recalls the last shift on Christmas Eve which always finished with the singing of carols at the pit bottom led by William Henry Beard of Scholes, 'the Striker Up':

> *We all used to sit waiting for Mr Beard and knew when we'd got a good party together, he'd strike up. He was always on the note, Mr Beard. We'd sing five or six carols on the pit bottom before going up. The management allowed it, but eventually they stopped it. We used to love it, 'cos the men could sing, even in the dirt.*[21]

Derek Renshaw (61 years) recalls that a few years later when the last shift before Christmas emerged from Thorpe Colliery at the Smithy Wood drift, the miners would gather in the fitting shop and, led by Alfred Jones, the foreman, with Bob Nesbitt, 'Greaves' from Ecclesfield, and Charlie Bailey, the winder, sing the local carols unaccompanied for an hour or two before going home. On one particular occasion (in the mid 1950s), Derek was the duty electrician on Christmas Day and a pump broke down.

> *There was myself, a couple of fitters, and more men on duty . . . Old Percy Burgin, the banksman, asked us to sing one while we were going down. We sang him 'Hail Smiling Morn'. We got nearly to the bottom; he enjoyed it that much he stopped the chair, brought us back up again and said, "Sing it again and I'll let you go!"*[22]

Between the two World Wars a number of groups toured the village singing and playing the local carols. In fact, all four religious denominations organised carol parties. The two strongest came from the Thorpe Street (Wesleyan Reform) and Hope (United Methodist) Chapels, whilst the Primitive Methodists from Zion Chapel attracted some support, despite the subsequent closure of their chapel. It is not clear how committed or involved Holy Trinity Church became, but they did have an annual carol service when some of the local carols were performed (with Arthur Walsh as organist, as noted above), and a band of musicians led by William Henry Beard (also mentioned above) and members of his family, played the carols around the village. Two other bands also toured the village at Christmas, the Salvation Army and Ecclesfield Brass Band, though it is not clear what proportion of their repertoire, if any, were local carols.

Among the chapel groups there was a strong feeling of identity even rivalry and a perception that each had its own territory. This was only true to a limited sense, such that each chapel party steered clear of the immediate vicinity of the other chapels. Thus, for example, Hope Chapel kept away from Thorpe Street, but all three groups sang on Barnsley Road and travelled out of the village to the hamlet of Barley

Hall. The usual pattern was to sing at houses where they would be made welcome and a donation could be relied upon. Usually two carols were performed at each house, two verses of each. The first would be the choice of the singers and the second would be the choice of the householder. If the carollers were invited in, they would perform an extra carol and be offered food. When the Hope singers performed at Kirkcroft Farm on Wentworth Road (Harry Smith's) they would be offered a slice from a huge iced cake. When the Primitive singers performed at Elliott's Farm (Kirkstead Abbey Grange Farm) where pigs were raised, a slice of pork pie was on offer. More usually, mince pies were given.

Although the groups mostly sang unaccompanied, the Hope singers led by Arthur Athey, sometimes carried a small 'American' pedal organ (a type of harmonium) which Clifford Chesman would play. The Primitives were accompanied on occasions by Mr Tingle on the flute. (It should be noted that there was, in the 1930s, a fife and drum band in the village associated with Holy Trinity Church.) Finding the correct pitch for a carol was considered to be very important such that the Hope Singers used a tuning fork. Previously Reg Beard would take his clarinet to help the singers find the prescribed pitch.

The primary occasions for singing carols around the village were Christmas Eve, Christmas morning, and New Year's Eve. Other occasions that were sometimes chosen included Christmas Day evening and the Sunday after Christmas. Derek and Janet Renshaw recalled that in the 1950s the Hope Singers would perform at Dropping Well, Hollywood, Back Lane, and perhaps Scholes on Christmas Eve; Hesley Bar and Hesley Lane on Christmas morning; and the Barnsley Road end of the village on New Year's Eve.

At certain houses the choice of carol was prescribed by custom and practice, usually because it was the favourite carol of the senior member of the household. Thus at Varah Cooper's house on Sykes's Row (No 2 Hesley Lane), whichever chapel party called, they knew to sing 'Mortals Awake'. Between the wars the Coopers must have been one of the poorest families in Thorpe Hesley with 15 children (11 of whom reached adulthood) and yet Mrs Cooper still managed to keep on one side three sixpences, one for each group of carol singers. Robert Chesman (85 years) remembers visiting Sam Burgin's house:

> *Old Pegleg Burgin's, that was a place to visit carol singing. He was the lampman at one of the pits. He'd had his leg off by the knee. It was the old fashioned stump . . . When we used to go singing there, we used to say, "Have you a favourite, Mr Burgin?" "You know what my favourite is, 'Old Israel?' "*[23]

Householders, however, did not always get their favourite carol, particularly if they chose one of the more difficult tunes. This was the case when Dennis Willis requested 'Fosters' from the Hope singers. Clifford Chesman recalled that they would pre-empt the request by singing an easier setting of 'While Shepherds Watched', namely 'Liverpool'.

Just as particular carols became associated with certain points of call, so they also became associated with certain singers. Dennis Willis's brother, Charlie, together with Bernard Wilkinson, sang tenor and they are remembered by the Chesmans for their singing of 'The Star of Bethlehem':

Clifford: ' "Shines the star!" and they were up on top A.'
Robert: 'You could hear them from one end of the village to the other. . . nearly up to the stars!'[24]

Another noted tenor singer was Joss Jenkinson of Thorpe Street Chapel.

Although both Hope and Thorpe Street Chapels produced a carol sheet, which contained the words to the local carols, plus a few of the well-known carols, these were for use at the Sunday carol service. In fact, all the churches had a carol service featuring the local repertoire on the Sunday before Christmas. The singers who performed the carols around the village did so entirely from memory without any prompts including those who sang the bass or tenor parts (contralto was rarely performed outside). In fact, when singers have been questioned about learning the carols none can remember consciously memorising them, probably because they were brought up with them in the home. Janet Renshaw's (57 years, née Goddard) childhood experiences in the 1940s provide an explanation:

> *We were singing them all the time. We never had any words. We always had a piano [accompaniment], if houses had got a piano. If they didn't, we just used to strike up. I can't remember learning them. When I was a very little girl, [we] used to go down to Grandma Goddard's and every Sunday night we sang. But then, when it got near Christmas, it was always the local carols, always. They just came. They're wonderful.*

Up until the 1950s the singing of carols was just one of several aspects of the seasonal Christmas celebrations, especially for the young people of the village. As soon as the buzzer went at Thorpe Pit to signal the end of the shift at 12 noon on Christmas Eve, boys would go round 'Wishing'. Walter Goddard, who was the sixth child in a family of eleven children, lived on Brook Hill: 'We began wishing, running to people's homes. You all had your own little patch in which to "wish". Certain people wouldn't have boys with light coloured hair because it was bad luck. Walter's version of the rhyme reflects his 'Sons of Temperance' upbringing:

We wish you a merry Christmas and a happy New Year
I'm a teetotaller, I want no beer.
A piece of spice cake, a small bit of cheese,
A glass of cold water and a penny if you please.
If you haven't got a penny, a ha'penny will do,
If you haven't got a ha'penny, God bless you!

There were traditional forms of rebuke for those householders who refused to open the door and give the boys a penny or two, such as:

We're coming to your door, we toured o'er wi' clog,
If you don't gi' us owt, we'll punch your dog!

or

We're coming to your door, we tum'led o'er the clart [mud],
If you don't gi' us owt, we'll have to go wiart[without]!

This custom was also practised to 'Let the New Year In', when a piece of coal was carried into the house and placed on the fire. Varah Cooper (85 years) notes that some older members of the community would not open their doors until they had been wished a Happy New Year.

Any evening in the week or so before Christmas, groups of boys would get together to do 'Six Jolly Miners'. This was a form of Christmas mumming that involved blacking faces, singing a song and performing at houses in the village in return for a donation. The boys did not wear any special costume nor did they carry any props. One of the boys sometimes carried a stick which he tapped in time with the song or rattled on the railings. A version of the song is transcribed in Figure 1.

The equivalent custom in which the girls were able to participate was a-wassailling (pronounced *wosselling*). The girls usually went round in pairs and carried a doll wrapped in a shawl, sometimes in an open box, as well as a purse for the collection. Varah Cooper commented: 'Mother bought a cloth doll for a penny from Piper's Bazaar in Rotherham, which we filled with rags, for me sisters.'[25] They knocked at the door, showed their doll and performed the wassail song. In large families such as Walter Goddard's, any money collected from these Christmas visiting customs was used to supplement the family income:

Money we got from wishing, it wasn't ours. That was for Mother.

Figure 1

Six Jolly Miners

As sung by Varah Cooper
10 July 1995

Original Key E ♩= 112 Transcribed by Ian Russell

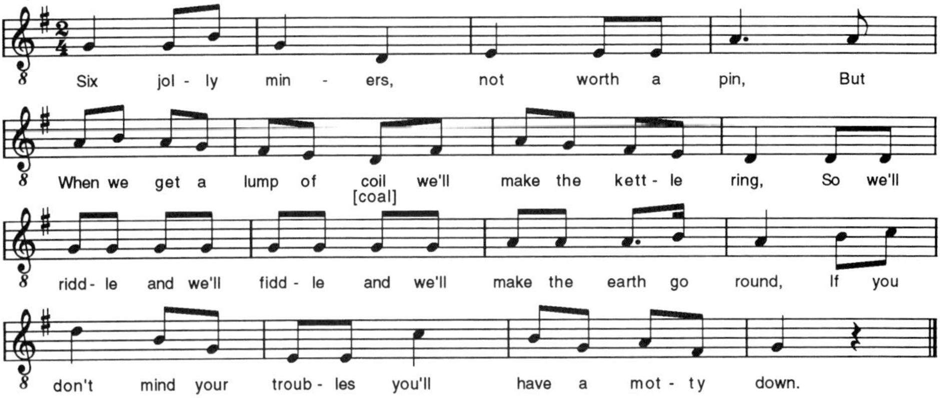

Two from Derby and two from Derby town,
The other two from Oughtibridge and they came firing down,
So we'll riddle etc.

> *Mother used to pool it altogether and buy us all a new jersey to go to school.*

Whichever Christmas custom was involved, it also provided the opportunity to reinforce the learning of the carols among the young. When Don Batty went out 'Wishing' or doing 'Six Jolly Miners', he went to the pubs: 'You'd to sing a carol or they wouldn't give us a penny. "C'mon, first two verses of 'Hark Hark' or you're getting nowt!"'

In the Appendix there is a listing of Thorpe Hesley carols based on the song sheets from the pubs and the chapels (words only), eight family manuscripts / collections, and recordings from oral tradition. Reference is also made to the old music manuscripts from Hope Chapel which are believed to date from the opening of the chapel in 1856. These manuscripts identify a group of carols that must be among the most established in the village tradition. This includes 'Old Israel' (the words are attributed to Richard Furness of Eyam and Dore in Derbyshire, 1791-1857), 'Martin' (the words appropriately are by Charles Wesley, 1739), 'The Star of Bethlehem' (the source of the words and tune have not been traced though the same setting is known at Green Moor near Stocksbridge and in Staveley in North East Derbyshire), 'Mortals Awake' (neither the words nor the music have any local connection), 'Good News' (the music is attributed to John Hall of Sheffield Park, d 1794), and two settings of 'While Shepherds Watched', 'Liverpool' and 'Fosters' ('Liverpool' has been attributed (erroneously) to John Hall and 'Fosters' is by John Foster of High Green, before 1820). These manuscripts also include a similar number of carols no longer associated with the village, for example there is another carol by Richard Furness (words and music), which is still sung at Eyam, 'Victorious Love'.

There is a popular misconception about local carols that needs to be corrected. This concerns the extent to which a village repertoire may be considered unique in that the bulk of it originated locally. In the first instance, Thorpe Hesley's carol repertoire has a lot in common with the repertoires of other nearby villages, such that about half the Thorpe carols are also sung in Ecclesfield (see the Appendix). Whereas it has been established that a number of carols originated in the wider region, including Sheffield, Rotherham and North Derbyshire, a greater number had their origins in parts of England remote from Thorpe Hesley. What we are left with are two or three carols about which information is not known and these may or may not have originated in the village. Of course, what gives Thorpe carols their uniqueness is their local provenance, the contexts of their performance, the way the carols have evolved locally in tradition, and the manner of their performance. It is right and proper that the local community should feel a sense of ownership for their carols and understandable that chauvinism would lead them to believe that ownership should imply origination.

Taking the repertoire as a whole, it numbers about 30 carols, four of which are fairly ubiquitous — 'Christians Awake', 'Hail Smiling Morn', 'How Beautiful Upon the Mountains', and 'Lyngham'. The three sets of words for which there exists more than one setting are James Montgomery's 'Angels from the Realms of Glory' (1816), (Montgomery was the editor of a radical Sheffield newspaper, the *Iris*), Charles Wesley's 'Hark the Herald Angels Sing', and Nahum Tate's 'While Shepherds Watched' (1700). Undoubtedly the visits by the Wesleys and the proximity of Montgomery accounted in part for the popularity of two of these sets of words, but there is no local rationale for the popularity of the other set. In fact, its widespread acceptance into local carol repertoires is largely due to its inclusion on countless broadsides and in chapbooks which were hawked by chapmen throughout the eighteenth and nineteenth centuries. Moreover, it was one of the few hymns which the Church of England permitted to be

Figure 2

Mount of Olives

Law Family MS

Transcribed by Ian Russell

Ye saints rejoice your Saviour's birth
In praise your tongues employ,
In praise your tongues employ,
In praise your tongues employ;
Clouds clap your hands, exalt ye plains
And shout ye hills for joy.
Clouds clap your hands, exalt ye plains
And shout ye hills for joy,
And shout ye hills for joy.

sung prior to 1820 that was not a metrical version of one of the Psalms. Its simple common metre form made it easy to set to different tunes.[26] Another example of a Thorpe carol, the words of which were popularised by the broadside press is 'Hark Hark What News'.

At the start of this account specific reference was made to the characteristic type of vernacular sacred music that the reformers tried to suppress, namely the exuberant 'fuguing' tunes. These can be identified in the Thorpe repertoire as 'Crown Him', 'Shaw Lane', 'Jacob's Well', 'Good News', 'Martin', 'Mount of Olives', 'Pentonville', 'Fosters', 'Liverpool', 'Lyngham', 'Northrop' and 'October'. The fact that several of these tunes are among the most popular in the Thorpe repertoire demonstrates how unsuccessful the Reform movement was. Moreover, tunes such as 'Crown Him' by Laban Solomon (1842-1903) of Elsecar near Barnsley and 'Northrop' by Abraham Northrop (1863-1938) post-date the reforms. An example of a fuguing carol is given in Figure 2.

The carol repertoire at Thorpe Hesley is eclectic such that alongside the fuguing tunes are a number of carols with a strong evangelical flavour. This style of sacred music is typified by the hymns of Moody and Sankey.[27] The carols often have repeated lines and a chorus section. Typical examples are 'World's Jubilee', 'Ring the Bells', 'Wondrous Story', and 'Messiah Was Born'. An example of an evangelical carol is given in Figure 3.

The truly eclectic nature of the repertoire is demonstrated by the fact that several items are included that either have no reference to Christmas or the Christmas story, and in one case has no sacred reference at all. In this respect Thorpe Hesley is no different from many other villages in the district. Thus we have, the stories of 'Jacob's Well' and 'The Prodigal Son', an example of a devotional hymn, 'A Charge to Keep I Have', and a secular glee, 'Hail Smiling Morn'. It would seem that, because other seasonal occasions for singing, sacred and secular, have largely disappeared, the Christmas repertoire has become the repository for favourite items that the community values and does not wish to lose. They have become carols by association and by usage over many years, and are a central element of the tradition.

Alongside the types of sacred music referred to above must be added anthems. The two obvious examples are 'How Beautiful Upon the Mountains' and 'The Prodigal Son', the latter became so popular in the pubs and with the Primitive Methodists that it was nicknamed 'Thorpe Anthem'. Two other carols that are 'anthem-like' in their scope are 'World's Jubilee' and 'Merry Christmas'.

Reference has been made to the fact that a number of carols in the Thorpe repertoire have origins that are remote to the village. 'Mortals

Figure 3

Messiah Was Born

Clifford Chesman MS

Transcribed by Ian Russell

Good news they bring to all the earth,
Good news to all mankind,
Good news to all mankind;
They told the shepherds where to go
That Jesus they may find,
That Jesus they may find,
That Jesus they may find,
That Jesus they may find. [Chorus]

Awake' ('Pentonville') is a case in point. It has words written by Samuel Medley in 1782, a Baptist pastor based in Liverpool, and is set to music written by William Marsh of Canterbury [c 1800].[28] Whereas the broadside press helped to diffuse the words for carols, the music was spread largely without the aid of print. (Prior to 1861 (*Hymns Ancient and Modern*), there was no such thing as a modestly priced, mass produced hymnbook with music.) The most probable explanation for this diffusion is that 'Pentonville' along with other music, song and oral tradition, was carried from village to village in the wake of the Napoleonic Wars, by itinerant preachers, by disbanded soldiers in search of employment, and by village labourers turned off their land as a result of the Enclosure Movement. It is ironic that more is known about Marsh, than the arranger of another carol, 'Mount of Olives', George James of Rotherham.[29]

An example of the confusion that surrounds the origins of a local carol can be seen in 'A Song for a Time'. In Thorpe this carol is attributed to Dr Alfred Gatty (1813-1903), Vicar of Ecclesfield from 1839 to 1903. However, no evidence has been found in family papers, local manuscripts or publications to substantiate the claim. It is far more likely that the carol is the work of his third son and namesake, Alfred Scott Gatty (1847-1918), who contributed over thirty carol compositions to his mother Margaret's famous annual for children, *Aunt Judy's Magazine*. Moreover, an Ecclesfield manuscript belonging to the Baxter family bears the ascription, A S Gatty.

Mention has been made of Clifford Chesman's manuscript, which was written in the late 1960s and 1970s, but not his reason for producing it. All earlier manuscript settings were pitched too high or inappropriately for modern performance practice. In fact, many were pitched in the key of C. Clifford was determined to remedy this and also to tidy up anomalies in the harmonies such as consecutive fifths. In this respect his motives mirrored those of John ['Jack'] Couldwell of Worrall, who edited a selection of his local carols for publication as *Ye Old Christmas Carols* [1969], to be used as a performance copy by the Bradfield Evening Institute Choral Society directed by Bert Sorsby. It is not surprising that Bert and Clifford were friends. Clifford's settings were also intended to be used for performance, but not just by the congregation of Hope Chapel. He brought together a quartet of singers, all of whom had trained voices. The original line-up was Mary Law Doughty (soprano), Janet Renshaw (contralto), Tony Scrooby (tenor), and Derek Renshaw (bass). A later line-up had Janet (soprano), Esme Brooks (contralto), Ted Johnson (tenor), and Derek (bass). The quartet would give performances of a few of the Thorpe carols each Christmas from 1977 to 1985 and they achieved quite a reputation for their efforts.[30] Derek Renshaw explained:

> *We polished them up. We got them more accurate and made some slight adjustments, a semi-tone here and there. But that's all we ever did with them.*

Nonetheless, however minimal the alterations were, the older generation found them difficult to accept. Janet Renshaw confessed:

> *We did try to get my family to sing them as we'd done them with Cliff, but that were a sheer impossibility. "We don't sing 'em like that! We've always sung 'em other way!" We're probably wrong, but it sounds better.*

For the last fifteen years the Thorpe Hesley carols have not been sung very often when compared with the previous fifty. In fact, the demise of the tradition has been a cause for some concern by all the carollers interviewed for this article. In the first place, their centres of worship have been lost and they see no future for the carols in the alternative locations. Annie Chesman (74 years) commented:

> *It seemed as if there was something missing these last few years when we've not had the old carols. Modern ministers won't have them.*[31]

They see the problems of performance in the local pubs in terms of both unsympathetic licensees and clienteles for whom the carols are alien. Don Batty identifies the dilemma:

> *They're building estates on [the village]. They bring them in from the towns. They don't know the carols. They don't want you to sing them, that's the trouble. It doesn't mean a thing [to them].*

Thus the demise of the carols is understood as a metaphor for more sweeping changes in society and loss of community values and identity.

> *Thorpe is no longer a village. We don't know the people. We used to know everybody that lived in the village when we were children.* (Gertie Chesman)[32]

> *All the old houses in the village, people are paying a fantastic price for them and having them restored. It's bad for the old atmosphere of the village.* (Robert Chesman)[33]

> *When we were young, you couldn't lock the door. The key was too big to fit in your pocket.* (Don Batty)

> *Everybody knew everybody else in village. [There was] No lock on the door. Me dad used to say if anybody came into our house and saw all the bills under the table, they'd go out fast.* (Walter Goddard)

> *We never hear a child sing, not even on Christmas Day. Children can't go knocking on strangers' doors.* (Mavis Firth)[34]

> *Your mother walked to Thorpe for groceries. Walked to Chapeltown. Walked to the bus. Walked for everything. The old days were good in a lot of respects, [though] everyone was poor. You [a woman] can't even walk across Chapeltown Park these days.* (Mavis Firth to Don Batty)

Should the nascent revival of Thorpe Hesley's carols among a younger generation be successful, as has happened at other villages in the district,[35] then this success perhaps should be recognised as a positive step towards the healing of a fractured community and the restoration of its identity and values.

Notes and References

1. A number of these traditions have been documented and information is available from Village Carols (address below), as well as a list of published recordings. See, for example, *A Song for the Time: Village Carols from the Black Bull, Ecclesfield*, cassette VC001, Village Carols, 1987, accompanying book by Ian Russell, 48 pp.; see also Ian Russell, 'A Survey of a Christmas Singing Tradition in South Yorkshire -- 1970', *Lore and Language*, 1, no 8 (1973), pp 13-25.
2. A number of villages sing their local carols in the West Country including Odcombe and High Ham in Somerset, and Padstow in Cornwall. I am grateful to Bob Patten for information on West Country carol traditions.
3. See Robert Chesman (in collaboration with Tom Doncaster), *Thorpe Hesley: Its Past, Present... and Future* (Thorpe Hesley: Hope Methodist Church, 1987); and *Fine Art and Industrial Exhibition: Easter Week, April 7th to 12th 1890* (Thorpe Hesley: Mechanics Institute, 1890).
4. See Melvyn Jones, 'The People of Thorpe Hesley and Scholes' in Stephen Cooper, Robert Chesman and Melvyn Jones, *Church, Chapel & Community: Thorpe Hesley and Scholes in 1840* (Thorpe Hesley: Holy Trinity Church, 1990), pp 21-34.
5. See Nicholas Temperley, *The Music of the English Parish Church*, 2 vols (Cambridge: Cambridge University Press, 1979), I, pp 151-163 and 201-206.
6. William Henry Monk (ed), *Hymns Ancient and Modern* (London: William Clowes [1861]), no 166.
7. See, for example, John Foster, *A Second Collection of Sacred Music* (York: S. Knapton [c 1820]), pp 25-33, Psalm 47.
8. See Alfred Gatty, *A Life at One Living* (London: Bell and Sons; Worksop: Robert White, 1884), p 34.
9. Robert Chesman interview, 7 April 1992. For a comprehensive account of church bands, see Kenneth Holland MacDermott, *The Old Church Gallery Minstrels* (London: SPCK, 1948).
10. John Hall attracted a very modest pension from Francis Hurt Sitwell of Renishaw Hall, but it was too little too late, see the *Sheffield Register*, 18 January 1792, p 3. See also E D Mackerness, *Somewhere Further North: A History of Music in Sheffield* (Sheffield: Northend, 1974), pp 21-22.
11. John Foster, *Sacred Music* (York: S Knapton [c1820]), title page. See also Rev J Eastwood, *The History of the Parish of Ecclesfield in the County of York* (London: Bell and Daldy, 1862), p 548; and Matthew Henry Habershon, *Chapeltown Researches, Archaeological and Historical* (London: Simpkin, Marshall, Hamilton, Kent; Sheffield: Pawson & Brailsford, 1893), pp 106-107.
12. See Vic Gammon, 'Babylonian Performances: The Rise and Suppression of Popular Church Music 1670-1860', in Eileen Yeo and Stephen Yeo (eds), *Popular Culture and Class Conflict* (Brighton: Harvester, 1981), pp 62-88.
13. Gatty, pp 34-38.
14. *Sheffield and Rotherham Independent*, 13 June 1840, cited in Robert Chesman and Stephen Cooper, 'The Methodists', in *Church, Chapel & Community*, pp 14 and 19.
15. Robert Chesman interview, 7 April 1992.

16. See Chesman and Cooper, 'The Methodists'; Chesman, *Thorpe Hesley*; [J R Chesman] *Hope Methodist Church, Thorpe Hesley, 1856-1956* (Thorpe Hesley: Hope Church, 1956); 'Bi-Centenary Celebrations of Methodism at Thorpe Hesley in the Rotherham Circuit, 1738-1938', in Rotherham Local Studies Library (Ref: 942.741.287 THH/287); and Robert Chesman, 'Thorpe Hesley, Its Past, Its Places, Its People' (unpublished typescript in Rotherham Local Studies Library).
17. See Stephen Cooper, 'The Parish Church' in *Church, Chapel & Community*, pp 4-13.
18. Varah Cooper interview, 10 July 1995. His father, also Varah, sang carols in the local pubs at the turn of the century.
19. Don Batty interview, 19 July 1995. All subsequent quotes are from this interview.
20. Gertie Chesman interview, 31 March 1992.
21. Walter Goddard interview, 19 June 1995. All subsequent quotes are from this interview.
22. Derek and Janet Renshaw interview, 12 June 1995. All subsequent quotes are from this interview.
23. Robert Chesman interview, 31 March 1992.
24. Clifford and Robert Chesman interview, 31 March 1992.
25. Varah Cooper interview, 10 July 1995.
26. The well-known 'Winchester Old' setting was combined with these words for the first time in 1861 in *Hymns Ancient and Modern*, no 62, which post-dates many of the local versions. The 1970 survey of local carols referenced above listed 16 versions being sung in oral tradition in South Yorkshire.
27. The classic collection is Ira D Sankey (ed), *Sacred Songs and Solos with Standard Hymns Combined* with *New Hymns and Solos* and *The Christian Choir*, 1169 pieces in one volume (London: Morgan and Scott, no date).
28. Published in William Marsh, *A set of new psalm and hymn tunes composed in a familiar style* (Canterbury, no date).
29. Alfred Rogerson (ed) *The Centenary Tune Book: A Selection of Old Methodist Tunes* (London: Charles H Kelly, 1897), no 6 'Celestial Concert' arranged by George James of Rotherham is 'Mount of Olives'.
30. Several copies of recordings of their singing have been circulated in the village. A set of copies of the original recordings, which were made by Clifford Chesman and Annie Chesman, are available in Village Carols archives.
31. Annie Chesman interview, 28 May 1992.
32. Gertie Chesman interview, 7 April 1992.
33. Robert Chesman interview, 7 April 1992.
34. Mavis Firth interview, 19 July 1995.
35. The community of Castleton in the Peak District has enjoyed a successful revival of its village carols in recent years. See *The Bells of Paradise: Village Carols from Castleton in the Derbyshire Peak*, cassette VC004, Village Carols, 1991, accompanying book by Ian Russell, 48 pp.

Acknowledgements

This account has been put together as a result of the support and encouragement of singers of Thorpe Hesley Christmas Carols. I am particularly grateful to Robert Chesman, Annie Chesman, Clifford Chesman, Gertie Chesman (née Wood), Derek Renshaw, Janet Renshaw (née Goddard), Walter Goddard, Varah Cooper, Graham Waller, Don Batty, Mavis Firth, Fred Ridge, and Bessie Ridge (née Burgin). Others who I would like to thank that have helped me with my researches for this study include: Tony Green, Gus Grenfell, Ruairidh Greig, David Ragsdale, Melvyn Jones, Joan Jones, Rotherham Local Studies Library, Sally Drage, Jeremy Blundell and other residents of Thundercliffe Grange. All the manuscripts and recordings have been deposited in the archives of Village Carols, Bridge House, Unstone, Sheffield S18 5AF which is directed by the author.

APPENDIX The Christmas Carol Repertoire of Thorpe Hesley

	FIRST LINE	Sung at Ecclesfield	Core Repertoire	TITLE	Masons - Words	Red Lion - Words	Sportsman - Words	Hope Chpl - Words	Thorpe St - Words	Church (Walsh?) MS	Almond MS	Burgin MS	Chesman MS	Cooper Ms	Law MS	Renshaw Collection	Waller MS	Hope Chpl Treble MS	Hope Chpl Alto MS	Hope Chpl Tenor MS	Hope Chpl Bass MS	In Oral Tradition	Source of Words	Source of Music
1	A Charge to Keep I Have	√	√	Southport		√			√	√	√	√	√		√							√	Charles Wesley (1762)	J. Davies (1889)
2	All Hail the Power			Crown Him						√			√			√	√						Edward Perronet (1779)	Laban Solomon (1842-1903)
3	All Hail the Power		√	Shaw Lane		√		√		√	√		√			√	√					√	Edward Perronet (1779)	Richard Thomas (?)
4	Angels from the Realms		√	Olivet									√			√						√	James Montgomery (1816)	G. Hirst
5	Angels from the Realms		√	Prospect						√	√	√	√	√		√						√	James Montgomery (1816)	
6	Angels from the Realms		√	World's Jubilee	√	√		√	√	√	√		√	√	√	√	√					√	James Montgomery (1816)	
7	A Song for a Time	√	√		√	√	√		√	√	√	√	√			√						√	Alfred Scott Gatty (?)	A. S. Gatty(?) (1847-1918)
8	At Jacob's Well	√	√	Jacob's Well	√	√			√	√	√	√	√	√	√	√						√	Hugh Bourne(?)	James Leach (1762-1797)
9	Awake My Harp		√	Old Israel		√		√	√	√	√	√	√		√	√		√	√	√	√	√	Richard Furness (1791-1857)	
10	Bright and Joyful	√	√	Malin Bridge		√			√	√	√	√				√						√	James Montgomery (1819)	
11	Christians Awake Salute	√	√		√	√		√	√	√	√			√	√			√	√	√	√		John Byrom (before 1750)	John Wainwright (1750)
12	Come Singers Make Bold		√	Merry Christmas		√	√	√	√	√	√		√		√	√						√		
13	Hail Smiling Morn	√	√																			√		
14	Hark Hark What News	√	√	Good News	√	√	√	√	√	√	√		√	√	√	√					√	√		Reginald Spofforth (1810)
15	Hark the Herald Angels		√	Mansions							√		√	√	√	√						√	Charles Wesley (1739)	John Hall (d.1794)
16	Hark the Herald Angels		√	Martin		√		√		√	√		√	√	√	√			√	√	√	√	Charles Wesley (1739)	
17	Hark the Herald Angels		√	Ring the Bells							√		√	√	√	√						√	Charles Wesley (1739)	
18	Hark to the Ringing		√	Christmas Bells		√			√	√	√		√		√	√						√		
19	Hark What Means		√	Wondrous Story		√		√	√	√	√	√	√			√							J. Cawood (1819)	
20	How Beautiful upon the Mts	√	√								√												Isaiah, 1ii, 7	R.A. Smith (c.1827)
21	I Will Arise	√	√	Prodigal Son	√	√	√	√	√	√	√		√	√	√	√	√					√	Luke xv, 18-19	
22	Joy to the World	√	√	Mount of Olives	√	√	√	√	√	√	√	√	√		√	√						√	Isaac Watts (1719)	(arr. George James)
23	Lo The Eastern Magi		√	Star of Bethlehem		√		√	√	√	√	√	√	√	√	√		√	√	√	√	√		
24	Messiah was Born		√	Christmas Morn		√	√	√	√	√	√		√		√	√						√		
25	Mortals Awake		√	Pentonville		√		√	√	√	√		√		√	√		√	√	√	√	√	Samuel Medley (1782)	William Marsh (c.1800)
26	Ring Out Ye Bells	√	√	Ring On		√	√	√	√	√	√	√	√			√						√		
27	While Shepherds Watched			(Buckley)																		√	Nahum Tate (1700)	
28	While Shepherds Watched	√	√	Foster's	√			√		√	√		√	√	√	√	√	√	√	√	√	√	Nahum Tate (1700)	John Foster (before 1820)
29	While Shepherds Watched	√	√	Liverpool	√	√	√	√		√	√		√	√	√			√	√	√	√	√	Nahum Tate (1700)	Edward Harwood (1786)
30	While Shepherds Watched		√	Lyngham						√												√	Nahum Tate (1700)	Thomas Jarman (1821)
31	While Shepherds Watched			Northrop																			Nahum Tate (1700)	Abraham Northrop (1863-1938)
32	While Shepherds Watched			October						√	√						√						Nahum Tate (1700)	

10. 'The Odd Confounded Speech of Rawmarsh Lane': Aspects of the Growth of Parkgate 1831-1891

by Tony Dodsworth

PARKGATE IS LOCATED THREE KILOMETRES north-east of Rotherham town centre. Today it lies well within the built-up area of Rotherham but for much of the nineteenth century it was a separate settlement. Before 1800 it has very little history of note, indeed its name indicates that the most significant aspect of its existence was that it lay close to one of the entrances to the emparked area surrounding Aldwarke House. Yet the nineteenth century saw Parkgate grow phenomenally (see Figure 1) as did a large number of other mining and industrial communities in South Yorkshire. Based on the quality of the iron, and later steel, manufactured at the works in Parkgate, it would not be an exaggeration to say Parkgate rose to national prominence. Certainly when the works rolled the plate for use in the construction of the *Great Eastern* steamship, launched in 1858, for a short period it was unique — the only works able to produce rolled armour plates. This industrial growth, and the demand for labour which accompanied it, attracted workers from all over the country and it was this migration that particularly accounted for its rapid growth during the nineteenth century. When P Rodgers was moved to eulogise about the wonders of Greasbrough Ings and New Park-Gate in his poem of 1831 the following lines set the scene, even at that early date, for what was to follow in the area as the century progressed:

Some with amusement hear, and some with pain,
The odd, confounded speech of Rawmarsh Lane;
Where Warwickshire, and Staffordshire, and York,
Like Nimrod's masons jabber o'er their work.

By using the sources that are available it is possible to become acquainted with some of the individuals who made Parkgate's rapid growth possible and to identify the patterns of migration that sustained this growth. This story, both of the lives of individuals residing in Parkgate and of the overall migrational routes, is the focus for this study.

Sources of data

The key resources when 'peopling' settlements in the past are the

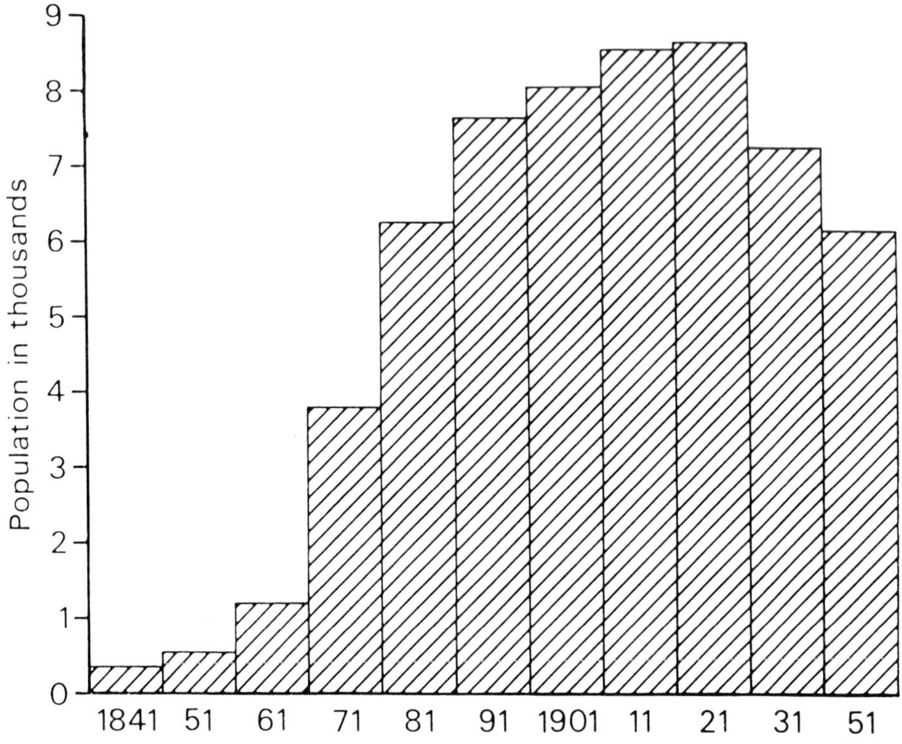

Figure 1. Population of Parkgate, 1841-1951, from Census returns.

enumerators' returns of the national census. A Census of Population has taken place every ten years (with the exception of 1941) since 1801. The returns have generally not survived for the 1801-1831 period and were not in fact particularly reliable as enumerators (the people whose task it was to collect the information) were left in some doubt as to whether to count persons normally living in their districts or only those actually there on census day. From 1841 onwards the instructions to enumerators were much more precise and from that date the returns do survive. Thus at that census, people sleeping in a house on the night of 5/6th June 1841 were to be entered as living there. Each enumerator was responsible for collecting the information from a relatively small area, usually with 50-100 households and a population of several hundred. It was important that the enumerator was seen by the Census authorities as a local person who could carry out his duties conscientiously, and by the population at large as someone to whom confidential information could be entrusted.

The generalised figures from the census would be published a few years after the census date, usually in the form of tables, so that it was possible to tell how many people lived in a particular town, their age distribution and occupations. What you could not find out from these generalised census returns were the names of the individuals living in particular houses, the occupations of individuals and the family relationships of individuals. All this information did exist in the enumerators' books but in the interests of privacy it was not released for one hundred years. Thus at present the most recent enumerators' returns available for inspection (usually on microfilm in the nearest central library) are those for 1891. The 1901 enumerator returns should be made available to the public in 2001.

The amount of information available in the enumerators' returns varies slightly between 1841 and 1891. So for example in 1841 it is only possible to find out whether a person's birthplace was in his home county or elsewhere, but from 1851 onwards it is possible to discover the actual county where a person was born and generally the exact village or town. Similarly the 1841 Census returns give individual ages rounded up or down to the nearest five years but from 1851 onwards exact ages are given (although it is apparent from looking between censuses at different dates that people were not always very accurate in the ages they gave). Taking the 1871 enumerators' returns for Parkgate as an example it is possible to discover the name of each street, a separate number for each household (at that time many houses themselves did not have numbers like today), the name of any individual (name and surname), the relationship of each individual within the household (e.g. head, wife, son, daughter, lodger, apprentice etc), their condition (married, unmarried, widower etc), their age (in years if over one, in months if under one), their occupation and their birthplace. A final column was also available to record if any individual was (1) Deaf and Dumb, (2) Blind, (3) Imbecile or Idiot or (4) Lunatic. This certainly seems to indicate a less sensitive attitude to people with disabilities then. Thus in the returns for Parkgate in 1871 we find living in Bear Tree Road the members of the Sambrook family (spelt Sandbrook in the census) (see Figure 2).

Part of the attraction of using census returns in a local history study is to speculate on aspects of individuals listed there and to try to discover more about those individuals. We know from other sources that Charles Sambrook was already resident in Parkgate in 1851 and that in 1860 he was responsible for a forge rolling department within the puddling department of the Parkgate Railmill. He was assisted in this role by his family and worked alongside other forge rollers working in family groups led by Robert Harris and Bowen Adams. Much more information

No.	Name	Relation	Status	Age	Occupation	Where born
47	Charles Sandbrook	Head	Married	54	Forge Roller	Dawley, Shropshi
	Elizabeth Sandbrook	Wife	Married	53		Rawmarsh, Yorks
	Frank Sandbrook	Son	Married	31	Forge Roller	Rawmarsh, Yorks
	William Sandbrook	Son	Unmarried	18	Forge Roller	Rawmarsh, Yorks
	Elizabeth Sandbrook	Daughter	Unmarried	10	Scholar	Rawmarsh, Yorks
	John C. Sandbrook	Grandson	Unmarried	6	Scholar	Rawmarsh, Yorks

Figure 2. Example of an Entry in the Census Enumerator's Returns for Bear Tree Road, Parkgate, 1871 Census.

about him waits to be found, meanwhile we might speculate about where Frank's wife was on the night of the 1871 Census and whether Charles worked in the iron industry in the West Midlands before moving to South Yorkshire and getting married.

Other sources which are particularly useful in 'peopling' the past are trade directories. The two main trade directories available covering the Parkgate area over the past 125 years are the various volumes of Kelly's *Directory of Sheffield and Rotherham* and White's *General Commercial Directory of Sheffield*. There is not continuous coverage available in Rotherham Library for all this period but either on microfilm (for early directories) or in the books themselves a good spread can be studied. Parkgate is defined as a separate area in the directories from the 1870s onwards but the early ones do not give addresses generally, only names and trades/shops. By the end of the nineteenth century it is possible to list the name, full address and type of shop/trade from the directories. Thus we know that in 1881 amongst the shops on Broad Street and Rawmarsh Hill were nine butchers (including four pork butchers), five shoemakers/cloggers, a china dealer cum cab proprietor and a medical botanist. Many of the shops mentioned in streets off Broad Street and Rawmarsh Hill were not in purpose-built shop/houses but in ordinary terraced houses.

One other very special source must be mentioned to complete this introduction and that is a book entitled *A History of Parkgate Iron and Steel Co. Ltd. 1823-1923*, written by George P Royston. One fascinating section in this book involves the author in recalling the outstanding personalities working in the ironworks in 1860 and includes brief descriptions of them and their jobs. Many of these same workers can be found in the census returns for 1851, 1861 and 1871 and once again this helps to put 'flesh on the bones' of local history.

The Parkgate Works

The first ironworks to be established in Parkgate was built there in 1823. The Parkgate Works was set up by two Sheffield men, Sanderson and Watson, and at about the same time a small works was set up by Oxley and this still trades to this day close to its original site. Both ironworks were sited to the west of the main road between Rotherham and Rawmarsh and just south of Taylor's Lane. The site was a good one with local coal, black-band iron ore and limestone quite close by and alongside a spur of the South Yorkshire and River Don Navigation (canal). Initially there was no rail link but by 1840 the old London-Midland-Scottish Railway ran past the site followed in 1871 by the London-North-Eastern Railway.

The fortunes of the ironworks were not consistently in the ascendant in the period 1831-1891 despite the apparent non-stop growth of the population of Parkgate in this period. The impact of local coal mines and ironworks on population growth is obvious from the graph in Figure 3. Tickhill, a small agricultural town without jobs in pits and

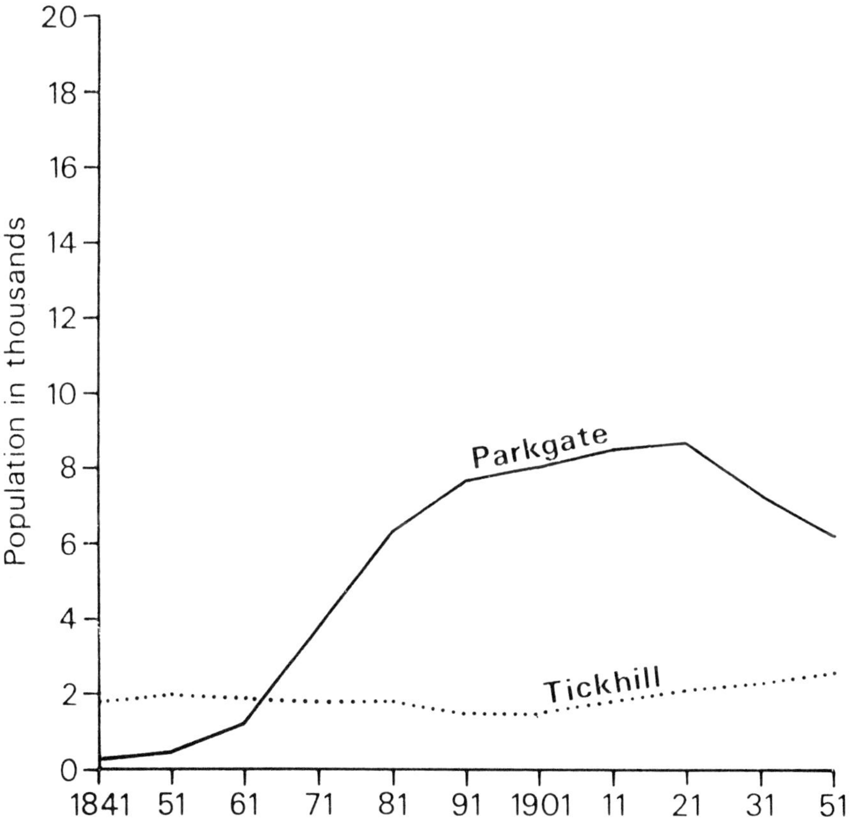

Figure 3. Line Graph showing Population Growth for Parkgate and Tickhill, 1841-1951.

works, stagnated throughout the nineteenth century scarcely growing at all while Parkgate clearly experienced a population explosion. Such rapid growth must be expected to be linked with a very strong flow of migrants into Parkgate and the census returns certainly confirm this. Yet within this overall pattern it is possible to sense there were fluctuations in fortunes for the works and workers of Parkgate.

By the end of the 1820s the ironworks was producing iron bars, iron castings and tin plate yet by 1832 Sanderson, by now the sole owner, was declared bankrupt and the mortgage on the works was foreclosed. It operated under the name of the Birmingham Tin Plate Company in the 1830s and the first blast furnace was built in 1839. Samuel Beale was partly responsible for the next major advance in the works, seeing the possibilities when Parliament authorised 2,800 miles of railway in 1845 followed by another 4,540 miles in 1846. A rail mill was built in 1845 which was capable of turning out 2,000 tons of rails monthly. This represented a huge capital outlay and before long iron rails became the chief product of the works. Large quantities were supplied to all the British railways and many foreign ones. The Holmes ironworks were first rented and then bought in 1854 to supply more pig iron from its two blast furnaces. At about this time a lease was also taken on the Chapeltown ironworks, which involved a blast furnace, foundry and three collieries. Tin plate was no longer manufactured but the production of iron plates for general purposes began in 1849.

In the 1850s the Parkgate works became a world leader in the production of rolled armour plate for naval ships. The request to produce the plates came from the Admiralty via Palmer Brothers of Newcastle upon Tyne and the first successful trial led to a rolled plate being sent to Palmers' in 1856. For five years Parkgate was the only works capable of producing rolled armour plates and in this period turned out some plates up to twenty-five feet long, four feet wide and one and a quarter inches thick for the famous *Great Eastern* steamship. Yet by 1865 this trade was given up as the market changed. This rapid reversal in fortunes illustrates one vital aspect of the heavy trades in metal manufacture, innovation throughout the century constantly 'moved the goalposts' and gave the advantage first to one works and then to another. One innovation could lead to a massive investment in plant being obsolete within a very short space of time. The fact that many of the migrants to Parkgate looking for jobs in the ironworks were from the West Midlands, and particularly Staffordshire, suggests that some of the works particularly in the West Bromwich-Tipton-Bilston area were caught on the wrong side of one of these 'innovation changes' and their employees consequently looked for a new location which appeared to have good work prospects for the future. As early as 1831 Rodgers refers to the presence of workers from Staffordshire in Parkgate and by 1841 far more of the heads of households in iron trades were born outside Yorkshire than in Yorkshire (see Figure 4), and many of these probably came from Staffordshire. Certainly in the censuses from 1851-1891 birthplaces of iron workers were often to be found in Staffordshire.

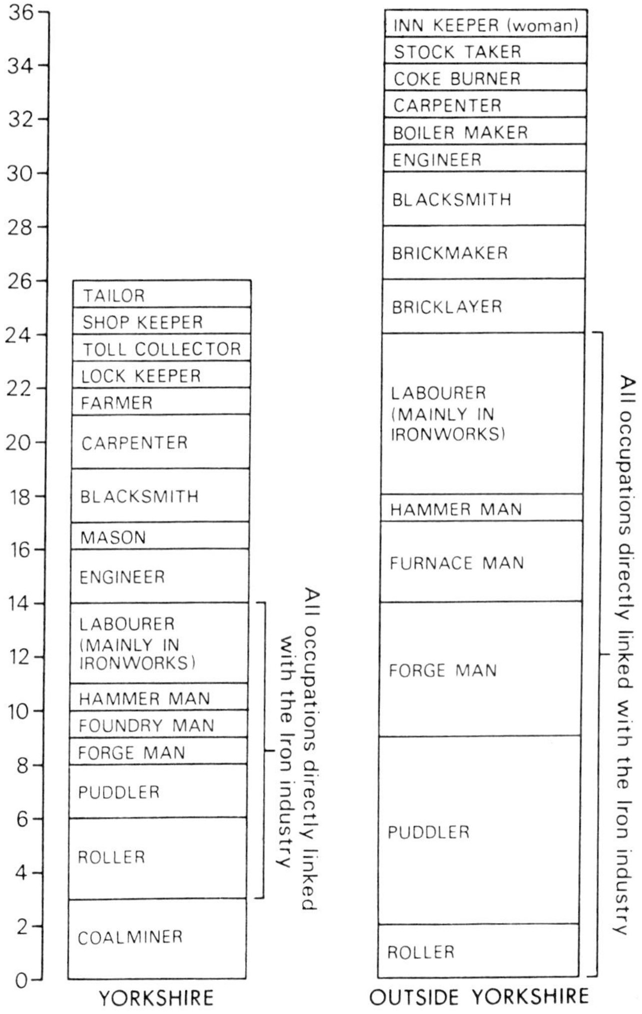

Figure 4. Birthplace and Occupation of Heads of Households in Parkgate, 1841.

Iron production in South Staffordshire particularly ran into difficlties as the century progressed with coal mining becoming increasingly uneconomic as flooding problems increased and ironstone reserves were exhausted.

As early as July 1843 a deputation of South Staffordshire ironmasters met the Prime Minister, Sir Robert Peel, to report to him the extreme falling off in the demand for iron, the great depression in the price and the consequent reduction in the wages of labour and contraction in the means of employment. The state of pauperism, as evidenced by the enormous increase of the poor rates in the unions comprising the district, was stressed by a number of the members of the deputation. Peel replied that 'he feared the production of iron had been forced by the requirements for railroads and other causes, so much beyond the ordinary demand that, now that these sources of consumption had been supplied, he could hold out no prospect of immediate improvement from any measures within the power of the Government'. Following this in the same year *The Times* of the 21 June reproduced an article from the *Monmouthshire Merlin* which stated that 'the present state of the iron trade annihilates hope — we see nothing but ruin before us and behind us'. (Remember that it was in 1845, just two years later, that a new rail mill was built at Parkgate — clear evidence of the vagaries of the trade cycle in heavy metal goods).

Even so the South Staffordshire iron industry did not reach its peak until 1859 when it was responsible for 22 per cent of British production but the fact that six iron firms in West Bromwich alone closed within five years at about this date clearly showed the problems the area was experiencing. At this time the industry in North Staffordshire was growing rapidly yet many of the unemployed iron workers chose to travel to Parkgate rather than move a much shorter distance northwards.

Both the Staffordshire area and Parkgate suffered particularly as a result of the new Bessemer process for making mild steel, patented in 1857. The type of ore used in the Bessemer process was not available in either Staffordshire or around Parkgate and the pendulum of change swung towards new steel-making areas like Middlesbrough. Steel was a superior material to wrought iron and Parkgate must certainly have suffered as a result of Bessemer's invention. Particularly from the 1860s onwards the ironworks were developed on a new site to the east of the Rotherham-Rawmarsh Turnpike Road (see Figure 5) and in the space of several years a new forge, puddling furnaces and two plate mills were erected, but it was not until 1888 that it was decided to start steel production at Parkgate. This late change must have had a profound impact on the success of the metal industry in Parkgate and Royston gives us a tantalising glimpse of this when he wrote 'many Parkgate workmen emigrated to America in the late sixties or early seventies' and that 'a soup kitchen for distressed work people' was operating at Parkgate at the same time. Elsewhere he writes of 'difficult times in the seventies'.

Ironworks trades and some notable ironworks personalities

Royston's book helps to bring to life these changes in the fortunes of the Parkgate works by describing some of the personalities involved in the works in the 1860s and the jobs that they did. He writes of the puddlers whose work 'was considered to be more arduous and exhausting than the other branches for the period of time they were engaged'. He describes how a puddler heated balls of iron in the furnace before withdrawing each separately and, gripping it with his tongs, dragged it across the floor plates to the metal-helve (a type of hammer). Here he lifted the hot ball with his tongs and swung it under the helve. This process he repeated with each ball until all was complete, then he fettled his furnace, charged it again and started once more until the turn's work was finished. It certainly required strength, endurance, skill and nerve to be a puddler but Royston states there was no shortage

Figure 5. The Parkgate Ironworks east of the Rotherham-Rawmarsh Road about 1870. *Rotherham Central Library, Archives and Local Studies Section*

as 'the higher wages, compared with some other industries, were an inducement for strong men to undertake it'.

Among the puddlers at this time was Richard Griffiths, born in North Wales in 1823/4 and married to a local girl, Elizabeth. In 1861 they lived in a cottage which stood alone between the crossing gates and the Railmill Inn (the Old Forge Tavern was later built beside it) with their four children aged between six and thirteen. Three of the children were born in Parkgate and the other in Leeds. His nickname of 'Rough Dick' suggests an interesting past but he had come under the influence of the Temperance Movement, which was of quite considerable importance locally, and had switched from 'excessive indulgence in strong drink' to total abstinence. His 'reformed habits' had enabled him to build his own cottage. There were at least two other families named Griffiths in Parkgate at this time with both heads of household being born in Wales and working as puddlers so it is tempting to imagine them working together as a team. The work of puddling the iron does seem to have been based on teams rather than individuals and family groups were quite common. William Hawk(e), born in Scholes, was described by Royston as working alongside Griffiths and being a tall, thrifty and industrious workman. He worked with his sons, Thomas (sixteen), Arthur (thirteen) and Charles (eleven) in the ironworks. We will discover more about William and his family later. The fact that Royston describes Hawk as a puddler while the enumerator in 1861 describes him as a furnaceman does indicate that care must be taken not to draw too many sweeping conclusions about people and their occupations at the time just based on one source. Certainly workers did change jobs within the works for Royston mentions William Kemp and William Lister as puddlers in 1860 but later becoming ball furnacemen. Other puddlers included Enoch Powell from Shropshire and Godfrey Walker and James Thompson from Greasbrough.

Another specialist trade within the ironworks was that of the forge roller. Bowen Adams was a roller and, assisted by numerous family members, was in charge of one of the forges. He was very unusual in being the only iron workman listed in the 1861 census enumerators' returns with two occupations i.e. forgeman and beerhouse keeper. Apart from his exacting occupation in the ironworks he also ran the Flying Dutchman Inn, no doubt assisted by his wife, Ann, and a fifteen-year-old servant from West Bromwich, Elizabeth Murphy. Both he and his wife were born in Stourbridge in Worcestershire with all six of his children living at home in 1861 being born in Burnhill, Staffordshire. Charles Sambrook, mentioned earlier (spelt Sambrock by Royston) was a forge roller in charge of another department who was living on Rawmarsh Hill in 1861 with his wife, Elizabeth, who had been born locally at Wath. Sambrook was born in Dawley, Shropshire but his four children living with him in 1861 were all born in Rawmarsh (the enumerator in 1861 did not list Parkgate births separately). The eldest of these, Frank, was twenty-one and worked as a roller with his younger brother Charles (sixteen). It seems fair to assume that Sambrook had moved to he Parkgate area by 1840 if not earlier. By 1871 he had moved just a few yards westwards into some of the first terraced houses to be built in Bear Tree Road and had been joined as a forge roller by his youngest son, William (by then eighteen). His six year-old grandson, John, was living with him at the time of the census.

Royston believed that the most notable workmen in the puddling department in 1860 were the shinglers. These again worked at the metal helve but were also required to manipulate the metal balls to a number of positions whilst the helve was still working. This again was rewarded with 'good wages' and only men of 'fine physique, good nerve and skill' were suitable. Amongst the shinglers were Aaron Parkes and his two brothers, William and Joseph. Aaron was born in Wednesbury, Staffordshire and was married to Elizabeth from Rowley in Staffordshire. His two eldest children, aged nine and seven, were born in Staffordshire while the youngest, Phoebe, was born locally. It seems likely therefore that Aaron moved to the area between 1854 and 1860. He lived in Holly Bush Mount with a number of other Royston 'notables' including another shingler, Joseph Field, born in Londonderry, Worcestershire. From his children's birthplaces it would appear he moved to the area between 1852 and 1859. Unusually, living with them was a nineteen-year-old servant, Catherine Lindley, from Tipperary, Ireland.

Much more can be discovered about these workers from 1860 but space is limited so before leaving them individually we will just become acquainted with two other 'notables'. Firstly, Edward Amies, a strong square built man, was noted for his ability in the use of a seventy pound hammer in cold rail straightening. He was living in Aldwarke Lane in 1861 having been born in Onibury, Shropshire. He had quite recently married a Barnsley girl, Sarah, and had two young sons born locally. Thomas Amies followed the same trade and lived in Station Row while Ann Amies, a thirty-eight year-old unmarried housekeeper (also born in Onibury) lived in the household of William Davis (another 'notable'), together with his two children. He was a widower born in Staffordshire and was described as an iron rod roller. These family connections across a number of different households crop up time and again when looking through the enumerators' returns for Parkgate. Edward apparently remained in Parkgate for the rest of his life and was laid to rest in the graveyard of St Mary's, Rawmarsh on 19 March 1893, aged sixty-four. Finally we find John Ping, a railmill furnaceman, who was living in

Holly Bush Mount in 1861. He, unusually, was a real 'southerner' from Buckinghamshire who moved into the area when young to work in a field other than iron making but, while still in his youth, was attracted to the Tin Mill. He later became a Railmill hammerman. He was quiet and unassuming but also a strict disciplinarian and was closely involved with the building of a new Methodist church at the foot of Rawmarsh Hill at its junction with Holly Bush Mount. He lived with his Sheffield-born wife and nine children all born locally apart from William, aged fifteen, who was born in West Bromwich, Staffordshire. Yet again there is a suggestion that people at this time may have been much more mobile than we would imagine. In St Mary's graveyard in Rawmarsh the gravestone of John Ping can still be seen (see Figure 6).

Figure 6. The Gravestone of John Ping and his family in St Mary's Graveyard, Rawmarsh. *The Author*

He lived to the great age of ninety-one (died 1907) having survived his wife by seven years. The actual gravestone was originally for his son Edwin who died aged 12 in 1865, being joined some years afterwards by another son, Lawrence Campbell Ping. It is interesting to note that by 1865 the family was well-off enough to be able to pay for a memorial stone.

Of the seventy Parkgate Works 'notables' mentioned by Royston, forty-eight can be found in the 1861 enumerators' returns for Parkgate. It seems likely that virtually all of the remainder would have been still living locally but beyond the boundaries of Parkgate itself. Using details given in the 1861 Census and adding a few extra pieces of information from Royston we can draw up a pie graph to show the birthplaces of fifty-three of Royston's 'notables' (see Figure 7). Simple analysis shows

Figure 7. Exploded Pie-Graph showing the Birthplaces of 'Royston's Notables'.

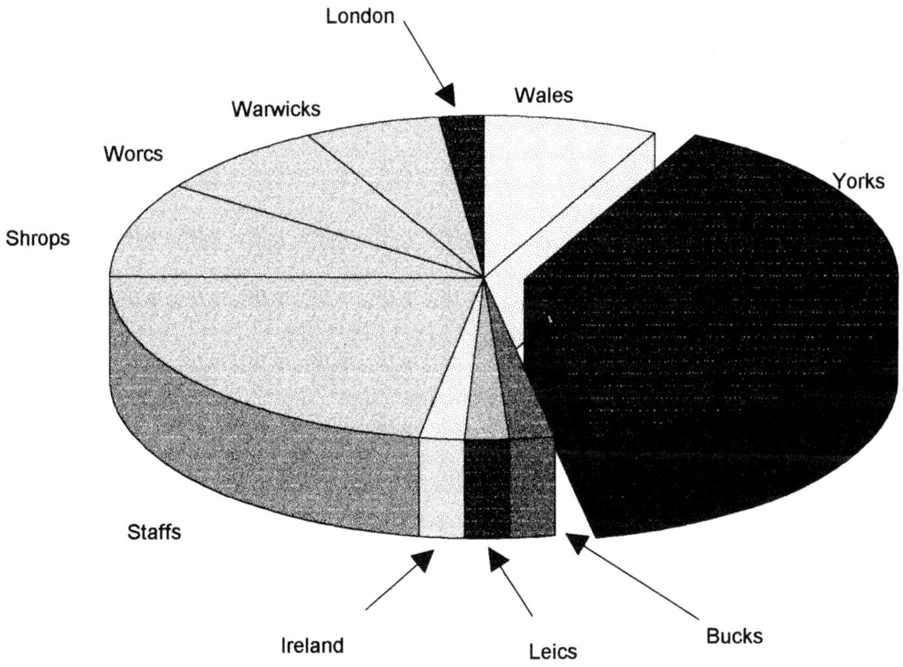

Birthplace	Wales	Yorks	Bucks	Leics	Ireland	Staffs	Shrops	Worcs	Warwicks	London
Number	4	21	1	1	1	12	5	4	3	1

the importance of men born in the West Midlands-Black Country area in the Parkgate iron trade but it should not be ignored that quite a large percentage were local (ie, born in Yorkshire), the figure being 40 per cent. Royston's criteria of picking out his 'notables', which seems to have emphasized church-goers and members of the Temperance Movement, may favour local men from more stable backgrounds and less prone to migration. Certainly the fact that he could remember them sixty-three years on, when he wrote his book, suggests that they were established in the works for quite a time.

A quick glance at the surnames of his 'notables' including Griffiths, Jones, Roberts, Evans and Edwards suggest that a 'Welsh connection' could have been a characteristic of some of the migrants, four indeed being born in Wales. It seems possible that some of those born in the Staffordshire/Shropshire area may in fact have been the offspring of Welsh fathers who themselves had moved to the Black Country for jobs in the ironworks from their birthplaces in Wales. Tantalising evidence for this type of migration is provided in the 1861 enumerators' returns for Parkgate, for living in two households beside each other in Aldwarke Road we find the following:

John Watkin Junior	Head 33	Furnaceman	Bilston, Staffs
Sarah Watkin	Wife 31		Rotherham, Yorks

....

John Watkin Senior	Head 60	Labourer at Steelworks	Newtown, Montgomeryshire
Mary Watkin	Wife 60		Oswestry, Shropshire

Further work could be undertaken to establish just how important the Welsh connection was to the Parkgate workforce.

A snapshot of Parkgate's population in 1871

The period 1861 to 1871 saw the rate of growth of Parkgate reach its peak with its population swelling from 1,204 in 1861 to 3,807 in 1871 (an increase of 216 per cent). In the same period the population of Tickhill fell from 1,914 to 1,844. To get a snapshot of the workers in Parkgate at that time a 25 per cent sample of heads of household was made using the 1871 enumerators' returns. This does not necessarily give an entirely balanced picture of the workforce in Parkgate at the time but it does establish major trends. It must not be assumed that every head of household lived with his family in a self-contained house, some families (with two or more heads of household) shared one house.

As in 1841 the iron trades still dominated the occupation structure of Parkgate in 1871 (see Figure 8), the percentage involved in these trades being broadly similar between the two dates. Not surprisingly, considering the way the settlement had grown, the range of jobs outside the iron trades and labourers had expanded from just under 50 per cent in 1841 to just over 50 per cent in 1871. There was a growing group of workers providing an increasingly diverse range of services and shops in Parkgate (see Figure 9). A new pit had been sunk at Aldwarke, very close to Parkgate in 1864 and this obviously led to an explosion in the growth of coal jobs and perhaps accounted most for such a rapid population increase locally in the decade from 1861. The single largest occupational group in the 1871 sample was the puddlers, there being no less than twenty-four heads of household described thus. More remarkable still only three of these were local men while eighteen were from the traditional ironworking counties of Staffordshire and Shropshire. The importance of this area for migration to Parkgate can be seen in Figure 10. With such a high percentage (75 per cent) of puddlers coming from the same general area one is tempted to assume a common cause and it has already been mentioned that in West Bromwich alone six iron firms closed down within five years at about this time. We also need to remember that about a third of the nation's puddling furnaces were located in South Staffordshire then. Six of the twenty-four Parkgate puddlers in the sample were from West Bromwich itself with another four from the neighbouring towns of Bilston and Tipton.

The furnacemen were a much more diverse group with only one from Staffordshire itself while three were local men. All five forgemen in the sample were Yorkshire born, four actually being local. The five more responsible ironworks jobs mentioned in the survey involved only one local man but three were from Staffordshire, a manager, a foreman and a contractor. The local coal industry attracted six miners in the sample from Staffordshire and Shropshire (out of twenty) while one from Great Snoring in Norfolk was listed as both a miner and a local preacher. This 'Norfolk connection' is a particularly interesting one being a development specifically of the 1861-1871 period. In the whole of the 1861 enumerators' returns for Parkgate there is only one person listed with a Norfolk birthplace — James Cousley from 'Snowring/Stiffkey' — living in Station Row, yet in the 1871 sample no less than eleven heads of household were from Norfolk and they continued to provide a significant presence in Parkgate right through to at least 1891. Even more surprising, the great majority of these migrants came from a small area of North Norfolk (see Figure 11). None of the eleven in

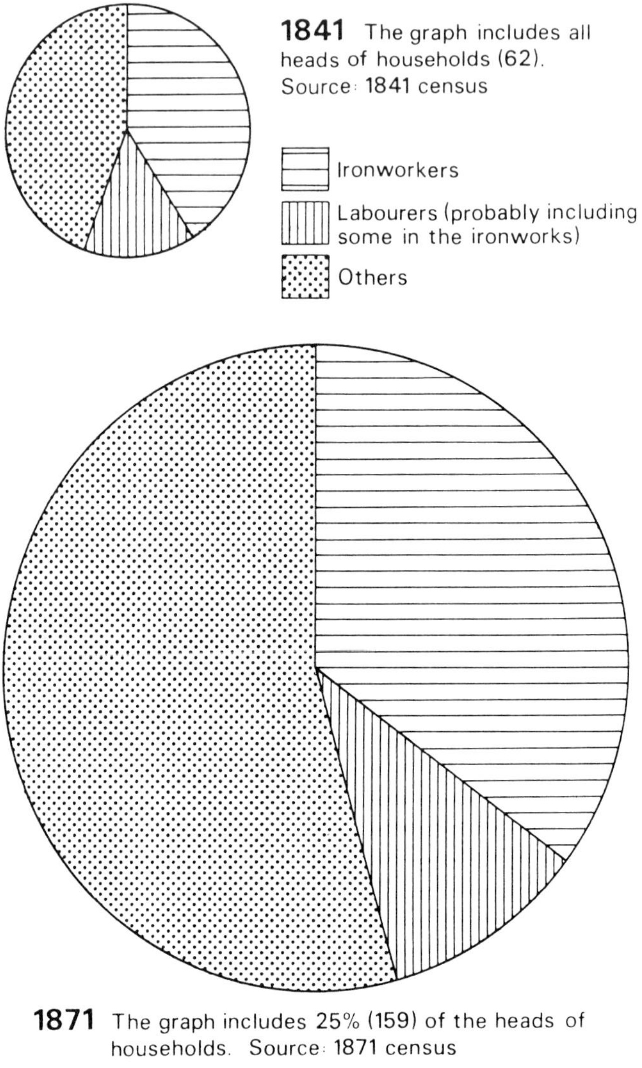

Figure 8. Pie-Graphs showing Occupations of Heads of Households in Parkgate, 1841 and 1871.

1871 had a skilled ironworks job and four were listed as labourers. In the nineteeth century many labouring jobs were taken by people on a seasonal basis, agricultural labourers in winter often coming to urban areas for temporary employment. A link may have been established between Parkgate and migrants from North Norfolk in this way and, when the demand for agricultural workers fell in areas like Norfolk, especially from 1851 onwards, some decided perhaps to make it a permanent move. Certainly the importance of continuing links between the two areas must be surmised from this migration. As an example we find James Graver from Syderstone, Norfolk living in Hall Street in 1891 with his wife, also from Syderstone. They had three unmarried lodgers living with them, William Baldwin (nineteen), Edward Hurns (twenty-four) and Fred Amies (eighteen) and all were born in Syderstone. Two of these lodgers were labourers.

The physical expansion of Parkgate 1850-1890

The housing area of Parkgate grew rapidly between 1850 and 1890 as shown by the detailed Ordnance Survey maps of those dates. In 1850 the entire population of Parkgate was concentrated in a small number

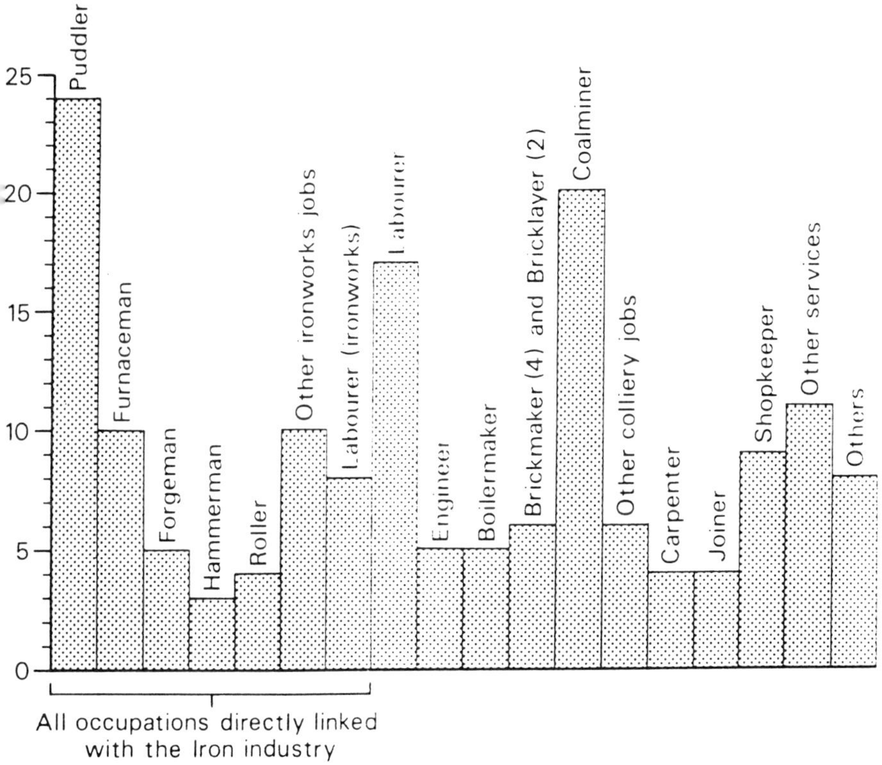

Figure 9. Occupations of a 25 per cent sample of Parkgate's Heads of Households, 1871.

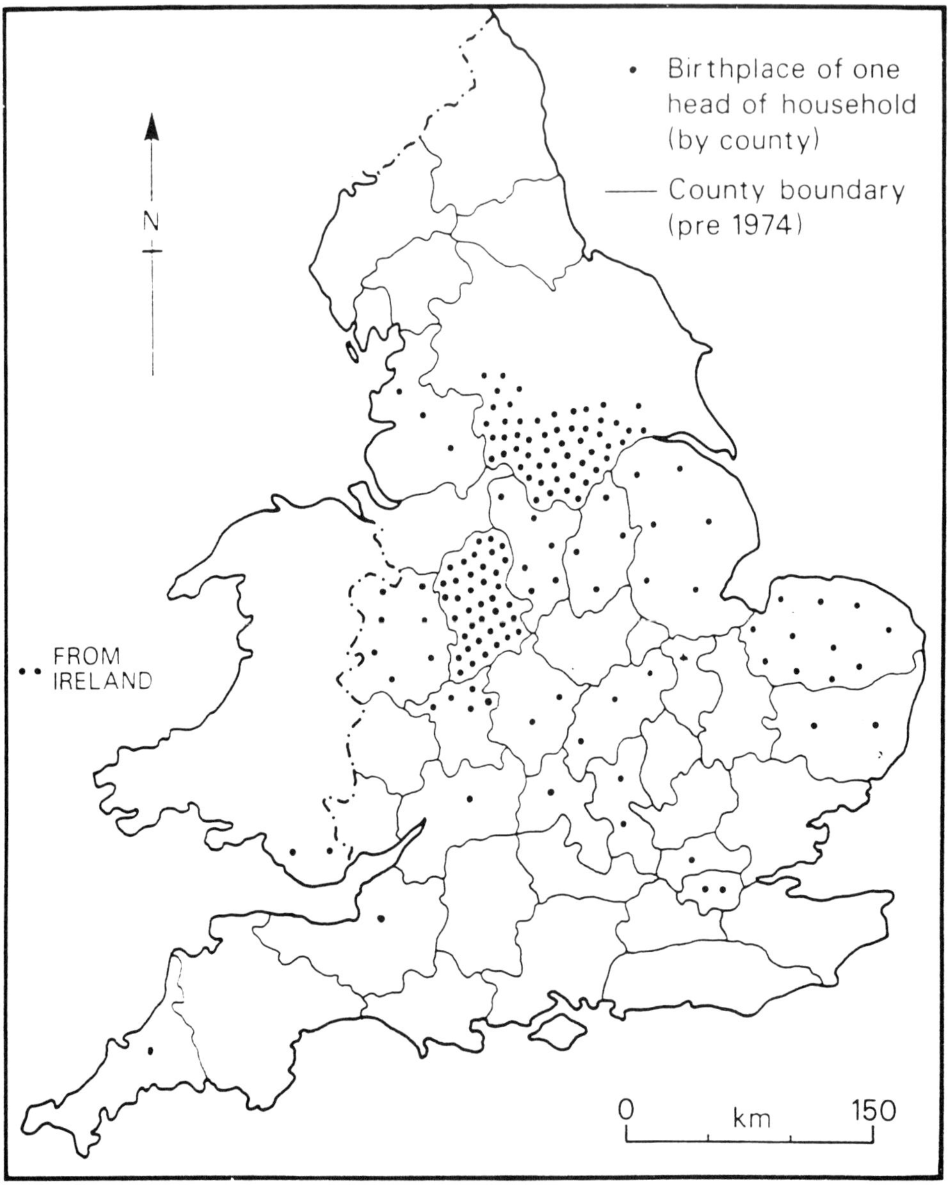

Figure 10. County Map of the Birthplaces of a 25 per cent sample of Parkgate's Heads of Households.

of terraced rows as shown in Figure 12 and including one just south of the map area — Little Bridge Row. By 1890 many of the fields north of the ironworks and sloping up towards St Mary's Church near the top of Rawmarsh Hill had been covered by numerous new rows of terraced housing. It should not be thought that this growth involved some large-scale provision by a rich industrialist or entrepreneur, much more it seems to have been the result of a large number of small-scale developments adding on a few new houses at a time to existing terraces. The names of the new rows or streets sometimes tell us something of the history of their construction; thus the 1850 OS map shows Francis Row (probably a spelling mistake for France's Row) just to the north of the Travellers Inn. In the 1861 Census we find Amos France, a forty-two-year-old stonemason, and his family living in 'France's' Houses in this location. It seems more than likely that he built at least a few of the original houses (France is still a local surname in the Rawmarsh/Parkgate area). Orgreave House was quite a large house lying just to the north-east of Parkgate House. In 1861 it was occupied by William Oxley, the steel manufacturer, who at that time employed seventeen men and three boys. In 1871 John Lloyd, a railway waggon builder, was living there with his family and in 1873 it was up for sale. On the same land in 1881 we find Lloyd Street, once again a connection seems likely. Hall Street just north of Lloyd Street was built slightly earlier, in the 1860s, and was apparently named from the Temperance Hall at its end on the main road. It is also interesting to note a Charles Wannop, a grocer living on Broad Street in the 1891 trade directory, close to where Wannop Street was developed.

Royston in his book on the Parkgate Iron and Steel Company also gives us tantalising glimpses of this gradual process of housing development in the area. He tells us that 'housing accommodation had not kept pace with the demands resulting from the increase of the works'. As a result of this the workers themselves, building on the habits of thrift and self- help developed with the Temperance Societies, turned their attention to building their own dwellings. In this way 'most of the houses in Holly Bush, Aldwarke Road and Hall Street' were built. No doubt inspired by this they went on to raise money and build the United Methodist Free Church on the corner of Hollybush Street and Rawmarsh Hill in 1867. This was no small undertaking costing a total of £2,500 and having seating for 900. Royston also tells us about William Brazier a contractor at the ironworks who built his own house. He left the works some time after 1861 and started speculative building but Royston reports 'Like many others who had ventured too much he came under difficult times in the 1870s'.

By studying a specific street in an area of interest and tracking it through different censuses it is possible to get much closer to the level of continuity and change there. Hall Street was developed in the 1860s just north of Parkgate House and Orgreave House. About thirty-nine terraced houses were built along the south side of the street, the north side being occupied by the yards of the houses on Aldwarke Road. East of Cross Street, and at the end of Hall Street, were Aldwarke Road Buildings and these nine dwellings have also been included in the street survey. At this level the importance of individuals becomes much more apparent and can add to the interest of a study.

Hall Street, Parkgate, 1871-1891

By studying population pyramids for Hall Street for the three successive censuses 1871, 1881 and 1891 (see Figure 13) it is possible to get a better insight into the main characteristics of the resident community. The shape of the pyramids changes very little between 1871 and 1891 with the large number of children under eleven and the tiny proportion of people over sixty being the most easily identifiable features. The bulge on the male side of the pyramids between the ages of eleven and forty is a characteristic often seen today in Third World cities and reflected the fact that many migrants were moving into the settlement in search of work and that these were more often men rather than women. The group described as lodgers in the censuses are almost exclusively male, single and between the ages of eighteen and forty. A number of migrants moved with their families and tracking the birthplaces of the children offers insights into the routes they may have followed. Many of the patterns of migration identified in the 1871 head of household sample are repeated here. The total population of the street did not vary dramatically, rising slowly from 224 in 1871, to 246 in 1881 and 253 in 1891. Of the 1871 population only thirty-eight were recorded as born in Parkgate and amongst them not a single head of household; thirty of them in fact were under sixteen-years old. Widening the local area for births to Rawmarsh takes in another thirteen residents but of these only one is a head of household. In total exactly half of the resident population was born in Yorkshire and amongst these were eleven heads of households. This compares with the thirty-seven residents with birthplaces in Staffordshire, including ten heads of household. This strong Staffordshire connection mirrors the situation in the whole community and reflects especially the attraction of specific ironworking jobs in the area. Significant numbers of migrants are also found from Nottinghamshire (sixteen including four heads of household) and Derbyshire (eleven including four heads of household). The Norfolk connection identified earlier is repeated in Hall Street with eight residents born there including two heads of household in 1871, rising

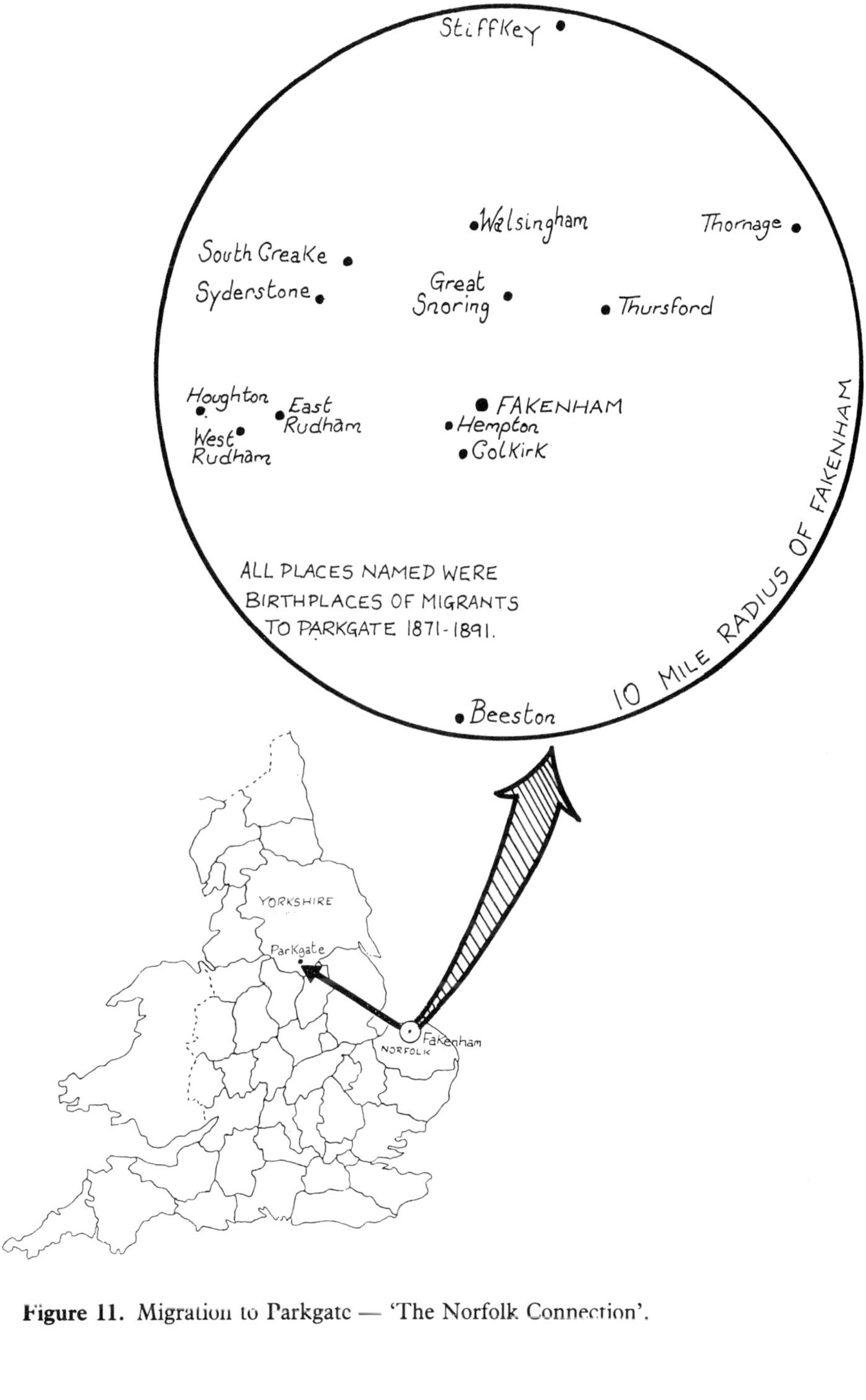

Figure 11. Migration to Parkgate — 'The Norfolk Connection'.

to sixteen and six heads of household in 1881 and falling slightly to fifteen in 1891 including five heads of household. There was also a rush of Lincolnshire migrants rising from just four in 1871 and three in 1881 to thirty-one in 1891 including eight heads of household. By 1891 the Staffordshire connection appears to have been in decline with just seventeen residents born there including five heads of household. Analysis of marriage patterns can give us further insight into the characteristics of the resident population. The married couples in Hall Street in 1871, 1881 and 1891 have been classified into those born in Rawmarsh (R) — which includes Parkgate, Locally (L) — within a twenty mile radius of Parkgate and Distant (D) — more than twenty miles from Parkgate. In each category the male birthplace precedes the female birthplace. In a few cases at each date households were headed by widows or widowers. By studying the table below the importance of migration to the residents of Parkgate at this time is reflected again.

Birthplaces of Married Couples in Hall Street and Aldwarke Road Buildings

	D/D	D/L	L/D	L/L	L/R	R/R	D/R	Single Head	Total
1871*	13	4	2	6	0	0	0	6	31
1881	30	5	5	3	1	1	0	3	48
1891	21	6	1	7	2	1	1	6	45

* Excluding Aldwarke Road Buildings

It should not be assumed from these figures that all the couples with distant birthplaces were married away from Parkgate and then moved to the area. In some cases both men and women, although born away from the local area, may have moved with their parents when young and have been living locally before their marriage. Any community growing rapidly through migration is likely to end up with this pattern of many 'distant birthplace' marriages and very few marriages of people born in the community itself. The pattern of occupations of Hall Street residents between 1871 and 1891 again generally reflected the findings of the 1871 Head of Household Sample Survey with some interesting changes between the two dates. Ironworking jobs and coal mining jobs dominate the list at all three dates but their relative importance does seem to alter as the century draws to an end. In 1871 twelve residents of Hall Street worked in coal mining while twenty-five were ironworkers including ten puddlers. By 1881 the number of jobs linked to coal mining had risen dramatically to forty-two while the ironworkers total slipped to eighteen including seven puddlers. In 1891 there were

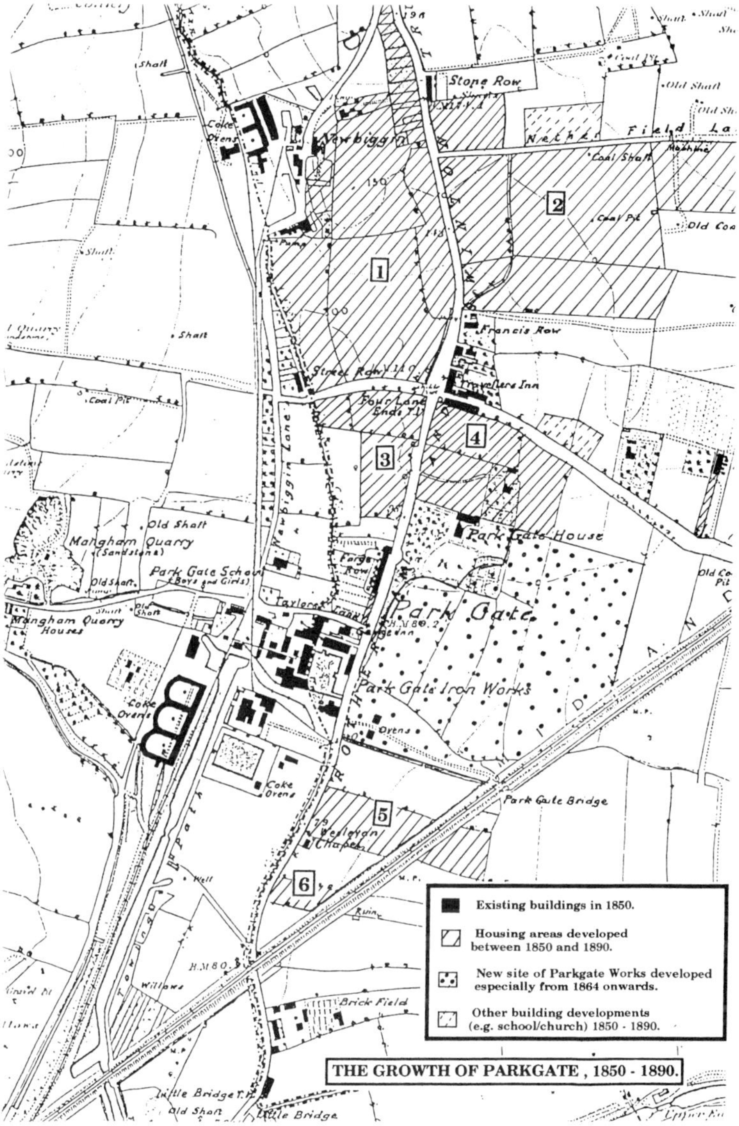

1 = Holm Flatt Street , Ashwood Road , Bear Tree Road.
2 = Netherfield Lane , Victoria Road , Albert Road , Hollybush Street.
3 = Wannop Street , Coleman Street , Foundry Street.
4 = Aldwarke Road , Hall Street , Lloyd Street.
5 = Stanley Street , Chapel Street , Dilks Buildings.
6 = Midland Street.

Figure 12. The Growth of Parkgate, 1850-1890.

thirty-nine coal mining jobs compared to eighteen ironworkers (no puddlers are listed, perhaps because the enumerator was less interested in listing the exact job done within the iron industry). This rapid increase in coal miners as residents of Hall Street may be related to further development of the Aldwarke pit that was opened in 1864. Hall Street would have provided some of the closest housing accommodation in Parkgate to the pit itself. The 1891 Census for Hall Street residents showed clearly a wider range of jobs apart from coal mining and iron working than in 1871, a development to be expected as the settlement grew.

Based on the census it would appear that few women over the age of fourteen who lived in Hall Street in this period had an occupation. Excluding visitors, boarders and lodgers, of the forty-eight females over fourteen in 1871 there were just five servants, one laundress, one housekeeper and one nurse recorded. This compares with sixty-one females over fourteen in 1881, amongst whom there were two servants, three dressmakers and one pianist/musician. The range of female occupations, if not the number, expanded slightly by 1891 so among the sixty females there were a labourer, a dressmaker, a shirt seamstress, a factory hand, a machinist, a straw bonnet maker and a servant. The accuracy of this recording is difficult to assess, some women may not have spoken of their occupations or some may have been unrecorded by the enumerator.

In terms of the people themselves the census allows us to get quite close to certain families. Ten years was obviously a long time in terms of being resident in the same house in the second half of the nineteenth century. Just five families are found in both the 1871 and 1881 census returns for Hall Street and perhaps significantly all five are still to be found living there in 1891. The links between 1881 and 1891 were stronger as the community settled down with thirteen families (including the five already mentioned) resident at both dates as well as two lodgers. The mobility of working people in places like Parkgate during the nineteenth century was obviously very high although the majority of moves probably involved very small distances within the community itself. Other links between inhabitants of Hall Street might also be noticed, such as members of the same extended family living at different addresses and also people born in the same small and distant village living close to each other. Thus living in Hall Street in 1881 we find George Gelder, a thirty-eight-year-old carter born in Whiston, living with his wife from Cawood and their four children under twelve. In 1891 George has moved from the street but now we find William Gelder, a forty-nine-year-old coal carter born in Whiston, living with his wife Jane from Whiston and their two children born in Dalton. In 1881 we

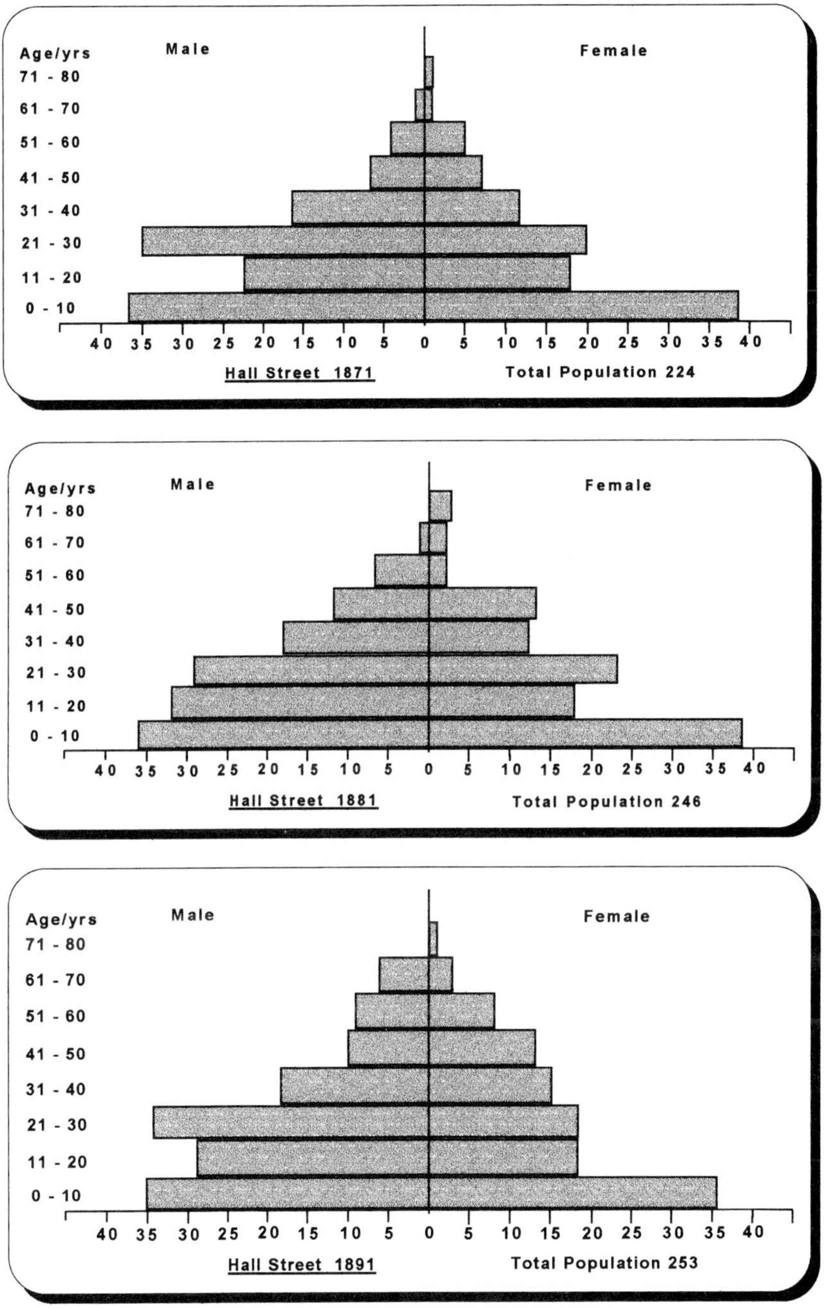

Figure 13. Population Pyramids for Hall Street, Parkgate, 1871, 1881 and 1891.

find Charles Tildersley, a twenty-seven-year-old miner from Sedgley, Staffordshire, living in Hall Street with his wife Elizabeth also from Staffordshire and two young children aged three and one. Just a few doors away we find William Tildersley, a five-year old born in Staffordshire, living as a boarder with William Wright and his wife. William Wright was a fifty-eight-year-old miner from Shropshire. Given the unusual surname it is probable there was a family link with Parkgate's most 'famous' Tildersley, Thomas, who was a medical herbalist and lived at 70 Broad Street for many years. Lydia Moors was just four years old in 1881, living with her family in Aldwarke Road Buildings. Her father 'Jas' was a coal miner and the whole family was born in Hyde, Cheshire (quite a rare example for Parkgate of migration across the Pennines). In 1891 Lydia was working as a domestic servant for Benjamin Wall, an ironworker born in Sedgley (just like Charles Tildersley), and his family including three children under eight.

One of the families that remained in Hall Street between 1871 and 1891 was that of Elisha Pickerell (he was listed as Elisha Pickershill in 1881 and Elijah Pickerell in 1891 — clear evidence of the likelihood of enumerator error). He was a coal miner from East Rudham in Norfolk and 38 years old in 1871. His wife, Mary, was the same age and was born in West Rudham, Norfolk, and they apparently had no children. In each of the three censuses they had someone else living with them, in 1871 there was George Craw, their eight year-old nephew from West Rudham and William King, a twenty-year-old boarder also from West Rudham. In 1881 there was Thomas Roadley, an unemployed boarder from Shropshire and in 1891 there were three unmarried labourers as lodgers, Reuben Curry, Frederick Cornwell and Walter Whitmore born respectively in Houghton, Syderstone and Rudham, all in Norfolk. In both 1881 and 1891 we find other residents of Hall Street born in these small Norfolk villages of West Rudham and Syderstone.

The only resident of Hall Street who is listed in trade directories in this period is Henry Clay, who was also one of the five household heads who stayed resident there between 1871 and 1891. He is quite exceptional as well in that he was part of a two person household throughout this period. Henry and his wife, Eliza, apparently had no children and very unusually for couples in this area do not appear to have taken in lodgers. Henry was thirty-years old in 1871 and a labourer born in Kirton, Lincolnshire, married to Eliza who was twenty-seven-years old and born in Beltoft, Lincolnshire. In 1881 he was described as 'an oil dealer and provision store' and in 1891 as a 'general hawker' (again we have to rely on the enumerator for what is written down). In trade directories around the turn of the century he is listed as a grocer, lamp and oil dealer of 24 Hall Street. It is interesting to note that in both the 1881 and 1891 censuses he is listed at Number 24 in the enumerator returns but at a totally different number in 1871. The numbers of houses on enumerator returns are known to be rather arbitrary in early censuses but it would appear from the evidence of Hall Street that more confidence can be placed in them from 1881 onwards. Much more could be written about Hall Street and its inhabitants at this time — of people like Edward Amies (no longer able or needed to wield the seventy-pound hammer mentioned earlier), one of 'Royston's men' found living in Hall Street in 1881 and by then a sawyer in the ironworks. We could use the trade directories to recreate the shops and businesses found just beyond Hall Street in Broad Street and Rawmarsh Hill (see Figure 14) but space is limited. To conclude then we will stay with 'Royston's men' and follow the fortunes of two families and one individual linked with Hall Street or its immediate environment.

The Hawkes and the Naylors of Parkgate

The Hawke family and the Naylor family had much in common in the period covered by this study. Both William Hawk(e) and James Naylor worked in the ironworks in 1860 and were written of in glowing terms by Royston. Both moved into Hall Street as soon as the houses were built (indeed may have been amongst those responsible for building their own houses) and they or their families remained resident there for the entire 1871 to 1891 period. They can be found initially living next to each other in Barrack Row in the 1851 Census. Barrack Row was on the same line as Station Row later in the century and was either replaced by this or extended and renamed. They were both described as puddlers but originally from very different areas. William was born in Scholes according to the 1861 Census although he later described himself as being born in Wentworth; on the other hand James was a distant migrant from Coseley in Worcestershire (it is actually just over the border in Staffordshire) according to the 1851 Census, but by 1861 gave his birthplace as Tipton, Staffordshire and in subsequent censuses was even less forthcoming just giving Staffordshire. Both were closely associated with the Temperance Movement in Parkgate according to Royston. Royston describes William as 'tall, thrifty, industrious' and as a 'good workman and citizen'. In 1861 William (forty) was living in Ings Road with his family and was by then a forgeman at the ironworks. His wife, Hannah, was the same age as William and was born in Wentworth. At this time there were eight children living at home. The two eldest, Thomas (sixteen) and Jessie (fifteen), were born in Wentworth while the remaining six were born in Rawmarsh (including

Figure 14. Broad Street and Rawmarsh Hill, Parkgate, taken about 1912. The United Methodist Free Church can be seen in the centre of the photograph. *Rotherham Central Library, Archives and Local Studies Section*

Parkgate). A W (probably Arthur from the 1871 Census) was the eldest child (thirteen) born in Rawmarsh so it seems reasonable to surmise that the Hawke family (the name changed from Hawk to Hawke between 1871 and 1881) moved from Wentworth to Parkgate between 1846 and 1848. In 1861 Thomas (sixteen), A W (thirteen) and Charles (eleven) were also listed as forgemen, no doubt assisting their father at work. James Naylor and his family were living in Aldwarke Road in 1861 and he was also described as a forgeman. His wife, Mary Ann, was 35, a year younger than James and was born in Tipton, Staffordshire. There were six children living at home at this time, ranging from Susannah (thirteen) to Agnes (eleven months) as well as an unmarried lodger from Tipton, Thomas Ward, who was also a forgeman. From the children's birthplaces it seems likely that the Naylors moved to Parkgate around 1850.

By 1871 the Hawkes and the Naylors were living about five houses from each other in Hall Street. The two eldest Hawke children had apparently left home by then, but the other six from the 1861 Census were still at home along with a new sister, Sevilla, aged six. Hannah would have been forty-four when giving birth to Sevilla. Arthur and Charles were both listed as forgemen like their father. By 1881 William had died for Hannah was now the head of household and a widow. Living with her were Allan, her twenty-year-old son, James Marsh, a ten year-old grandson and perhaps the son of Jessie, William Haley, a boarder and Isaac and Phoebe Fletcher as lodgers. Phoebe was Hannah's daughter who had married Isaac, a roller from the ironworks who was born in West Bromwich, Staffordshire. Arthur and Charles were both living close by (in fact in a house where the backyard was on the north side of Hall Street) in Aldwarke Road. By 1891 Hannah was one of the oldest residents of Hall Street and still in the same house. Isaac and Phoebe Fletcher were still living with her as lodgers and now had two children aged nine and seven. Isaac was now described as an ironworker,

Figure 15. Workmen from Parkgate Steelworks c1900-1912.
Rotherham Central Library, Archives and Local Studies Section

as was James Marsh, still there and now described as a lodger. By this time Thomas, her eldest son, living elsewhere in Parkgate, was a foreman in the ironworks and married to Sarah from Sunderland. Figure 15 shows a group of workmen from the steelworks at Parkgate at about the turn of the century. (At least two of the workers shown are descendants of 'Royston's men', in this case both being related to William Cattle — he was in charge of the engines and machinery on one shift at the railmill in 1860). No doubt Hannah was pleased to have living next door her neighbours for twenty years, Henry and Eliza Clay, as well as the Naylors just five doors away, whom she had lived next door to fully forty years ago.

By 1871 Susannah, the Naylor's eldest daughter, had apparently left home but the other five children from 1861 were still there as well as three younger children, John, Alice and Minnie. Ten years later Mary (fourteen in 1871) and Thomas (twelve in 1871) were missing but all the rest of the family were still at home with Richard (thirty-one), Sam (twenty-seven) and John (seventeen) all puddlers and unmarried like Agnes (twenty), their sister. Quite amazingly by 1891 the same six 'children' were still at home unmarried despite now all being in the age-range from twenty-two to forty-one. It certainly must have been crowded round the dinner table! All the men including James (now sixty-eight) were described as ironworkers, a rather vague description that reflects the thoroughness or otherwise of the enumerator rather than anything else.

These two families are surely very good representatives of those who helped in the growth of Parkgate and took part in the shaping of the community. Beyond the wall at the end of their backyards was Parkgate House.

Sir Charles Stoddart

In 1871, the head of the household at Parkgate House was Charles Stoddart living with a housekeeper and two servants. Stoddart was also one of 'Royston's men', being particularly important in fact as holder of some of the most important executive positions in the ironworks in the latter half of the nineteenth century. Royston tells us that Stoddart entered the London offices of Samuel Beale and Company (these were owners or joint owners of the Parkgate Ironworks for some years around the middle of the century) as a junior clerk; he had been born in Clerkenwell in London. When the works was transferred to the new Limited Company, Stoddart was appointed Secretary and came to live in Parkgate House. Despite having initially a very limited practical knowledge of ironmaking he learnt about it quickly. After some years he took control of the blast furnaces and later of the whole works, becoming General Manager. Stoddart married between 1871 and 1881 and moved with his wife, Fanny, into Granby House on Aldwarke Lane. Fanny had been born in Wentworth just like Hannah Hawke but was over thirty years younger. Stoddart was especially important in keeping the company afloat in the 1870s and 1880s when it suffered because of the failure to move from ironmaking to steel. He was later appointed a Director of the Company and interestingly, like so many others in his position nationally, moved away from his home close to his workplace and, in this case, to one of the smartest houses in Rotherham — Blenheim House in Doncaster Road. The remainder of his exploits can be followed in detail in the pages of the *Rotherham Advertiser* for he went on to be Mayor of Rotherham and in fact was the first person to be elected Freeman of the Borough in 1907. He was also Knighted. He died in 1913 having financed the building of the spire at St Stephen's Church, Eastwood not long previously. It may be of interest to note that the new road beside the Station Hotel in Parkgate has been named Stoddart Way.

Conclusion

In conclusion we can see that through investigating the roles of individuals like Stoddart, families like the Hawkes and Naylors, street communities like Hall Street, occupational groups like 'Royston's men', migrant groups like those from North Norfolk and Staffordshire and a whole local industry like iron manufacture we can get close to bringing a past community to life and see just how a place like Parkgate grew from a tiny village to a town whose expertise in metal manufacture won it fame throughout the world for a time.

Notes and References

1. Census of Population for England and Wales Enumerators' Returns for 1841, 1851, 1861, 1871, 1881 and 1891
2. *Kelly's Directory of Sheffield and Rotherham 1891.*
3. P Rodgers, *Greasbrough Ings or An Excursion to New Park-Gate — A Poem* (1831).
4. George P Royston, *A History of Parkgate Iron and Steel Co. Ltd. 1823-1913.*
5. *White's General Commercial Directory of Sheffield.*

All the above can be consulted in the Local Studies Section of Rotherham Central Library. The censuses are available on microfilm. The photographs, with the exception of Figure 6, are all from the photographic archive in Rotherham Library's Local Studies and Archives Section.

Acknowledgements

I would like to thank Mel Jones for his help and advice in preparing this study as well as all the staff in the Local Studies and Archives Section of Rotherham Central Library. Thanks also to Mrs Gordon, a descendant of one of 'Royston's men' for permission to use the photograph in Figure 15, and to the Geographical Association and Keith Palfreyman for help with other illustrations. Finally, thanks also to Jane, my wife, for all the hard work — the checking and word-processing.

11. A MAN AND HIS WORKS: THE LIFE OF GEORGE WILTON CHAMBERS OF ROTHERHAM

by John Goodchild M Univ

GEORGE WILTON CHAMBERS (Figure 1) was an incomer to Rotherham, yet like so many influential citizens of the newly industrialising towns of the West Riding, he was to have a major impact commercially, socially and administratively upon the town of Rotherham in which he settled as a young man. His story is well worth the telling.

He was born in 1812 into the comfortable middle class: his father, a barrister, was a salaried magistrate in London and able to send his clever and ultimately only surviving son to be educated at Charterhouse School and then on to University College, Oxford, where he graduated in 1831. The young Chambers came to Rotherham in 1832, virtually straight from his education. His father had an interest in the Greaves or Holmes Colliery in Wortley Road and at Garrowtree, and the young Oxford man came down to manage these interests of his father's. Of this work he made a considerable success, modernising the pits, including introducing wire ropes for shaft haulage, an innovation of which his workmen were initially most suspicious; he also became a member of the then new Yorkshire Geological Society, which was undertaking research work of great interest to colliery owners and managers. The colliery's surface layout as Masbrough Colliery is shown on the Six-inch Ordnance Survey Sheet of c1850, but a few years later it was taken over by one of the newly-introduced joint stock companies, the Rotherham, Masbrough and Holmes Colliery Co Ltd and Chambers ceased to run it. This colliery was to be one of the largest employers among the collieries of the West Riding, with some 900 men and boys on its payroll in 1876, but it closed in 1881; it had worked the 3 ft 8 ins of hard coal in the Barnsley Seam, which was a steam-raising coal of the very finest quality. The site of one of the Chambers' pits was taken in 1856 by Robert Jenkins, who began boiler manufacturing there: G W Chambers advanced £300 to help set that business going.

On giving up the colliery, Chambers transferred his financial interests to the stove grate manufacturing concern of George Wright & Co at the Perseverance Works at Rotherham, where he was for long the senior and active partner, latterly with two sons and a grandson in the business too; the Wright business had removed from Sheffield to Rotherham in 1864.

Figure 1. George Wilton Chambers. *Ivanhoe Review*, Vol 1, 1898, p 38.

But Chambers' business interests were not confined to the colliery, the boiler works and the stove grate works: he was an investor in and a first director of the Sheffield & Rotherham Railway Company, promoted in 1834 and opened in 1838, and for some time he was that railway's vice-chairman, although he seems not to have become a director of the successor Midland Railway Company. He was also a director of the North Central Waggon Company, a waggon and locomotive hiring company, which was very successful, and vice-chairman of the directors of the Sheffield & Rotherham Banking Company, one of the new joint stock banks formed under legislation of the early 1830s. His legal training doubtless proved useful in these

Figure 2. Clough Hall, the home of George Wilton Chambers, as depicted in the 1857 sale particulars. The house was described as comprising 'the fine ancestral mansion ... approached by a handsome Carriage Drive, and beautifully situated in tastefully arranged pleasure grounds, sheltered on the north by a chain of hills, the declivity of which is picturesquely clothed with hanging woods. The mansion, which is of architectural elevation, has a projecting portico adorned with columns, and is built of stone in the most substantial manner, overlooks the town of Rotherham and commands an extensive prospect of the richest scenery; and being within fifteen minutes walk from Rotherham and from the Masbrough station of the Midland Railway, and within twenty minutes ride of Sheffield, is admirably adapted for the abode of the wealthy Manufacturer or Professional Gentleman, to whom a residence in the immediate neighbourhood of the mineral districts is indispensable. *John Goodchild Collection*

offices, as in his voluntary offices.

Chambers married in 1840 when he was about twenty-eight and she, Anne, a Cheshire gentleman's daughter, twenty-two; there were to be eight children. The present writer's particular interest in Chambers arose first when he bought on one of his forays in search of West Riding historical manuscript material, the Chambers family's personal household account book, which was used from the year of the marriage (1840) to 1922. The book tells of an early £15 a month household allowance and the purchase of food which included chickens, turkeys, fish, cream, cheese, sugar, ginger, lemons, biscuits, yeast, etc, etc, the payment of a washerwoman, the buying of cloth for clothes-making (and payment for sewing work), of crockery, turpentine, lucifer matches, black lead, blue for washing, pots, gin, brandy and porter, payment for holidays, a dog kennel, and silver and plated wares. Even the family's charitable payments are recorded in the volume. Keeping lists of the household linen and an eye on the servants were among Mrs Chambers' tasks too, and the book records interestingly the servants' comings, their wages, and their goings. In 1841 there were three female servants; in 1854 there were five; the cook was paid £20, a nurse £16, a housemaid £10 10s 0d, another housemaid £6, and a nurserymaid £5 10s 0d.

At the time of the 1881 census, a bachelor son of thirty-four and three spinster daughters were living at home with mother and father, and they were served by a married butler of thirty-seven, an unmarried footman of eighteen, a groom of twenty, a cook of forty-one (born at Inverness), a lady's maid from France, two housemaids and a kitchenmaid. The family lived at Clough House, a minor mansion built in the 1770s by the local architect/builder John Platt for an earlier coalmaster: the house and its park were leased to Chambers until, upon its being offered for sale in 1857, he purchased it. The sale particulars survive in the present writer's Collection and extracts from these are shown in Figures 2-4.

Chambers, the successful employer of labour, also worked actively in local society. He had been nominated to the then exclusive West Riding magistracy and qualified in 1847, and he was thenceforward an active justice, as well as becoming a Deputy Lieutenant for the Riding. He had a Justice's Room at Clough House for the holding of Petty Sessions, took an active part in the work of the Rotherham Bench and was its chairman for many years. Indeed, he also acted as Chairman of Quarter Sessions, the direct predecessor of the County Council, and took a special interest in the Riding's new South Yorkshire Pauper Lunatic Asylum at Wadsley and its detailed administration. In later years, like many of his class and administrative experience, he was

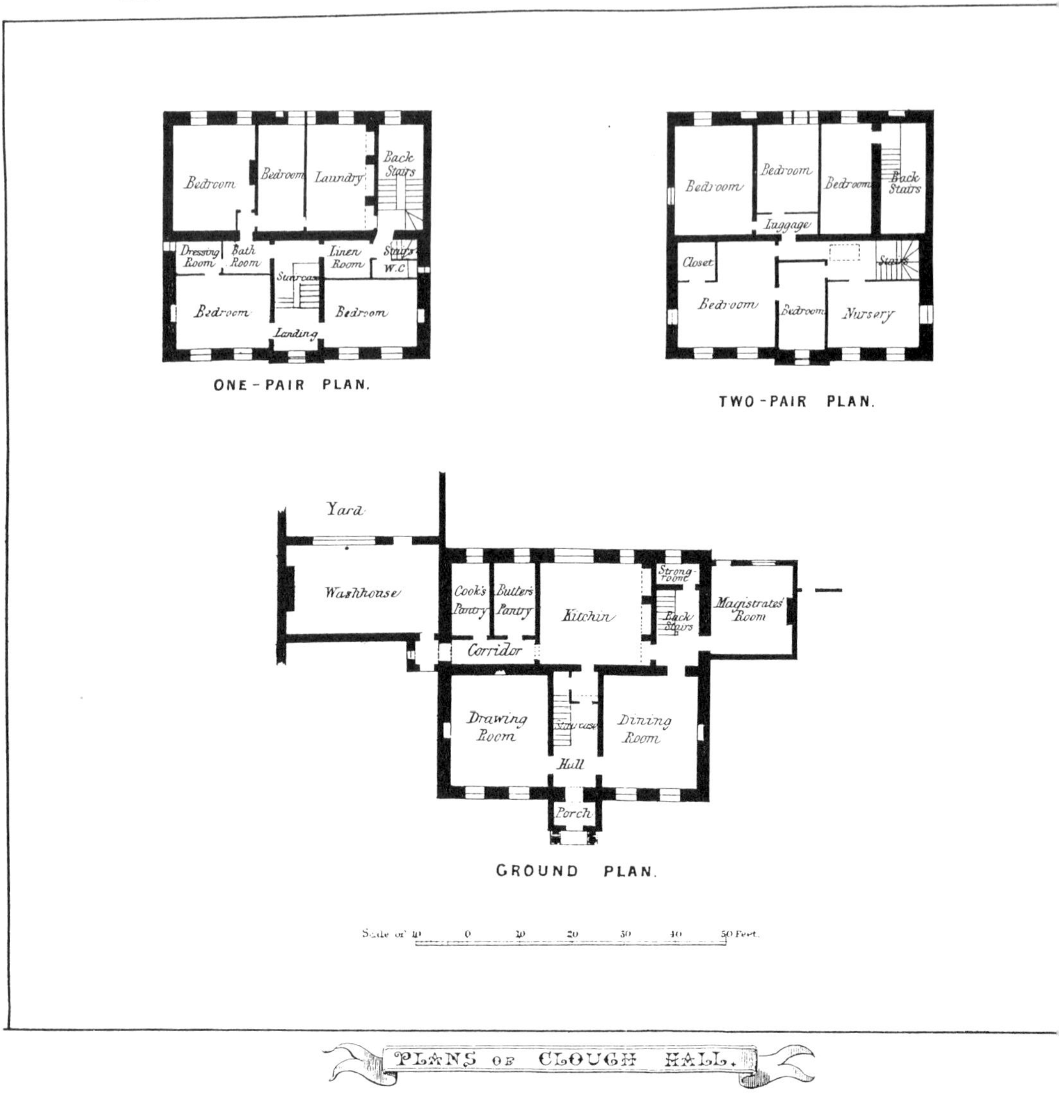

Figure 3. The layout of Clough Hall as portrayed in the 1857 sale particulars. On the upper floor, the children's nursery, measuring 21 ft by 19 ft, was described as 'spacious and airy'. On the first floor the main room at the front of the house was the principal bedchamber with en suite bath and dressing rooms. The laundry, approached by the servants' stairs, was also on this floor; it contained ironing stoves and presses. On the ground floor was a 'spacious hall with a handsome staircase', a 'noble dining room' and an 'elegant drawing room'. These rooms all contained 'rich Derbyshire marble' mantelpieces. The ground floor also contained Chambers' magistrate's room, with a separate entrance from the yard. In the basement of the house were 'capacious vaulted ale, beer and wine cellars'. *John Goodchild Collection*

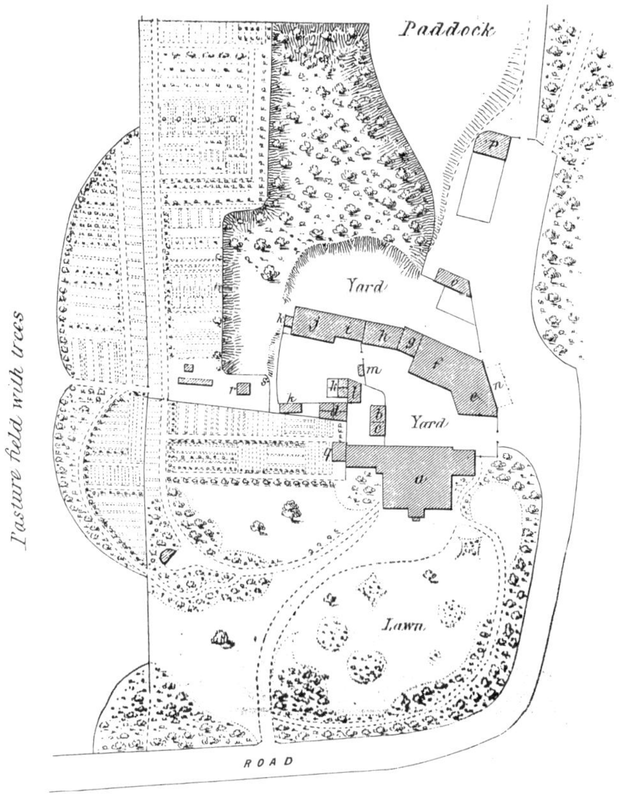

Figure 4. Clough Hall and its grounds. Key: a — mansion; b — dairy; c — larder; d — ash pits & privies; e — tool and fruithouse, cellar under; f — four stall stable and harness room, with hay-loft over; g — carriage house; h — two loose boxes; i — cowhouse for four cows, loft over; j — six stall carthorse stable with loft over; k — piggeries; l — boiling houses; m — stone trough, water laid on; n — wagon shed; o — cart shed; p — shed; q — greenhouse; r — seedhouse; s — liquid manure pump and tank. The outbuildings were screened from the house by well grown shrubs.

The 'pleasure grounds' were described as comprising ... 'the Lawns, tastefully interspersed with beds of rich flowers, shaded and surrounded with borders and clumps of choice shrubs and evergreens, grouped with ornamental trees. On the sloping side Lawn is a semi-circular temple of classic design overshadowed by a venerable yew, and above is the terraced Flower Garden, with its Greenhouse, separated by a wall from the extensive and productive Kitchen Garden, plentifully stocked with standard, espalier and wall-fruit trees of the most noted qualities. In the large Kitchen garden are a seed house, forcing frames, hotbeds, liquid manure pump, &c...'.

Beyond the outbuildings was a deep dell containing a wood. The wood contained a well which supplied the house with spring water. On the west the gardens were bounded by a 'park-like enclosure' of about 12 acres 'shaded with noble Timber Trees in clumps and belts' and on the north by a paddock of about one and a half acres. *John Goodchild Collection* elected a first County Councillor in 1889 — unopposed — for Kimberworth. He was also a trustee of the Sheffield Infirmary, a trustee and the chairman of the Rotherham Hospital, and generally concerned with philanthropic activity in Rotherham and its surrounding communities. Chambers was the chairman of the Rotherham School Board from its establishment in 1875, and his wife opened that Board's first school, at Masbrough Common. He was an active Poor Law Guardian, deriving that office from his magistracy; in politics he was a Tory. It was he who had to read the Riot Act sentences when there occurred the great West Riding election riot at Rotherham in 1865.

Chambers lived to the patriarchal age of 92 and died in September 1904, but he was still sufficiently active to take the chair at the North Central Waggon Company's meetings in the year of his death.

Chambers was accorded a long and detailed obituary in the *Rotherham Advertiser*, although much of the detail there seems to have been derived from an earlier account in the *Ivanhoe Review*. He had been successful not only as a man of business, but as a local administrator, a well-wisher to his neighbourhood, and a country gentleman — his name appears in that acme of Victorian landed respectability, *Burke's Landed Gentry*, and also in *Walford's County Families*. His interest in matters military locally had again been typical of his class and time: as a junior officer in the Loyal Wath Wood Yeomanry Cavalry, as part of a mounted guard when the Princess Victoria had visited Wentworth Woodhouse, and later as Captain Commanding the two companies of Rotherham Volunteers from 1859. He represented a situation common to many of the newly industrialised towns, and he lived his life fully and — so far as its detail may now be recovered — well.

Sources

The John Goodchild Collection, Wakefield: Chambers family account book and estate sale particulars.
Fred T Larder, 'George Wilton Chambers, JP, DL, Rotherham', *The Ivanhoe Review*, Vol 1, 1898, pp 38-40.
Rotherham Advertiser, 3 September 1904, p 6.
Census returns.
Burke's Landed Gentry, various editions.
Walford's County Families, various editions.

12. THE STIRRINGS IN THORPE HESLEY ON SATURDAY NIGHT

by Stephen Cooper

MANY PEOPLE WILL HAVE SEEN *THE STIRRINGS* at the Crucible Theatre in Sheffield, concerning the outrages perpetrated by William Broadhead's Sawmakers' Union, and the Royal Commission which inquired into those events in 1867.[1] The stirrings in Thorpe Hesley in 1861-2 are less well known than their Sheffield counterparts, but Thorpe did experience its own outrages, though they were connected with the trade of nail- rather than saw-making, nailmaking having been established in Thorpe since at least Tudor times.[2]

On Saturday 21 December 1861 two nailshops in Kirby Lane and Thorpe Street were blown up, by crude bombs made from tin cans and gunpowder. No-one was hurt, but there was considerable damage to property and John Hattersley and Charles Butcher were put out of business.

The background to this was that Hattersley was a foreman employed by a Mr Favell (or Flavell) of Westgate in Rotherham, who was in the horse-nail trade. Favell paid wages which were less than those recommended by the Nailmakers' Union, which had its headquarters

Figure 1. Old nail shop, Thorpe Hesley.

in Belper but had a branch in Thorpe.[3] The Union men had called a strike, which produced a hostile atmosphere in the village. On 19 October 1861 Thomas Jenkinson had been asked by a Union man whether he intended to begin making nails for Favell. Jenkinson had confirmed that he did, once he had 'worked up his common iron'. Despite being told that he had 'better be on strike and have 8s from the box per week', Jenkinson had insisted that he intended to take the chance of work while he had it, to which the reply had been: 'If you do, it will be the worse for you'.

Men from Belper visited Thorpe on more than one occasion, to persuade the 'knobsticks' (or blacklegs)[4] to join the strike. As Butcher explained: 'The Union men wanted us to leave off work because we were working under them in prices'. The Unionists held meetings in local pubs, in particular on 28 October 1861, but the 'knobsticks' refused to attend. Men from Belper and Chesterfield who were present at this meeting were heard to vow that they would 'blow the b—s up'. Later that night, someone placed a can of gunpowder in the chimney of Charles Butcher's workshop, so that it would explode next day when the fire was lit. On this occasion the 'infernal machine' was discovered in time and no damage was done. Hattersley and Butcher still refused to take industrial action; but, as we know, the bombers struck again on the Saturday before Christmas, this time successfully.

The outrages in Thorpe had a different outcome from those in Sheffield. The latter could not be dealt with by the ordinary system of criminal justice, because a code of silence was observed by the Sheffield sawmakers, and no-one would testify. This was not true in Thorpe Hesley, where there were witnesses who were willing to come forward, most notably a courting couple who had been out walking nearby when the bombs went off. Because of this the stirrings in Thorpe became the subject of court proceedings in Rotherham and York, which were fully reported in the *Rotherham Advertiser*.[5]

* * *

Sarah Ann Butcher lived with her father at Thorpe. On the Saturday before Christmas 1861, at about 11 pm, she was in Kirby Lane[6] with her 'sweetheart' William Frost, who was a miner from Wentworth. In the moonlight, she saw three men running away from John Hattersley's nailshop, which exploded shortly afterwards. She recognised these men because they were 'not Thorpers' — she clarified this by saying that 'she did not like their looks, because they were not belonging to Thorpe'!

The police arrested two brothers, Emmanuel Isaac Watson and James Watson, and Joseph Tomlinson. They were nailmakers, living in

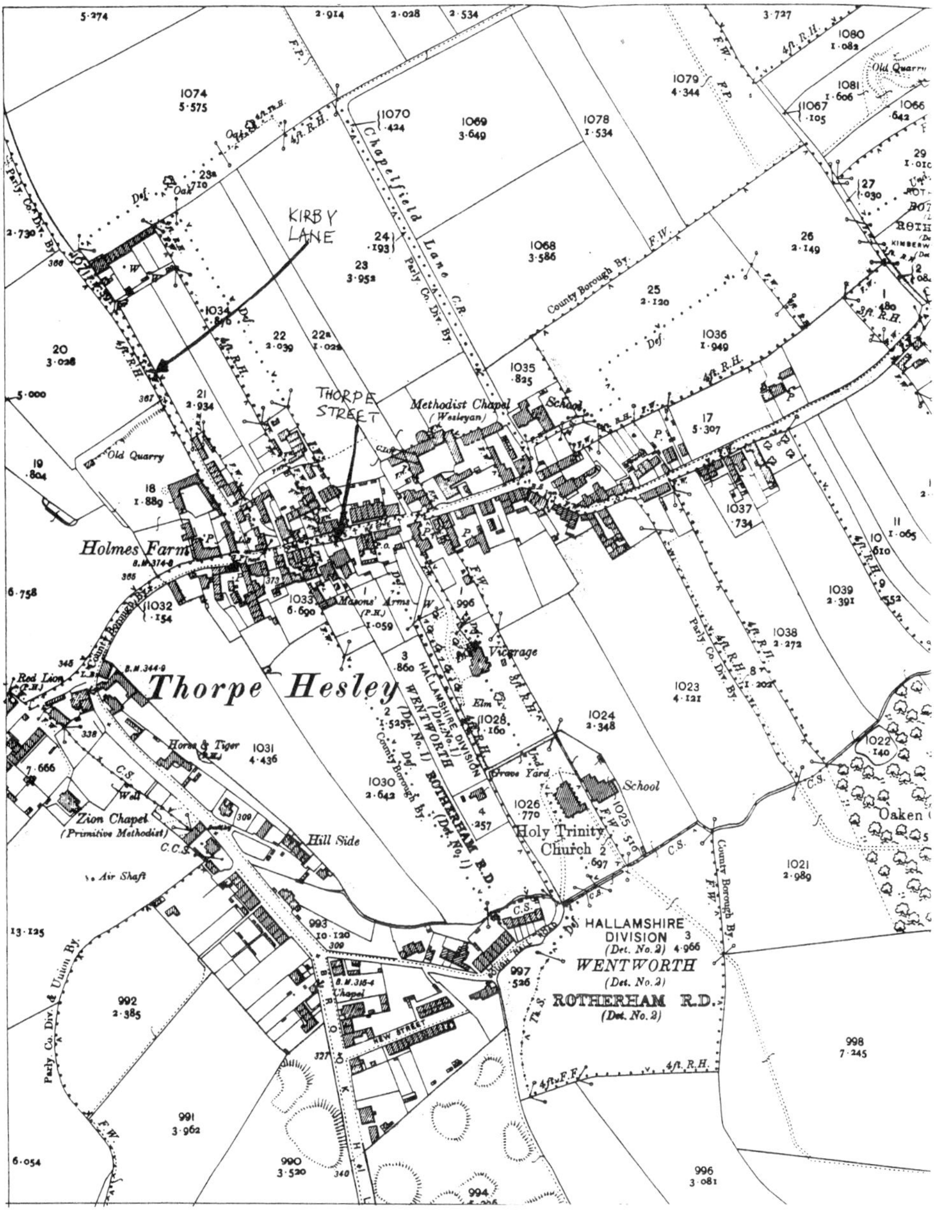

Figure 2. Thorpe Hesley in the late nineteenth century, showing Thorpe Street and Kirby Lane.

Chesterfield and Belper. All three were brought before Rotherham magistrates early in January 1862, charged with an offence under the new Malicious Damage Act of 1861, section ten of which specifically made it an offence to attempt to destroy buildings with gunpowder.

THE ROTHERHAM AND MASB

Police Intelligence.

COURT-HOUSE, ROTHERHAM.

MONDAY.—Before the Rev. H. PARTINGTON, and G. W. CHAMBERS, Esq.

THE TRADE OUTRAGES AT THORPE HESLEY.

EXTRAORDINARY CONFLICTING EVIDENCE.

The hearing of the charge against Emanuel Isaac Watson, Joseph Tomlinson, and James Watson, the two former of Chesterfield and the latter of Belper, was resu... to-day. At the previous hearing, the att... prisoner (Mr. J. G. Walker, of ... or a... respectable

YORK ASSIZES.

(Continued from page 3.)

CROWN COURT.

TUESDAY.—Before Mr. Justice MELLOR.

THE OUTRAGES AT THORPE HESLEY.

JOSEPH TOMLINSON, and ISAAC EMMANUEL WATSON, of Chesterfield, and JAMES WATSON, of Belper, were charged with throwing gunpowder into two shops at Thorpe Hesley, on the night of the 21st December last. Mr. MAULE and Mr. VERNON BLACKBURN (instructed by Mr. Whitfield) prosecuted; Mr. PRICE, Q.C., and Mr. CAMPBELL FOSTER (instructed by Mr. J. G. Walker, of Belper) defended the prisoners.

Mr. Maule stated the case as it was developed in ... following witnesses. ...

Figure 3. Headlines from articles in the *Rotherham Advertiser* of 11 January 1862 (top) and 22 March 1862 (bottom) giving details of the court proceedings.

The enactment of this new legislation shows that bombings such as that in Thorpe had unfortunately become common in the industrial areas of England.

The accused were represented by a solicitor from Belper. Several people from Thorpe gave evidence for the prosecution, including the Butchers and the Hattersleys, Joseph Allott (a beerhouse keeper), Thomas Jenkinson the nailer, and Police Constable Strange, who had been on duty on the night of the crime. He said that he had met the Watsons on the road near Thorpe Common before the explosions had taken place, and asked them who they were. James Watson had replied that he was from Wales and had begun to talk in a language which Strange took to be Welsh, though (like most Englishmen) he could not understand it.

A certain amount of forensic evidence was given. PC Strange testified that when the ruins of Butcher's shop in Thorpe Street were searched, Matthew Waller found a piece of tin, which Superintendant Gillett was able to match with fragments of metal found in the accuseds' premises in Chesterfield. Strange explained to the court that Gillett 'put the two pieces of tin on an iron mould and flattened the surface with a hammer', before comparing them. He was cross-examined about this dubious procedure as follows:

Defence Solicitor: '*And if they did not fit he hammered them again?*'

PC Strange: '*Yes*' [Laughter in court].

Solicitor: '*He hammered it until it did fit?*'

Strange: '*Yes*' [More laughter].

This line of questioning seems reasonable enough, but it was greatly resented by Superintendant Gillett. When the defence solicitor criticized the procedures employed by the local police in his final speech to the court, Gillett called out:

'*It only shows his ignorance of the criminal law*'

to which the solicitor replied:

'*I shall take the insult and pocket it; but it will not prevent me from doing my duty to my clients.*'

The Rotherham magistrates were not impressed by this advocate's eloquence, nor by the alibi produced by his clients. At one point the chairman of the bench inquired rhetorically:

'*Do you take us all for Irishmen?*'

All three defendants were committed to stand trial at York Assizes.[7]

* * *

According to the *Rotherham Advertiser*, the three accused appeared in court in York on Monday 10 March 1862. They brought seventeen witnesses with them but the case had to be adjourned because the chief prosecution witness from Thorpe, Sarah Anne Frost née Butcher, had gone into labour that morning. Sarah gave birth the following day and the trial resumed a week later, the witness being allowed to remain seated while she gave her evidence.

The trial lasted two days. It was a serious case and the accused were represented by a Queen's Counsel. The evidence given before the magistrates was repeated but there were several additional witnesses for the defence, some of them from Thorpe Hesley or nearby Scholes: Mary Anne Senior (wife of a publican on Thorpe Common), Jonathan Burgoyne and Charles Moxon (miners), Benjamin Burgoyne (an ironstone miner who lived only 150 yards from Hattersley's exploded nailshop), John Fieldsend and John Evans, and William Wood (a collier from Scholes). So the trial was not simply *'Thorpe v Belper'*.

Superintendent Gillett gave evidence, referring to his altercation with the defence solicitor in Rotherham in January. The judge stopped him, pointing out that this had nothing to do with the case. Gillett was also accused of having 'lectured four or five jurymen upon this case at Gray's Hotel', but he denied this.

At least one of the accused had a strong alibi. Emma Smith of Belper said that on the night in question she had seen James Watson at the top of Belper market at ten past ten, when Watson had asked her where her husband was. She was sure of this, because she had just gone out to 'hunt' for her husband, who was out drinking. Watson had also asked her who had won the toss for a race which was to be run the following Monday.

Doubt was also cast on the value of the forensic evidence; and at one point there was some discussion amongst the lawyers as to whether the case against Tomlinson was even strong enough to be put to the jury. The judge's summing up was very favourable to the defence: he pointed out, with regard to Sarah Frost's evidence, that there was no gas-light in Kirby Lane, so that she might be mistaken in her identification. According to the newspaper report, it was generally expected that the verdict would be 'Not Guilty'.

The jury was out for only forty minutes and returned to find all three prisoners guilty. The judge then sentenced each of them to the maximum penalty prescribed for the offence — fourteen years' penal servitude! The *Advertiser* reported that: 'The prisoners, who were confident of an acquittal seemed to be completely overwhelmed by the result of the trial and sentence.'[8]

So ended the stirrings in Thorpe. One is left to wonder about the verdict. Someone undoubtedly blew up John Hattersley's and Charles

Butcher's nailshops on Saturday 21 December 1861; but was it the three men who were convicted and sentenced for the crime?

Notes and References

1. JP Bean, *Crime in Sheffield*, Sheffield City Libraries, 1987, pp 57-61.
2. For a nailer in Thorpe in 1589 see T Walter Hall, *A Descriptive Catalogue of Charters relating to Sheffield and Rotherham*, J.W.Northend, Sheffield, 1916, p 223.. See also David Hey, *The Rural Metalworkers of the Sheffield Region*, Leicester University Press, Department of English Local History Occasional Papers, second Series, Number 5, 1972. When Joseph Hunter described Thorpe Hesley in 1831, he wrote: 'Here is a populous village inhabited for the most part by nailers and agriculturists'. For the last nailmakers see JR Chesman, *Thorpe Hesley, Its Past, Present and Future*, Hope Methodist Church, Thorpe Hesley, 1987, p 38.
3. Men from Thorpe Hesley played a leading role in establishing a Horse-Nail Makers' Union in 1822, Rule 28 of which provided 'That these Societies do recommend to all who have joined the Union, a strict adherence to its laws, at the same time to discountenance such, who, from motives far from laudable, stand aloof, and will not join in a cause absolutely necessary to save the trade from inevitable ruin': David Hey, *The Village of Ecclesfield*, The Advertiser Press Ltd, Huddersfield, 1968, pp 55-60 and p 119. I do not know if there was continuity between this Union and the one which is referred to in the present article; but the spirit of Rule 28 certainly seems to have survived.
4. A knobstick is a stick, cane or club, with a rounded knob for its head; or a blackleg: *Oxford English Dictionary*. Churchwardens carried knobsticks as a badge of office: WE Tate, *The Parish Chest*, Phillimore, 1983, p 216, p 316.
5. *Rotherham Advertiser*, 28/12/1861, 4/1/1862, 11/1/1862, 22/3/1862.
6. Kirby Lane is now known as Barnsley Road. Before the enclosures in the early nineteenth century, it was known as West Field Road: see Kimberworth Enclosure Award 1796, Kimberworth and Wentworth Enclosure Act 1814 and the awards which followed; Sheffield City Libraries, Newman and Bond Collection 382 W5, 62, 482.
7. In the nineteenth century a person accused of a serious criminal offence appeared before the magistrates and was then committed for trial at the Assizes or else at Quarter Sessions. Both were abolished when the Crown Courts were created by the Courts Act 1971.
8. Penal servitude — imprisonment coupled with an obligation to do unpaid work such as breaking rocks or work in the Royal dockyards — had been enshrined in English law for the first time in 1853: Clive Emsley, *Crime and Society in England 1750-1900*, Longman, 1987, p 229.

13. COAL IN THE VALLEY: COAL MINING IN THE DEARNE VALLEY AT WATH

by Alex Fleming

THREE COLLIERIES DOMINATED THIS PART of the Dearne Valley during the century which witnessed the supremacy of 'King Coal' in South Yorkshire; they were Manvers, Wath and Cortonwood. They came into production during the 1870s and by the end of the 1980s all had closed down. Together they provide a massive seam of historical material, not least, of course, the dramatic final chapter, but our story begins long before they were dreamt of.

Coale pitts and gyns

For the very earliest years 'Coal in the Valley' is misleading, because the first workings exploited outcrops of coal on the hillside. Trenches or quarries were dug along the outcrops, until deeper workings in the form of bell-pits were necessary. Among the local outcrops exploited from those times were the Newhill, Wath Wood, Swinton Pottery and Abdy seams. Indeed, workings in the Newhill seam at Wath Colliery were not abandoned until 1986.

The first documentary reference to coal being worked locally is an entry in Wath parish register:

> *1606 Septebr. Buried Jo: Beamonte kyld in Abdy Colepitt*

Although there is no indication of the circumstances of his death, the dangers of coal mining are made a little clearer by another burial recorded in the register:

> *1616 Jan. Thomas Dickinson who dyed (as yt pleased God) by the dampe of a coale pitt*

Here we have, probably, a reference to 'choke damp', suffocation by carbon dioxide gas. This gas is typical of shallow workings and such problems of ventilation were referred to in mining literature as early as the 1550s:

> *We also have in the northern parts of Britain certain coal pits, the unwholesome vapour whereof is so pernicious to the hired labourers that it would immediately destroy them, if they did not get out of the way as soon as the flame of their lamps becomes blue...*[1]

The tragedy of Joseph Beamonte serves to focus attention on an important area of coal mining at Wath in the earliest period for which we have records. There was much mining activity near Abdy in the early eighteenth century, particularly in and around Wath Wood. Coal mining leases dating from 1715 mention 'Wath Common' and 'Wath Wood Bottom' (Figure 1). We also have an inventory of the property

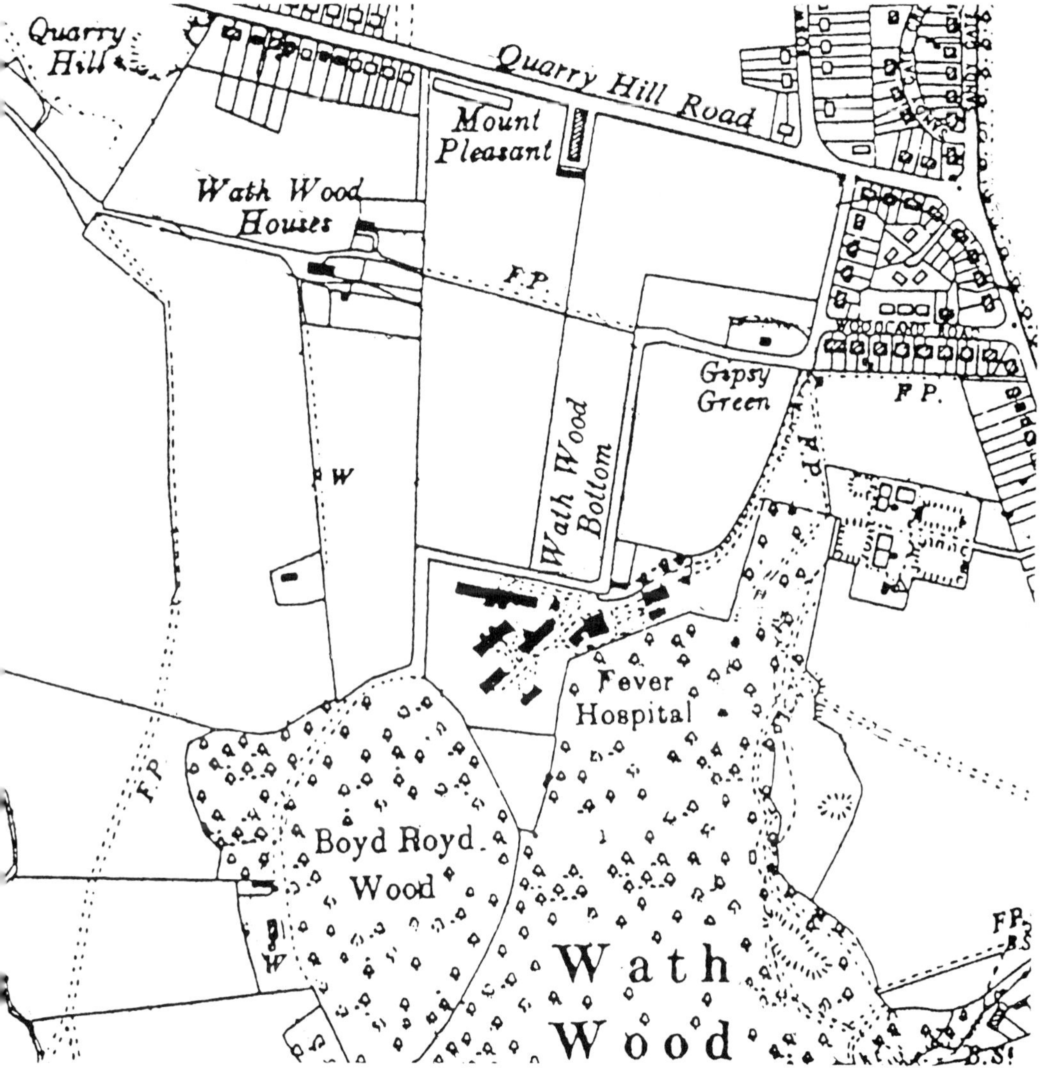

Figure 1. Wath Wood and Wath Wood Bottom, the scene of small-scale mining for coal in the eighteenth and nineteenth centuries.

of William Wharam of Abdy, who died in October 1723. The list of his goods refers to

Wood on ye Coal pitt hill Sturstakes Corves Gyn & Bricks...[2]

Such equipment points to the existence of a mine deep enough to need winding gear and containers for transporting the coal. 'Gyn' is an abbreviation of engine, indicating a simple winding wheel. 'Corves' were baskets or tubs for moving the coal.

By the early eighteenth century the old method of digging a trench or quarry along an outcrop had disappeared and even working by bell-pits would have been insufficient to meet demand. Consequently, the sinking of relatively shallow shafts was becoming common. Such was the demand for coal as fuel by potters, brewers, nail makers, lime burners and domestic users that it was worthwhile to go to the expense of sinking and equipping a mine shaft. By combining information from leases and documents relating to coal working at Wath Wood Bottom, Wath Common and Swinton Common during the period 1715 to 1725, the operation of a typical, small colliery at Wath in the early eighteenth century can be reconstructed.

Robert Cutts, William Newbolt of Swinton, John Holland and his son John from Newhill, leased land at Wath Wood Bottom for the purpose of sinking pits to get coal. For the privilege they paid £20 a year, plus delivery of about twenty tons of coal annually, to the lords of the manor, Wentworth and Tolson. Working only one pit at a time, taking great care not to mine within fifty yards of Boyd Royd Wood or be fined £50, they would sink a shaft eleven to eighteen yards deep and support the sides with timber. It would cost them 10d a yard to sink and timber each shaft.[3]

A sough would drain the pit, with Richard Axe being paid 6d a day for drainage work. In the pit three men would 'get' the coal while three boys 'hurried' the coal to the pit bottom by carrying or pushing greased corves. One man would wind the coal to the surface, possibly using a simple horse gin. Haulage ropes would have cost 16 shillings for two. On the surface coal would be taken by barrow to the bank, ready for sale. Surrounding the top of the shaft would be a low stone wall, and in bad weather the top might be covered by a rough shelter of straw thatch called a 'fleake'.[4]

When a pit was exhausted it was filled in carefully so that, '...the ground to be so as it was when they began to sink pitts there.' Filling a disused pit would cost three shillings to eight shillings and was essential if they were not to be in breach of their lease. During 1720 fourteen pits were filled in and during 1724 '...in getting 144 loads of coal (c 150 tons) four new pits were sunk.'[5] One such pit worked near Wath

Wood Bottom revealed itself dramatically in October 1965. A shaft seventy feet deep and seven feet wide was discovered under the kitchen floor of No 1 Wath Wood, marked on the map as Wath Wood Houses. The NCB poured 250 tons of red shale into the shaft and topped it off with concrete.

Of the men working the pits some were not always the most reliable of people. For example, one of them was John Parratt and he was described as 'A sad fellow', who 'did nothing but drink and spend money'. He went missing and was tracked down to an ale house in Swinton where he had been for several days!

In 1725 there was also a working colliery at West Melton, but it was not an important centre of coal production and little is known beyond the bare fact that coal was worked intermittently and on a small scale.[6] From 1745 a small mine called 'Wath Wood Colliery' was worked in conjunction with Edward Butler's 'Tile and Pot works', later famous as the Rockingham Pottery. Supplying fuel for firing the kilns, the colliery operated until 1806 when a meeting resolved:

> *That no more coal be got at Wath Wood Colliery and the pits be railed round...That all the engines and everything belonging to us be removed from the Colliery to the pottery premises.*[7]

These small and somewhat scattered mines were restricted in their development because of high transport costs. The price of coal doubled with every mile it was carried from the mine and so the major obstacle to the development of the South Yorkshire reserves, until the late eighteenth century, was the absence of an adequate transport network. Coal owners were anxious to improve transportation so as to reap the benefits of selling in a wider market. Consequently, they gave enthusiastic support to the development of the Dearne and Dove Canal, sanctioned by Act of Parliament in 1793. The Act expressly stated that the object of the canal was to: '...open an easy communication between several valuable coal mines and the towns of Rotherham and Sheffield and the port of Hull...'[8]

Partly opened in 1797, the canal was completed in 1804 and although it had the desired effect of making coal cheaper the reduction was small. For example, it sold in Sheffield at 8s 6d per ton. Wath became an important shipping point, collecting coal from Brampton and West Melton as well as from its own workings. During the second half of 1801 Wath sent 759 tons down the canal, though in the same period Elsecar sent 10,000 tons![9]

A much greater blessing to the industry was the expansion of the railway network during the 1840s. Giving easy access to national markets, railways made it profitable to undergo the expense of sinking deep shafts to the rich Barnsley seam. The first railway line through Wath was the North Midland in July 1840 (linking Derby and Leeds). Next came the South Yorkshire Railway, opened to coal traffic on 1 February 1849, really it was part of the MSL (Manchester, Sheffield and Lincolnshire). At first these lines would have served the Newhill, West Melton and Brampton collieries and a closer look at such mid-nineteenth century workings provides an insight into the problems of mineral rights and of colliery identity.

The workings at West Melton have had a variety of names, all relating to the same place: Cottage of Content Colliery, Ashcroft Pits, Melton Field Colliery, and Ashcroft New Pit. At least from 1851 the Wath Wood (Meltonfield) seam was worked, until abandonment finally came in May 1928 under the title 'Ashcroft Pit'. In 1864 George Law was the owner and he proved less than honest towards the George Ellis Trust which owned coal adjacent to his land. Law's workings had entered the Wath Wood seam belonging to the Ellis Trust and the Trust took action against him. On the 27 May 1864, Henry Briggs of Brampton wrote to Charles Newman, solicitor to the Trust:

> *In reply to yours of yesterday respecting the Price of West Field Coal. The Lund Hill Co. are paying me £130 per acre and I think Mr. Carnley asked Law the same price for his, but I am not aware they have yet made a bargain.*
>
> *I never heard of more than the above price being paid and he deserves to pay the highest rate, or even more for having stolen it.*
>
> *Yours truly,*
> *Henry Briggs.*

On the 1 July, 1864, Law signed a lease with the Ellis Trustees normalising his affairs.[10]

Newhill Colliery, whose letterhead is shown in Figure 2, was the pit

NEWHILL COLLIERY,
Near Wath-upon-Dearne, Dec 30th 1876
Mr Smith West Melton
To the Newhill Coal Company

Figure 2. Letterhead of Newhill Colliery.

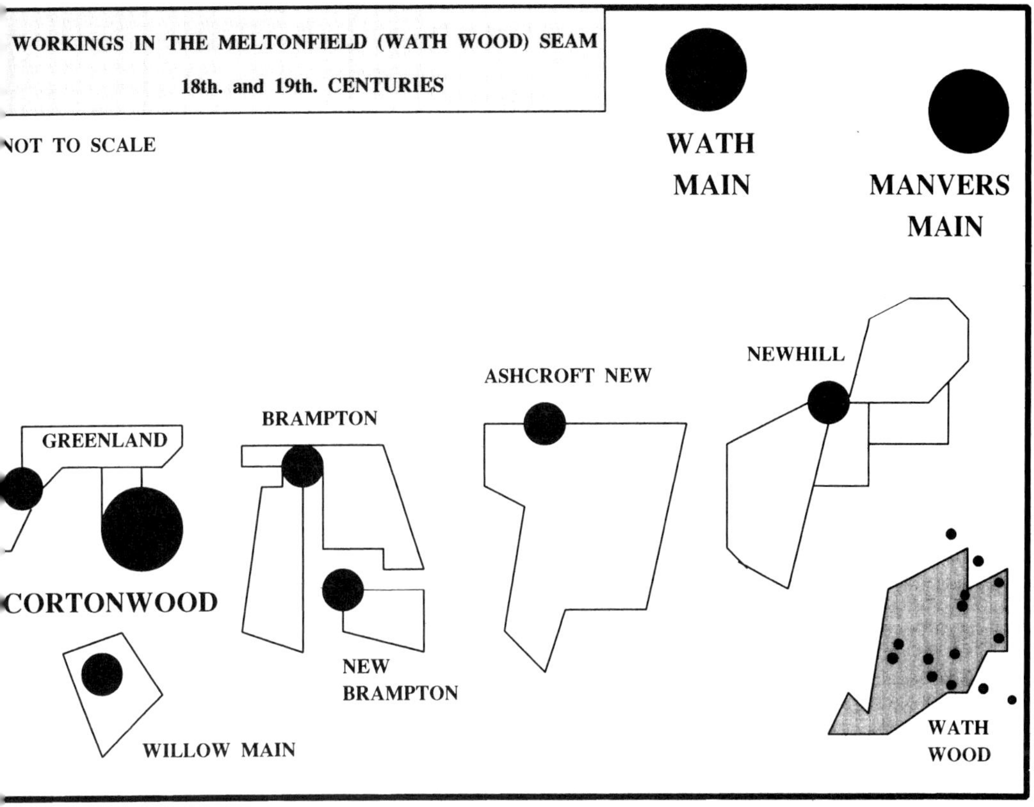

Figure 3. Workings in the Meltonfield (Wath Wood) seam in the eighteenth and nineteenth centuries.

closest to the centre of Wath and was sunk during the autumn of 1866. In 1873 George Pearson Nicholson, solicitor in Wath, leased land to the Newhill Coal Company for working the Wath Wood seam, at £120 per acre per annum. That same year there was a fatal winding accident at the pit, which drew a stinging report from the inspector of mines for the district, Frank Wardell. He lived in Wath and his name appears in several inquiries into accidents at pits in the Barnsley area. Development of the colliery continued so that in August 1877 negotiations were completed for the working of a new shaft to the Meltonfield seam (Figure 3). Reorganisation took place a few months later when the Newhill and Melton Main Coal Company was formed with a capital of £30,000. Three of the directors were from Wath:

Charles Adams	corn miller
James Bamford	fellmonger
George Willis	colliery manager[11]

Ten years later, as the Milton Colliery, all workings were abandoned on 12 August 1887. The key to its failure was that it was too small an enterprise, lacking the capital to sink deeper shafts to the more valuable seams.

The lure of the Barnsley Bed

Land owners had long been aware of the riches beneath their feet and the prospect of exploiting an 8 feet thick seam of coal was an overwhelming temptation. The lure of the Barnsley Bed was quite irresistible. Consequently, Earl Manvers commissioned a report on his estate at Adwick, where he was lord of the manor. His family had acquired the land early in the seventeenth century, but the family seat remained Thoresby Hall, near Ollerton in Nottinghamshire. Reporting to the Earl on 7 August, 1865, Ben Sellars observed:

The Estate comprises near 1050 acres of land, the whole containing mines (seams) of Coal...compact and well adapted for the site of a colliery...its position with regard to facilities of conveyance by rail and water is in every way convenient and advantageous.

The 'Barnsley Main' Coal, the mine (seam) of greatest importance in the district, underlies the whole of this property, at depths of 350 yards...

The thickness of the Barnsley Coal in this Estate is not at present known — at smaller depths it is usually 8 feet...and is easily and cheaply wrought; the area and position of this coal for working, would render a colliery judiciously planted, and properly carried on, capable of producing a very large quantity annually...[12]

In November 1867 the third Earl Manvers (Sydney William Herbert Pierrpont) wrote to the developers of the colliery: 'I have no objection to the proposed name of the Manvers Main Coal Company at all, and shall be very glad whenever there is anything really doing to go & inspect the works.'[13]

Thus, Manvers Main Colliery came into being (Figure 4). It was the first of the three 'main' collieries which were to dominate the Dearne Valley at Wath for more than a century (Figure 5). When sinking began in 1868 the scale of its operations opened a new chapter in the story of local mines. Consequently, when the third Earl died at Thoresby

Figure 4. Manvers Main Colliery and the Dearne and Dove Canal, looking east, c 1920. Number 2 shaft is on the left and number 4 shaft is in the centre. *British Coal*

Park in January 1900, aged seventy-five, Manvers Main had easily fulfilled the expectations so clearly set out in the Barnsley Chronicle in December 1869:

> *...a very large plant is being formed between Wath and Mexbro', at what will hereafter be known as the New Manvers Main Colliery... The Colliery, when opened out, will rank amongst the largest in South Yorkshire... the company has leased about 2,000 acres of coal... Two beautiful shafts, 13ft. in diameter, are being sunk. Although the sinking operations have not been going on for more than eighteen months — being commenced in May, 1868 — one of the shafts has been sunk to a depth of over 200 yards, and the other has been prosecuted to a distance of 175 yards. Both the shafts have...metal 'tubbing' for a distance of fifty yards, in addition... the shafts have been bricked inside the metal...each block (of tubbing) measures little more than a yard square yet weighs 3 cwt. The casting of this immense quantity*

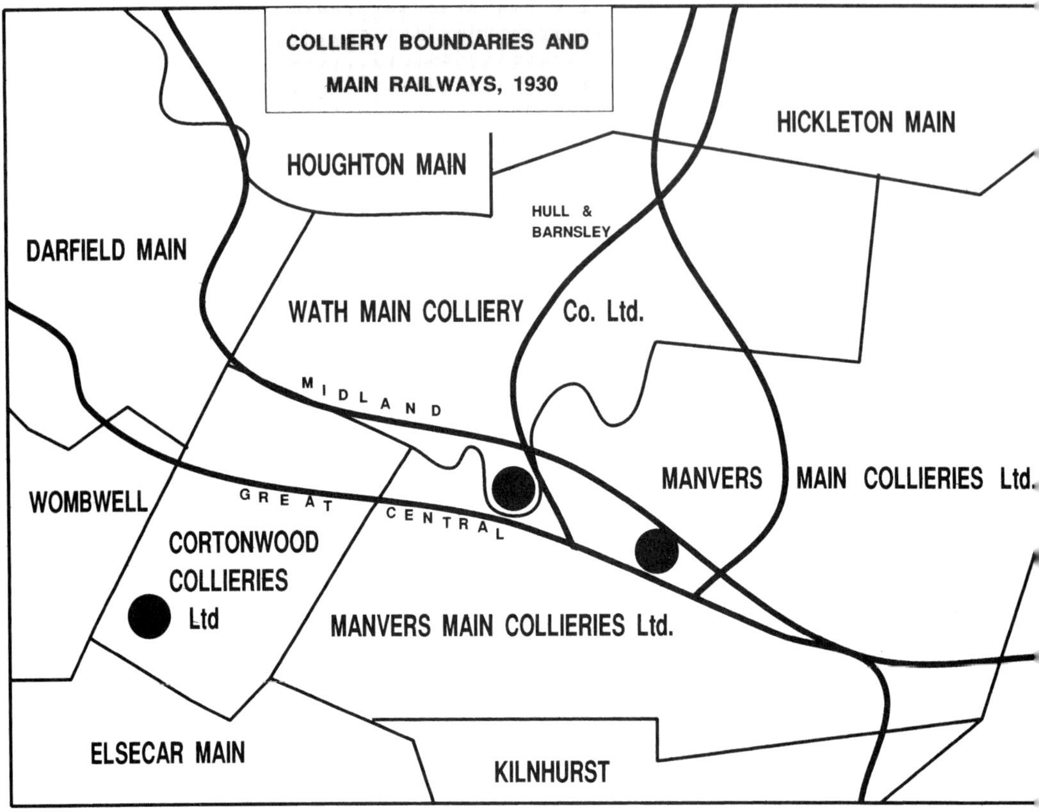

Figure 5. Boundaries of colliery workings in the Dearne valley and main railways, c 1930.

of metal has been entrusted to a Sheffield firm, and has been conveyed by water. The rest of the shafts are bricked and made water tight.

At Manvers Main four shafts were sunk eventually. Shafts one and four were in the south-eastern part of the colliery, while two and three were in the north-western part. Sinking began in 1868 to the Barnsley seam at shafts 1, 2 and 3. Sometime during the very early period a furnace shaft for ventilation was sunk to the Barnsley seam near number 1 shaft and subsequently filled in. Number 1 shaft itself was capped in 1955. Figure 6 shows the headgear of this shaft in 1912 with the underground officials in the foreground. Shaft number 2 was deepened to the Swallow Wood seam in 1942 where production finally ceased in March 1988. This was the last face worked at the Manvers Complex and its ending constituted abandonment of the mine. Meanwhile, number 3 shaft had reached the Parkgate seam in 1895 and the Silkstone seam in 1951. Number 4 shaft was sunk to the Parkgate seam during 1899-91, being deepened to the Silkstone level during 1953-54.

Cortonwood came into existence in 1872 with the foundation of the Cortonwood Colliery Company, specifically to exploit the Barnsley seam. Charles Bartholomew, Samuel Roberts and Robert Baxter of Wombwell Colliery joined forces with six others e.g. :

Henry Davis Pochin	Manufacturing chemist, Bodnant Hall, Denbighshire.
Benjamin Whitworth	Merchant, Holland Park, London
John Devonshire Ellis	Steel manufacturer, Sheffield.
James Holden	Merchant, Wilmslow Cheshire.

Their deed of partnership is dated 12 July 1872, with the original intent of calling the venture the Brampton Colliery Company.

Some details of the financial costs involved can be obtained from leases brought to the new company by the partners. Bartholomew, Roberts and Baxter had paid a total of £13,985 to the Earls Fitzwilliam and Wharncliffe for five leases, dated between 1854 and June 1872. In

Figure 6. Manvers Main, 1912. Background: number 1 shaft; foreground: underground officials. *Tom Nelson*

the memorandum and articles of association for the Cortonwood Collieries Company Limited, dated 20 March, 1879, the capital of the company was set at £250,000. That capital was formed of 12,500 shares of £20. Each partner held 100 shares each, totalling £2,000 per person and comprising 5.6% of total capital.[14]

To put such sums of money into perspective it is useful to note that in evidence about wages given to a Parliamentary Select Committee on Coal in 1873, it was stated that hewers earned nearly 9 shillings a day at thick seam collieries, but only 5 shillings a day at thin seam collieries.[15]

Development of the colliery began in 1873, when two shafts were sunk to work the Barnsley seam lying at 213 yards. Number 1 shaft (downcast) was twenty feet in diameter, with number 2 shaft (upcast) being fifteen feet. Barnsley coal was wound up number 1 shaft until the seam was exhausted in 1921. During sinking cast-iron tubbing was installed in both shafts to eighty-five yards, for protection against possible water from old workings in the Meltonfield seam near the shafts. The remainder of the shafts were then bricked. The old workings belonged to Greenlands Pit, Brampton Pit and Willow Main Colliery.

In 1907-8 both shafts were deepened for working the Parkgate seam at 481 yards. This coal was wound up number 2 shaft until the seam was exhausted in 1941. Beginning in 1917 the Haigh Moor seam was worked. Correctly re-named Swallow Wood in 1971, it was last worked on 18 April 1975. During 1925-27 number 1 shaft was deepened even further, to its limit of 606 yards in the Silkstone seam. The coal was transported via a drift to the Parkgate level and wound up number 2 shaft. Modernisation of winding equipment in 1934 and 1961 led to Silkstone coal being transferred from one shaft to another. When the Silkstone seam ceased production on 25 October, 1985, it was number 1 shaft which was being used.

Wath Colliery's two shafts were being sunk to the Barnsley bed in 1876, though such operations probably began in 1873. When Barnsley coal was reached at 346 yards the seam was a very profitable 8 feet 6 inches thick. The colliery did not swing into production properly until 1879 and some idea of its relative size may be gauged from the records of the West Riding Miners' Permanent Relief Fund. Wath Main does not figure until 1881, when the following numbers are recorded:

Manvers	1080 members
Cortonwood	114 members
Wath	76 members[16]

Of course not all miners belonged to the Relief Fund, but the contrast in size of operation between the three pits is clear. A further illustration of differences between local collieries is provided by these figures:

PRODUCTION JANUARY — SEPTEMBER 1900

Manvers Main	94,768 tons
Wath Main	52,896 tons
Wombwell Main	44,504 tons
Cortonwood	37,904 tons
Mitchell Main	13,128 tons

Shaft deepening to the Parkgate seam took place during 1912-15, with a final extension to the Silkstone seam in 1923 (see Figure 7). That seam, however, was never exploited. Development was scarcely halted by the Great War, in fact Doncaster Races caused more disruption to

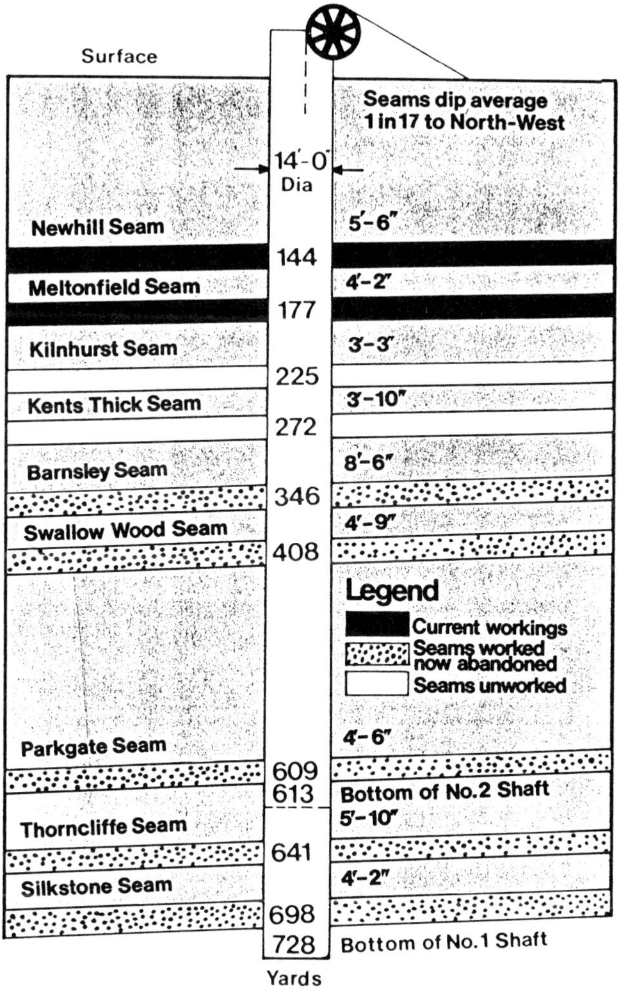

Figure 7. Section through the workings at Wath Colliery, c 1976. *British Coal*

production! In September 1914 the general manager complained that during race week lost production totalled 3,000 tons of coal.

During the early days of sinking shafts flooding was a problem and in certain seams it remained so. As late as 1980 water from the Oaks Rock was pouring into the Newhill and Meltonfield seams. Such was the flow that each year nearly six tons of water were pumped for every ton of coal mined. Productive years of the seams are summarised as follows:

Barnsley	8ft. 6in.	1879-1944
Swallow Wood	4ft. 6in.	1896-1954
Parkgate	4ft. 7in.	1915-1952
Meltonfield	4ft.	1929-1977
Newhill	6ft.	1962-1986
Silkstone	4ft. 2in.	Not Worked

Such a decline in fortunes was reflected in name changes. From the beginning the pit was known as Wath Main Colliery. After 28 March 1977 it was simply Wath Colliery until 1 January 1986 when it became the anonymous Manvers Complex West.

Getting coal

When these mines began operating the method of getting coal was by pick and shovel. As colliers hacked coal from the seams, in short-face workings about eight yards long, their trammers filled it into corves (tubs holding half a ton) which were pushed into the roadways to a passbye. There they left the full tubs and took empty tubs back onto the face. Ponies pulled loaded tubs to another passbye on a main roadway, then the tubs were dragged by rope haulage to the pit bottom, for winding up the shaft. At Manvers the Barnsley seam was worked out in this way and the same method was used in the Parkgate seam. Consequently, at one period there were over 100 ponies working underground.

A clear account of pony-life underground is given in this extract from an interview with Charlie Taylor, who began his working life at Wath Main in 1921 when he was fourteen. He was interviewed by the author in 1981.

> *It was all collar work for the pony and he wasn't allowed to walk when pulling two tubs of coal. He had to get moving fast and run all the way back for the next two tubs, a distance of three to four hundred yards. There was hardly a pause, it was slog, slog, slog all the time for a whole shift. At the end of the day shift the ponies were taken to the water tub for a drink, then tied to their feed boxes near the workings.*

When the afternoon shift came on it was another shift of slogging for the ponies.

I've seen ponies with sore chines (backbone) caused by scraping along the low roof in various places. I've seen ponies having to work with sore shoulders caused by particles of shale getting between their shoulders and the collar of the harness.

Some of their names were Blazer, Badger, Ben, Blucher, Damper, Digger, Joss, Scorcher, Skipper and Tim.

Many years passed before there was any significant mechanisation of coal getting at the actual face. At Manvers when the Meltonfield seam was opened in 1925 cutting machines and conveyors were introduced and this system eventually became the standard way of mining coal. Mechanisation of coal faces at Wath began about 1930 with the introduction of Siskol coal cutters, again opening up the Meltonfield seam. Earlier signs of a new technology include the recommendation by the directors of Wath Main in December 1909 that electrical power be adopted for haulage, at an estimated cost of £5,700. One illustration of the results of increased mechanisation is provided by the figures for output per man shift at Wath:

1939	*28.23 cwts*	
1945	*24.15 cwts*	
1964	*98.5 cwts (face)*	*overall 34.4 cwts*
1978-79	*220.4 cwts (face)*	*overall 48.6 cwts*

The price of coal

What of the people during this century of colliery development? From the very beginning there were the all too familiar accidents. At Manvers, for example, two of the sinkers were killed at Christmas 1869. In August 1877 Henry Burtoft of Wath was almost blinded by bursting coal, Edward Hartwell of Newhill was severely crushed between two corves and Michael Walker of Swinton injured his spine and hand when there was a roof fall. Between 1868 and 1893 there were fifty-six fatalities at Manvers, but only eight at Wath.[17] Given the size of the Manvers operation and a correspondingly high fatality rate it was natural that the joiners' shop had a macabre sideline, making coffins. In 1903 it was W Astley who made them for those killed at the pit. The coffin was supplied free to the victim's family.

The first fatality at Wath Colliery was in 1879, when William Watson was crushed by corves. His tragedy could have only emphasised the need for friendly society benefits. Not all men belonged to the Miners' Relief Fund, but there were several similar groups in Wath such as the

Druids and the Oddfellows. Men from Newhill could well have belonged to the Beehive Sick and Dividing Society, formed in 1883. Based at the Beehive Inn at Newhill, membership was restricted to those between sixteen and forty-five and the subscription was a shilling a fortnight.

One way in which employers attempted to reduce accidents was to enforce severe penalties for misconduct. On 24 August 1877 William Long and William Mitchell, colliers at Manvers Main, appeared before Rotherham Police Court for neglecting to set a sufficient number of spraggs in the workings of the colliery. They were working in a bank twenty yards long. Eight yards had been 'holed out' and no spraggs had been set. When questioned by Mr Robson, the underviewer, they said they were sorry the place had been found in such a state and hoped nothing would be said about it. Both were fined 10s and costs. In 1897 Manvers Main prosecuted a 'bye-workman' for having a pipe in his possession and he was fined 5s with 10s-6d costs. At the same time they prosecuted a 'driver' for riding on tubs; he was fined 10s with 11s-3d costs.

Punitive action could not, however, overcome completely the inherent dangers of working the deepest coal and none of the three collieries escaped the tragic consequences. A comparatively safe pit, Wath Main's worst disaster happened on 24 February 1930. An explosion of 'fire damp' in the Barnsley seam, two miles from the pit bottom, killed seven men. John Poole was in charge of the Wath Rescue Station and we can scarcely imagine his anguish on finding the body of his son, Algernon. The victims were:

John Algernon Poole	21	Wath
Herbert Allott	27	Wath
Ernest Cusworth	31	West Melton
John Dyson	37	West Melton
John Russell	42	Bolton
Leonard Unwin	46	Mexborough
Thomas King	55	Mexborough

Poole, Cusworth and King died in the explosion. Allott, Dyson, Russell and Unwin were brought out alive, but died at Mexborough hospital.

Valuable though its coal was, the Silkstone seam was notorious for its methane gas discharges and at Cortonwood the miners paid with their lives. In 1932 a roof fall in the seam led to a build up of gas which exploded when the face was being reopened. Six men were killed and three injured. An outburst of methane gas in the same seam on 19 June 1961, following a roof fall, affected seven miners. The gas killed four of the men and there began an epic of self-rescue which led to Granville

Mason of Brampton being awarded the George Medal. Fatalities in that tragedy were:

Robert Arnott	35	Elsecar
John Kellett	38	Barnsley
John Holmes	46	Brampton
Albert Bailey	50	Brampton

Manvers Main suffered disaster when a severe gas explosion killed five men on 4 March 1945, but it was not always the men underground who were at risk. For example, there was an horrific accident at Manvers in 1955 in the winder house of Number 3 shaft. On 13 September a winding rope slipped and trapped three men by their legs against the winding drum. Dr Kevin Maher from Wath and Dr Iain Campbell from Swinton were called to the colliery and had to perform emergency amputations to release the men: R Elliott and J E Gilbert, both of Mexborough, and W H Gething of Wath. Within a few days Elliott and Gething had died.

Mercifully, there was a much happier outcome from an incident at Wath Main in July 1960, when a roof fall in the Meltonfield seam trapped three miners. Hugh Outram and George Cooke of Wath, together with Lawrence South of Hoyland were in considerable danger of suffocating until one of their rescuers, Harold Lister, remembered the pipeline to the face carrying a compressed air supply for pneumatic picks. Following instructions shouted to them, the trapped miners used the air supply literally as a life-line. After four hours of digging frantically the three men were released.

Faced with earning a living under desperately difficult conditions it is no surprise that wage rates and terms of employment were never-ending sources of friction for the men and their employers. During the early days, especially with large new mines being sunk and developed, there was great scope for disagreement as to rates for different jobs. A complicating factor was a general trade recession which affected the coal industry badly at the end of the nineteenth century. Figure 8 shows the rates of pay in the Parkgate seam at Cortonwood Colliery in 1911.

A lengthy dispute at Manvers Main in 1878 was eventually resolved by referring it to the arbitration of A J Mundella, M P. His award was not liked by the men, for example 1s 5½d for getting a ton of coal. One of the men commented:

We cannot work on this award for it is impossible to make wages at some of the prices. We are 25% worse off at Manvers Main, than at most other collieries, owing to the manner in which the pit is worked.

Cortonwood Colliery

PARKGATE PRICE LIST

		s.	d.
1	Getting Coal, Bord, Cross, or End, and Tramming eighty yards, free from bat or stone, and setting and drawing timber .. per ton	1	4
	The above price only applies to coal section down to 4ft. 6ins. in thickness, under 4ft. 6ins. to be paid for each 3 inches less in thickness extra per ton	0	1
	Dirt between the top of bat and rock to be propped up if possible, but when taken down and cleared away from the face to be paid for each 2 inches in thickness .. .. per ton	0	0¼
	The average thickness to be taken if it varies in the Bank.		
2	Men working shifts in Banks .. extra per ton	0	0½
3	Heading—End worked up to 1 in 3 off bord, per yd.	6	0
	Bord .. .. ,,	4	6
	Dirt between the top of bat and rock filled into tubs to be paid for each inch in thickness per yard	0	1½
	Men working in headings 2 or more shifts extra per yard	0	6

Trammers to work in less than 30 yards of face, except by arrangement between the management and collier in charge.

The above are standard rates and district percentages to be added.

One ton of Home Coals to be allowed free to Colliers and Trammers who are householders each Calendar Month (not including carting).

Colliers and Trammers each to pay for the use of lamps when lighted .. per week 0

For half a week or less .. .. ,, 0

Colliers find all picks, blades and shafts, and to pay for sharpening .. .. per week 0

All work not provided for in this list to be arranged for between the management and workmen.

Failing a settlement a deputation to be arranged to meet the management.

Signed on behalf of the Owners—
J. E. CHAMBERS,

Signed on behalf of the Yorkshire Miners' Association—
JAMES MURRAY,
GEO. HY. HIRST.

Signed on behalf of the Workmen—
THOMAS ABBOTT,
JOHN SAGER,
JOHN WM. HALL,
ARTHUR PHILLIPS,
LUKE ROYSTON,
WILLIAM COPLEY.

December 4th, 1911.

Figure 8. Rates of pay in the Parkgate seam at Cortonwood Colliery, 1911.
Mrs C Porter

Our trammers cannot get the coal away, the pass byes are so crowded and we have to lie idle. If things were differently managed a trammer could fill three corves where he now fills two.

Another miner said that a man and his trammers had only made 4s-3d per day for nearly three weeks. In connection with the award there was a meeting at the *Lord Nelson Inn*, Nash Row, at the end of June 1878. A miners' deputation met the manager of Manvers, Mr Thompson, and it was agreed, 'In future the system would be two gates for every thirty-five yards... two colliers and two trammers in one gate, for fifteen or sixteen yards...'

A similar dispute at Cortonwod was also referred to the arbitration of Mr Mundella. Included in the award was an increase 'For getting coals in the Banks and Straitwork places one farthing per ton.' An ominous sentence, however, prefaced the details of the Cortonwood award: '...subject to any general reduction of prices that may have taken place in the district.' As there was talk already of a 12.5 per cent reduction in pay the prospects were grim, especially as it was noted in the *Mexborough & Swinton Times* in January 1879, '...tradespeople and persons of influence in South Yorkshire are sympathising with the men, believing that they are at present earning a very scanty living'.

In that context this must have seemed heaven sent:

> **Manvers Main Miners' Tea, No. 2 Lodge**
> Monday Feb 10th. 1879
> A Public Tea will be provided in the Congregational School-room Mexboro'
> Tea on the tables at half-past four o'clock.
> The following is a complete list of what the Committee propose to provide:-
> 27 stones of plain bread, spice ditto, seed ditto, buns, tarts & etc,
> 7 hams, 100lbs beef and mutton, 24 tongues, 12lbs tea, 80lbs sugar, celery and other good things.
> Tickets 1s each.

Adequate lighting at the coal face has always been a problem and it was not helped, at first, by the introduction of safety lamps. For example, the Davy Lamp only gave a very poor light. The Stephenson Lamp was brighter, but even it was not as strong as a naked candle flame, though it was certainly safer than a candle! Introduction of new safety lamps at Manvers in December 1877 caused trouble lasting several months. At a meeting of Manvers men in Swinton in April 1878 it was claimed that,

> *...8 Davy lamps were only equal to 1 candle ...no lamp gave as good a light or was as convenient as a candle. A man is not allowed to put his lamp where he liked so as to shed the most light, but had to fix it according to rule.*

Cortonwood was equally strict about rules governing the use of lamps. For example, Benjamin Birchall of Brampton Bierlow was charged at Rotherham Police Court that on 28 January 1878, he infringed the special rule that when a safety lamp became unfit or unsafe, the light must be put out and the lamp taken to the lamp keeper. To do so meant loss of working time and loss of pay, so many men continued to work, as Birchall did with a Stephenson lamp which had a broken wire gauze. He called a witness to prove that the lamp had fallen from a prop, but he was ordered to pay 10s in fines or serve 14 days. A minimum week's wage would be 15s to 20s.

Insistence on correct use of safety lamps gave rise to a curious case involving men at Cortonwood in February 1878. A miner named Lockwood claimed he had been given a safety lamp without any glass in it and did not realise the fault until he reached the coal face. Consequently, the lamp keeper, William Harper of New Wombwell, and the deputy who checked lamps at the pit bottom, John Fish of Brampton Bierlow, were summoned to appear in court at Rotherham. Under questioning Lockwood admitted that his route to the coal face took him against the return air flow. It was pointed out that even if he had carried a Stephenson lamp with a complete glass, '...it would have taken him all his time to prevent it being blown out, and to keep it from being extinguished he would have had to shade it with his hand.' Another important point to emerge was that the colliery had only just resumed work after being idle for several weeks because of a wages dispute. During that dispute Fish, the deputy, had continued working and there was, '...a considerable amount of ill-feeling against him on that account.' The case was dismissed.

For all those miners and their families whose lives hinged on shillings and pence, a fraud in their midst involving thousands of pounds must have been beyond belief, yet there was such a case in 1889. That there was wealth to be had from coal is clear. Thus, the 8 feet 6 inches Barnsley seam was valued at £260 to £300 per acre. So that, for example, the estimated value of Barnsley coal belonging to the Ellis Charity and to be worked by Cortonwood stood at £39,622-13s-4d. in 1880. The value of Earl Fitzwilliam's royalty for the Barnsley seam at Cortonwood was £53,000.[18] Consequently, it is not surprising that some fell prey to temptation. Such was the tragedy of James Crawshaw, secretary of and partner in Wath Main. He manipulated the Wath Colliery accounts to finance personal speculation in the corn trade, taking £9,624-8s-11d. of company money. He lost everything. Unable to face the public disgrace which was inevitable, he committed suicide. On the morning of Thursday 14 February 1889, a platelayer on the Wath Midland line found Mr Crawshaw, '...leaning down on the sleepers. He had not fallen down. Blood was issuing from the right temple. He was quite dead. He had a pistol in his right hand.'

A few years later, in 1893, Wath Main was headline news once again when it suffered the consequences of one of the longest disputes the industry had known. An editorial in the *Mexborough & Swinton Times* of 6 January 1893 predicted a gloomy new year:

> *...during 1892 the influence of the falling off of trade seems to have touched colliery owners ...Hard coal is fully a shilling per ton lower and looks like declining still further.*

As usual the owners' response was to reduce wages and they proposed a massive reduction of 25 per cent. Notice of the pay cut was given to the 700 men and boys of Wath Main on 8 July, with a deadline of 28 July. Since all the Yorkshire miners rejected arbitration there was a lock-out and from 11 August not a ton of coal was drawn in Yorkshire. On Wednesday 6 September several hundred miners gathered at Wombwell with the intention of marching to Denaby to prevent the Midland Railway loading coal from stock. When the marchers reached Wath they heard that the Midland was loading coal at Wath Main. In a body estimated as 1500 to 3,000 they entered the colliery and took their vengeance, causing an estimated 7,000 worth of damage:

> *The office windows were most scientifically smashed... A mass of torn correspondence and account books strewed the yard... while the (office) furniture was in many instances reduced to matchwood.*

A bonfire was lit in the colliery yard and the saw mill was set on fire. The rioters also burst open the gates at the head of a shaft and threw down an estimated 80 corves. Local men subsequently arrested and charged were:

Isaac Jevons	West Melton	charges withdrawn
Reuben Turner	Brampton	charges withdrawn
Henry Frost	Wath	8 months
Edwin John Warren	Wath (photographer)	15 months hard labour

During those early September days there were violent incidents involving large crowds at several pits in the Wombwell-Barnsley district. Regular soldiers, volunteers and the police were deployed to protect colliery premises and eventually some calm returned. Troops and police would not, however, have been needed to control the 660 children aged four to fourteen who went to the grounds next to West Melton Primitive Methodist Chapel at 5 pm on Monday 11 September,

> *...with mugs, basins and spoons and were treated to a hearty meal of hot, nourishing soup with bread. Over 100 gallons were prepared. The juveniles were seated on the grass in long rows and enjoyed themselves heartily.*

The dispute ended finally on 17 November, after sixteen weeks, without any reductions. A successful stand by the mining communities, but at great cost to themselves.

It was to be 1926 before an even greater struggle tested once more the mettle of miners and their families. Some indication of the scale of that conflict is indicated by the fact that at the beginning of July

1926, the secretary of the Wath Distress Fund reported a total of 32,793 meals had been provided for children on three days per week. On a typical day some 2,800 children in Wath and West Melton would be fed. Other aspects of life then include young men marching to Rotherham to demand assistance from the Poor Law Guardians and the working of outcrop coal at the side of Newhill Road, immediately to the west of Newhill Park.

Working coal by outcropping was the starting point of this account and it is a sad reflection on the human condition that a few hundred years on people felt compelled to resort to such primitive ways. Of course, you will be saying that is exactly what happened again during the great strike of 1984-85, but that is yet another chapter.

Notes and References

Technical details of shaft sinking, seams worked and sequence of working at each of the three 'main' collieries are based upon information issued by them during their operation. With the closure in 1992 of the Mines Records Office at Golden Smithies Lane, Wath, an invaluable local resource was lost. All of the regional offices have been closed and a national centre established at Bretby, Burton on Trent. Details of court cases, strikes, disasters and contemporary accounts are taken from the *Mexborough & Swinton Times (South Yorkshire Times)*, unless otherwise indicated.

1. Quoted in A Burton, *The Miners*, Deutsch, 1976.
2. Dr D G Hey, lecture at Wath, 1975.
3. Sheffield Archives, WWM D 1762A.
4. R. Cox 'Development of the Coal Industry In South Yorkshire Before 1830'(Unpublished MA thesis, University of Sheffield, 1960).
5. Sheffield Archives, WWM D 1762B.
6. Cox, thesis.
7. H W Quarrell, *A History of Swinton*, 1954.
8. Cox, thesis.
9. Cox, thesis.
10. Sheffield Archives, Newman Bond Collection 515.
11. *Mexborough & Swinton Times*, 1877.
12. Nottingham University Library, Manvers Papers, MAB 498.
13. Nottingham, Manvers Papers, MAB 493.
14. Sheffield Archives, NCB 961.
15. F Machin, Yorkshire Miners, vol 1, 1958, p 17.
16. *Mexborough & Swinton Times*.
17. Inspector of Mines Report.
18. Sheffield Archives NCB 965.

Acknowledgements

My friend and former colleague Bob Cox was indispensable in helping me deal with the earliest period. I should also like to thank the following for their help: staff of Sheffield Archives; Barnsley Local Studies Library; Rotherham Central Library, Archives and Local Studies Section; Nottingham University Library; British Coal; and various former employees at Manvers, Wath Main and Cortonwood.

14. ROTHERHAM'S RAILWAY TRADES: AN EARLY CHAPTER IN HEAVY ENGINEERING

by Trevor Lodge

IF RECENT PUBLISHED WORKS are any guide, the heavy engineering trades rate low indeed in the priorities of those researching the economic and industrial history of South Yorkshire. Yet in real terms the contribution these industries made to the wealth of the region has been very significant, particularly from the middle of the last century.

Railway rails, components for locomotives and rolling stock (especially tyres, wheels, axles and springs), ships' armour, ordnance and engine forgings are all recognised as the former staple products of Sheffield's so-called Heavy Trades. The manufacture of such items is generally thought to follow in the wake of the region's adoption, from 1860, of Bessemer's pneumatic method for bulk steelmaking. Nothing could be further from the truth, for all were being produced locally before the advent of tonnage steel — by the region's iron industry, principally centred on Rotherham. And, just as ordnance casting for the Royal Navy formed the mainstay of Rotherham's eighteenth century heavy foundry industry, the coming of the Railway Age acted as the single biggest stimulus for the town's nineteenth century wrought, or malleable, iron trades.

Nothing has appeared in print which deals comprehensively with the full spectrum of Rotherham's railway trades; in particular, no previous author has attempted to indicate the size or tenure of Rotherham's railway steel industry.

Guest, in *Relics and Records*[1] wrote enthusiastically about Dodds and Owen, two of the town's pioneer railway engineers. This account, however, appeared in the trade's adolescent years and Guest could not have foreseen how the whole business would develop. A fuller account of Dodds' locomotive building activities was given by Snell[2], but Rotherham's rolling stock builders — who plied a less romantic but collectively much more important economic role — still await a knowledgeable author to chronicle their story. More recently, the present author dealt with other aspects of these trades particularly rail production and tyre and wheel manufacture — as part of a broader treatment of Rotherham's iron and steel industries.[3] Finally, Rotherham's Archivist, Tony Munford, has considered briefly Rotherham's wheelset manufacturers in response to the recent discovery of some preserved examples of their wares.[4]

The Coming of the Railways

Railways of a sort have existed in South Yorkshire from the eighteenth century, but the earliest lines were isolated, primitive affairs which linked coal pits with canal staithes or land sale yards. They were invariably lightly engineered and tended to follow the existing contours of the land. The track consisted of either longitudinal timber baulks (often faced with wrought iron strips), or cast iron plates. Motive power was provided by gravity, a stationary engine, horses or men, or a combination of these. A local example of an early wooden railway, mentioned by Guest, connected Fentons' coal workings (probably in the Bassingthorpe area) with the original canal course just to the north of Rotherham's present day Centenary Way.

The nature of these early lines was such that they could not be integrated into a national transport network capable of being operated safely at speed hauling commercially viable loads. The locomotive worked public railway as we understand it did not come until 1830, when the Liverpool and Manchester Railway opened. This event actually followed several years of successful operation of the Stockton and Darlington Railway, primarily a coal-carrying line which used high pressure steam locomotive traction quite widely.

The promotion of South Yorkshire's first public railway, the **Sheffield and Rotherham Railway** (S & RR), provided the first real opportunity for the region's engineers to participate in what was then the leading edge of technology. In the event, local concerns barely responded to the challenge of supplying the engineering infrastructure, with one notable exception — Davy Brothers of the Park Ironworks in Sheffield, who eventually supplied a solitary steam locomotive. Perhaps it should not come as too much of a surprise that the line's other capital equipment — locomotives, rolling stock and rails — was produced at manufactories elsewhere which had 'grown up' with the infant railway industry, and had already supplied such equipment to pioneering lines such as the Liverpool and Manchester Railway.

When it opened in October 1838, the S & RR was isolated from the country's embryonic rail network. In truth, though it carried passengers it was, like the Stockton and Darlington Railway, little more than a glorified coal railway. It had been promoted in the first instance by Earl Fitzwilliam, who was keen to transport his Park Gate (Stubbin) coals to Sheffield by a more efficient means than the Don Navigation, and thus break the virtual monopoly on the trade enjoyed by the Duke of Norfolk, who supplied the town from his Manor pits. Fitzwilliam's promotion of the line as a public passenger carrying line was nothing short of a sop to gain Parliamentary approval for the venture in the first instance.

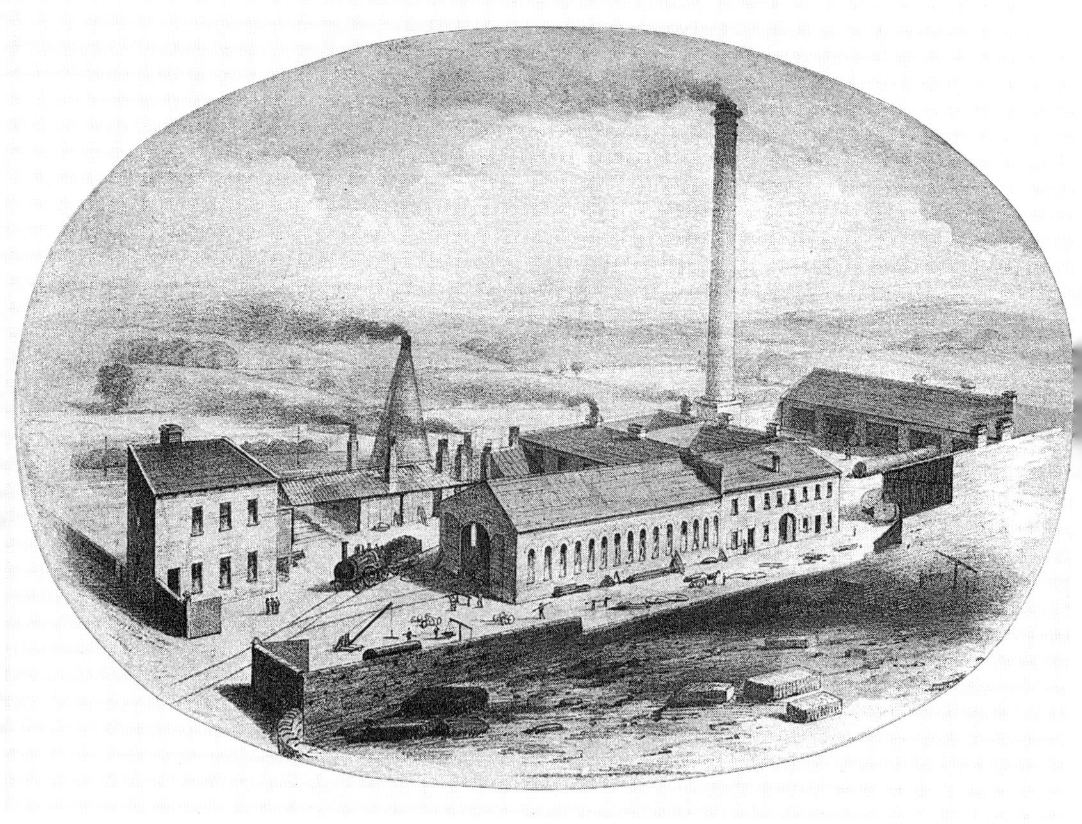

Figure 1. Artist's impression of the Holmes Engine Works, looking south-west.
Courtesy A J Booth

Indeed, the line was so 'geared' to Fitzwilliam's requirements that all but one of the coal wagons which ran on it belonged to the Earl.[5] To work this traffic he even acquired his own brand new locomotive in 1839, a six-coupled freight engine built by Tayleur & Company of the Vulcan Foundry at Newton le Willows, Lancashire.

The event which put Rotherham well and truly on the nation's railway map was the opening in 1840 of the **North Midland Railway** (NMR), a trunk line running from Derby to Leeds via the Rother valley with which the S & RR made a junction at Masbrough. In 1844 the NMR, which by this time had effectively absorbed the S & RR, merged with the Birmingham and Derby Railway and the Midland Counties Railway to form the Midland Railway, which grew to become one of the UK's largest pre-grouping networks.[6] The youthful MR was destined to play a significant role in the fortunes of Rotherham's railway trades.

With the coming of the **South Yorkshire Railway** (SYR) in 1854 the town's basic railway network was established. Later to become part of the Manchester, Sheffield and Lincolnshire Railway, the SYR ran roughly west to east, linking the rich South Yorkshire coalfield around Barnsley to Doncaster and beyond. Much of the coal traffic originating on the SYR passed to London by way of Doncaster and the Great Northern Railway main line.

Early Manufactories

Because of the isolated nature of the infant S & RR, it was realised that first-class workshop facilities for maintaining and overhauling the equipment would be needed. Rotherham's first railway manufactory, the **Holmes Engine Works** (Ordnance Survey grid reference SK411923) shown in Figure 1 was created by Isaac Dodds (Figure 2) to satisfy this need.

A native of Felling in County Durham, Dodds worked as a youth for his uncle Ralph Dodds, viewer at Killingworth Colliery in Northumberland, where he first became conversant with Stephenson's high pressure steam technology. He went on to serve an engineering apprenticeship under George Stephenson at the newly-established workshops at Forth Banks in Newcastle, which soon evolved into the world famous locomotive factory of Robert Stephenson & Company. The S & RR was an early 'Stephenson' line, ie, one for which George Stephenson had acted as consulting engineer, so it was no mere coincidence that Dodds, who by now had gained considerable further experience, was appointed as Superintendent and Resident Engineer, with responsibility for locomotive and rolling stock maintenance.

The first three service locomotives built for the S & RR had to be supplied in kit form from Robert Stephenson & Company of Newcastle. They were sent by coaster, completing their journey on the South Yorkshire Navigation. It has been said that they were assembled in Sheffield, but I question this since the S & RR never had any engineering workshops in Sheffield. I suspect that the operation took place at the Holmes Engine Works, which was immediately alongside the Navigation and ideally placed to accept water-borne deliveries. It has also been claimed that delays in receiving these locomotives were the reason that Dodds built his first locomotive, a 2-2-2 called the 'Old Cutler'. This was supposed to be a contingency arrangement for the official opening of the S & RR — should the Stephenson engines not have been assembled in time — but the local press reported that a locomotive was in use on the S & RR in July 1838[7], assisting the contractors to move spoil in connection with the building of the line, and this was likely to be the 'Old Cutler'.

Dodds appears to have supplied maintenance and repair facilities for

Figure 2. Isaac Dodds.

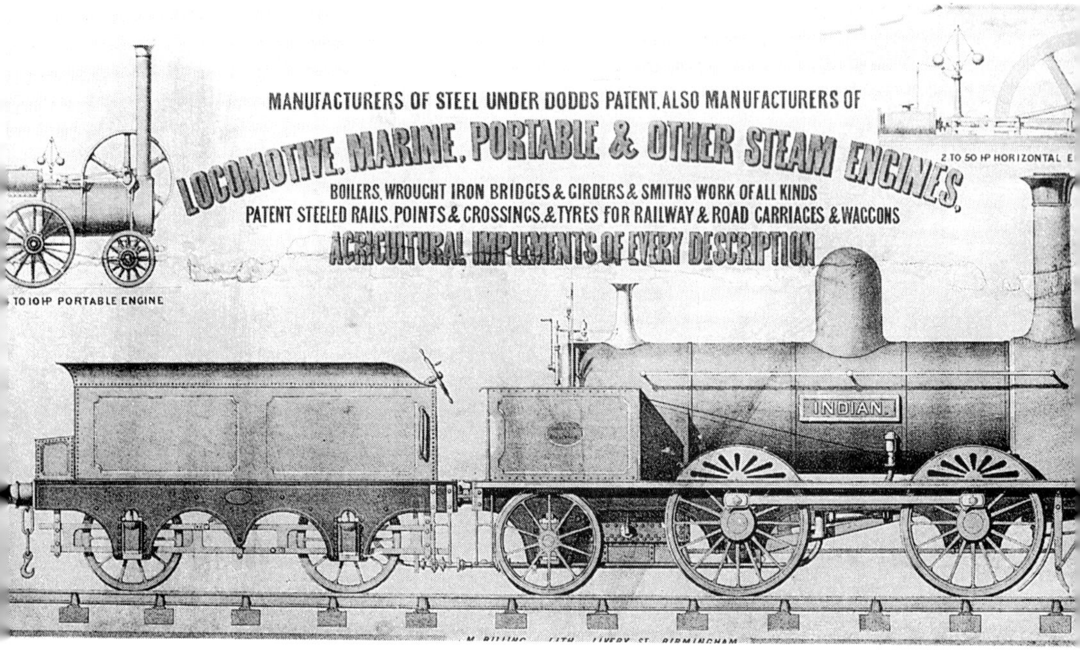

Figure 3. Part of Dodds' advertisement showing an 0-4-2 locomotive thought to have been supplied to India. *Courtesy A J Booth*

the S & RR on a contract basis, and remained relatively free of the railway company's immediate control. He was able to solicit outside engineering orders, and this arms-length approach became even more noticeable after the S & RR lost its independent existence and was absorbed by the NMR.

Ultimately, the Holmes Engine Works became a specialist manufactory of stationary and locomotive steam engines for customers at home and abroad, and it also made items of ordnance and general engineering equipment. Some of Dodds' more notable customers for railway locomotives included the Newport, Abergavenny and Hereford Railway, the Great Indian Peninsular Railway (Figure 3) and the Isabel II Railway in Spain.

Sadly, the business went into liquidation in 1866 because of unpaid bills for railway contracts carried out on behalf of the Spanish Government before the outbreak of the Carlist Wars which virtually destroyed Spain's entire economic infrastructure. No Dodds company records are known to survive, and railway historians have estimated the firm's output of railway locomotives, at some 70 machines.

Another Rotherham engineer who catered for the lucrative railway market from early days was William Owen (Figure 4), based at the

Figure 4. William Owen.

Phoenix Works (SK427933). According to Guest (*op cit*), Owen had served his time with iron founders Yates and Sandford at the Phoenix Works, where he took over as manager of their newly opened forge in 1832. The works soon became well known for large nautical and other steam engine forgings in wrought iron — paddle wheelshafts up to eighteen tons weight, crank axles to twelve tons and crank throws to six tons. Most of the early developments attributable to Owen occurred in the field of railway engineering, several in connection with Isaac Dodds.

In particular, Owen and Dodds collaborated in patenting improved methods for the manufacture of railway wheels and the forming of crank throws and crank shafts. These methods incorporated Owen's ideas, which did away with the need for complicated welding, resulting in a more dependable product.

Owen became a partner in the Phoenix Works with Charles Sandford in 1838, after which time railway wheel and axle manufacture, commenced two years earlier, began to predominate.

Examples of Owen's 'Patent railway wheels, three feet in diameter, made of wrought-iron' were shown at the Great Exhibition of 1851.The firm — by now Sandford, Owen and Watson — was careful to point out the wheels were 'welded into one piece' and that 'The manufacture is effected by machinery...'

Owen's biggest single success seems to have been the solid wrought iron weldless tyre, which was shown at the Great Exhibition of 1862. Three years later production capacity was boosted when the plant's solitary tyre mill was augmented by the installation of two more. Significantly, by this time tyres, axles and general castings were also being offered by the firm in steel (Figure 5).

Details of a few interesting early orders executed by Sandford & Owen for the Stockton and Darlington Railway have survived.[8] The latter ordered 80 sets of wheels and axles (complete with tyres and assembled) in 1857 for incorporation into ten ton trucks (30 sets at £23 14s 0d each) and timber-carrying wagons (50 sets at £22 14s 0d each). At this time Rotherham had no rolling stock builders of note, and the completed axle trees were sent to Matthew Crawford, Elswick Iron Works, Newcastle and Bray, and Waddington & Co, New Dock Works, Leeds, for assembly into the trucks and timber wagons respectively. The steel springs for the timber wagons were supplied to Bray by Charles Cammell of the Cyclops Works in Sheffield.

From about 1864 the firm traded under the style of Owen's Patent Wheel, Tyre and Axle Company Ltd, but was in liquidation by about 1872. A new firm, founded by George Dyson Owen and Robert Dyson — son and nephew respectively of William Owen — established the

	Solid weldless No 1	Solid weldless No 2	Solid weldless No 3	Yorks	[illegible]	[illegible]	Lowmoor, Bowling, & Coopers	Farnley & Taylors
Tyre Bent welded and Rolled To 3½ Cwt.	25/	20/	16/	16/	19/	21/6	27/6	26/6
To 4	30/	24/	20/	20/	23/	25/6	31/6	30/6
To 5	33/	28/	24/	24/	27/	29/6	35/6	34/6
5 to 7	37/	32/	28/	28/	31/	33/6	39/6	38/6
7 Cwt & upwards	41/	36/	32/	32/	35/	37/6	43/6	42/6

Figure 5. Phoenix Works price list for weldless wrought iron tyres. The eight columns refer to various grades of wrought iron which were available, with West Yorkshire brands (especially Low Moor and Bowling) commanding the highest prices.

Rother Iron Works (SK420917) on Fullerton Road about 1875 to continue in much the same line of business as the Phoenix Works (Figure 6). It is difficult to avoid the conclusion that William Owen was in some way connected with Owen & Dyson, but proof is lacking.

In the early days of the Rother Iron Works a speciality product was the cold spoked wheel, hydraulically pressed, built up, machined and usually supplied complete with tyre and fitted as a pair on the axle. The axle and wheel sets complete were often referred to as an axle tree assembly (Figure 7).

Owen's succession of business undertakings did not quite enjoy a monopoly in Rotherham's tyre manufacturing trade. The **Rotherham Forge** (SK426929), on the aptly-named Forge Lane, also developed a

Figure 6. Group of employees at the Rother Iron Works, c 1880. In addition to the more usual cold spoked wheels, visible at the extreme ends of the picture, four examples of carriage wheels (with teak centres and Mansell bolted ring fastenings for the tyre) are also shown.

Figure 7. Group of axletree assemblies by Owen & Dyson for Indian State Railway, December 1880.

specialism in this field. Originally part of the Walker iron and steel empire, the forge was acquired about 1832 by partners George Knowles and John Brown, who continued the business as 'iron manufacturers, rollers and slitters'. By the late 1840s the concern was trading as John Brown & Son, and later still as George and John Brown. There is, incidentally, no known link between this concern and the famous John Brown of the Atlas Works in Sheffield. The earliest specific end product from Rotherham Forge on record is the solid weldless wrought iron tyre, which according to Guest, was produced on a patented machine introduced in 1859. Guest goes on to claim that this was the first solid weldless railway tyre ever produced.

Unlike the various Owen enterprises, which specialised in the production of axle tree assemblies to the virtual exclusion of all other goods, Rotherham Forge had a broader range of products, including boiler plates and sheet iron. Ultimately it began rolling sheets and rods from cast steel, and became an early producer of lucrative crinoline steel wire feed stock. These early excursions into steel rolling proved to be the salvation of the forge, which was able to complete the transition from iron to steel successfully once the demand for the former, especially as large forgings, began to dwindle.

In 1844 a partnership between Henry Sandford and a Mr Beatson established the **Midland Iron Works** (SK417929) at Masbrough. This developed into a large supplier of wrought iron bars for forging and re-rolling, and ultimately made railway wagon three-link couplings as part of a range of products (Figure 8).

Figure 8. A typical example of the thousands of mineral wagons built and used in South Yorkshire. Though Midland Iron did not build wagons, by the 1890s it was already supplying wrought iron spokes and Mansell rings (for wheels), forged axles, and bars and strapping—all components used in wagon building.

Though I have not been able to verify a link between Charles Sandford of the Phoenix Works and Henry Sandford it is probable that the Phoenix Works would be supplied with bar iron by the Midland Works. By the same token, the earlier collaboration between Owen and Dodds is likely to have engendered trading between them also, with Phoenix supplying forgings for engines built by Dodds. Such interdependence within the local iron trade developed to an even greater extent in railway wagon building, as discussed below. At this point we need to mention several short-lived (and ill-documented) concerns which operated in quick succession from **Northfield Works** (SK429937). In 1855 the owner was listed in White's Directory as the Yorkshire Tire [sic] and Axle Company. By the 1860 edition, this entry had been replaced by one for the Swedish Steel Iron Company, and one year later yet another new name appears — that of the Northfield Iron & Steel Company. Of these, at least the last two businesses shared common management. Guest, (*op cit*), quotes from an article in *The Times* newspaper which detailed a celebrated product from Northfield — large (70 cwt) anchors made to the patent of a Captain Rodgers, and used by the Admiralty on ironclads. Northfield did produce railway materials, but its output is thought not to have been particularly significant. The Northfield Iron and Steel Co Ltd appeared in White's Directory for 1868, but had gone by the time of the 1871 edition. Finally, a Northfield Iron & Tyre Co Ltd was in existence in 1875, and a Northfield Iron Company, founded in 1879, was wound up in 1881!

Rotherham's Rail Mills

According to several economic historians, the demand for wrought iron railway rails in the 1830-1860 period was probably the largest single stimulus which affected the growth of Britain's iron industry. Quite a claim, especially when one remembers that there was then no bulk steelmaking industry.

During this time the **Park Gate Iron Works** at Rotherham was one of the country's larger producers of such rails, having installed in 1845 a railmill (SK434946) capable of rolling 2,000 tons per week (Figure 9). This early move into rail production came as a result of the foresight of one man — Charles Geach.

Born in 1808, Geach began his career with the Bank of England, where he was elected for a clerkship in 1826. Five years later he was serving as Second Inspector at the bank's Birmingham branch, and in 1836 ambition drove him to found the Birmingham and Midland Bank, which was soon known simply as the Midland Bank.[9]

Geach's first dabblings in the iron trade occurred in 1838, when he led

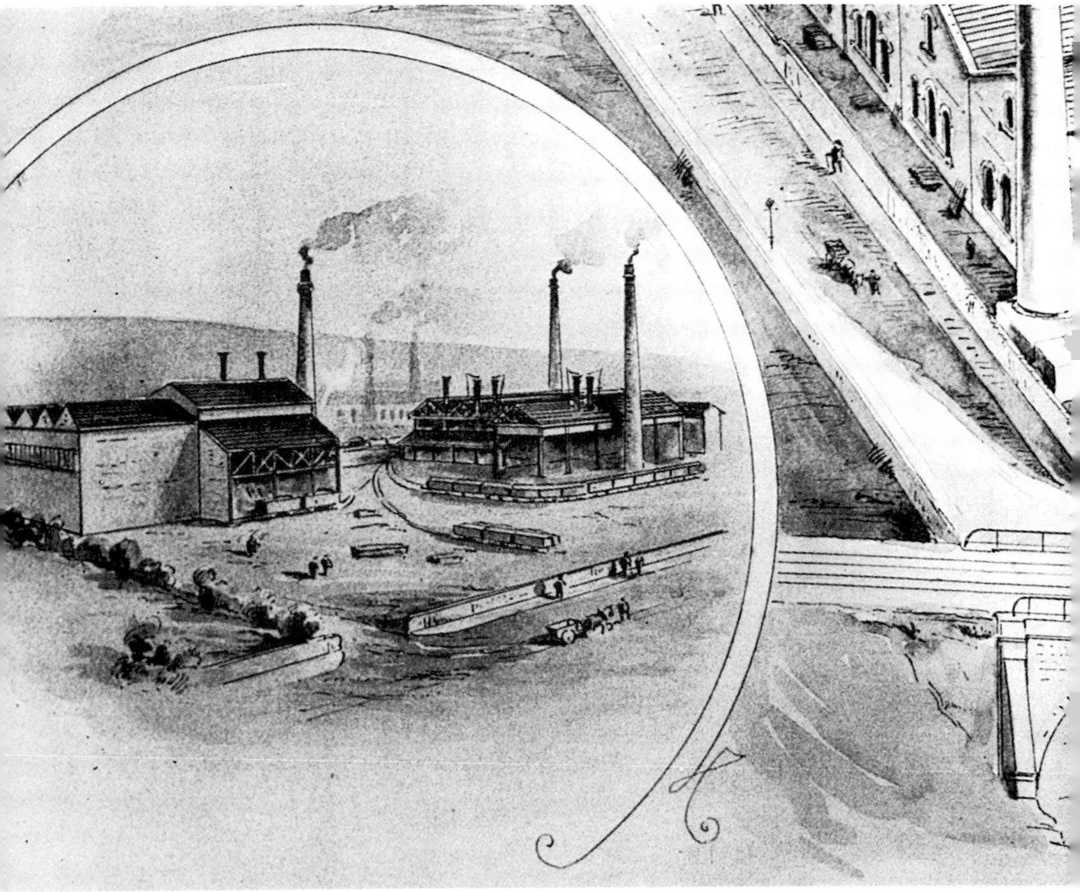

Figure 9. Artist's impression of Park Gate rail mill (right) and slag processing plant, c 1870. View taken from the Midland Railway embankment, looking north, with Rotherham Road in the foreground.

a group of Birmingham businessmen in purchasing the business and plant of an ailing West Midlands manufacturer of heavy duty iron axles. The concern was reconstructed as the Patent Shaft and Axletree Company and was soon enjoying new-found prosperity supplying to the infant railway industry. A major trunk route, the London and Birmingham Railway, opened in 1838 and this, together with the 1840 Manchester and Birmingham Railway must have presented golden opportunities for new business.

Geach soon realised that railways offered great business opportunities to the iron trade more generally. Apart from being used for the track itself, iron in various forms was needed for locomotives and items of rolling stock, not to mention permanent fixtures and fittings associated with the civil infrastructure (bridges, stations, etc). In 1842 Geach learned of the imminent failure of the Park Gate Iron Company at Rotherham, brought about by a collapse in iron prices. Together with Samuel Beale, a business colleague, he moved swiftly to acquire a controlling interest in Park Gate (Figure 10). So depressed were market conditions that Geach was later said to have 'bought the whole concern for an old song'. Not content with this acquisition, Geach consolidated his iron empire in 1844 by buying out his partners at Patent Shaft. His timing could not have been better. In 1845 Parliament authorised approximately 8000 miles of new railway construction in a period still known by economic historians as that of 'Railway Mania'. Nor could his choice of partner be faulted. Samuel Beale was ideally placed to promote Park Gate's rail business. His father had been one of the promoters of the Birmingham and Derby Railway, and Samuel served for many years as Chairman of the Midland Railway until his retirement in 1864. Even then his influence did not cease, for he remained a

Figure 10. Artist's impression of Park Gate Iron Works, looking north-west. The complex was bisected by Rotherham Road/Broad Street, which run across the view. The blast furnace (left) and forge beyond the road were the items of plant acquired by Geach and Beale in 1845. The buildings in the middle foreground housed a rolling mill (installed 1849) on which the hull plates for Brunel's *Great Eastern* steamship were rolled. The rail mill (not shown) was to the left of this view, approximately a quarter of a mile nearer to Rotherham.

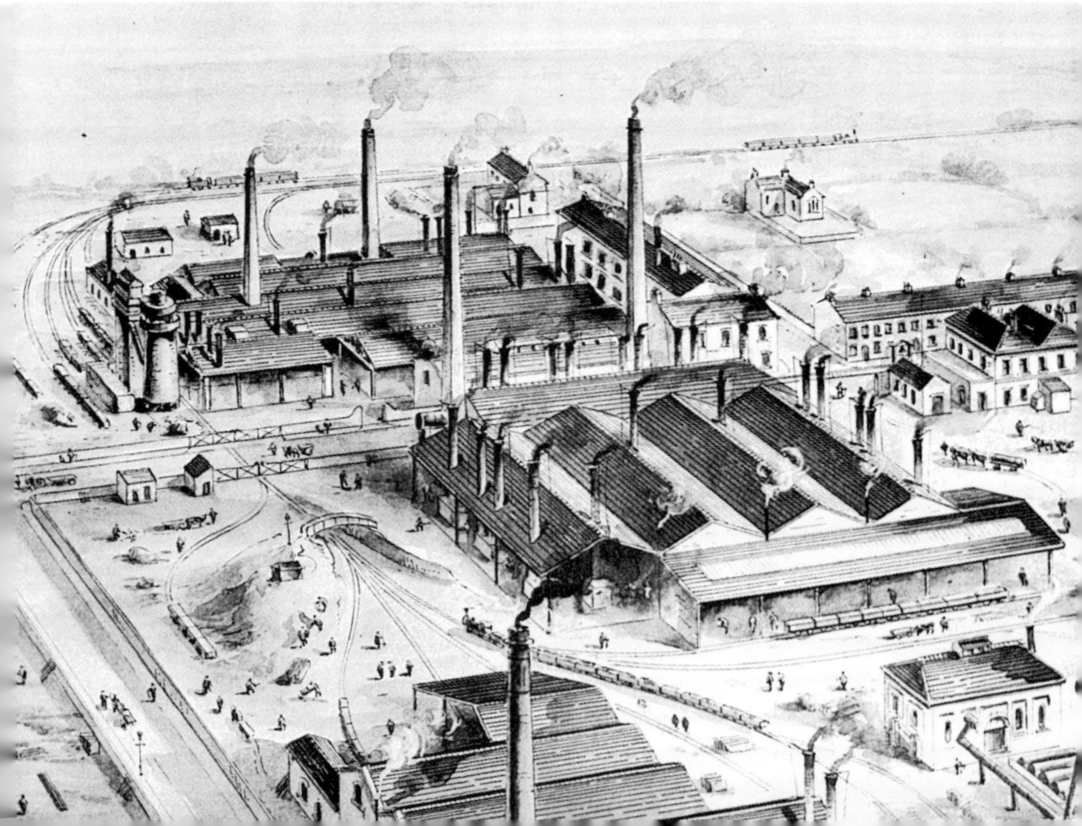

director of the Midland Railway. By 1850 Beale was also one of the Midland Bank's largest shareholders.

So deep was the involvement of Geach and Beale in inter-related matters of public railway company promotion, banking and rail manufacture, that under today's 'rules' of business ethics their techniques would have been considered questionable, to say the least! This closeness with both supplier of finance and goods to the railways was not seen as a problem at the time, however, and Geach in particular always took steps to ensure that the Bank of England, as well as his own bank directors, were cognisant of the arrangement, and that his position as Manager of the Midland Bank was not subservient to his interests as a trader.

Regrettably, firm details for Park Gate's early rail contracts do not survive, though it is said that in 1845 Geach took three orders for a total of 30,000 tons of wrought iron rails at £12 per ton, twice the cost of production — a huge quantity by any standards. Through Geach, Park Gate also soon became involved with supplying rails for the lines built by Thomas Brassey, the first of the big civil engineering contractors. By 1847 Brassey had built one mile out of every three in Britain, and by 1850 no less than three out of four in France.

Even in the early 1870s, by which time steel was rapidly ousting wrought iron for rail manufacture, Park Gate was still supplying iron rails to UK railway companies, and also occasionally fulfilling export orders. The Midland Railway was at the top of its list of railway customers, as might be expected. Between 1868 and 1874, for example, the Midland purchased some 44,000 tons of Park Gate rails. These were generally priced about £6 10s 0d to £7 10s 0d per ton, though in the boom period around 1872 prices were considerably higher — between £10 5s 0d and £1 17s 6d per ton. Other home customers at this time were the Great Northern Railway (7,500 tons in 1869) and the Lancashire & Yorkshire Railway (2000 tons in 1872-73). Details survive of just one export order — 3000 tons for the New South Wales Railway (Australia) in 1869.

In 1860 an event took place which was destined to turn the iron rail trade on its head, and eventually drive Park Gate out of rail rolling altogether. As part of his efforts to gain recognition for his revolutionary method of steelmaking, Henry Bessemer supplied 500 tons of steel blooms for rolling at the London & North Western Railway's rail mill at Crewe. Though twice as expensive as iron rails to produce overall, steel rails were shown to be vastly superior, lasting up to ten times longer in service trials.

For a variety of reasons, Bessemer's process got a mixed reception from established wrought iron producers. Some saw it as a future threat

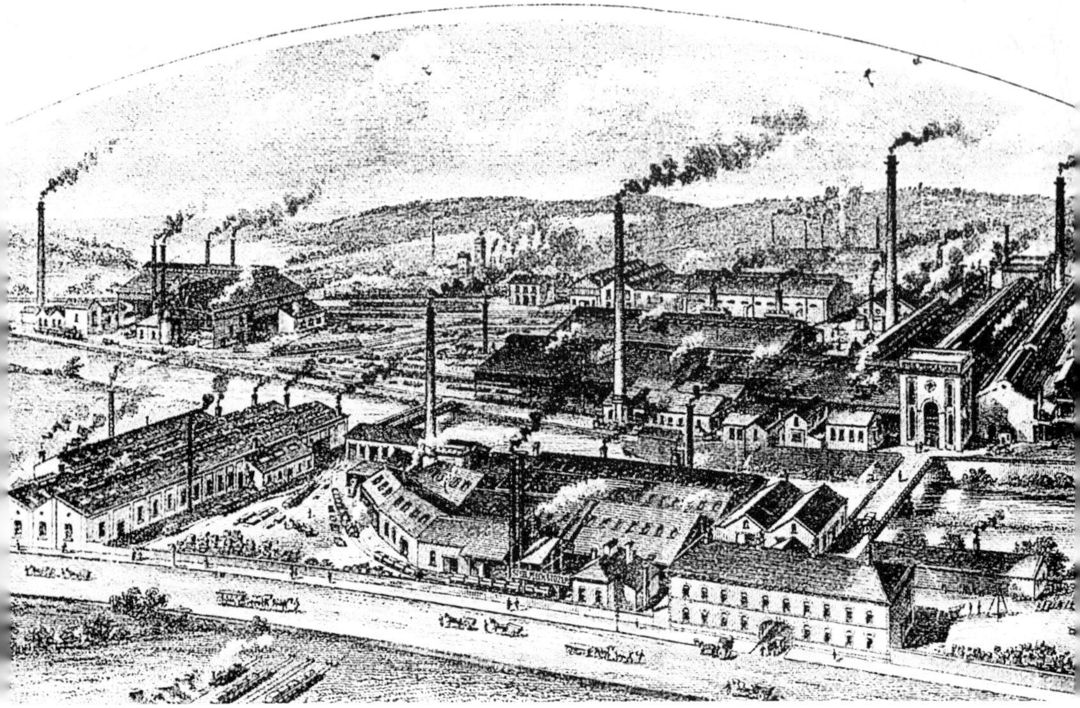

Figure 11. Artist's impression of Ickles Bessemer Works, looking north, with Sheffield Road in the foreground. The works was bisectd by the River Don.

to their trade, so took out licences for the process and became steelmakers in their own right. Others, Park Gate included, chose to spurn the new technology altogether, and stuck with the *status quo*.

Over half the initial Bessemer steelworks established in the early years of the process, from 1859 onwards, were located in the Sheffield region, making the area for a brief decade the world's largest producer of steel rails. Following this initial flush of success, several more Bessemer plants were built in the early 1870s, including **The Ickles Bessemer Works** (SK418919) as shown in Figure 11.

The first twelve years of Bessemer steelmaking at The Ickles proved to be a momentous period in which the production capacity of the plant increased almost ten-fold, from some 300 ingot tons per week from two converters in 1872 to 2,750 ingot tons per week from six converters by 1879. Such an increase in capacity was not achieved without struggles, and the plant was operated by no fewer than four distinct partnerships / companies in this period, a situation partly brought about by varying trading fortunes. The original equipment, consisting of two Bessemer converters, each with a capacity of two tons per blow, was owned and operated by partners Hampton and Radcliffe. The steel ingots produced must have been sold for forging or rolling elsewhere, since initially the plant did not possess a forge or rolling mill.

In July 1872 arrangements were made to float a company known as the Phoenix Bessemer Steel Company Limited for the purpose of purchasing and operating the Ickles Works. At this time, extensions to the plant were already in hand which would effectively double ingot production and it is likely that the original partners' plans for expansion could only be achieved by an injection of fresh capital, ie, the creation of a limited liability company of shareholders. With large shareholdings in the new company Hampton and Radcliffe retained some measure of control over its affairs and became directors.

Matters then continued uneventfully until a falling off in demand for ingots caused the directors to install a rail mill in 1873, with a capacity of 800 tons of rails per week. Initially the cast steel ingots produced in the melting shop were forge cogged by steam hammer to blooms, for subsequent reheating and rolling through the rail mill stands. Ingot reheating facilities at the mill call for no special mention, consisting of a number of vertical coal-fired soaking pits.

In August 1874 Phoenix Bessemer entered into a contract to supply 5,000 tons of rails to a firm of London iron merchants, Gilead A Smith & Company. The contract was to have far-reaching repercussions, for Gilead A Smith & Co ceased trading soon after this as a result of the failure of a South Wales iron company, and Phoenix Bessemer was left with a bad debt of over £14,000. This in itself would not have been sufficient to necessitate the liquidation of Phoenix Bessemer but came at a time when the company was trying to raise £30,000 by issue of preference shares.

Unfortunately, the company had already borrowed a considerable sum of money on the strength of the latter share issue, and on 3 July 1875 it was publicly announced that a petition had been filed for the official winding up of Phoenix Bessemer. The plant, now under the control of liquidators, continued to operate at a small profit, but eventually stopped working on 31 October 1875. On 3 November it was announced that the works had been sold to a Mr Henry Steel (Figure 12), a Turf Commission Agent, for £36,500.

Steel was no ordinary 'bookie'. The reputation he gained for sound dealings early in his career was such that in later years he became a leading member of Tattersalls and had numerous transactions with no less a person than Prince Edward (later King Edward VII).

Henry Steel proceeded to invite Edward Tozer and Thomas Hampton to form a new company with him to operate the works, and on 15 December 1875 the firm of Steel, Tozer & Hampton Limited (STH)

Figure 12. Henry Steel.

was registered. A Mr Henry Peech — an almost life-long business associate of Steel — was included as a director.

Steel's choice of partners was most shrewd and typified those aspects of his character which had already enabled him to build up a considerable private fortune from his earlier venture. The inclusion of Edward Tozer's name in the firm's title, for example, gave the new company considerable prestige, since from 1871 onwards he was elected consecutively as Town Councillor, Alderman, Master Cutler and Mayor of Sheffield. He was made a Justice of the Peace in 1881, and retired from Sheffield Town Council the same year. Tozer also possessed useful industrial experience, latterly as Managing Director of the Sheffield steel firm Sanderson Brothers & Co Ltd. Similarly, Thomas Hampton, former Managing Director of the Phoenix Bessemer Steel Company possessed considerable experience of steel making and was in an unrivalled position when it came to a knowledge of the Ickles plant and its capabilities. In 1883, after completing his eight year contract with STH, Hampton left the board with a 'golden handshake' and the name of the company was changed to Steel, Peech & Tozer Limited (SPT).

Steel managed the affairs of STH (and later, SPT) with sound business acumen. In April 1876, a new Bessemer Shop (which became known as 'B' Shop) was sanctioned, with two 2 ton converters. Other quite substantial expenditure was incurred on plant at this time. Two additional (and larger) converters for 'B' Shop were purchased in February 1878, and several improvements were made to the mill in the late 1870s to increase rolling capacity. By 1879 a cogging mill had been installed, consisting of a three-high stand incorporating 30-inch diameter rolls driven by a vertical compound steam engine of 260 hp rating. The associated rail mill comprised a stand of two-high bolting (ie, roughing) rolls and a similar finishing stand, both sets being driven by a 550 hp horizontal compound steam engine. The rail mill rolls were reversed through a hydraulic friction clutch supplied by W & J Galloway of Manchester, equipment which was very much a novelty at this time. Power driven rollers transferred the stock between the cogging mill and rail mill, and thence to the saws beyond the cooling banks. Machinery for punching, shearing and sawing rails to length was also installed. In 1879, the production plant comprised two melting shops, with a total of six Bessemer converters fed from thirteen cupolas (used to melt the pig iron feedstock); six steam hammers; a cogging mill; a rail mill; and a 14-inch bar mill. Thus equipped, the works had a capacity of some 2,750 tons of steel ingots per week, and could roll 2,500 tons of steel rails weekly.

At this stage we should explain that a cogging mill was used to cog, or break down, the as-cast structure of the ingot to produce an intermediate product called a bloom. The roughing, or bolting mill rolled the re-heated bloom to a section which approximated to an oversized end product and this, still hot, was sent to the finishing mill where it was rolled to the final desired profile.

The initial Ickles cogging mill had a relatively short career, for in 1880 a new mill and steam engine drive were supplied by Davy Brothers of Sheffield for a total of £7,897. STH must have been satisfied with the equipment for when the rail mill drive was modernised in 1881 by the purchase of a reversing engine, it too came from Davy Brothers, at a cost of £5,600.

More capital expenditure was the order of the day when yet another new cogging mill (with 36-inch rolls) and engine were installed in 1893 to replace the twelve years' old Davy equipment. Additions or replacements were also made to the rail mill, which latterly consisted of three stands of 30-inch reversing rolls, all driven by one engine (Figure 13). The last major modification to the cogging mill was the installation of a German (Demag) duplex compound steam engine for drive, a move which was in hand when the 1914-18 war broke out.

The mill complex was capable of rolling rails, billets (mostly for supplying to the plant's 10-inch and 14-inch bar mills), axle blooms and round bars. Doubtless the mill's universal nature helped it to compete more favourably than mills designed to roll rails only: a similar situation obtained at Penistone and Stocksbridge, two other local works which survived as rail producers into the present century.

We do not have a comprehensive picture of SPT's rail order book. The company's last major home order for rails, however, was a massive one it shared with two other local producers. In 1894 the Manchester, Sheffield and Lincolnshire Railway began its grandiose extension from Nottinghamshire to London, in consequence of which it soon changed its name to the Great Central Railway. The London Extension order for rails — 35,000 tons of them at £4 7s 6d per ton — was shared between SPT, Samuel Fox & Co Ltd of Stocksbridge and Charles Cammell & Co Ltd of Penistone.[10]

Rolling stock manufacture

It has been estimated that even as early as 1863, some 160,000 to 170,000 wagons were running on the UK's railway system, the vast majority of which had entered traffic in the previous 20 years. When it is considered that many of these were built by private contractors, rather than in the railway companies' own workshops, the full potential of this business, both to the wagon builders and their suppliers, can be appreciated.

Figure 13. Ickles rail mill, c1925.

Rotherham eventually boasted several railway rolling stock manufacturers who were important customers for the town's railway materials producers. Much more research is required, however, before a comprehensive account can be given of their activities.

The best known of these was **Harrison & Camm**, with premises at the Holmes (SK410924) on the north side of the former Sheffield and Rotherham Railway. William Harrison, one of the partners, had served since the mid 1850s concurrently as both secretary for the short-lived Yorkshire Tire and Axle Company at Northfield, and Manager of the Midland Wagon Company, railway wagon hirers of College Hill. Using expertise gained from these two posts, Harrison set up in business with Samuel Camm, of whom we know little, and who first appears in local directories in the 1860s.

Guest, in his *Historic Notices of Rotherham*[11], provides some contemporary information on the business. He states that Harrison and Camm commenced in 1860 — the company's advertisements claimed 1861 — and originally intended to employ 120 men to make fifteen wagons a week. As a consequence of increased trade, the partners put down plant in 1866 to manufacture railway wheels and axles and make themselves independent of other suppliers of such items. By 1871 the works employed almost 500 hands and produced 30-40 wagons per week, in addition to 80 sets of wheels and axles. Guest concludes: 'The present capacity of the works is fifty railway wagons and one hundred sets of wheels and axles per week'.

Harrison & Camm remained the town's largest private rolling stock builder, not only catering for the home market but also supplying colonial and other overseas railways. An advertisement for the business which appeared in White's Directory for 1871 (Figure 14) gives a good indication of the early product range.

Private wagon building and/or repairing was carried out elsewhere in the town by a number of other concerns, including the **North Central Wagon Company** at The Ickles (SK421914), and the **British Wagon Co Ltd** at Northfield (SK426937). Both concerns were established in the1860s. The **Great Central Railway** also operated quite extensive wagon building and repair facilities at Northfield (SK427938), from c 1900 to c 1920.

We should also remember that the larger coal/iron/steel empires, for example Park Gate Iron & Steel and Aldwarke Main Colliery, operated sizeable wagon repair shops for the maintenance of their own rolling stock, since efficient operation of mineral wagons consituted the 'life-blood' of their busnesses.

Another facet of the rolling stock business which we can only mention here is that of wagon financing. This business developed as a natural

HARRISON & CAMM,
ROTHERHAM,
RAILWAY WHEEL & AXLE MAKERS,
AND
RAILWAY CARRIAGE AND WAGGON BUILDERS;
MANUFACTURERS OF WROUGHT IRON CENTRE & OTHER
RAILWAY WHEELS,
AND EVERY DESCRIPTION OF
Railway Rolling Stock & Railway Iron Work.
HEAVY AND LIGHT FORGINGS,
PLAIN SHAFTS, SINGLE CRANK SHAFTS, & OUTSIDE CRANKS,
DOUBLE & SINGLE CRANK AXLES,
PISTON RODS, CROSS HEADS,
MOTION OR SLIDE BARS, SHARE, HAMMER, & ARM MOULDS, &c., &c.

Figure 14. Harrison and Camm advertisement, 1871.

adjunct to wagon building, and provided the mechanism by which deferred payment for the wagons was arranged. Suffice to say that railway wagons were the first 'goods' which could be purchased on an instalment basis which allowed the customer, often a colliery owner, to begin using the wagon in revenue-earning traffic (effectively on hire) as soon as an initial down payment had been made to the finance company. Today, 'hire purchase' is a universally accepted means of High Street shopping for domestic consumer durables, but owes its origins to the nineteenth century wagon trade. Indeed, there are numerous reminders of this practice in present day financing. Lombard North Central, for example, with premises on Moorgate, is a successor to the North Central Wagon Co Ltd and operates a diversified loans portfolio which includes most items other than railway wagon hire purchase! A similar concern, Wagon Finance Limited, has a name which relates more closely to its origins, though doubtless the relevance is lost on its present day clients.

Consolidation (1880-1920)

The period from 1880 to 1920 was largely one of consolidation, though there were several notable changes, technological and others, and one further independent railway materials plant was established in the town.

Openhearth steelmaking was introduced during the period at both Park Gate (1888) and SPT (1892). Whilst at Park Gate this was of no relevance to the rail trade — abandoned in 1876 — the company was now able to roll steel plates of sizes suitable for fabricating locomotive frames and boilers. At SPT Bessemer steels were gradually superseded by open hearth steels for more general applications, but remained the preferred material for rail manufacture.

Mindful of the dwindling opportunities in the rail trade, SPT diversfied into tyre, wheel and axle manufacture. Steam hammers were quite widely employed at SPT by the early 1880s, forging plain and crank axles, piston rods and similar items (Figure 15). Spring manufacture commenced about 1885 (Figure 16), and a tyre mill was installed in 1888/89. (This could, however, have been SPT's second, or 'new' tyre mill, for tyre ingots were being cast in 1883 (Figure 17).) A wheel mill, costing £¼ million, was installed in 1905 and generally modernisation proceeded apace in much the same way that it was necessary to update Bessemer steelmaking and rail rolling facilities at the plant, as detailed earlier.

Rotherham's last significant undertaking for the manufacture of railway materials to arrive on the scene was the **Brinsworth Iron and Wheel Works** of John Baker, established in 1884 (SK422924).[12]

Born in Nottingham in 1843, Baker served his apprenticeship with locomotive builders Sharp, Stewart & Co Ltd in Manchester. He gained further experience at rolling stock plants at Gorton (Manchester), Preston and Derby before coming to Rotherham to manage the Phoenix Works of Owen's Patent Wheel, Tyre and Axle Company. Keen to 'go it alone', he went into partnership with one Thomas Burnett, assembling wheels and axles from bought in forgings using rather cramped premises at Conisborough. In 1884 Baker acquired premises in the New York district of Masbrough, in which he established his Brinsworth Works. Following a period of prosperity, in 1903 he purchased a site at Kilnhurst where he developed steelmaking and forging facilities to complement the Brinsworth Works.

The biggest single business change relevant to our story to take place during this period was the bold move to create the United Steel Companies Limited (USC). During the latter part of World War One, government pressure and economic factors had brought together SPT and fellow steelmakers Samuel Fox & Co Ltd of Stocksbridge (Sheffield). In 1918 this partnership acquired iron and steel plants at Scunthorpe and Workington, together with various colliery companies, in order to stabilise their sources of raw materials. The full effect of the consortium created (USC) would first be felt in the post-1926 Depression Years. For SPT, the move would ultimately guarantee its role in railway

Figure 15. Forging wagon axle under steam hammer at Steel, Peech & Tozer Ltd.

Figure 16. Shop for assembling heavy duty laminated railway springs at Steel, Peech & Tozer Ltd.

Figure 17. Rolling a wagon tyre on the tyre mill at Steel, Peech & Tozer Ltd.

materials manufacture for the remainder of its quasi-independent existence, ie, up to 1967.

Twentieth Century Retrenchment

As UK railways declined in relative importance, largely from the 1920s onwards, companies supplying this once massive service sector were faced with the alternatives of developing new markets overseas or switching to non-railway products. Rotherham's two largest steelworks, SPT and Park Gate, illustrate well this dichotomy of approach.

SPT specifically promoted sales to overseas railway companies, both within the colonies and in South American countries (such as Argentina) which had been developed with British capital. In 1907, SPT took a financial share in the neighbouring company of Owen & Dyson Ltd, which by this time possessed a strong export business for finished wheel sets and axle trees[13]. The tie-up made sense, since SPT was already supplying quantities of 'black' (ie, as-rolled and forged) tyres, wheels and axles to Owen & Dyson's Works, where they were finished, machined and assembled. Acquiring a major stake in Owen & Dyson helped guarantee this particular outlet for railway materials from SPT's Ickles Works. The move is of particular significance to our story, for it marked the point at which steel, rather than iron, dominated rolling stock production — the last significant outlet for wrought iron. As time went by the two businesses worked ever closer together until full merger of their interests took place in 1961. The strength of this 'combine' was such that in the 1950s it could proudly and justifiably claim in adverts to be 'known wherever there are railways' (Figure 18).

Ultimately, even export opportunities for railway materials dwindled in the face of aggressive overseas competition through the 1950s and 1960s. To its credit, the British Steel Corporation (BSC), which inherited the assets of USC in 1967, did invest to modernise the industry. A completely new computer controlled precision forging machine was installed in the 1970s at The Ickles to manufacture railway axles (the RAM Project, an acronym for Railway Axle Manufacture), and tyre and wheel manufacture was later concentrated at Trafford Park, Manchester, where BSC had its most modern ring and disc mill plant.

Such moves, though, could do little to arrest the dwindling order book from British Railways, which by then was BSC's largest customer for railway materials but was being starved of investment. Though the plants at The Ickles and Trafford Park both survive under new owners

Figure 18. United Steel Companies Ltd stand at the Birmingham Trade Fair in the 1930s. Most of the railway materials visible were rolled or forged at Steel, Peech & Tozer Ltd, with the exception of the Workington-produced pressed steel sleepers.

they have never enjoyed levels of activity in the manufacture of railway products once so commonplace at SPT in its heyday.

The fate of Rotherham's steel rail trade was decided in a much more 'clinical' fashion. Following the Depression of the mid 1920s, SPT's parent company, USC, rationalised production throughout the group on economic grounds. Under this scheme SPT gave up its rail orders to USC's Workington Works, but in return received the tyre and axle orders previously dealt with at Stocksbridge. Closed officially in November 1928, the Ickles railmill actually re-opened for a short run on street tramway rails in 1929 to relieve local unemployment.

Park Gate provides us with the classic textbook example of pursuing an alternative to the option taken by SPT, namely to move out of railway markets and develop a broader market base supplying steels for more general engineering applications. This move had really started as early as 1876, when Park Gate ceased to roll wrought iron railway rails in the face of competition from superior Bessemer steel rails. Despite the move away from railways, however, Park Gate remained firmly tied to transport-oriented products. Increasing amounts of Park Gate steel went to the automotive industry, particularly from the 1950s onwards, and today's successor to the Park Gate Works — the Aldwarke/Roundwood/Thrybergh complex of British Steel Engineering Steels — is a dominant supplier in this market, with 60 per cent of its one million tonnes per annum output of engineering steels going ultimately into automotive applications, both at home and abroad.

Independence v Integration

In view of the strong supplier/customer chain which existed between Rotherham's iron and steel makers, the manufacturers of railway materials, and the rolling stock builders there was considerable scope for amalgamation. Few attempts to achieve this are on record, and most concerns continued to operate as discreet entities until they disappeared from the scene. The amalgamation of Owen & Dyson with SPT — cited earlier — was an unusual exception. This general situation was in marked contrast to that pertaining in the West Midlands, an area which boasted the UK's highest concentration of railway rolling stock manufacturers. A number of those concerns gradually acquired an interest in the Patent Shaft and Axletree Co Ltd from 1864 onwards. In 1902 Patent Shaft became a wholly owned subsidiary of the Metropolitan Amalgamated Railway Carriage and Wagon Company Ltd, a consortium which included three rolling stock builders in the Birmingham area. Patent Shaft, said in 1906 to make 'twice as many wheels and axles as any other works in Britain'[14] was used to provide the consortium with railway materials until 1920, when the Metropolitan group acquired a more modern producer of tyres and wheels and began to phase out its existing supplier. I know of only one comparable Rotherham-based merger, very much an eleventh hour episode and, in the event, still-born.

In February 1927 George Baker, Managing Director of John Baker & Co (Rotherham) 1920 Ltd acquired the defunct wagon building business of Harrison & Camm. According to the technical press of the day, the move was 'a private speculation and at the moment (he) has not definitely decided the form that its activities will take in the future'.[15] In reality, Baker was considering the idea of restarting wagon building at the Holmes as a means of providing a captive outlet for the wheels, tyres and axles made at his company's Kilnhurst Works. Unfortunately, the company's other customers — established wagon builders — reacted so sharply to this potential threat that he reluctantly dropped the idea in case these angered customers took their business elsewhere. Strangely, this was the second time that the Baker undertaking had run foul of the wagon building trade. In 1912 the company had put down its own wagon assembly plant at Kilnhurst, but was forced to discontinue this for identical reasons.[16]

The Baker company's subsequent acquisition of the Sheffield-based firm of steelmakers and forgemasters Henry Bessemer & Co Ltd looks on the face of it to be a further fusion of interests in steelmaking and railway materials manufacture, but was in reality largely a paper transaction. Baker's were keen to acquire the Sheffield company's order book, along with the considerable goodwill associated with the name of its founder. As John Baker & Bessemer Ltd (Figure 19), the successor company remained a key player in the UK's railway materials sector until it ceased trading in the mid 1960s, when it in turn was bought out for its order book by its larger rivals, the English Steel Corporation Ltd and the United Steel Companies Ltd.

There were, of course, other means by which business alliances could be created for mutual benefit. William Owen was one of four Rotherham businessmen who founded the Midland Wagon Company in 1853. Though the company initially only hired wagons, it established its own wagon building works in Birmingham in 1864, and Owen's position as Chairman for many years can only have helped the business prospects of the Phoenix Works and Rother Iron Works. Similarly, George Brown of the Rotherham Forge was a director of the British Wagon Company. For several years a director of SPT, he served as a board member with locomotive builders Robert Stephenson & Hawthorns Ltd, and USC had a similar arrangement with the Sheffield-based Yorkshire Engine Company Ltd prior to this company being fully absorbed into the USC group from the 1940s.

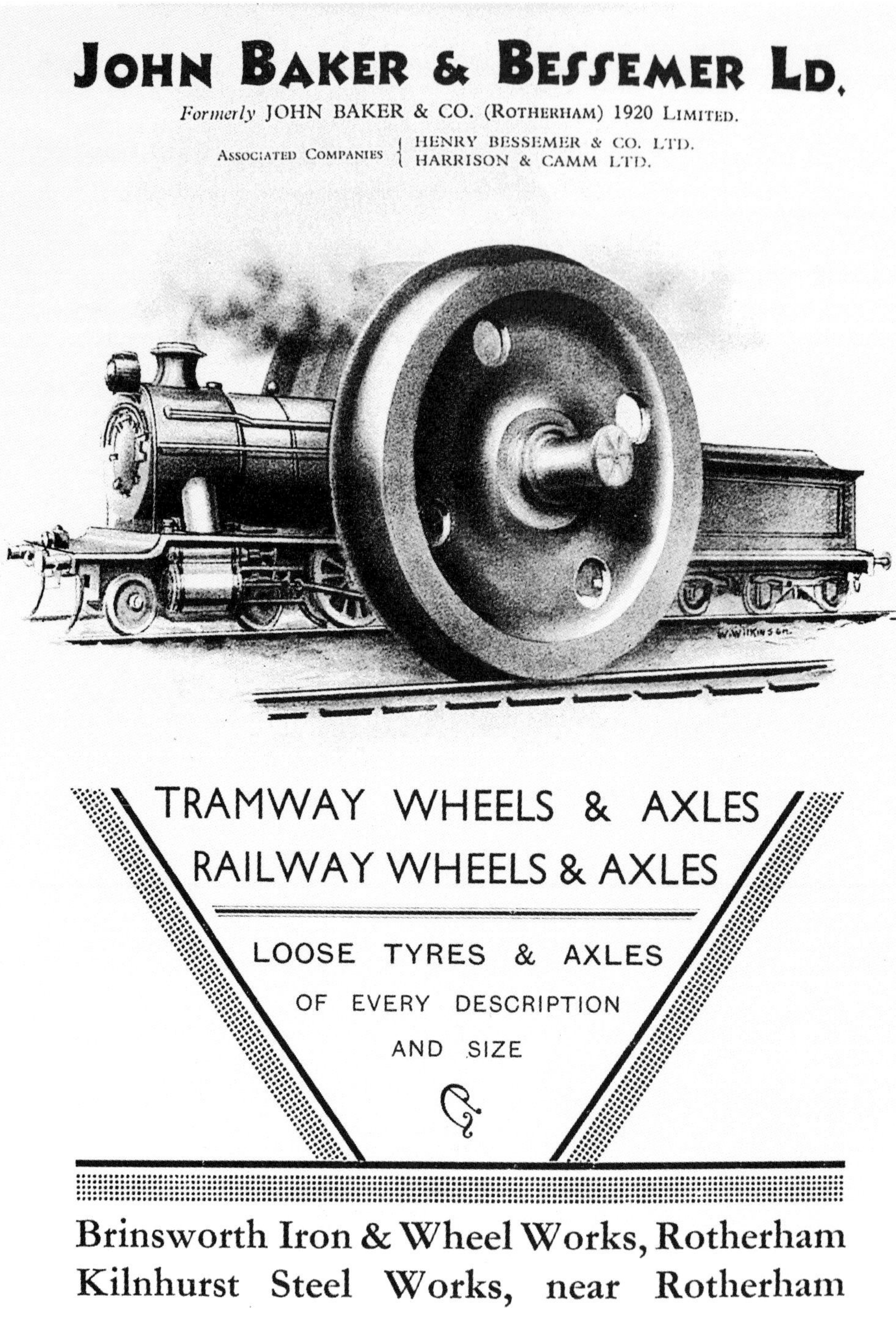

Figure 19. John Baker & Bessemer Ltd advertisement, c 1930.

Rotherham's rolling stock builders had a particularly tough time from the mid-1920's Depression onwards, ultimately suffering total annihilation. It had been the rail-borne transport of minerals, principally coal, which created and sustained the demand for their products. Once coal began to decline in importance as a universal fuel for industrial and domestic consumption, the wagon building trade fell on evil times, and the inevitable repercussions quickly passed back to the iron and steel manufacturers.

Tailpiece

The very rapid contraction of the UK rail network from the 1960s onwards (ie, post Beeching) rendered much capital equipment surplus to requirements. Railway rolling stock and locomotives are ideal sources of steel scrap, and several Rotherham companies made a specialism of breaking up such items for re-cycling. Through the 1970s and 1980s this scrap formed some of the raw material for South Yorkshire's special steels industry, which in turn supplied much of its output to the automotive industry. As a consequence, the episode provides us with the ultimate industrial phoenix.

As when the bird of wonder dies, the maiden
phoenix her ashes new create another heir.

Shakespeare's words, taken from *Henry VIII* (Act V Scene V), could not be more appropriate. Thus 'reborn', the former railway steel, much of which was originally melted and shaped at Rotherham anyway, served anew in automotive applications. It was the unseen triumph of road over rail, and provides a final, ironic twist to our story.

Notes and References

1. J Guest, *Relics and Records of Men and Manufactures at or in the Neighbourhood of Rotherham.* Originally published by A Gilling, Rotherham 1866, re-published 1980 by the Metropolitan Borough of Rotherham, Department of Libraries, Museum and Arts.
2. S Snell, *A Story of Railway Pioneers*, published by Selwyn & Blount, 1921.
3. T J Lodge, *The Rotherham Works Story*, serialised in the Rotherham and Wolverhampton edition of *Steel News*, published by the British Steel Corporation. See especially issues 141 (12/1983), 144 (3/1984), 155 (2/1985), 156 (3/1985), 157 (4/1985), 164 (11/1985) and 165 (12/1985).
4. A P Munford, 'Made in Rotherham', *Ivanhoe Review* No. 2, Winter 1992, pp 25-28.
5. F Whishaw, *The Railways of Great Britain and Ireland*, J Weale, 1842.
6. F S Williams, *The Midland Railway: Its Rise and Progress*, reprinted by David & Charles, 1968.
7. *Sheffield Independent*, 28 July 1838.
8. G W Green, private correspondence.
9. A R Holmes and E Green, *Midland: 150 years of Banking Business*, Batsford, 1986.
10. G Dow, *Great Central*, Volume 2, Locomotive Publishing Company, 1962.
11. J Guest, *Historic Notices of Rotherham*, 1879, Worksop.
12. H Baker, *The 'Steel' Bakers of Rotherham*, privately published, 1960.
13. Official Board of Trade returns show that in 1907 UK exports included 92,000 tons of tyres, wheels and axles (51 per cent of total production) with a value of £1.34 millions. A significant proportion of this originated in Rotherham.

14. J H Price, *Tramcar, Carriage and Wagon Builders of Birmingham*, Nemo Productions, 1982.
15. *Iron & Coal Trades Review*, 25 February 1927.
16. H Baker, private correspondence.

Various editions of *White's Sheffield District Directory, Rylands Directory, the Stock Exchange Year Book and Bradshaw's Railway Manual, Shareholders' Guide and Directory* have been consulted.

The sections relating to the Park Gate Iron & Steel Co Ltd, Steel, Peech & Tozer Ltd, Owen & Dyson Ltd, and their predecessors are based largely on the author's archive of manuscript material relevant to these businesses assembled over the last thirty years. The information has been verified and/or amplified as necessary by reference to Company Minute Books and other official records in the archives of British Steel plc. A comprehensive account of the first 100 years of the Park Gate undertaking is given in *A History of the Park Gate Iron & Steel Co Ltd 1823-1923* by G P Royston (printed by the Times Printing Co, Mexborough). Those readers wishing to learn more of the general history of Steel, Peech & Tozer Ltd should see Andrews and Brunner, *Capital Development in Steel*, published by Blackwell (Oxford) in 1951.

Acknowledgements

In addition to those individuals cited under Notes and References, the author also wishes to thank Ron Dyal, former Press and Public Relations Officer for BSC's Sheffield Division, and Bill Dunn and Liz Green, former Manager and former Archivist respectively at BSC's Northern Region Record Centre, Teesside, for assistance. He is grateful to British Steel plc for permission to quote from the company's extensive archive holdings on SPT and Park Gate.

15. From Slums to Council Houses: the Rotherham Experience

by Tony Munford

IN COMMON WITH MOST NINETEENTH CENTURY industrial towns, Rotherham had its fair share of urban slums. Most of the industry was concentrated on the Masbrough side of the river. Masbrough Street and College Road in Masbrough had their share of slum housing but some of the worst slums were to be found in the town centre. Here developers had crammed courts of ill-lit, undrained cottages onto almost every scrap of spare land. The elegant shops and town houses fronting the town centre streets gave no indication of the horrors hidden behind them. With no planning controls, there was nothing to stop property developers maximising their profits by building as many cheaply constructed cottages as possible on their land.

The names that were given to these courtyards often belied the grim conditions within. The 1851 Ordnance Survey 5ft plan of the town shows a succession of yards on either side of Bridgegate, Westgate and Wellgate (see Figure 1). Some were named after the men who built them — Styring's Yard, Brunt's Yard, Naylor's Yard. Other names were more exotic. True Briton Yard on Westgate took its name from the public house on the street frontage. The nearby All Nations Yard probably took its name from the variety of individuals who lived there. In 1851 there were sixty-one individuals, mostly Irish, living in the eight houses in the yard. Garden Row off Wellgate was so called because of its proximity to Garden Road and the allotment gardens in the area. In 1871 Garden Row contained fifteen houses with a total population of seventy-two. By 1881 eight of the houses were empty but the remaining eight dwellings were housing sixty-seven people. One house contained a widowed charwoman with five children, two grandchildren, three visitors and a boarder in its four rooms. Some of the yards changed their names from time to time. Garden Row, for instance, later became Pass's Yard. By the late nineteenth century, nearly all the yards had been given numbers, so Garden Row ended up as Court Twenty, Wellgate. Styring's Yard became Court Six, Westgate, while Wild's Yard became Court Eight, Westgate.

Over the river in Masbrough similar courts were to be found along Masbrough Street and College Road, bearing names such as Square Yard, Old Holland, New Holland, Pool Green, Jubb Fold, Rabbit Burrow, Phoenix Square and Windmill Yard.

Figure 1. Wellgate in 1851 showing the courts packed in on either side of the street and the Water Works on Quarry Hill. *From the Ordnance Survey 5 ft to 1 mile plan*

The piecemeal development of back yards and gardens can be traced in the title deeds of town centre properties. Among the most avid developers of slum housing were the various members of the Badger family. Thomas Badger had been tollbar keeper at Tinsley and was later licensee of the *Travellers Inn* on Westgate. His sons and several of his grandsons entered the legal profession, combining the law with property development. In May 1840 three houses on Westgate, nos. 66-70, were sold to Benjamin Badger for £297. When he sold them to John Booth, stone mason and builder, in September the same year, three cottages had been erected and the price had risen to £650. When Booth mortgaged the property in 1842 it was described as three messuages and ten cottages 'recently erected'. The development was known as Booth's Yard, later Court Sixteen, Westgate.[1]

Further north on Westgate the history of Courts Seven and Eight (originally Brunt's and Wild's Yards) can be traced from the early eighteenth century. In 1711 the future Court Seven consisted of a house, stable and orchard. The house was rebuilt in 1713 and by 1744 had been divided into four dwellings. In 1854 the property was sold to Mary Slack of Sheffield for £320 and was described as a house on Westgate with four cottages and three unfinished cottages at the rear. By 1881 no 53 Westgate had nine cottages behind it.[2] Court Eight in 1716 was described as a house and croft. By 1755 it had grown to 'several messuages' with five tenants named. These had been replaced in 1773 by three newly erected houses, rising to four houses in 1797 and seven in 1819. By 1883 the property comprised three shops on Westgate (nos 55-9) with eleven cottages at the rear extending to the bank of the Don.[3] The site of Courts Seven and Eight is now covered by the Telephone Exchange.

The area between Bridgegate and Howard Street contained two courts of back-to-back cottages.[4] The most northerly of the two was known as New Zealand Yard, possibly because the British Army were fighting the Maoris at the time they were built. In 1842 the site was sold to John Wragg, joiner, by Catherine Calton and her daughters. A year later, when Wragg mortgaged the property to George Hodgson for £1,900, he had erected sixteen back-to-back cottages on what had been the garden of a town house on Bridgegate. A further six houses were erected between 1843 and 1846.[5] To the south of New Zealand Yard lay the walled garden behind the town house that formerly belonged to the Buck family. In 1847 Joseph Henry Sales, druggist, purchased the land behind the house from Elizabeth Sales for £170. In 1850 he was able to mortgage the property for £700, having erected fourteen back-to-back cottages. These houses were variously known as Sales's Yard or New Brighton Yard.[6]

None of the cottages in these courts had running water, proper drainage or sanitation and all suffered from poor ventilation. Many of them were back-to-backs and others were 'single backs' with no openings in the rear walls. These conditions were exacerbated by the practice of keeping pigs in sties within the courts. While this undoubtedly gave a little variety to the inhabitants' poor diet, the animals only increased the problem of waste disposal. Diseases such as typhus, dysentery and diarrhoea were ever present. The poor sanitary conditions in the town undoubtedly contributed to the outbreak of cholera in 1832.[7] Rotherham was probably lucky that the cholera outbreak was relatively mild. Only some thirty people died in Rotherham compared with the 402 victims in Sheffield. There was a further outbreak of the milder English Cholera in the Pool Green area of Masbrough in 1847.

Not all the slum housing was owned by private developers and landlords. Some of the houses on Oil Mill Fold were owned by the trustees of Down's Row Chapel. These developments were only possible because there were no planning controls and no unified system of local government to enforce minimum standards of building and public health. What local government there was in Rotherham was in the hands of the manor court, the parish (overseers of the poor, highway surveyor and constable), the Feoffees of the Common Lands and the Commissioners for Lighting and Paving the town of Rotherham. The highway surveyor made some attempts to install drains and the constable carried out inspections under the *Nuisances Removal Act* of 1848 but they did not have the money or staff to make much of an impact.

All in all, Rotherham must have been a very noisome and unpleasant place in the middle of the nineteenth century. Conditions were so bad that a petition signed by the Earl of Effingham, the vicar of Rotherham and 358 inhabitants was sent to the General Board of Health who sent William Lee to conduct an enquiry under the *Public Health Act*. Lee held his enquiry in the Court House between 7 and 12 August 1850 and his report gives an excellent picture of the state of the town in the middle of the nineteenth century.[8] Mr Lee took evidence from all strata of society and the witnesses did not pull any punches when giving their evidence.

The report contains a complicated table comparing the mortality figures of the town with the figures for Pateley Bridge, Ripon and Knaresborough. The rates of death per 1,000, averaged over the years 1841-9 were 26.8 for Kimberworth and 24.1 for Rotherham compared with 17.7 for Pateley Bridge. One in six of all babies died before they reached their first birthday and the average age of death was twenty-seven years and six months in Kimberworth and twenty-two years and eleven months in Rotherham. Anyone who survived beyond twenty could expect to live to be fifty-three against sixty in Pateley Bridge. The inspector calculated the total loss to the community through deaths over the nine years in the two townships at more than £180,000.

It soon became clear that one of the main problems in the town was the lack of proper drainage for foul water and sewage. The overflow from house drains and privies had to find its own way downhill, often passing through other peoples' houses on the way. At the highest point of the town, the Crofts, was the cattle market which had an annual sale of some 3,000 fat sheep, 200 fat cattle and appreciable numbers of lean cattle and pigs. The effluvia from this livestock had to find its own way down to the Don or the High street. There was only one properly constructed sewer in the town, in Masbrough Street, but very few houses were connected to it. The surveyors of highways had constructed a public drain in Oil Mill Fold but only one person had used it. In most cases the drains that did exist in the streets were shallow and above the level of the floors of the cellars on either side which were, as a result, subject to flooding.

The evidence given by some of the inhabitants of the yards and courts was very graphic. John Hagan and his wife lived in All Nations' Yard which was owned by Maclachlin. The houses were small with no through ventilation and there was an open drain running into an open cesspool in the centre. Mrs Hagan stated:

> *The privy soil comes through the wall, and I have to lade it up. Yesterday my husband had only some tea and a bit of bread for his dinner, but the stench was so bad that he could not eat it. We are poisoned with the stench from the privy in our bedroom.*

It was reported that in Wellgate, near the *Masons' Arms*, were two cottages owned by Mrs Holland and occupied by Scott and Pearson. Level with their roofs on the hillside above them lay Ward's Place and immediately above the cottages was a privy and five pig sties. The liquid waste from these percolated downhill through the two cottages. Scott's wife said:

> *We have to keep our victuals in that nasty place. I wash for hire and we fetch water from the well 150 yards below and from the brook for slopping. I am most in the house and have been ill several times. I have had worse health since we lived here than before.*

Eight cottages at the Butter Market Foundry of Guest and Chrimes, between the Market Place and the Don, got their water from the river and a pump. A privy frequently overflowed into the well. In John Brook Greaves's property in Millgate, occupied by 'notoriously bad people' there were foul piggeries, large accumulations of filth, no drainage and no pavement. At Old Holland, Masbrough, there were three privies to thirty dwellings with numerous offensive piggeries below bedroom windows. William Lee made personal visits of inspection to many of the courts and yards. In Gillott's yard, Masbrough, described as a fever locality, he found:

> *Two slaughter-houses, and manure place; blood and garbage; drain stopped; filthy privy under bedroom. Six dwellings: water from the river for cooking; pump within 4ft. 6in. of a privy within an open cesspool, and the water unfit for anything. There is a tap from the water-works, but very little pressure. The neighbours say they have been three months together without water, but not lately; and that the pipe comes through a pottery, so that the supply is warm.*

As the foul water was free to find its own way where it would, it was not only the slum housing that suffered. Edward James Shearman, one of the most prominent doctors in the town, reported that there was no common sewer in the Market Place where he lived. All the sewerage in the street ran into an old well under his kitchen. As it had been running into the well for more than twenty-five years, it was expected to be completely full by the next winter. Dr Shearman fully expected to have to move house when this happened. Edward John Heseltine was manager of the Sheffield and Rotherham Bank at the bottom of the High Street.[9] He lived over the bank and claimed with justification that half the water closets in the High Street drained into his cellars. Even though the cellar floor had been raised, the cellar regularly flooded and had to be pumped out six or seven times a day. In summer conditions were so bad that he had to send his children away from Rotherham. Further up the High Street, pork butcher Mr Brankley reported:

> *We have no privy or water closet at all. We kill pigs in the house. We have water in the cellars, and three weeks since had a man up to the neck in it fetching bacon out of the cellar.*

One local character, Maria 'Lady' Barton makes several appearances in the report. She kept a lodging house on Millgate, reported by John Foster, house surgeon to Rotherham Dispensary, to be 'dangerous to the town'. When William Lee visited her establishment she was in the House of Correction for receiving stolen goods from one of her lodgers. One room contained four beds occupied by eight men. Another room had five beds occupied by eight males and seven females, one bed having six occupants. There were forty such lodging houses in the town. John Foster reported having seen forty individuals of both sexes crammed into two small bedrooms, six or seven to a bed in a state of nudity.

The lack of proper drainage was coupled with the lack of any proper water supply. In his evidence Edward James Shearman MD made it clear that the intermittent supply provided by the Water Company only served to exacerbate the sanitary problems. Prior to the formation of the Water Company in 1827, the main water supply in the town came from the springs that rose in Wellgate. The water flowed down Wellgate, College Street[10] and Bridgegate into the Don. In the eighteenth century the water was put into a conduit with access points at intervals. Reminiscing in 1870, John Guest praised this supply of 'crystal water' which gushed from five or six iron spouts along the conduit 'in all its sparkling purity'. The main supply point was the spout near the steps leading up to the old Town Hall, below the church. According to Guest, this was the town's 'Telegraph Station' where the 'buxom servant lasses, in their short striped bedgowns, with short sleeves and round red arms within them' met to fetch water and exchange the latest gossip.[11] Dr Shearman felt that the overflow from these springs and others ran down the roads and served to wash away accumulations of filth.

The Water Company diverted the springs into a reservoir under the road and erected a 4hp steam engine on Quarry Hill, pumping the water to a reservoir in the Crofts and thence through pipes to some parts of the town. The supply from the Water Company was at best intermittent, even after the original engine had been replaced with a 30hp engine. This was partly because the springs supplied 180,000 gallons a day, two-thirds of the quantity required to supply the town. The pumps could only lift half the necessary amount and the main pipes could only convey one-eighth of the demand. The Water Company was easily able to let off part of the power from their engine to Guest and Chrimes. Initially Guest and Chrimes worked the engine themselves and reported that there was seldom enough water to work the water pumps more than three or four hours a day in summer. Richard Chrimes gave it as his opinion that the houses that could be supplied by the Water Company could only expect water for an hour or two on alternate days. William Lee found that the company was supplying a total of 36,000 gallons a day comprising thirty gallons a day to 500 cottages, at a price of 5s [25p] per year, fifty gallons each to 300 houses at 10s [50p] and 60 gallons each to 100 houses at 20s [£1]. The charge of 5s a year for cottages only applied if the tap was outside. It rose to 7s 6d [37p] for an inside tap. Lee also calculated that households which had to fetch water from a pump or well used twelve to fifteen gallons a day, whereas those who had a tap, albeit outside and with an intermittent supply, used forty gallons. The Water Company's regulations, however, expressly forbade the use of its water for cleaning purposes.

Families who did not have the advantage of a piped supply often had to carry water for cooking or drinking for a considerable distance from a clean supply. Before the Wellgate Spring was diverted by the Water Company, people came from Masbrough to fetch water. At Kimberworth the supply to some wells was cut off when coal mines were sunk in the area. George North gave evidence that he had to get up at 2am or 3am to go to a well 200 yards from the village. If he got there first, he could get two or three gallons to get him through the day. If others had been there first, he would be lucky to get two or three quarts.

In the conclusion to his report, William Lee found that 'all the local arrangements having reference to the health of the inhabitants are exceedingly defective.' He recommended that the *Public Health Act* of 1848 be applied to the townships of Rotherham and Kimberworth and that the Act be extended to Brinsworth for the purposes of main sewerage only. Lee calculated that the cost of providing a constant supply of tap water to each cottage, with proper drainage and sanitation, and proper paving and cleansing of the courts would be 2¾d per cottage per week. He particularly recommended a self-acting water closet manufactured by Guest and Chrimes. Lee was also of the opinion that the town's sewage could provide an appreciable revenue if sold for use as manure on the surrounding agricultural land.

The report was to result in a rapid improvement of conditions in Rotherham. The General Board of Health accepted Lee's recommendation and the Rotherham and Kimberworth Local Board of Health was established in 1852, with six members each from Rotherham and Kimberworth and three from Brinsworth. Election to the Board was confined to residents having real and/or personal estate worth at least £700 or paying the poor rate on property valued at least £25 per annum. The Board first met on 11 August 1852 and consisted mainly of substantial tradesmen, viz Robert John Bentley (brewer), James Hodgson (corn merchant), John Kerr (draper), John Guest (partner in Guest and Chrimes), George Haywood (iron founder) and Thomas Turner (farmer) for Rotherham, William Beatson (manufacturing chemist), George Brown (iron manufacturer), Micah Barber (coal owner), George Shaw (timber merchant), James Yates (iron founder) and John Spencer (manufacturer) for Kimberworth and John Haywood (druggist), Robert Marsh (solicitor) and John Waring (railway contractor) for Brinsworth. William Beatson was elected as the Board's first chairman. The first surveyor and inspector of nuisances to be appointed by the Board was John Booth, builder, of Booth's Yard, Westgate. In February 1853 Edward Shearman was elected as the town's first Medical Officer of Health, defeating John Foster by four votes to three. His annual salary was £10. He was a pioneer of the use of the microscope in medicine and his examination of the local water caused great alarm when it revealed the 'disgusting filth that people were drinking'. His rigid adherence to the path of truth earned him enemies on the Board and he was eventually forced out of his post. On his death in 1878, the *Rotherham Advertiser* held that 'he had thoroughly opened the eyes of the people to the unsanitary condition of the town as regarded sewage and water and paved the way for a new and better era.'

One of the first acts of the Board was to purchase the Water Company. The Company's hand was forced by a demand from the Board that it supply the town with 87,600,000 gallons a year, twenty gallons per head per day. This the Company was clearly unable to do and the works were sold to the Board for £2,400. In 1854 tenders were invited for the erection of a new pumping station on Frederick Street with service reservoirs at Boston Castle and Kimberworth. The Wellgate Springs remained a major source of supply but were soon supplemented by further supplies from Pinch Mill near Whiston, Dalton Brook and a new reservoir at Ulley. A main outfall sewer was erected along Effingham Street, with sewers down the High Street and Wellgate, and at Masbrough. The sewers deposited their contents into the Don which did nothing to improve the state of the river. Unfortunately, the Local Board's enthusiasm for improving the condition of the town does not seem to have been matched by its financial control. In December 1856 the Sheriff's officer seized the Board's works in execution of a judgement obtained by the Earl of Effingham and several of the contractors for the sewerage and water works. The total debt was £6,400, including £3,587 due to the Earl, presumably for the purchase of the waterworks site. It transpired that the money to pay for the works had been borrowed as a mortgage on the rates but had been 'misappropriated to other purposes'.[12] The Board admitted that it did not know what had happened to the money and was forced to borrow further money to pay the creditors.

Although the Board was able to provide an improved water supply and adequate sewage disposal it could do little about the state of the River Don. In 1864 the Board petitioned the Secretary of State requesting that a Bill be introduced into Parliament to prohibit the deposit of sewage in rivers. The Board claimed that the Don brought down 'an immense quantity of sewage which flows into it from Sheffield and is deposited in the bed of the river near Rotherham, polluting the stream and poisoning the air.' The Bill never materialised and the Board certainly did not stop depositing Rotherham's sewage into the river. The Local Board could also do little about the state of the houses in which a large proportion of the population was forced to live. The sanitary inspectors could issue enforcement notices on unfit dwellings or privies and middens that had not been emptied but these only offered short-term improvements. On the whole the owners of the property had little interest in improving the houses from which they drew an income.

In the second half of the nineteenth century, large areas of Masbrough and the St. Ann's and Eastwood areas of Rotherham were developed for housing. From 1850 the Earl of Effingham began to develop his land to the north of College Street. Benjamin Badger and his son Thomas Smith Badger purchased the Eastwood estate from Joseph Need Walker for £30,000. They laid out roads (Fitzwilliam Road, Cottenham Road, Cranworth Road) and attempted to sell the land in building plots. Sales were initially slow but one of the first plots to be developed was a triangle of land to the west of St. Ann's Road. On this plot a development of artisans' dwellings was built, known as Shaftsbury Square. Benjamin Badger was also responsible for developing the land to the east of Masbrough Station, including Station Road and James Street. The rents demanded for the new terraced houses remained out of the reach of the poorer sections of the population. With the increased availability of water, an increasing number of houses were built with water closets and numbers of earth closets were converted. The shortage of cheap housing, however, was such that the large part of the population who could not afford a new or improved house had to settle for one of the unimproved courts. The population of the town rose from 13,277 in 1851 to 27,004 in 1871 and 54,348 in 1901.

A public meeting in the Court House on 22 September 1870 unanimously resolved that the limited powers of the Local Board of Health were insufficient to govern a town the size of Rotherham and called on the Local Board to petition the Queen in Council to grant a charter of incorporation to the area of the Board. This the Board did, resulting in the creation of the Rotherham Borough Council which met for the first time in November 1871.

The housing situation did not change greatly after the Borough Council replaced the Local Board. As late as 1909, Dr R Sweeting reported[13]

> *the houses are generally brick and slated; with usually four rooms, two on a floor. Many of the older dwellings have damp walls, whether through their position (built up against banks), from inadequacy of eaves spouting, or from the absence of a damp proof course.*

Dr Sweeting stated that there were 359 back-to-back houses in the Borough and numerous other houses with no through ventilation. Since 1892 only 137 houses had been demolished under the *Housing of the Working Class Act 1890*. There were still 2,248 privy middens in use.

Only one street, Steel Street, was not sewered and galvanised rubbish bins had recently been introduced. Unfortunately the municipal rubbish destructor, erected in 1892, could deal with only forty-eight tons of the sixty-eight tons of rubbish generated every day. The remainder built up into a large tip beside the destructor.[14] The Wellgate Spring had been abandoned as a public supply in 1894[15] and the Dalton Brook had to be abandoned when it was polluted with sulpho-cyanide of copper from Silverwood Colliery. The town began to take water from Langsett Reservoir in 1905. Dr Sweeting was particularly scathing about the performance of the sanitary inspectors, reporting that the senior inspector, C E Parkin senior, 'is altogether too tender and lenient towards property owners, especially if they happen to be borough councillors or aldermen.'

The inspectors were seriously hampered in their work by the shortage of housing. If the Council took the extreme course of ordering an unfit house to be demolished, the inhabitants would simply be forced to find accommodation in another unfit house. The *Housing of the Working Class Act* had given local authorities powers to clear insanitary areas, paying compensation to owners, and carry out rehousing schemes on the cleared site or elsewhere. They could also deal with single houses or groups of houses by repair or closure notices and buy land for the erection of houses for letting or sale. Many nineteenth century philanthropists recognised that it was not enough to provide new houses. The tenants must be educated to live in them. Octavia Hill, who did much work among the slums of Marylebone, was a great advocate of tenant education, believing that if tenants were simply transplanted to new houses, they would pollute and destroy them. The *Public Health Act* of 1875 placed on the owners of houses let to the working classes, the duty of keeping them in repair and empowered local authorities to inspect, demand improvements and, ultimately, to declare a building unfit and order its demolition.

Rotherham Borough Council had made a start with municipal housing in 1905 when ten houses were built in Lord Street. These houses were erected under powers conferred by the Section 56 of the *Rotherham Corporation Act 1900*. This required that, before the Council could purchase any houses occupied by the 'labouring classes' for clearance purposes, they had to provide sufficient new housing to accommodate the occupants of the cleared houses. The original plan was to erect sixty houses. In July 1903 the Improvement and Property Committee accepted the designs of Joseph Platts for three classes of houses which would cost from £150 to £190 each to erect. The rents were to be 6s [30p] and 5s [25p] per week. The Local Government Board approved the scheme in November 1903. However when a survey by the Borough Surveyor revealed that there were 221 empty houses within a mile of the Parish Church it was decided that the full scheme was not necessary. A public enquiry held in April 1904 allowed the Council to reduce the scheme to fifteen houses, of which ten were to be built immediately. William Thornton and Son's tender of £2,356 was accepted in December 1904 and the houses were completed by the end of 1905. The houses in question, nos. 59-77 Lord Street, are ordinary terraced houses, little different from the other houses in the Clifton area. The other five houses do not seem ever to have been constructed.

A Housing Committee was established in 1913 and concentrated initially on the demolition or repair of unfit houses. Between 1913 and 1919, 237 houses were found to be unfit for habitation with 190 closure orders being issued. During the First World War the Committee began to turn its mind to building houses to relieve overcrowding. In May 1916 the Town Clerk was empowered to negotiate for the purchase of nine acres of land near the Pumping Station in Doncaster Road from the Earl of Effingham. The Earl was agreeable to sell at £80 per acre and offered further land in the area. In March 1917, the Council applied to the Local Government Board for sanction to borrow £1,750 to purchase the site. A plan to invite competitive schemes from architects was shelved and the Borough Engineer was instructed to draw up the plans after consultation with local architects. He was empowered to appoint an architectural assistant at £200 p a. The same year also saw the Committee negotiating with the Earl for the purchase of eighty acres at Hill Top, Kimberworth. In 1918 the Committee accepted that it would be necessary to establish a Housing Department, recommending an initial establishment of an architect and two assistants.

During the First World War the Government was also turning its attention to post-war housing needs and the Tudor Walters Report estimated that there would be a shortfall of 1,000,000 houses in the country as a whole.[16] The *Housing and Town Planning Act 1919* required all local authorities to prepare schemes to erect the necessary number of houses within their areas, the building to be completed by 1922. The financial liability of the authorities was to be limited to the product of a rate of 1d in the pound, with the government making good any shortfall. The cost of rehousing was kept low by limiting the compensation to be paid to slum landlords to the value of the cleared site. In the same year the *Housing (Additional Powers) Act* made a total of £15,000,000 available to fund grants of £130 to £160 to private persons or bodies for each house completed within the next year. When Rotherham surveyed its housing needs in 1919, it was estimated that 3,000 houses would be needed. This figure was made up of 2,090 houses to meet unsatisfied need, overcrowding and population growth,

Figure 2. Houses in Far Lane showing the variety of houses built on the original East Dene Estate in the early 1920s. *Rotherham Central Library, Archives and Local Studies Section*

441 to rehouse people displaced by the clearance of unhealthy areas, 161 to replace dwellings unfit for human habitation, two to replace obstructive buildings, 156 to replace houses which were not unfit for human habitation but which fell below a reasonable standard, and 150 to meet deficiencies caused by industrial expansion. There were 1,410 houses in the town occupied by two or more families. The houses planned in 1916-7 would obviously be inadequate to meet this need and the scheme had to be expanded.

A site on Doncaster Road, near Far Lane, was selected as suitable for housing development. In February 1919, the Housing Committee heard that the Earl of Effingham had offered to sell 109 acres between Doncaster Road and Badsley Moor Lane for £12,000 while the Feoffees were prepared to sell a further 25 acres at £120 per acre. Charles A Broadhead had been appointed Housing Architect at a salary of £600 p a. In February he was asked to prepare a scheme for the erection of 1,000 houses, 30 per cent to be five-roomed and 70 per cent six-roomed. Both types of houses had three bedrooms, the six roomed houses having a parlour as well as a living room. The estate was laid out to the standards recommended by the Tudor Walters Report which emphasised light and spacious design and a low density. A varied mix of house designs was used (see Figure 2). In May the Committee appointed an Advisory Committee of Women to make 'suggestions of a practical nature as to the interior arrangements and details'. May 1919 saw the Committee resolve to build an initial batch of 100 houses forthwith, the first instalment to be erected between Doncaster Road School and Far Lane. The name 'East Dene' was chosen for the new estate. In June 1919 the Council applied to the government for loan sanction to borrow £110,000 to cover the cost of erection and the preparation of roads and sewers and a further £20,500 for the purchase of the land. The contract for the first block of 124 houses had been awarded to J H S Randall and Co who tendered a price of £4,293 for the roads and sewers and prices of £661 to £905 per house, dependent on type. Some problem must have occurred with Randall's contract for in July the contract was transferred to E T Small and Co of Patrington.

In the July the Housing Commissioner suggested alterations to the specifications and sizes of the houses for economy reasons. The Housing Committee objected that the alterations would increase maintenance charges in the future and 'rob the houses of all the features tending to relieve the scheme from monotony.' The builders had initial problems attracting enough workmen because an agreement between the Sheffield and Rotherham Master Builders' Association and the building operatives prohibited the payment of overtime. A rail strike caused a shortage of materials. In April 1920, the first two houses were ready for occupation and a sub-committee was appointed to choose the tenants. The first house to be occupied was 1, First Avenue. Unfortunately the minutes of the sub-committee's first meeting have not survived so the names of the first tenants, who moved in on 15 May, have not survived. In July 1920 the Housing Sub committee reported that one of the first four tenants, Mr Holland, had obtained his house by false pretences and had taken in eight lodgers. They resolved to evict Mr Holland and offer the house to Mr Burton. The second four houses were offered to Joseph Bennett of Eastwood Lane, Oliver Hobbs of Clifton Grove, Garvin Bilton of Sherwood Crescent and John Stamp of Doncaster Road. The tenancy agreement contained the following conditions:

Tenants shall keep forecourts properly cultivated and neat. Tenants shall keep all paths, hedges and fences properly cleaned and trimmed. No permanent or temporary structures or fence of any kind shall be

erected without the sanction of the committee.
No ashes or rubbish shall be thrown upon the gardens, paths or streets.
Tenants shall use every endeavour to preserve the property and shall keep it in a clean, fit and proper condition.
The tenants are reminded that the cost of all repairs falls upon the rental, and any unnecessary costs will have to be paid by the tenant.
Any tenant or person living in the houses who cause unnecessary neighbourly friction are liable to eviction.

The Council had a disagreement with the Ministry of Health over the rents to be charged for the new houses. The Housing Committee wanted to charge 7s 9d [38p] a week for three bedroom non-parlour houses, 8s 9d [43.75p] for three bedroom parlour houses and 9s 9d [48.75p] for four bedroom houses. The Ministry believed the minimum rents should be 10s [50p], 12s 6d [62.5p] and 15s [75p]. A tribunal finally settled the rents as 8s [40p], 9s 3d [46.25p] and 10s 6d [52.5p]. By the end of the year 31 houses had been completed with another 200 under construction. A further 225 houses were finished by the end of 1921. In all 555 houses were built by the Council under the 1919 Acts, all on the East Dene Estate. By the end of 1925, 1,016 new houses had been built in the borough (192 of these were built by private enterprise). By 1925 there was a waiting list of 1,500 with 20 applications a week being received. The number of council houses rose to 2,540 by the end of 1929 and 4,943 by 1939.

Even before the first houses had been started on Doncaster Road, the Council was considering alternative construction methods. As early as March 1919 the Housing Committee resolved to send a deputation to view houses at York and Chepstow constructed with concrete blocks. These were reported to be 20 per cent cheaper than brick. In May 1920 the committee resolved to ask E T Small and Co and local builders W H Treherne to erect ten houses each using the 'Lean' system. In the same month the Committee agreed to the Housing Commissioners' proposal that they erect 100 steel-framed, concrete houses, using a system developed by Dorman Long. May 1920 saw the number of Dorman Long houses reduced to fifty, with the contract being awarded to Frederick Hopkinson (Worksop) Ltd. In September the committee resolved that, after the first twenty-four Dorman Long houses were finished, no further houses would be built because of the 'unsatisfactory type of construction and materials'. The houses that were built gave endless trouble, particularly the steel frames, and were to become known as the 'sink of East Dene.' Inspections of houses at Blackpool on the trussed concrete system and at Liverpool on the Clifton Ewart system did not result in any houses of these types being built in Rotherham.

Further experiments were made in the mid-1920s. A number of ironworks had developed systems for constructing iron houses in an attempt to replace lost armaments orders after the end of the War. At its meeting in September 1924, the Committee asked the architect to submit a report on iron houses. Later in that year Alderman Caine recommended that the Council build six cast iron houses of a type developed by the Tenter Foundry of Rotherham.[17] These would cost £840 a pair and could be erected in half the time of a conventional brick house. When approached the Ministry of Health stated that it would not object to the erection of one pair for experimental purposes. Early in 1925 the Council accepted tenders for the erection of two of these houses in Meadow Bank Road. In the following year the Ministry, through the Committee on New Methods of House Construction, was actually urging councils to erect experimental metal houses. Rotherham initially agreed to erect some houses on the 'Weir' system. In July 1925 however they agreed to try two 'Telford' steel houses, a system developed by Braithwaite and Co of West Bromwich. The houses were to be erected next to the earlier iron houses in Oakdale Road on the Meadow Bank Estate, in place of the proposed 'Weir' houses. The company claimed that fifty of the houses could be erected within twelve weeks. As the inner walls of the houses were lined with asbestos sheets, they would be unlikely to receive approval today. The houses were completed by February 1926 and, in accordance with Ministry instructions, were then open to public inspection for a month before being let. The metal houses were not an unqualified success and in January 1932, the two cast iron houses at 2 and 4 Oakdale Road were reported to be in bad condition owing to internal dampness. Other less extreme experiments included the completion of six houses on the East Dene Estate as 'all electric houses' in 1925.

Further houses, totalling 278, were built under the terms of Neville Chamberlain's *Housing Act* of 1923, which offered a subsidy of £6 per house for twenty years. These houses were all of the three bedroom, non-parlour type, as the subsidy was not available for parlour houses. More generous subsidies were introduced by the Labour Government with Wheatley's *Housing (Financial Provisions) Act* of 1924. This offered a subsidy of £9 per house for forty years. Under this act the East Dene Estate was completed and the Council began to build three bedroom, non-parlour houses on the land it had purchased on the Herringthorpe Estate (see Figure 3). They also built numbers of two bedroom houses for the 'lower working class' at Hartington Road, Masbrough, Meadow Bank Road and Canklow Road. These houses were intended for families with a disposable weekly income of £2 to £2.50 and the rents were set at 8s [40p]. Under the 1925 *Housing Act* the Council was the first local

Figure 3. Later estates were much more uniform in their design. This is Sheridan Drive on the Herringthorpe Estate in the 1930s. After the War, the fields in the background were covered by the East Herringthorpe Estate. *Rotherham Central Library, Archives and Local Studies Section*

authority to erect colonies of old people's bungalows. A total of 272 bungalows were built in groups of six. Each group had its own reading or common room. The Council was only the second authority in the country to adopt the Octavia Hill Estate Management Scheme which was adopted on all estates, except East Dene, in an effort to reduce rent arrears. Each estate had a female estate manager with a team of female rent collectors who also assessed the condition of the houses and arranged for repairs.

The cost of house building fell throughout the 1920s. The first three bedroom parlour houses cost £899. This high price was caused partly by the post-war shortage of building materials and skilled workers. By 1925 the houses erected at Canklow Road were costing £325 and in 1934 the Council could erect houses at Eastwood for only £305 each. In 1920 the Council had tried to finance its housing programme by issuing 6 per cent National Housing Bonds under powers in the *Housing (Additional Powers) Act 1919* but there were few takers. The programme was mainly financed by the issue of local authority stock at 5 per cent or 6 per cent, government subsidies, mortgages and rent and rate income. By 1930 26 per cent of the Borough Council's income was being spent on housing, compared with 13.69 per cent in 1921. In England and Wales the national average of houses provided by local authorities was 16.5 per 1,000 of their 1931 population. In Rotherham the figure was 32.98 per 1,000, twice the national average.

The first flush of council house building was primarily intended to relieve overcrowding and homelessness. Large numbers of slum houses remained. In 1920 there were 13,149 houses in the town, of which 11,000 were classified as working class houses. As a result of the 1919 Survey, seven insanitary areas had been identified.[18] The first of these, the Square Yard area of Masbrough, was cleared in 1923. The infant mortality in this area had been 249.9 per 1,000, against a Borough average of 115.8. Fifty-five houses were demolished, the tenants being rehoused in fifty-six new cottages on the Meadow Bank Road Estate. The Medical Officer of Health reported that the transplanted tenants were pleased with the new houses but were 'not so favourably inclined towards the increased rent.' In 1929 there were 335 houses in the remaining insanitary areas with a further 367 houses in other areas. Attempts were made to improve the best of the old houses. Thirty-two back-to-back houses in the Lyme Street/Phoenix Square area were converted into sixteen through houses with WCs in 1929. Several landlords expressed their willingness to improve their property but were understandably reluctant to spend money on houses where the tenants had run up large arrears of rent.

A picture of life in a working class house in Rotherham is provided by Margery Spring Rice who conducted research into the life of working class wives in the 1930s, taking several of her examples from Rotherham.[19] Mrs N had six children under fourteen and paid 9s 5d [47p] rent out of weekly housekeeping of 42s 6d [2.12p]. She drank a great deal of tea, had an imported egg twice a week, a bit of fish once a month, no supper and lived largely on bread and marge. Her husband had been out of work for four years and their house, in a 'congested district', was damp, with a broken fireplace, forcing her to do all her cooking in the oven. Mrs B, the wife of a greengrocer, lived with their five children in a four roomed old cottage, paying 8s 2d [41p] rent out of her 30s [£1.50] housekeeping. A typical weekly diet for the family was:

> Breakfast: cup of tea, bacon and bread.
> Dinner: joint with vegetables three days, other days eggs and tomatoes.
> Tea: cup of tea, cheese, boiled mutton or fish, kippers.
> Supper: fish and chips, bacon. Tinned food: — salmon or fruit occasionally.

In contrast Mrs C had been rehoused on one of the new council estates. She had eight children and her husband, a labourer, had been out of work for two years. The rent was 7s 10d [39p] out of £2 5s [£2.25] housekeeping. Her own diet was:

> Breakfast: tea, don't usually eat any breakfast.
> Dinner: bread and lard or margarine; dinner occasionally included stewed meat and potatoes but by the time the other nine had been fed, there was little left for her.
> Tea: Tea, bread and butter, tinned tomatoes and black pudding.
> Supper: 3d of chips and 1d fish for five or six of the family three times a week.

Mrs C suffered from headaches, rheumatism and tuberculosis, blaming her poor health on the bad housing conditions they had previously endured. She was obviously not impressed with the new house's gas fire:

> *you burn money on an' still no rooms get heated or dried. Only living room to dry clothes in and back kitchen so small. Children unable to attend school, having no boots and unable to get any. Teachers always sending and grumbling.*

Life in a slum house was a constant battle against decay and indifferent landlords. In 1929 Ernest Bywater of 7, Court Six, Westgate (also known as Three Horse Shoes Yard) wrote a letter to the Minister of Health:

> *Please could you be so kind as to have my oven and fireplace seen to as I have told my landlord until I am tired of telling him. It won't cook*

a think [sic]. There is six of us in the family and I have to buy shop bread. You can't do no meat pies or anything and it smokes us all out of the house, is just as if it's on fire when the door opens and we have all sore eyes with it. It's terrible. I don't know how we all keep our health with it.

It is interesting that, even in the slum districts, the inhabitants expected to bake their own bread. The letter did not get to the Minister but was delivered to the local Sanitary Inspector. Moving to a council house was obviously not the complete answer for the inhabitants of the slums but most slum dwellers happily swapped their damp, dark courts for a new house on a council estate.

In 1927 Dr William Barr, the Medical Officer of Health, contrasted 'the older type of long, continuous, monotonous rows immediately abutting on to the street footpath or in unpicturesque cul de sacs' with the varying groups of new houses erected by the Council, predicting that the council housing 'cannot but help have an electrifying influence on the populace.' When, in 1929, Dr Barr looked back at the 1919 housing needs survey, he found that the Corporation had erected 2,540 houses in the ten years and there were now only 352 houses shared by more than one family. The worst of the housing shortage had been solved and the Council began to turn its attention to slum clearance. Many towns began slum clearance campaigns in the 1930s following the *Greenwood Housing Act* of 1930 which offered a subsidy of £2 5s [£2.25] per person for forty years towards the construction of houses to replace dwellings demolished as unfit. Starting with one clearance order, covering fifty-three houses in 1933, the Rotherham campaign continued with eleven clearance orders covering 258 houses confirmed in 1934, with 241 houses demolished before the end of the year. This was followed by eighteen orders (248 houses) in 1935 and twenty-eight orders (289 houses) in 1927. By 1939 a total of 1,196 unfit houses had been demolished since 1923. The courts along both sides of Wellgate and Westgate were swept away, as were Down's Row off Moorgate, Thomas Street, Mary Street and Albert Street at Masbrough. Many of the sites were to remain empty as their steep nature did not attract new developers. The sites of Courts Six, Seven and Eight, Westgate, were soon to disappear under the new telephone exchange.

Luckily the Corporation photographed the unfit houses as part of its evidence for the clearance orders, so we have very good evidence of the conditions in which people were still living in the 1930s. Two of the courts off Westgate, demolished in the 1930s, are shown in Figures 4 and 5, shortly before they disappeared. The report on Down's Row stated that the twenty four-roomed houses contained between three and eight occupants in 1933. Repair notices had been issued in 1914 but

Figure 4. Court 8, Westgate (formerly Wild's Yard) photographed in 1933, shortly before demolition. *Rotherham Central Library, Archives and Local Studies Section*

the houses were found to have porous walls, no damp proof course, ceilings below bylaw height and infestations of bugs and cockroaches. When Ernest Bywater's house in Three Horse Shoes Yard was inspected in 1933, the household had grown to seven with the addition of a lodger. He was paying 5s 7d [28p] a week rent. The court, which was owned by the executors of Matilda Jarvis, consisted of seven single back houses and a former lodging house, at a density of sixty-one houses per acre. Four of the houses had only kitchen and bedroom, the others had kitchen, scullery and two bedrooms. The occupants shared six insanitary trough closets. Mr Bywater's kitchen range still had a door that would not close and the house was infested with bugs, fleas, cockroaches and rats. His landlord made no objection to the clearance order, but George Machin Gill, who owned Court Eight nearby, made vociferous protests. The eleven single back houses that he owned reached a density of seventy-one per acre.

The Council was concerned that bugs and cockroaches should not be transferred to the new council houses. They entered into a contract with the London Fumigation Co and all new tenants had their furniture and bedding collected at 7.30am on the day of their move. The specially adapted furniture vans were driven to the fumigation centre where the contents were fumigated with Zyklon B gas.[20] It was then aired and delivered to the new house by 4.30pm, except for bedding, carpets and upholstered furniture which was allowed to air until the following day. The new tenants were provided with towels, soap and temporary bedding for their first night. They were also urged to have baths in their new houses while waiting for the furniture. The new houses to take the displaced slum dwellers were erected at Eastwood, South Street, Herringthorpe and Canklow. As the new tenants would not be able to afford high rents, these houses were all non-parlour houses, let at low rents.

Private house builders were also active between the Wars and considerable numbers of detached and semi-detached houses were erected on the outskirts of the town by builders such as Bilton, Dunk and Parkin. On Parkin's Sitwell Estate, houses were priced between £450 and £1,000. In other areas of the town houses could be had for as little as £415. In 1936 a Parkin house costing £415 could be had for a small initial deposit and 14s 6d [72p] a week for twenty-five years. A deposit of £5 and weekly payments of 13s 3d [67p] would have secured one of Donald Dunk's houses on Broom Lane. Between 1919 and 1939, 2,524 houses were built in the town by private enterprise with government subsidies and another 321 without subsidy. Home ownership came within the reach of the middle classes but the new houses were well out of the reach of the slum dwellers who relied on

Figure 5. Washing day in Oil Mill Fold, off Westgate, in 1933. *Rotherham Central Library, Archives and Local Studies Section*

the Council to rehouse them. The Council had estimated in 1919 that 3,000 council houses would be needed. Many local authorities never achieved their 1919 estimate but by 1939 Rotherham Borough Council had constructed approximately 5,000 houses. When war broke out again and put an end to Council house building, the Housing Committee could reflect with pride that they had erected two-thirds of the houses built in the town between the Wars against a national average of one quarter.

As soon as the end of the Second World War came in sight, The Housing Committee began to plan their post-War housing campaign. Further estates were planned at East Herringthorpe, Thorpe and Blackburn, with work starting in February 1945 on the roads and sewers at East Herringthorpe. To cater for the initial demand, 100 'Phoenix' type prefabricated houses were erected at Mowbray Gardens in March 1945 followed by 211 of the 'Arcon' type. The building of conventional houses started at the same time. Six houses were erected at East Herringthorpe by building apprentices from Rotherham Technical College, assisted by craftsmen. In May 1947 the Council was able to invite Aneurin Bevan, Minister of Health, to open the 600th house to be completed since the War. House building continued in the 1950s and 1960s with the estates at Broom Valley, Kimberworth Park and Wingfield. Apart from Beeversleigh on Clifton Lane, the Council was not tempted into building tower blocks although a number of blocks of low-rise apartments were erected.

The fight against slum housing also continued as many of the terraced streets built in the second half of the nineteenth century came to the end of their life. At the end of 1954 the Medical Officer of Health reported that there were 11,578 houses in the Borough that had been constructed before 1900. There were still 26 houses using pail closets and 136 with privy middens. By December 1968 there were 2,264 houses of clearance standard and a clearance rate of 300 a year was proposed. One of the areas to be cleared in this second round of slum clearance was Shaftsbury Square. Ironically, the St. Ann's Flats that replaced Shaftsbury Square lasted barely twenty years before they too had to be demolished.

Notes and References

1. Rotherham Central Library, Archives and Local Studies Section, 213/C71/7-23.
2. Rotherham Central Library, Archives and Local Studies Section, 415/B7/1-20.
3. Rotherham Central Library, Archives and Local Studies Section, 415/B8/1-10/6.
4. Back-to-back cottages were constructed with a shared rear wall so that there were no rear windows or through ventilation. Most had only one room on each of two floors, although there were a few (e.g. Albert Street, Masbrough) that were of three storeys.
5. Rotherham Central Library, Archives and Local Studies Section, 213/C46/1-9.
6. Rotherham Central Library, Archives and Local Studies Section, 213/C16/1-4.
7. For further details of the cholera outbreak see Freda Casson, 'The cholera burial ground' in *Ivanhoe Review* no.5, 1993, pp 36-41.
8. *Report to the General Board of Health, on a Preliminary Inquiry as to the Sewerage, Drainage and Supply of Water, and the Sanitary Condition of the Townships of Rotherham and Kimberworth,* HMSO 1851.
9. He was also father-in-law of Anthony Trollope, the author.
10. Known in the Middle Ages as Brookgate.
11. *Rotherham and Masbrough Advertiser*, 24 September 1870, p 2.
12. Rotherham and Kimberworth Local Board of Health minutes, 23 February 1857.
13. *Dr R Sweeting's report to the Local Government Board on the sanitary circumstances and administration of the County Borough of Rotherham, with specific reference to the continued prevalence of enteric fever,* HMSO, 1909.
14. The tip was known locally as 'Spion Kop' or 'Mother Kush'.
15. The abandonment of the Wellgate Spring led to a reduction in the annual deaths from diarrhoea from seventy-six to seven.
16. The history of government housing policy between the wars and its application in Rotherham is discussed in J. Bott, *Government policy and the development of working class housing in the inter-war period, with specific reference to Rotherham County Borough* (BA dissertation, University of Sheffield 1994) — a copy is available for study in the Archives and Local Studies Section, Rotherham Central Library.
17. Photographs of a similar cast iron building system, devised by Newton Chambers of Chapeltown, will be found in J & M Jones, *A Most Enterprising Thing*, Chapeltown and High Green Archive, 1993.
18. The insanitary areas identified in 1919 were Amen Corner and New Holland (98 houses); Square Yard and Jubbs Fold (63); Oil Mill Fold and Down's Row (68); Greasbrough Road and Primrose Hill (68); Lyme Street, Dorset Place and Phoenix Square (55); Badger's Row (32); Sales Yard and New Zealand Yard (23); Albert Street (40); Brunswick Lane and courts (25). These areas included 170 back-to-back houses.
19. Margery Spring Rice, *Working class wives: their health and conditions* (Penguin Books, 1939, republished by Virago 1981).
20. This gas was later to become notorious from its use in the gas chambers of German concentration camps.

16. ROGER DATALLER OF RAWMARSH

by Ray Hearne

ROGER DATALLER WAS THE PEN-NAME chosen by A A (Arthur Archibald) Eaglestone: steelworker, mineworker, Oxford graduate, historian, adult educator, university lecturer and above all writer, of widespread repute and renown.

Born in Parkgate in 1892, son of an ex-mineworker who had set up a small local mineral-water business, he soared to celebrity in 1925 with the publication out of the blue of his first book *From A Pitman's Notebook*, a journal-cum-diary which chronicled a whole year of mining life and lore based around his experiences underground at New Stubbin Colliery, Rawmarsh, where he worked as a time-keeper. The book received astounding reviews particularly in America where some seemed even then almost hysterical; eg, from the Detroit News,

MINER WRITES FROM BURROW

and from the breathless Providence Journal,

BLIND MOLE THINKS[1]

By the time of his death in 1980, having added a further two volumes to his pitman's trilogy: *A Pitman Looks at Oxford* and *Oxford into the Coalfield*, his remarkable literary output included two weighty and eminently readable South Yorkshire novels: *Uncouth Swain* and *Steel Saraband*, (the former described as 'like Dickens but not so verbose'[2] the latter turned in 1941 into the film *Hard Steel*); four plays, all on 'industrial' themes, two books of criticism, two series of BBC radio broadcasts, countless articles, reviews and short stories, as well as an authoritative history of Rockingham Pottery (written jointly with his son-in-law T A Lockett). In addition to this substantial and diverse corpus, and representing a valuable indicator of the esteem in which he was held by fellow writers such as J B Priestley and Phyllis Bentley, he served for five years as president of the prestigious Association of Yorkshire Bookmen (sic), before completing, towards the end of his life, a rich and fascinating, though poignantly unpublished account of his own earliest days growing to adulthood in Parkgate and Rawmarsh.[3]

Despite the demonstrably high quality of all his writings, every one of Dataller's books is long out of print; certainly copies can be found for consultation in Rotherham's Local Studies Library, but none is available to be taken out by the general public. Like Ebenezer Elliott before him, in the years since his death Dataller has been sadly neglected by his own community, the very subject of his best work! Indeed it is more than ironic that on the occasion of Elliott's centenary in 1949 it was Dataller who wrote and presented, both in Rotherham and in Sheffield, splendidly memorable celebratory lectures, 'accompanied by readings from the poems by Mr Paul Eddington'.[4] Tastes change inevitably, but for all the occasional faults one might detect in some of his work, an excess of pedantry perhaps, and a niggling pomposity at times, it seems to me irrefutable that Dataller's contribution to the literature of this part of the world, and to the possibilities of a broader collective sense of a South Yorkshire culture, deep-rooted and ever evolving, was by any measure first class and deserving of substantially more widespread recognition.

Curiously enough perhaps, the two texts which offer most insights into Dataller the writer and Eaglestone, the man behind the pseudonym, are his first and his last; the *Pitman's Notebook* and the unpublished autobiography, *A Yorkshire Lad* written some fifty years later. The latter's first chapter, 'Intimations of Coketown', with its overt allusion to Dickens's *Hard Times*, tries to evoke the smoke and muck of 1890s Parkgate viewed through a child's eyes from number twelve Lloyd Street:

> *It was just another industrial street, built to serve the works adjoining. Steel odours lingered in every yard and doorway. My earliest recollections were of peering through the window curtains at men with flushed and toasted faces — furnacemen and rollers — as with neatly laundered sweat towels (like the plain cravats of the Age of Anne) they clip-clopped steadily to the great gates around the corner. When they returned, the neckcloths had been screwed into shapeless folds, and the toasted features disguised with dust and grime. Our parlour window opened not upon faery lands forlorn, but on the blistered scales of the furnace door, and the rust-streaked columns of the chimney-stacks.*[5]

Gritty and colourful, committed to an earthy and emotional realism, yet so characteristic of all Dataller's work, in its ready embrace of historical and literary reference; here, 'faery lands forlorn' is a direct transplant from Keats's *Ode to a Nightingale* and works subtly and effectively as a foil to the furnace; elsewhere on occasions when he seems unable to write a page without showing us how many books he has read and how much history he has imbibed, the impulse jars somewhat and represents to my mind his greatest literary weakness. At one level of course this is understandable; one of his central themes particularly in the *Notebook* is to try to get across to an alien, principally middle-class book-reading public the notion that people in mining communities are actually capable of rational thought, informed opinion and articulate discussion! Taking on indeed, what one might call a widespread 'blind

A A Eaglestone (1892-1980)

mole-ism'. For me though, Dataller's writing is at its best when it simply describes, or re-enacts unliterary lived experience:

> *The street had been thrown together in the early seventies by a speculative builder, who had succeeded in packing the greatest amount of living accommodation into the smallest possible space. This achievement included tiny wash-kitchens, and bare, earth-trodden yards, brightened occasionally by clumps of marigolds, and fitful borders of nasturtiums. And the inevitable 'hen hoile'. Gas lamps prinked the mathematical line of the houses, a front broken only by the modestly retiring red-brick, stone-faced Primitive Methodist 'Bethel'. ...The street had sprung directly from the turf; one year grass-roots, the next macadam and*

asphalt. Encrusted with soot, when it rained the water streamed in a jet black torrent along the gutters; and when the west wind blew from off the Pennines, clouds of dust shot up and billowed between the grimy houses... The women fought the atmosphere with scrubbing brush and wash-tub, a battle in which there was no armistice and no mercy. They welcomed, of course, the annual holidays, but those who went away always announced as the brief spell drew to a close, how delighted they were to return. For sound and heat and soot despite, the street was home. When they fell asleep it was to the clashing echo of barrows from over the wall, the slithering of ore down the chutes, and the eldritch wailing of the Company's locomotives. Those who remained at home during the holidays found it difficult to sleep at all. Only when the wheels began to turn did they find peace again. They lived to mechanical rhythm(s).[6]

There is an enviable sense of 'place' rendered with an undisguised admiration for its people, and for their wondrous abilities to endure and to adapt despite the dictatorial proclivities of the industrial machine. The relentless war against muck waged scrupulously here by the women was matched by the men in their own daily labours, both in the adjacent Parkgate Iron and Steel Works and more pointedly down the pit at nearby Aldwarke Colliery, which remained:

A furtive thing, tucked away as though by conscious design behind the railway station in Aldwarke Road. The Iron Company exposed itself with the utmost frankness; there were few boys of my generation who on the plea of carrying snap-baskets to relatives had not penetrated its utmost recesses; but no outsider ever wandered into the mine. From time to time stray echoes of underground warfare would reach our ears — falls, explosions, strikes and things — but only in the sense of rumour passed on. All that we saw of the mine was in the sweat-streaked dust of the colliers' faces, a flashing glimpse of teeth and eyes, pit-pants flapping through leathern belts ('I'll belt thee!'), and the clank of dudleys, as with Elizabethan swagger, they made for home.[7]

Something of that yeoman 'swagger' transfuses itself into his prose; it is not difficult to detect the growing child's pride in, if not love for the enigmatic and unpromising muck-hoile that was his home;

The air, like that of Prospero's magic island, was full of twangling, if somewhat discordant, noises, intoxicating enough to a young person...A cloud by day, a pillar of fire by night, the Don Valley still smoked and glowed in the background; but that was the normal setting. If any Economics student had come along to assure us that we were the 'victims' of the Industrial Revolution we should not have believed

> *him. We didn't feel in the least like victims, and while the sulphurous atmosphere in which we lived was the price that Parkgate paid for Cheltenham, it was implicitly agreed that you couldn't make steel without fire, and fire without all the attendant pother...*[8]

Dataller's undeniable literary gifts have vouchsafed us a marvellous array of poetic insights into this lost native community, some as provocative as they are unique; most memorably perhaps as he tries to isolate the defining characteristics, indeed what he perceives as the 'marked difference in attitude between the two classes of workman — the eyes of the iron worker, steady, level, serene; and those of the miners, ironical, alert and watchful'.[9] And later, in an almost too good to be true passage where, after the success of the *Notebook* he was invited to apply for a university scholarship courtesy of the newly established Miners' Welfare Scheme, and was interviewed in London by a panel of astonishing worthies including Lady Mabel Smith, R H Tawney, President of the Yorkshire Miners' Association Herbert Smith, and Lord Chelmsford; ('in a flash I remembered a picture that I had often studied in an old volume of the *Illustrated London News* of a grizzled Chelmsford in a pith helmet sitting on horseback to a vista of Zulus!'). Asked to comment on the difference he had drawn between the psychology of the miner and that of the steel-worker his response is inspirational:

> *...I think that a familiar spirit must have dictated my reply for I answered: 'The steelworkers may I think be termed the Children of Light and the miners, the Children of Darkness!*[10]

The scholarship was of course in the bag!

At home in both elements, though it might be said, not always so comfortably, Dataller felt that he had more than paid his dues to each, having worked at Parkgate Forge for ten years and at Stubbin Pit for a further seven. The autobiography preserves a series of vivid portraits of shift-work in the mill, material that Dataller was later to work up into his novel *Steel Saraband*; also preserved are a number of delightful, almost self-mocking cameos in which the writer describes his young book-struck self, stock-taking absent-mindedly, filling in dockets, labels and chitties, head full of poetry and butt of many a shop-floor joke; in one passage redolent of the young Wordsworth he re-enacts nipping out off the night-shift:

> *A little distance down the canal, on the Rotherham side a flat-boat had been tethered, and sometimes early in the gentle summer mornings, while it was still grey, I would tread the path softly, and watching the windows of the little house where the owner lived, ease out the*

post (for it was loose in the ground) to which it had been chained and padlocked, lay the whole in the bottom, and with a strip of matchboard for a paddle,move Crusoe-like up and down the misty water...I slid unhurriedly upon the canal surface, watched the dawn emerge behind the distant smoke-stacks, and delighted even in the liquid swirling and glugging of the murky water. Years later, learning to punt in Oxford, and gliding along the shadowed waters of the Cherwell, the old flat boat came once again in mind. But stolen fruit is sweetest. I always drew to the landing stage with a slight quickening of heart, watching closely the drawn curtains... Whoever he was...(the owner) slept soundly enough...[11]

In another context, significantly different, at the outbreak of war in 1914, we are able to witness the mixture of endearing impetuosity and ardent moral courage that ignites the spirit of the artist as a young man, as single-handedly he sets about organising a spontaneous and much derided peace-protest at the bottom of France Street: 'We passed a resolution, which I sent to the Prime Minister.'![12]

Of the two beguiling cultures however, it was the rebarbative ambiguity of the mine's darkness which provoked his imagination most roundly. He had hardly started at the pit, it seems, when the idea occurred to him of writing in some form or another a realistic account of miners' lives underground; what seems to have fired his passion specifically was his strategic closeness to the 'ambulance cupboard':

...every day we were confronted by a succession of split thumbs, burst eyeballs, ripped shins, (the blade slipping), and other injuries... The routine would become horribly familiar. A slow shuffle of steps outside the door, a faint whispering, then the entry of some collier or trammer, ashen under his coal-dust, with a bloody bandage around his head or the injured limb.[13]

Dataller never seeks to disguise his lasting outrage that men should have to work in such an environment 'where every passing day is a battle-ground', little wonder that he comes to define the miners' lot at its worst as a 'community of misfortune, a fellowship of poverty, a Guild of Grief.'[14] Begging the question of whether or not anything could be done to change things, the world at least ought to know the facts!

Needless to say, no management would have wished 'its day by day activities to be recorded for the public eye'[15], so, in order to keep a veil over his activities, New Stubbin became New Tollgate Colliery and A A Eaglestone became Roger Dataller:

...partly because Roger was old English, partly because Dataller represented the type of worker paid by the day, and whose pace was

generally regarded (sometimes unjustly) as significantly slow.[16]

'Sharing the secret only with my future wife' (the shadowy 'M' to whom the published book was dedicated) 'Week by week the journal grew'.[17]

Throughout the *Notebook*, with great consistency, Dataller employs 'battleground' imagery in order to communicate his sense of miners as constantly on the front line of human experience; unknown heroes, frequent casualties, waging a thankless and unyielding war on behalf of a largely ignorant and ignoring public:

> *They rode home in the olden days, with battle-battered casks and sword-indented breastplates. Their coming was heralded with the shrilling of invocatory trumpets. Fair lips smiled, and small and lily hands made bright the way with flowers. Nowadays the flinging of roses has fallen somewhat into disuse. But I never look upon colliers returning home from labour, save as one thinks of tired and triumphant warriors departing from some hard-fought battlefield. There are few perceptible casualties, but the evidence of an earthly warfare is upon them. One sees it in their clothing, disreputable, ragged, combed by impish talons, sometimes torn out of all recognition; in their clogs ridged and abraided, bright of sole where the ceaseless thrusting and spurning of the flat-sheet or the coal itself has brightened the iron fortification; in their 'Dudleys', those round and corded tin receptacles holding just a quart of water and slung around the shoulder as one slings a haversack...*[18]

And in a majestic pit-bottom clog-swipe at American psychologist and philosopher William James who in a moment of vapid metaphysical speculation had posed the question, 'How are we to find a moral equivalent for war?' This might be 'a problem... as far as the upper reaches of Society are concerned',

> *As for the miner, the question has no especial significance*
> *...He's got* his *equivalent all right.*[19]

Despite such passages, Dataller's view of mine-workers whether as individuals or in their collective 'warpaint' never becomes sentimental or romantic. Although he did work underground for seven years, he remained a time-keeper, detached to some extent, from the greater body of coal-getters; this, added to his early pop-factory background, along with, it has to be said, a certain sense of his own scholarly superiority, served to maintain that distance and enabled him in his writing to preserve a distinct degree of objectivity. As well as the doughty rough-hewn heroes, Dataller introduces us to the pit's share of inevitable rogues; petty pilferers, the odd boozer; examples of the idle and the feckless, even a character or two from the ranks of that 'black, black, treacherous breed of deputies!'[20] (In one priceless passage he informs us of Methodists he knew who refused to become deputies 'on the plea that such an office and Christianity were quite incompatible.'!)[21]

On occasions though, some of these judgements seem supercilious, his asides tendentious; partly perhaps because the mineworker-writer's sense of relative separation from his fellows is further intensified by their political divide; Dataller was no class-warrior; he seems always to have been instinctively and profoundly Liberal; though radical indeed in many values and beliefs, he seems to have felt most intellectually comfortable in the same ideological chapel as eighteenth century reformers like Major Cartwright;[22] fiercely independent and individualistic; a natural anti-Tory, but with a certain soft spot, perhaps for reasons of local history, for aristocratic whigs such as Rockingham and the Fitzwilliams, and an equally vehement opponent of the socialism burgeoning all around him; he seems as an enthusiastic youth to have taken to heart the ponderous pronunciations of Nealy (Cornelius) Bott at Four Lane Ends, 'one late evening in November, when a bitter east wind swept down the colliery road, and shook the gas-mantles in and out of incandescence overhead... Socialism' he declared was 'nowt in the end but a glorified workhouse!'[23]

Dataller's politics were shaped and coloured unquestionably by his own Christian beliefs; a deeply-felt non-conformism, originally Methodist in its perspective, is rarely far from the surface of his exquisitely honed narratives and adds an ever detectable spiritual dimension to his vibrant perception of the miners' dark warfare; 'I MUST reveal the light I have within' he says at one point in the *Notebook*[24] and gradually as the text unfolds, the archetypal miner's lamp itself begins to gather added resonances, and becomes suggestive, symbolic even of the very 'light' of revealed 'truth' and 'faith'; the individual collier, it might be argued, becomes increasingly an allegorical Christian soul led back to the light by his unerring lamp, placing Dataller for me, in a tradition of writing which stretches directly back to Bunyan and possibly beyond.

The *Notebook* is a tremendous read; there is as much pit-banter and anecdote as there is blood and gore; the fact that passages depicting the latter remain the most memorable is perhaps inevitable. As a representative year 1923 experienced its share of coalfield tragedy; roof-falls, explosions, injuries and fatalities. Dataller's undiluted wrath towards the carelessness with which some non-mining folk greeted occurrences such as the Maltby Main disaster, makes memorable literature,[25] and individual horrors such as *Casualty* and *Like the gourd that Jonas had* are as good as anything in the canon. This was widely recognised when the book came out (interestingly enough one of its few bad reviews came from the *Sheffield Independent*!)[26], though Dataller himself made clear that the key to its successful publication was the keen interest sections of the manuscript had aroused in John Middleton Murry, friend of D H Lawrence and celebrated editor of *The Adelphi*. It was Murry indeed, as the writer's influential champion, who placed the book with the publisher Jonathan Cape. Dataller's reputation was established; in the relative whirl which followed, in the year of the General Strike, he married his beloved 'M', and the couple moved into a magnificently placed new house in Rawmarsh, overlooking the Haugh Valley where, apart from his time at Oxford, he was to remain for the rest of his life, and from which he was to produce all his other books.

Two further anecdotes exemplify perhaps the calibre of the man at this period. He describes in the autobiography how he was encouraged and supported during his Oxford days by a bunch of tutors of almost mythical repute including; Gilbert Murray, H A L Fisher, G D H Cole, A L Rowse and C S Lewis, though one even greater name was to seek him out for a word. A Welsh acquaintance asked:

> *if he might bring a friend of his to my rooms, a miner from South Wales who wished to avail himself of a Miners Welfare scholarship...his name, Aneurin Bevan...So one night Bevan came and sat upon the settee...his mouth in a perpetual faint smile, dangling his hat beneath his knees and questioning with the utmost assurance...*[27]

And, almost a decade later in 1936, by this time back in the South Yorkshire coalfield organising courses as a tutor for the Workers' Educational Association (WEA), he is able to record the following:

> *One day the postman brought me a bulky parcel of manuscript, and opening this I found that it was (via R H Tawney) from George Orwell and entitled* The Road to Wigan Pier. *'I want', he wrote, 'the man who calls himself Roger Dataller to vet the mining chapters for me'. This was quite an unusual exercise, particularly for the Goldthorpe Class, for there I consulted some of the miner members. We spent quite a time on the manuscript, and in due course I returned it. Eventually Gollancz published the book, but while I have a great admiration for the author of* 1984, *I regret to announce, that I never received a word of thanks. Perhaps Orwell was busy at the time.*[28]

John Field has since pointed out that Orwell was indeed 'busy' — fighting Fascists in Spain, and getting shot in the process![29] Needless to say, the story underlines Dataller's status as a writer to be reckoned with.

In summation, it is true that Dataller might not have achieved either the breadth or the consistency to be classed as a 'great' writer, but to my mind there are elements of greatness about him; his mission, to give a literary voice to his own voiceless people, the 'Mighty Inarticulate' as he terms them, might have been flawed in some ways in its conception and patchy in parts in its performance, but as an aspiration it was inherently noble and all but unique even now in these parts. For me, Dataller's emotional commitment to this notion of 'his people' vastly outweights any minor perceivable weaknesses in his writing. In this final passage we see him at his best; in a single haunting image that echoes the Trojan Women of Euripedes, he manages to embody the tragedy that was the very nature of working class life at this period; at the same time his final 'stray lines' carry an implicit message to all of us, most particularly perhaps to the writers and artists amongst us; to remember, to record, to articulate and thereby to keep alive the whole truth of our own people's experiences:

I heard a woman weeping in the darkness of this place a week or two ago. She was standing well within the shelter of an alleyway so that her face was hid from sight, but not the outline of her form nor of her head which was shawl covered and very slight. I might have halted, but I just dared not. It seemed to me that sorrow was very sacred in that moment, so I took my blundering feet away as lightly as I could. She was crying because her little son had been compelled to work on the night shift at the local ironworks. She had patted him away with fear and foreboding. For the first time in his life he would not sleep within his mother's house, within the territory of her tender fingers. And she, good woman, fearful of the loco's [sic] and the molten metal, had crept into the alleyway...to weep.

I find it impossible not to think of her, but I know that save for these stray lines her sorrow goes with small remark...[30]

Notes and References

1. Unpublished autobiography *A Yorkshire Lad*, p 90.
2. Quoted in *Sheffield Star*, December 1964.
3. *A Yorkshire Lad*, available in manuscript in the Archives and Local Studies section of Rotherham Central Library.
4. Centenary programme and Elliott monograph (Rotherham Central Library).
5. *A Yorkshire Lad*, p 1.
6. Ibid.
7. Ibid, pp 1-2.
8. *A Yorkshire Lad*, p 29.
9. Ibid.
10. Ibid, p 100.
11. *A Yorkshire Lad*, p 54.
12. Ibid, p 66.
13. Ibid, p 85.

14. *From a Pitman's Notebook*, p 158.
15. *A Yorkshire Lad*, p 88.
16. Ibid, p 88.
17. Ibid, p 86.
18. *From a Pitman's Notebook*, p 22.
19. Ibid, p 212.
20. Ibid, p 175.
21. Ibid, p 63.
22. Subject of Dataller's B. Litt. thesis at Oxford.
23. *A Yorkshire Lad*, p 38.
24. *From a Pitman's Notebook*, p 157.
25. Ibid, p 233.
26. *From a Pitman's Notebook*, p 89.
27. Ibid, p 107.
28. *A Yorkshire Lad*, p 135.
29. 'Education For A Tolerable Society', Northern College, 1986.
30. *From a Pitman's Notebook*, p 183.

Acknowledgement

I wish to thank Mrs Ruth Hunt and Mrs Isabel Lockett, A A Eaglestone's daughters, for permission to quote from their father's unpublished autobiography, for commenting on the text and for supplying the photograph which illustrates this essay.

The Contributors

1. Thomas Rotherham's College 1482—1550
and
12. The Stirrings in Thorpe Hesley on Saturday Night

Stephen Cooper was born in 1948 and was educated at the Holt Grammar School, Liverpool and Balliol College, Oxford, where he read Modern History. He qualified as a solicitor in 1972. He was in private practice in Sheffield for a number of years, but joined the Government Legal Service in 1989. Stephen married his wife Gaye in 1970 and they have two daughters, Elizabeth and Rosemary. The family has lived in Thorpe Hesley since 1979. Stephen's interest in local history was awakened in 1985 by the chance discovery of a document relating to a disputed will. This led to the publication of *A House Divided* in 1987, a story of madness and litigation in the late eighteenth century. Stephen's other publication is *Burglars and Sheepstealers* (1992), which concerns crime and transportation in the early nineteenth century. Apart from history and law Stephen's other hobbies include walking and running.

2. Some Travellers to Rotherham from the Sixteenth to the Eighteenth Centuries

Freda Casson was born in Rotherham and received her education at the High School for Girls. An Associate of the Library Association, she has worked, both full-time and part-time, in most departments of Rotherham Library, culminating in the position of Local Studies Librarian. She has written (some under a former name) many pamphlets and articles on different aspects of the history of Rotherham. It has given her great pleasure to have been able to help many students and researchers and to have had her help acknowledged in books and theses written by them. She was both touched and honoured to have had a recent book dedicated to her. Having recently retired she is hoping to be able to devote more time to her family and friends and to being able to continue work on her own family history after many years helping other people to do theirs.

3. EARLY WATERMILLS OF THE MALTBY AREA

Alice Rodgers was born and brought up in Burton-on-Trent on the borders of Derbyshire and Staffordshire. She came to South Yorkshire in the late sixties after qualifying as a teacher and, for ten years, lived and worked in Sheffield eventually marrying a local. In 1978 she and her family moved to Maltby where, in her spare time, she has been able to pursue her life-long interest in local history. In 1981, she co-founded Maltby Local History Society whose regular monthly meetings now draw people from the wider Rotherham area and beyond.

Research into the history of the local 'miners' church led to her contribution, in 1990, of an article on the 'South Yorkshire Coalfield Church Extension Committee' to the South Yorkshire Industrial Mission publication *God's Coal*. This, in turn, sprang from her work on Maltby Colliery Disaster. She is now employed part time as a lecturer and community outreach worker at Rother Valley College at Dinnington.

5. SANDBECK HALL AND PARK

TOM WILLIAM BEASTALL was born in Doncaster and brought up in Tickhill. After attending Maltby Grammar School and Manchester and London universities he made study of the Lumley archives a major leisure time interest. He published *A North Country Estate : the Lumleys and Saundersons as landowners* in 1975 and *The Agricultural Revolution in Lincolnshire* in 1978. He contributed to the *Victorian Countryside*, volume 2 in 1981 and has edited publications on the history of Tickhill for the University of Sheffield. A book, *Tickhill: Portrait of an English Country Town* is due out in September 1995. A churchwarden at St Mary's Parish Church Tickhill, he was deputy headmaster of Maltby Comprehensive School after teaching history at Chichester High School for Boys, West Sussex.

4. THE DOMESTIC COMFORTS OF A SEVENTEENTH CENTURY KIMBERWORTH FARMING FAMILY

Joan Jones (neé Gregory) was brought up in Charlton Brook near Chapeltown and was educated at Ecclesfield Grammar School, Matlock College of Education and what is now Sheffield Hallam University. She has taught in primary schools in the West Riding, Nottingham and Sheffield, latterly as Deputy Head at Bankwood School. She is currently on secondment to Sheffield Hallam University where she is a Senior Lecturer in the School of Education attempting to unravel the mysteries of National Curriculum History to B Ed and PGCE students. She is Honorary Secretary of the Chapeltown and High Green Archive which was founded in 1987 and consists of a large collection of photographs, films, documents and artefacts relating to the economic and social history of Chapeltown, High Green and surrounding areas. The Archive is noted for its wide range of local history publications and Joan was joint author of *A Most Enterprising Thing* (a history of Newton Chambers at Thorncliffe) and joint editor of *Chapeltown and High Green: The War Years* (1994), *Ecclesfield Parish Pictorial* (1991) and *Ecclesfield Parish: People and Places* (1994). In 1983 she co-ordinated a local history curriculum development project on *Childhood in Chapeltown and High Green* which resulted in the publication of a series of teachers' guides, resource packs and pupil worksheets. Between 1983-86 Joan acted as adviser to the award-winning BBC TV's schools history series *Now and Then*.

16. ROGER DATALLER OF RAWMARSH

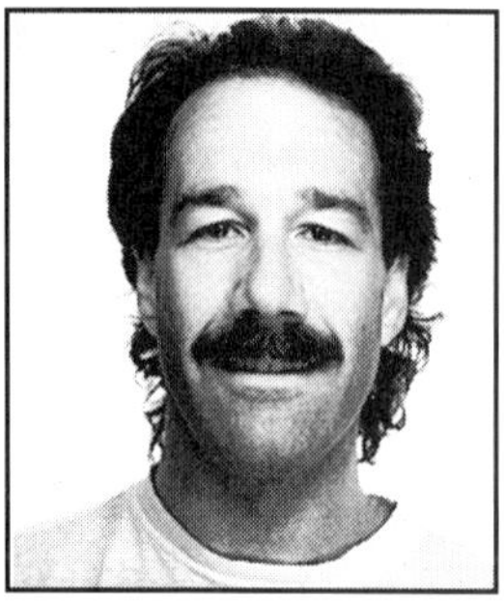

Ray Hearne is a poet/singer-songwriter from Parkgate, now living in Wath. He has worked across South Yorkshire for the Workers' Educational Association since 1981 teaching Literature and Writing. He contributed an essay on 'Ebenezer Elliott, Corn Law Rhymer' to *Aspects of Barnsley 1*.

6. Matters of Concern: The Life Story of the Third Earl of Effingham
and
11. The Life of George Wilton Chambers

John Goodchild, M Univ, is a native of Wakefield and was educated at the Grammar School there. He has been active in local historical research since about the age of thirteen, and he is the author of some 130 books and published essays on aspects of the history of the West Riding. He was the founder-Curator of Cusworth Hall Museum near Doncaster, and subsequently Archivist to Wakefield M D C; in his retirement, he runs a Local History Study Centre at Wakefield which houses his immense collections of manuscripts and research materials, and which is open to all to use, free of charge by appointment. Mr Goodchild holds an honorary Master's degree from the Open University, awarded for academic and scholarly distinction and for public services. Outside historical research, his interests lie in Freemasonry and in Unitarianism — and in his dog.

13. Coal in the Valley: Coal Mining in the Dearne Valley at Wath

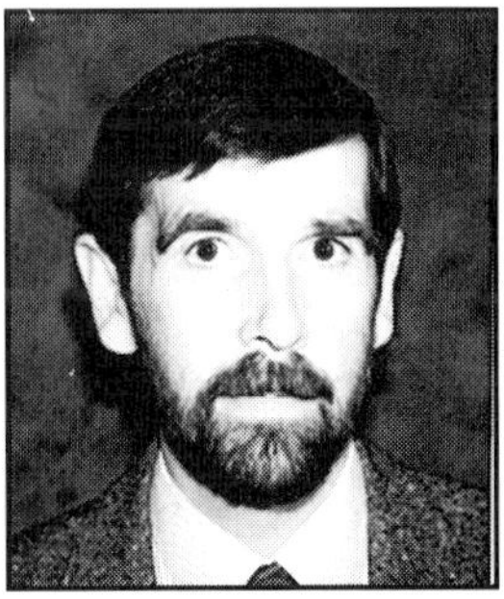

Alexander Fleming was born and educated in Liverpool. After obtaining graduate and post-graduated qualifications from London, Newcastle and Keele Universities he joined the staff of Wath Comprehensive School in 1972, where he is Head of History. As secretary of Wath History Group since its inception in 1979 he has given many illustrated talks at its quarterly meetings and organised several local history exhibitions at Wath library. His published contributions include a Wath town-trail, a photographic history of the town (jointly with Steve Hird) and commentaries on reprints of old Ordnance Survey maps of the area. A long-term project is the creation of an oral history archive for Wath. For many years a long-distance runner, Alex tries to spend as much time as possible walking, climbing and cross-country skiing with his wife Susan in Scotland and the Alps. Last winter in 'The Great Snow' he achieved a long-nurtured ambition by skiing down the Hoylandswaine by-pass!

4. THE DOMESTIC COMFORTS OF A SEVENTEENTH CENTURY KIMBERWORTH FARMING FAMILY
and
7. THE FIRST MARQUIS OF ROCKINGHAM'S RENT ROLL BOOK

Melvyn Jones was born in Barnsley and educated at the Holgate Grammar School and the universities of Nottingham and Leeds. He taught for seven years at Myers Grove, Sheffield's first comprehensive school, and then for nine years at Sheffield City College of Education before its amalgamation into Sheffield City Polytechnic in 1976. He is now Head of Academic Resources in the School of Leisure and Food Management at Sheffield Hallam University. He is a geographer by training, a countryside management specialist by profession and a landscape historian by inclination. He has written extensively on the economic and social history of South Yorkshire. Recent publications include *A Most Enterprising Thing* (an illustrated history of Newton Chambers) and a revised edition of the widely acclaimed *Sheffield's Woodland Heritage*. A new book on *Rotherham's Woodland Heritage* has just been published by Rotherham Libraries, Museum and Arts. He also contributed pieces on the riots at Newton Chambers' pits at Thorncliffe in *Aspects of Barnsley 1*, on the history of the Welsh community in Carlton and Smithies in *Aspects of Barnsley 2* and on ironstone mining at Tankersley in *Aspects of Barnsley 3*. When not doing his day job or toiling over a word processor in the evenings and weekends, he lavishes his attention on his wife, his cat, his garden and the ancient house in which he lives at Thorpe Hesley (but not necessarily in that order! — Joan Jones).

8. KIVETON: THE SEAT OF HIS GRACE THE DUKE OF LEEDS

Brian Elliott was born in Royston, near Barnsley but spent his childhood and youth in the neighbouring villages of Carlton and Monk Bretton. He was educated at Carlton Primary School and Edward Sheerien Secondary Modern where he first became interested in local history. After an undistinguished spell as an apprentice professional footballer he obtained a proper job, working for Barnsley Corporation in a Dickensian office next to the Cleansing Department. He studied part-time at Barnsley College of Technology and gained a place at Matlock College of Education where he met his Barnsley-born wife, Angela. Brian was Head of Geography at Royston Comprehensive School for almost fourteen years before taking up a post in Further Education at Rother Valley College where he is Head of Division (General Education). He has published many articles and his recent books include *The Making of Barnsley* and *Barnsley's History From the Air*. He has initiated, edited and contributed to *Aspects of Barnsley* (1993-95) and is a regular contributor to the quarterly *Yorkshire Journal*. He cites his greatest achievement as beating Seb Coe in the 1992 London Marathon. Brian lives near Doncaster and has two daughters, Natalie and Hannah.

15. FROM SLUMS TO COUNCIL HOUSES : THE ROTHERHAM EXPERIENCE

Tony Munford was born and raised in Surrey but claims to be a semi-Yorkshireman as his mother was born in the county. Educated at Dorking County Grammar School and the University College of Wales, Aberystwyth, he began his working life at the Derbyshire County Record Office, later moving to the South Yorkshire County Record Office. Since 1986 he has been head of the Archives and Local Studies Section of Rotherham Central Library. His other published works include *Victorian Rotherham* (1989), *Rotherham: a pictorial history* (1994) and *A walk round Rotherham: the town centre* (1994). He also edits *Ivanhoe Review*, the Archives and Local Studies Section's biannual local history journal.

9. CHRISTMAS CAROLLING AT THORPE HESLEY

Ian Russell is the Headteacher of a Rotherham primary school (Anston Greenlands). He was born in Aberdeen, lives in Derbyshire, and is married with a son at university. He has been researching the local carolling traditions of South Yorkshire and North Derbyshire for over twenty-five years. His doctorate was based on local singing traditions including carolling (Leeds University, 1977). He has broadcast, made films, and written on the subject of local carols both at home and in America, as well as on other related interests including folk song, traditional drama, folk dance, and traditional humour. The fruits of his carol research, which includes hundreds of hours of field recordings and dozens of manuscripts and local carol collections, are currently being organised into a major archive called Village Carols and copies of the recordings have been placed in the National Sound Archive (British Library) and in the Archives of the Centre for English Cultural Tradition and Language at the University of Sheffield. To date there are ten Village Carols publications including books, audio-cassettes, a CD, and a carol collection, and more are planned. The most recent village study to be published is of the carolling tradition of Foolow in the Peak District, *On This Delightful Morn* (audio-cassette and book, further information from Village Carols, Bridge House, Unstone, Sheffield S18 5AF). Ian was the editor of *Folk Music Journal* from 1980 to 1993, and in 1994 directed the highly successful Festival of Village Carols at Grenoside. He is currently undertaking research into the carol singing at Coal Aston in Derbyshire and writing for the new edition of the *New Grove Dictionary of Music and Musicians.*

10. ASPECTS OF THE GROWTH OF PARKGATE 1831-1891

Tony Dodsworth was born in Crystal Palace and grew up in South London. He attended St Joseph's College, Beulah Hill, before studying for a combined degree in Geography and History at Birmingham University. He began teaching in London but moved north in 1974 and has now taught for twenty years at Pope Pius X School, Wath upon Dearne, where he is Head of Humanities. It was under the influence of Professor Harry Thorpe at Birmingham University that he developed a keen interest in the historical geography of England and learned to recognise ridge and furrow at more than twenty paces! This interest has continued to grow through membership of English Heritage and the National Trust and he is an enthusiastic visitor of churches, particularly as a member of the Church Monuments Society.

14. ROTHERHAM'S RAILWAY TRADES

Sheffield born and bred, **Trevor Lodge** was educated at Abbeydale Grammar School, and Manchester and Sheffield Universities. An industrial chemist by training, he had an early career which comprised spells of teaching interspersed by a memorable (but all too brief!) period as research chemist with Newton, Chambers & Co Ltd at Chapeltown. He eventually 'found his feet' in South Yorkshire's special steels industry, retraining as a metallurgist in the early 1970s, largely through development work carried out at British Steel's Templeborough Steelworks. Possessing considerable working knowledge of many of South Yorkshire's other steelworks, both past and present, he currently works as an information officer in South Yorkshire's special steels industry. A growing interest in all matters mechanical and industrial has led him to carry out research since the mid 1960s into the UK's heavy industries (coal, steel and engineering) and the railways that served them. In a related capacity, Trevor Lodge is Vice-Chairman of the Industrial Railway Society, whose quarterly journal he edited between 1971 and 1979. His most notable published works — the histories of the Park Gate Iron & Steel Co Ltd, the Steel, Peech & Tozer Co Ltd, and Samuel Fox & Co Ltd — appeared in serialised form in British Steel's *Steel News* and United Engineering Steels' Journal, *Stocksbridge Gazette* between 1981 and 1993.

INDEX OF PEOPLE

Abercrombie, John, 145
Adams family, 184
Allott family, 217
Amies family, 185
Ansell, Robert, 95
Aram, Peter, 144
Aram, William, 144
Athey, Arthur, 162
Aveling, J W, 52, 62, 67, 71

Badger, Benjamin, 275, 282
Badger, Thomas, 275
Badger, Thomas Smith, 282
Bailey, Marmaduke, 111
Baker, George, 269
Baker, John, 264
Bale, John, 17
Barkworth, Richard, 90
Barnsley family, 78
Barr, Dr William, 292
Batty, Don, 158-59, 165, 171
Beale, Samuel, 180, 254
Beard, Reg, 162
Beard, William Henry, 161
Bessemer, Henry, 255
Birchall, Benjamin, 237
Birks, Samuel, 157
Bokyng, John, 14, 16
Booth, John, 275
Bosville, Thomas, 26
Brand, Daniel, 141
Brathwaite, Richard, 33
Briggs, Henry, 224
Bright, Mary, 124
Brooks, Esme, 170
Brown, 'Capability', 58, 72, 89, 97
Brown, John, 251
Buck, Samuel, 38
Burdett, Peter Perez, 119
Butcher, Charles, 213, 219
Butcher family, 157
Butcher, Sarah Ann, 214, 218
Byng, John (Viscount Torrington), 43, 45

Camden, William, 26, 32
Carnebull, Henry, 14, 15, 19, 24
Carr, John, 94
Cartledge family, 66-67
Castleton, Earl of, 56
Chambers, George Wilton, 206-212
Chesman, Annie, 158, 171
Chesman, Clifford, 160, 162, 163, 170, 171
Chesman, Gertie, 160, 171
Chesman, Robert, 162, 171
Chrimes, Richard, 279
Clay family, 200-01
Clerkson, Simon, 17
Clifford, Sir George (Earl of Cumberland), 49
Collins, William, 95
Cooper family, 162, 164
Crawshaw, James, 238

Daniell, John, 50
Dataller, Roger, 298-308
de Busli, Richard, 50
Defoe, Daniel, 37, 129
Dewhirst family, 62-63
Dodds, Isaac, 244-45, 248
Doughty, Mary Law, 170
Drapper, William, 19, 20
Dyson, Robert, 248

Eaglestone, A A (see Roger Dataller)
Edes (Eades), Richard, 32
Edward IV, 10, 11-12, 13
Effingham, Earl of, 99-112, 276, 281, 282, 284
Elizabeth Woodville (Queen), 10, 11-12
Elliott, Ebenezer, 298
Elliott, William, 49
Eyre, Jervase, 50

Field family, 185
Fiennes, Celia, 35, 131
Finch, Mary (Marchionness of Rockingham), 115
Firth, Mavis, 171
Fitzturgis, Richard, 50
Fitzwilliam, Earl, 36, 37, 122, 156, 229, 242
Foljambe, Thomas John, 103
Foster, John, 156, 158, 166
Fowler, Robert, 91
French, George, 49
Fretwell, James, 52
Fretwell, Ralf, 49

Gatty, Dr Alfred, 170
Gatty, Alfred Scott, 170
Geach, Charles, 252-55
Gibbs, James, 140
Gillett, Superintendant, 217, 218
Goddard family, 160
Goddard, Walter, 160, 163, 164, 171
Greybarn, William, 14, 16
Griffiths, Richard, 184
Guest, John, 26, 32, 241, 242, 248, 262, 279

Hall, John, 156, 166
Hampton, Thomas, 257
Hatchett, Charles, 36-37
Hattersley, John, 213, 218
Hawk(e) family, 184, 201-04
Henry VIII, 17, 67
Heseltine, Edward John, 278
Holden, Thomas, 19
Holderness, Amelia, 150
Hoole, Charles, 24, 26
Hopkinson, John, 93
Hunter, Joseph, 26, 32, 67, 100, 149-50

Ingram, William, 19, 26

Jackson, Edward, 92
James, George, 170
Jefferys, Thomas, 53, 55, 56, 61, 62, 134, 137, 152
Jelfe, William, 95
Jenkinson, Joss, 163
Jenkinson, Thomas, 214
Johnson, Ted, 170

Kirkstead, Abbot of, 15
Knight, Henry Gally, 43, 67

Laguerre, Louis, 133
Law, George, 224
Leach, Arthur, 26
Ledger, Gervase, 95
Ledger, Thomas, 95
Lee, William, 276-80
Leeds, Duke of, 40, 41, 43, 129-54
Leeson, William, 144, 145
Levet, Richard, 49, 52, 54
Leyland, John, 10, 30-31
London, George, 142, 145
Long, William, 234

McRitchie, Rev William, 37
Manvers, Earl, 226
Marshall, Robert, 90
Maw, Thomas, 145
Mitchell, William, 234
Montgomery, James, 166

Naylor family, 202-04
Neville, Robert, 15, 17, 18, 19
Newman, Charles, 224
Nicholson, George Pearson, 224
Noble, Francis, 144
Norfolk, Duke of, 81, 242
Northrop, Abraham, 168

Osborne, Thomas, (see Duke of Leeds)
Owen, George Dyson, 248
Owen, William, 246-48, 269

Paine, James, 89, 92-95
Parkes family, 185
Parkin, C E (Senior), 283
Peel, Sir Robert, 182
Perfect brothers (Nurserymen), 108, 144
Pickerell family, 200
Pilley, Thomas, 19
Ping family, 185-86
Platt, John, 91, 102

Platts, Joseph, 283
Pococke, Richard, 41-42
Procter, Catherine (Lady Effingham), 99-112
Pursglove, Robert, 23, 24
Rawson, William, 14, 16
Renshaw, Derek, 159, 160, 161, 162, 170, 171
Renshaw, Janet, 159, 160, 162, 163, 170, 171
Richard of Gloucester (Richard III), 12
Richinson, William, 52
Rockingham, 1st Marquis, 113-28
Rockingham, 2nd Marquis, 40, 41, 100, 115, 127-28
Rodgers, P, 175, 180-81
Rose, Joseph, 95
Rotherham, Bartholomew, 108
Rotherham, Thomas, Archbishop of York, 10-27, 39
Royston, George P, 178, 193, 201
Sambrook family, 177-78, 184-85
Sandford, Charles, 248
Sandford family, 131
Sandford, Henry, 248
Saunderson, Bishop, 42
Saunderson, Sir Nicholas, 49, 90
Saunderson, Robert, 52, 71
Scarbrough, Earl of, 58, 60, 64, 89-98, 156
Schopenhauer, Johanna, 35-36
Scrooby, Tony, 170
Sellars, Ben, 226
Senes, William, 18-20
Shearman, Edward James, M D, 279, 280
Sherbrooke, Michael, 16, 24, 26, 27
Short, Thomas, 40-41
Shrewsbury, Earl of, 18, 19, 24
Smith, Emma, 218
Snetzler, Mr, 104
Solomon, Laban, 168
Southwell, Edward, 145, 146-47
Spurr family, 67-68
Steel, Henry, 256-59
Stoddart, Sir Charles, 204-05
Strafford, 1st Earl, 131
Strafford, 2nd Earl, 113, 122, 124
Strange, P C, 217
Stuart Wortley, Lady (Caroline Creighton), 148-9
Swallow, Richard, 60
Sweeting, Dr R, 282, 283
Swift, Robert, 24, 25
Swift, Thomas, 15
Talman, William, 129-54
Taylor, Charlie, 232
Taylor family, 56
Tijou, Jean, 133
Tomlinson, Joseph, 214, 218
Tozer, Henry, 257
Tucker, Samuel, 40
Tyas, George, 53
Walker family, 36, 37, 103
Walker, Joseph, 37
Waller, Matthew, 217
Walpole, Horace, 104
Walsh, Arthur, 158, 159, 161
Wardell, Frank, 215
Watson, Emmanuel Isaac, 214
Watson, James, 214, 218
Wentworth, Hon Thomas (Senior), 113-14
Wentworth, William, 129
Wesley, John, 33-35, 157
Westby, George, 40
Wharncliffe, Lord, 157, 229
Willis, Dennis, 163
Willoughby, Cassandra, 145
Wilkinson, Bernard, 163
Wise, Henry, 142
Yates family, 60
Yeardley family, 77-88
Young, Arthur, 39-40, 148

INDEX OF PLACES

Abdy, 220,221
Airmyn, 91
Aldwarke Colliery, 262, 301
Almondbury, 13, 14, 20, 22
Alric Hall, 37
Angel Inn, Rotherham, 33
Aston, 142
Barley Hall Colliery, 155, 160
Bawtry, 39, 73, 91
Boston Castle, 99, 110-11
Braithwell, 91
Bramley, 43
Brampton, 122
Brinsworth, 15
Bugthorpe, 69-71
Bull Inn, Rotherham, 33
Canklow, 294
Catcliffe, 15
Chapeltown Furnace, 127, 180
Chatsworth, 129, 136, 145
Chesterfield, 216
Clough Hall, Kimberworth, 208-11
College Inn, Rotherham, 27
Conisbrough, 43, 49
Cortonwood Colliery, 220, 229-30, 235, 236-37, 238
Crown Inn, Rotherham, 39, 45
Dearne and Dove Canal, 223
Devil's (Dane's) Bank, 39
Doncaster, 37, 39
Doncaster races, 106
East Dene Housing Estate, 285-86, 287
Eastwood, 282, 294
Ecclesfield, 13, 15, 77, 156, 157
Elsecar Colliery, 223
Firbeck Mill, 64-67
Flying Dutchman Inn, Parkgate, 184
Glentworth (Lincs), 93, 97
Greasbrough, 122
Great Central Railway Works, 262
Guest and Chrimes Foundry, 277
Guilthwaite Spa, 40
Hall Street, Parkgate, 194-201
Harrison & Camm Works, 262
Harthill, 131
Hellaby, 47, 48, 49
Herringthorpe, 288, 292, 296
Higham Ferrers (Northants), 124
Hodsack Woodhouse, 144
Holmes Colliery, 206
Holmes Engine Works, 244-46
Holmes Hall, 99-112
Holmes Ironworks, 180
Hoober Stand, 118-19
Hooton Levitt, 47, 48, 49, 50, 52, 53
Hooton Levitt Mill, 50-54
Hooton Roberts, 122
Hope Chapel, Thorpe Hesley, 158
Hoyland Nether, 122
Ickles Bessemer Works, 256-57, 266, 267
Jamaica, 112
Kildare (Ireland), 122
Kilnhurst Works, 269
Kimberworth, 43, 77-88, 99, 122, 280, 284, 296
Kimberworth Park Gate, 77-88
Kirkcroft Farm, Thorpe Hesley, 162
Kirkstead Abbey (Lincs), 79, 102
Kirkstead Abbey Grange, 77-88
Kirkstead Abbey Grange Farm, 162

Kirkstead Abbey Mews, 78
Kiveton (Hall and Park), 129-54

Laughton-en-le-Morthen, 26, 58, 62, 64, 134
Laxton, 13, 14, 21, 22
Lincolnshire, 196

Maltby Mill, 49-50, 51
Maltby parish, 47-76
Maltby village, 43, 48, 49, 50
Malton (N Yorks), 124
Manvers Main Colliery, 220, 226-29, 232, 233, 235-36, 237
Masbrough, 273, 278, 281, 282, 288, 290
Masbrough Colliery, 206
Mason's Arms, Thorpe Hesley, 158
Meadow Bank Housing Estate, 288, 290
Middlesbrough, 182
Midland Iron Works, 251-52
Mill at Roche Abbey, 56-58
Monks' Fulling Mill, 54-56

Newhill Colliery, 224
New Stubbin Colliery, 298
Norfolk, 189-90, 192
North Anston, 134
North Central Wagon Company (Ickles), 262
Northfield Works, 251
North Midland Colliery, 243

Orgreave, 15

Parkgate (Rawmarsh), 175-205, 298-308
Park Gate Iron (& Steel) Works, 178-88, 252-56, 264
Perseverance Works, Rotherham, 206
Phoenix Works, 248

Railmill Inn, Parkgate, 184
Rawmarsh, 16
Red Lion Inn, Tickhill, 158, 159
Reindeer Inn, Doncaster, 37
Roche Abbey, 13, 43, 45, 47, 48, 49, 55, 58-59, 63, 69, 71, 73, 90, 97, 142
Roche Abbey Mill, 58-62
Rockingham pottery, 223
Rotherham Bridge, 11, 31, 39, 45
Rotherham Chapel on the Bridge, 11, 31
Rotherham College, 10-27, 31, 32
Rotherham Forge, 249-50
Rotherham Parish Church, 13, 31, 35, 104
Rother Iron Works, 249
Rufford Abbey, 17, 18

Sandbeck Lodge, 69-71
Sandbeck Park, 43, 47, 48, 50, 89-98, 142
Scholes, 81
Scholes Lane, 78
Skegness, 98
Slade Hooton, 59
South Anston, 134, 143
Sportsman Inn, Thorpe Hesley, 158, 159
Sprotborough Hall, 142
Stainborough, 129
Stainton, 49
Stone Mill, 62-64

Tankersley, 122
Templeborough, 42
Thorpe Hesley, 155-74, 213-19, 296
Thorpe Hesley chapels, 161
Thorpe Hesley, Holy Trinity Church, 161, 162
Thorpe (Hesley) Pit, 155, 160, 161, 163
Thorpe Salvin, 131, 132
Thrybergh, 20
Thundercliffe Grange, 99-112, 159
Tickhill, 43, 49, 179
Tinsley, 15, 24, 122
Tinsley Forge, 127
Todwick, 134
Travellers Inn, Rotherham, 275
Travellers Rest, Thorpe Hesley, 155

Ulley, 281

Walker Foundry, 36, 37, 39-40, 43, 45, 106
Wath, 122, 220-40
Wath Common, 221, 222
Wath Main Colliery, 220, 230-32, 233, 234, 235, 238-39
Wath Wood, 221
Wath Wood Bottom, 221, 222, 223
Wath Wood Houses, 223
Wentworth, 122
Wentworth House (See Wentworth Woodhouse)
Wentworth Woodhouse, 34, 36, 37, 40, 41, 42, 113-128, 131, 156, 212
West Melton, 223
Whiston, 281
Wicklow (Ireland), 122
Wingfield, 296
Wimbledon, 141
Worksop, 43

Yews Mill, 67-69